Courses
for
Change
in Writing

**A Selection from the
NEH/Iowa Institute**

For Siy,
Guiding spirit of the
whole affair.

Carl & Nancy

Courses
for
Change
in Writing

A Selection from the
NEH/Iowa Institute

Edited by
CARL H. KLAUS
University of Iowa
and
NANCY JONES
University of Iowa

BOYNTON/COOK PUBLISHERS, INC.
UPPER MONTCLAIR, NEW JERSEY

in cooperation with

THE INSTITUTE ON WRITING
OF THE UNIVERSITY OF IOWA

This publication was supported in part by a grant from the National Endowment for the Humanities. Its contents do not necessarily reflect the views of the National Endowment for the Humanities.

Library of Congress Cataloging in Publication Data

Main entry under title:

Courses for change in writing.

Bibliography: pp. 286-291
1. English language—Rhetoric—Study and teaching—
Congresses. I. Klaus, Carl H. II. Jones, Nancy
(Nancy L.) III. University of Iowa. Institute on Writing.
PE404.C64 1984   808'.042'071073   83-15711
ISBN 0-86709-121-5

For information address Boynton/Cook Publishers, Inc., 52 Upper Montclair Plaza, P.O. Box 860, Upper Montclair, New Jersey 07043

Printed in the United States of America

84 85 86 87 88 10 9 8 7 6 5 4 3 2 1

Foreword

James Britton

I was fortunate enough to be invited to teach at the University of Iowa, and to take part in the Institute on Writing during the first two years of this project, in the spring of 1979 and 1980. In prospect, this was an intriguing opportunity. Heads of writing programs in colleges and universities from many parts of the United States were to come together for six months in Iowa City, committed to a strenuous study of theory—rhetorical, linguistic, psychological and more—and then to the production and eventual execution of a writing program newly designed by them for their own institutions. Moreover, what struck me forcibly was that it was not only the members of the Institute who were committed; so also were their parent institutions, as it was a part of the contract that the appropriate dean or head of division visit the Institute, keep in touch and undertake to provide support for the new course in succeeding years. From the prospectus alone it was clear that this was a project that meant business.

In the event, I discovered how seriously the participants also meant business. Talking and writing became for them deliberate modes of learning, vigorously pursued, a practical demonstration of the principles on which the pedagogy of the course itself was based. Harvested in this collection are some of the outcomes of the learning that took place during those initial years. Furthermore, in the years that have intervened the courses planned then have been carried through, modified in the light of the experience of the originators, their colleagues and the students themselves, and taught again. Reading between the lines of these reports, I recognize the ripple effect that has taken place in many institutions, an extension of the learning by talking and writing—and now by teaching—that characterized those initiating years. Believing as I do that change in any educational system depends on the degree to which each institution becomes a center for professional development for its own staff, I cannot overemphasize the importance of this effect. (Here in England, when the Bullock Report presented a challenge to the *status quo* in education, a teacher wrote to *The Daily Telegraph* to say that "failure to implement the Bullock Report is built into the timetable." By and large, the experience of the past ten years has proved her right: time for staff consultation within a school or college remains an urgent priority.)

Moving from program to program in the text that follows, I have a lively sense of moving from classroom to classroom, each very different from the others, yet holding certain things in common. The differences—in clientele, in content area, in teacher orientation and expectations—will be evident enough and are of value in suggesting how adaptable the central ideas are to a variety of demands. But it is what the programs have in common that will define the central idea itself.

It hardly needs saying that what these programs show above all is a concern for the quality of the experiences their students will undergo in their writing, for the kinds of attitudes toward themselves as writers that will develop, and for the quality of learning that will result. A number of them imply also processes of *un*-learning—notably Jack White in his concern to help his students "transcend the artificial conceptions about writing" they bring with them, conceptions which, interestingly, he sees as regional: "by virtue of being Mississippians, they...have a very strong sense of propriety and civility, a code of manners as strict as the southern code of honor, which strongly colors their attitudes about writing, particularly in a university setting" (p. 49). By encouraging them to relax into comfortable use of their regional language as a starting point for their writing, he hopes to turn a stumbling-block into a source of strength.

Many programs similarly refer to a planned progression from relaxed personal writing, often in the working context of journals, to tackling philosophical topics (Philip Keith), or to the handling of public affairs (Ruth Lucas); or, stated taxonomically, from expressive to transactional discourse (Karen Pelz). Gracia Grindal uses an explicit instruction to this end. In a curriculum that looks high-powered and intellectually demanding she nevertheless makes use of an assignment worded, "This is not an organized essay! You are writing to one another and your teacher" (p. 79).

It is not only a concern for comfortable approaches to the writing task that leads to an emphasis on personal writing. It must, first, be recognized that expressive writing (an intimate, person to person form of discourse) is particularly appropriate to *discovery*. Being a relaxed form, it allows the writer to take risks; taking risks is necessary to discovery. Nor is that the end of the argument. As a number of the programs in this book have recognized, first-hand experience is an important foundation-stone for all learning. Whatever we study, we are likely to have to take a great deal of information on trust from other people's experience. Only if such belief rests on a familiar sense of how we learn from our own first-hand experience is it a secure understanding.

Thus, Trudy Dittmar introduces each of a multi-disciplinary series of writing projects by involving students in some kind of direct participation or observation—as for example attending a court of law—and makes this comment: "Although it is true that students could usually gain such an introduction through reading, it is also the case that direct experience helps to stimulate their personal involvement and disposes them to engage with the subject, to think about it, rather than simply to take in information passively" (p. 176).

From the Woods Hole Conference and Bruner's *Process of Education* (1960) came the notion of "the spiral curriculum"—an idea that is referred to by a number of the Institute writers and seems perhaps applicable to all the programs. The image is intended to indicate the kind of learning sequence in which skill and knowledge gained in a given area at a given time provide a jumping-off point for further learning when the student returns to it after a planned interval. The application of the idea to writing and re-writing is obvious. Its broader application is illustrated when Henry Silverman describes his program thus: "For each segment of a course, students find themselves looking at a particular thematic issue from various perspectives, not only in their reading but also in their writing. And the culmination of each course gives students an opportunity to synthesize their earlier writing and thinking in a major essay" (p. 70).

Philosophically speaking, the basic idea of the programs is that of *representation,* the notion that language is a principal mode of representing to ourselves our experiences of the world. For some time we have recognized *talking* in this context and now we are seeing how it operates also through *writing.* In our writing we share experiences and in the course of sharing them we *shape* them; and having learned how that pays off, we may write to shape without any further audience in mind. Echoes of this conception can be heard in many of the introductory statements in this collection: Patricia Carlson, for example, sees the role of writing in problem-solving as relying on "our ability to represent the world, and our ability to manipulate these representations" (p. 119); and Rebecca Faery, introducing her course, "Women Writing," says: "I want them to see…that they make reality for themselves (and others) in the way that they use words to define experience." And again, "Helping them to establish an authentic relationship with the words they produce on paper, and to understand the importance of these words in creating a sense of self, are thus the broadest and most important goals of the sequence" (p. 108).

* * *

So much, then, has been achieved: I think it is right and proper at this stage to ask, "Where next?" And here the editors, Carl Klaus and Nancy Jones, and each of the contributors would have their own answers and I can only speak for myself—the opinion, then, of an onlooker. I have two suggestions to make and I shall hope to show that each represents a foreseeable extrapolation of ideas already embodied in this collection.

The first might be crudely described as a move to further loosen the stranglehold that the expository essay has maintained over writing in American higher education. As Susanne Langer (1967, p. 148) attempted to correct a popular misconception when she claimed that logic is a mode of verifying our thinking and not a mode of thinking, so I would claim that the kind of discovered knowledge that an expository essay might demonstrate and present to the public is more likely to be arrived at by using forms of discourse that are not themselves expository. And if today's winds of change are any indication at all, *narrative* will be a candidate for a leading role among those forms of discourse. The American psychologist Gordon Bower (1978) claims that narrative provides us with "a royal road to an understanding of the human mind," while the British psychologist R. L. Gregory (1974) goes so far as to suggest that the proper subject of study for human psychology would be the *fictions* by which we anticipate and interpret events. It is of these fictions that Patricia Carlson writes in introducing her program, "Problem Solving and Writing": "By virtue of being human, we are all—from birth to death— engaged in an endless round of making and remaking hypotheses about our existence and the nature of our universe" (p. 119).

This new interest builds, of course, on ideas that have been with us for some time. James Moffett, writing in the mid-sixties, suggested that judgments arrived at through rational and logical processes by the adult are paralleled by what the handling of stories can do for young children. But if we take account of the vast size of the fiction-reading and fiction-viewing public, we are scarcely justified in limiting that mode of activity to young children.

Nor can we limit our concern to fictional narratives. There is an unbroken continuum, it seems to me, from autobiographical narrative to fictional. In recounting real experiences in gossip with family or friends, we invariably embellish the account (heightening in it the coloring of our own feelings); and on the other hand, our wildest fantasies must reflect in some degree, however camouflaged, the nature of our first-hand experiences.

Story-writing finds a place in a number of the programs presented in this collection. "Exploratory writing" as Karen Pelz conceives it must feature narrative when, in addition to reflecting on literary texts, students explore and reflect on their own experiences, "with the intention of discovering and developing their own attitudes, beliefs, feelings and ideas about experience" (p. 59). But it is perhaps a brief comment by John Thomson and William McCarron that comes nearest to the heart of the matter regarding the importance of stories. In explaining their focus on personal writing in a program for a military academy, they write: "We want [the students] to confront the issues that typically arise out of the conflict between an individual desire for personal expression and the military need for corporate loyalty. This dilemma is, after all, one that these cadets will struggle with in one form or another...throughout their professional lives" (p. 144). But it is not only cadets that face such conflicts of loyalty and desire. Story-writing, insofar as it employs artistic means and approaches the status of art, is a principal means by which such conflicts may be resolved. As such it seeks to fulfill an important, and rarely recognized, educational goal. (Traditionally, we have recognized the value of *response* to works of literature—an emphasis that parallels the way our society, from the invention of the printing press onwards, has tended to maximize the number of readers of fiction while minimizing the number of writers. I believe that as educators we must counter this tendency and that today we have the reprographic means to do so.)

It is the drift of this argument to suggest that stories—autobiographical and fictional—do not have to enter our writing programs only as approaches to expository or transactional writing. Pursued in the direction of literature—the shaped story, the verbal object—and given the support of a local readership, they have an essential educative purpose to fulfill: they constitute, in fact, a second major form of learning.

* * *

Indications of my other suggestion—my second finger-post to the future—are to be found in a single sentence in Frank Hubbard's introduction: "What I hope is that [the students] will take responsibility for their own learning" (p. 6), and in a student's comment after completing Leone Scanlon's course, "Work and Play": "I learned a great deal about having to think on my own, take complete charge of my work" (p. 91). Relevant also are the comments several contributors made to the effect that students were allowed some choice of writing task, or that assignment sequences were treated as *flexible*.

A great deal of thought on the part of directors and teaching staff goes into the preparation and presentation of assignment sequences. It is understandable that the more labor we put into preparing these, the more eager we are that what we offer our students should be accepted and used by them. But—here's the rub—it is a characteristic of human creatures that they show a singular capacity for doing whatever it is *they* want to do—and what others want of them can never set the adrenalin flowing in the same way. Increasing recognition of this human peculiarity has led educational practitioners to begin talking about a *negotiated curriculum*. Assignments are likely always to provide useful starting points for work with a newly formed group. Can we now investigate ways of making our sequences more open-ended—providing more choice, becoming more open to negotiation—and, even, more readily abandoned? Can we work towards an ideal in which individual intentions can be so orchestrated that each member of a group of students makes a distinctive contribution to a corporately planned undertaking?

* * *

Let me in conclusion share in the sense of pride in what has already been achieved as it is represented in the pages that follow. For me they are a vivid reminder of a notable teaching-and-learning experience, as I am sure they will be for many others. But of course, the real purpose of this volume lies well beyond that. I commit it to that purpose with confidence and with every good wish for its success.

REFERENCES

Bower, G.H. "Experiments in Story Comprehension and Recall." *New Directions in Discourse Processing*. Vol. I. Ed. R.O. Freedle. Norwood, N.J.: Ablex, 1978.

Bruner, Jerome S. *The Process of Education*. New York: Vintage Books, 1960.

Gregory, R.L. "Psychology: Towards a Science of Fiction." *New Society*, 28 (May 23, 1974), 439-441.

Langer, Susanne K. *Mind: An Essay on Human Feeling*. Vol. I. Baltimore: Johns Hopkins Press, 1967.

Moffett, James. *Teaching the Universe of Discourse*. Boston: Houghton Mifflin Company, 1968.

Acknowledgments

This collection offers a sampling of the courses that have been developed and the programs that have been carried on by the Institute on Writing since its inception in the fall of 1977. So it may be said to reflect the efforts and support of all the persons and institutions that have contributed to the work of the Institute. Accordingly, we have many to thank for having helped bring this book into being.

For its major support of the Institute, we are especially grateful to the National Endowment for the Humanities, and to its program officers—Blanche Premo, Dorothy Wartenberg, and Cynthia Wolloch—who have gathered and given good counsel. For its generous support of the Institute, we are grateful as well to the University of Iowa. In this connection, we are particularly indebted to William Farrell for his special assistance in conceiving, planning, and launching the Institute.

For their unstinting commitment to the Institute and for their profound influence on the courses in this book, we are indebted to our colleagues on the Institute staff: Paul Diehl, David Hamilton, Lou Kelly, Richard Lloyd-Jones, and Cleo Martin. For their expert contributions to the Institute, we are grateful to our other colleagues at the University of Iowa: Keith Achepohl (Art and Art History), Dudley Andrew (Broadcasting and Film), Kenneth Dowst (English), Wayne Franklin (English), John Harper (English), Rex Honey (Geography), Richard Hootman (Rhetoric and English), James Jakobsen (Mathematics), Linda Kerber (History), Margaret Keyes (Home Economics), James Lindberg (Geography), Keith Marshall (Anthropology), Donovan Ochs (Rhetoric and Speech), Sherman Paul (English), Elizabeth Robertson (Rhetoric and English), Eugene Spaziani (Zoology), James Van Allen (Physics and Astronomy), and Robert Wachal (Linguistics). For helping to administer the numerous affairs of the Institute, we are also grateful to the following staff at the University of Iowa: Lyell Henry, Felicia Lavallee, Mary Jane McLaughlin, Don McQuillen, Norman Sage, and Melody Scherubel.

For the wide-ranging knowledge and experience they brought to the Institute, we are indebted to the specialists in writing who served as visiting consultants and staff members: James Britton (London, England), William E. Coles, Jr. (University of Pittsburgh), Charles Cooper (University of California—San Diego), James S. Davis (State of Iowa Writing Project), Winifred B. Horner (University of Missouri—Columbia), William Irmscher (University of Washington), Erika Lindemann (University of North Carolina at Chapel Hill), Andrea A. Lunsford (University of British Columbia), Stephen M. North (SUNY at Albany), and W. Ross Winterowd (University of Southern California).

For the creativity, knowledge, and energy they have invested in the Institute, and in the collaborative development of these courses, we are especially grateful to all the writing program directors who have participated in the project: Lois Barry (Eastern Oregon State College), Beverly Beem (Walla Walla College), Mel Bertolozzi (Loyola Marymount University), Owen Brady (Clarkson College), Alma Bryant (University of South Florida), Patricia Burnes (University of Maine at Orono), Harry Caldwell (Trinity University), Patricia Carlson (Rose-Hulman Institute of Technology), Leo Cheever (Stephen F. Austin State University), Elizabeth Ciner (Carleton College), John Cole (West Liberty State College), Priscilla Davidson (Roosevelt University), Frank Devlin (Salem State College), Marjorie Dew (Ashland College), Trudy Dittmar (Brookdale Community College), Sandra Doe (Metropolitan State College), Timothy Donovan (Northeastern University), Rebecca Blevins Faery (Hollins College), George Fouts (Western Piedmont Community College), Gracia Grindal (Luther College), John Hanes (Duquesne University), Jim Hanlon (Shippensburg State College), Frank Hubbard (University of Wisconsin—Milwaukee), Lynda Jerit (Oakton Community College), Margaret Kantz (Carnegie-Mellon University), Philip Keith (St. Cloud State University), John Lang (Emory and Henry College), Ruth Lucas (Kapiolani Community College), Virginia Markel (University of Nebraska at Omaha), Donald Maxwell (J. Sargeant Reynolds Community College), William McCarron (United States Air Force Academy), Tom Miles (West Virginia University), Mary Frew Moldstad (Ashland College), Sally Nelson (University of Louisville), Hugh Owings (West Georgia College), Jane Parks-Clifford (University of Missouri—St. Louis), Jon Patton (University of Toledo), Karen Pelz (Western Kentucky University), Sister Ann Redmond (College of St. Catherine), Leone Scanlon (Clark University), Henry Silverman (Michigan State University), Lana Silverthorn (University of South Alabama), and Jack White (Mississippi State University). And we are grateful to all of the institutions that have supported these people throughout the design and implementation of their courses.

For contributing to the development of this book, we are grateful to the United State Air Force Academy which graciously hosted our editorial conferences, to Jan Cooper (University of Iowa) who helped prepare the bibliography and read proof, to Vic Schwarz who designed the book, and to Bob Boynton who kept us in line and in good humor throughout the course of bringing it into print.

For keeping the Institute in line and this book in plain language, we are grateful to Kate Franks Klaus.

And for the good influence they have had on these courses, we are grateful to the hundreds of collaborating faculty who have taught them, and to the thousands of students who have taken them.

C.H.K.

N.J.

Contents

V

VI

Introduction

On the Design of Writing Courses

Carl H. Klaus

You need only skim through a college catalogue or listen to conversation in a dormitory room or faculty lounge to realize that one of the most basic units of experience and value in academic life is the "course." Faculty speak about *offering* or *giving* them, students about *taking* them, as if courses were palpable objects, like presents or pills. You can also hear talk of being *in* them or getting *through* them, as if courses were three-dimensional spaces, like rooms or tunnels. And, as befits anything that figures so prominently in the experience of a particular group, courses are also spoken of in the colorful terms of personification. *Grind* or *snap, bear* or *mickey-mouse, bitch* or *bummer*—the language bears witness to the intense personal reactions they arouse. And not just in students. After all, faculty salaries and school budgets are often heavily influenced by course enrollments. And even when enrollments are not an issue, we are still intensely concerned with how our courses are *going,* for our sense of well-being depends upon how they *work out*.

Yet most of us who teach, especially those of us who teach writing, are usually so caught up in the hectic pace of our activities—the class sessions, the assignments, the papers, the late-night reading, the commenting, the conferring—that we rarely have an opportunity to stand back and reflect on where we have been and where we are going in our courses. And why. Indeed, we probably have occasion to see our courses whole—from beginning to end—only when we are planning them and when we are done with them. Even on these occasions, the circumstances of our work and of our lives—the end of vacation, the beginning of registration, the end of a term, the beginning of vacation—may well prevent us from reflecting very long or very closely on the overall planning and working out of our courses. The world is too much with us.

The materials in this book cannot, of course, do anything to alter that state of affairs, for the pressure of restricted time is an inherent condition of the academic year, made all the more intense by the special circumstances that obtain in the teaching of writing. But these materials, embodying as they do an integrated set of ideas for course design and instruction in writing, can contribute to the discovery and development of strategic ways to work within the constraints—ways that may prove to be productive and intellectually satisfying for both students and teachers. The designers of these materials repeatedly take account of such constraints, for their experience as directors of freshman writing has made them attentive to the wide range of special contexts—individual, institutional, and temporal—that must be considered in planning any general education course, especially one in freshman composition. So it is, for example, that Ruth Lucas of Kapiolani Community College, having recognized the "linguistic disorientation" that afflicts many of her Hawaiian students, makes this problem "one of the central aspects of language" that she addresses in her course (p. 38). So it is, too, that Gracia Grindal of Luther College, having acknowledged that the College's freshman program " is taught collaboratively by faculty from the English and history departments," designs assignments that call upon students to use writing both as a means of "exploring and explicating texts" and as a means of learning to reason about "historical ideas, issues, problems, and sources" (p. 75). And so it is that Timothy Donovan of Northeastern University, having recognized that he is limited to a week of pre-semester orientation for his new graduate teaching assistants, takes what he believes to be "the *most* direct route to understanding writing and how it is taught" by offering his TA's an "experiential program"—one that calls upon them to write and respond to each other's writing "in conferences, in small groups, and on the papers themselves" (p. 236). Each course in this collection unmistakably embodies its audience and situation. They are intensely rhetorical.

This rhetorical awareness is reflected not only in the fundamental way that each course has been designed to incorporate significant aspects of its academic situation, but also in the fact that each course, though fully drafted at the Institute on Writing in 1979 or 1980, has been repeatedly modified and refined on the basis of classroom experience. Henry Silverman of Michigan State University is typical in remarking that his course has "undergone various changes from the time I designed it in the spring of 1979, and first offered it in pilot form with a handful of colleagues in the fall of 1979" (p. 70). And the changes, as might be supposed, have been occasioned by the reactions of both colleagues and students. Leone Scanlon of Clark University, for example, notes that "In the first version of the sequence, all the assignments were on play and work. As the TA's and I taught the course, however, it became clear that the students found spending a semester on one subject restrictive. Thus to let them tap their own interests, an essential element in their seeing their writing as their own, I modified the curriculum to provide more choice of subject, though not always of genre. Some of the TA's have also made their own changes..." (p.89). These courses, in other words, have been, and continue to be, so responsive to their circumstances that the content, arrangement, and wording of assignments as they appear here probably no longer reflect exactly the character and makeup of each course. The materials in this volume, then, are offered not so much as literal models, but as manifestations of a set of ideas. And so the cautionary remarks by Phil Keith of St. Cloud State University apply to all the materials in this collection:

Despite all the plotting that has gone into this sequence, it is very important that this program be considered as more heuristic or suggestive than rigidly fixed. No exercise sequence, it seems to me, can work very well if its method is not the teacher's own method, and the best way for a prospective user to go about relating the method here to his or her own method is to add or substitute other examples, to reshape the pattern of assignments in part or in whole, and to alter the wording or overall style of the assignments (pp. 25-26).

Though each of these courses has been shaped by a different academic setting and situation, they are collectively informed by a shared body of ideas about the nature of writing—ideas that arose out of reading and discussions that took place among Institute staff and participants during their residence in Iowa City. These ideas, which were just beginning to be widely disseminated to writing teachers when the Institute was in session, have by now become so familiar that they need no detailed explanation. James Britton takes note of them in his "Foreword" (pp. v-ix), and sources for them are listed in the "Bibliography" (pp. 286-291). Thus the outline of these ideas here is meant only to identify them as clearly as possible and to explain as directly as possible the sense in which they constitute a matrix that informs the design of courses in this collection.

The controlling assumption of these courses is that writing is above all else a mental activity that involves the total sensibility of a human being in using language to engage the world of experience. Implicit in this assumption is a set of interrelated ideas: (1) that writing is a profoundly personal activity—a process that arises out of a human being's unique experience, mental behavior, and way of using language; (2) that writing is also a profoundly social activity—a process that enables human beings to use language as a way of carrying on transactions with others in the world of affairs; (3) that writing is a way of learning—an activity that enables human beings to use language as a means of apprehending the world and making sense of it for themselves; and (4) that writing is formative—an activity in which human beings shape their sense of experience by the way they form it symbolically in language.

Given this set of ideas about writing—a set in which it is conceived as a mental activity inseparable from experience—the Institute courses are designed to offer instruction in writing that is experientially oriented. In this respect, the courses may be said to be heavily influenced by the educational philosophy of John Dewey, as well as by the curricular theories of Jerome Bruner. Accordingly, they draw on personal experience and first-hand observation as a fundamental source of learning and understanding—"as the center of knowledge" (Frank Hubbard, p. 7). They emphasize learning through the process of engaging in mental activity rather than by adherence to authority. By extension, they involve students in a variety of language-using activities and situations that entail problems which are open to multiple solutions rather than calling for obedience to models and rules.

This approach to writing instruction is most visibly and distinctively embodied in the sequences of assignments that make up the bulk of this collection. These sequences typically begin with assignments inviting students to write about a particular experience. The experience may be drawn from the past, as in Frank Hubbard's course, which opens by asking his students at the University of Wisconsin-Milwaukee to recall an English teacher from their past "who had a 'hobby horse,' some word or phrase that was harped on at length" (p. 8). Or it may be based on first-hand observation that is called for by the assignment, as in Karen Pelz' sequence which begins by asking students at Dartmouth to "spend half an hour this afternoon or tomorrow in one of the more 'natural' areas on campus—down by the river, or at Occam Pond, or over in the woods near the Bema. While you are there, write down your observations of the place" (p. 61). The experience may have intense feelings associated with it, as in Mary Frew Moldstad's sequence, which begins by asking her students at Ashland College to write "about a time when you won something, or lost something, that you wanted very much to win" (p. 101). Or it may entail observation of a scene or situation that is relatively free of emotional attachments, as in Trudy Dittmar's sequence which begins by having students at Brookdale Community College observe and write about "a place you're not very familiar with, a place generally frequented by a group of people you don't belong to" (p. 182).

Whatever the origin or nature of the experience might be, it generally serves as a significant point of entry into the assignments that follow, an embodiment of topics, subjects, problems, or activities that will be of major concern in the whole sequence or a substantial portion of it. Hubbard's students, for example, move from writing about the verbal "hobby horse" of a past English teacher into a sequence of assignments that focus on " 'automatic language'—on the words or phrases or structures or texts that we make routine as ways of accomplishing some limited ends" (p. 3). Similarly, Pelz' students move from recording their observations about a river, or pond, or wooded area on the Dartmouth campus to a sequence of exploratory writing devoted largely to Thoreau's *Walden*. Moldstad's students turn from their recollection of having won or lost something to a sequence of assignments that explore the problematic nature of winning and losing in a variety of personal, fictional, and popular contemporary situations. And Trudy Dittmar's students move from observing an unfamiliar place and group of people into an interdisciplinary research course that begins with a set of assignments based on the observational and analytic techniques of anthropology. Thus each of these courses proceeds according to an organizational strategy somewhat like the musical form of theme and variation.

Much as the musical form typically moves through increasingly complex harmonic, melodic, and rhythmic expressions of its theme, so these courses typically move through progressively more complex perceptual, conceptual, or rhetorical re-engagements with a topic, subject, problem, or activity implicit in the initial assignment. Hubbard's students, for example, move from recalling and writing about a teacher's pet word or phrase to recalling or encountering increasingly complex pieces of automatic discourse, ranging from the Pledge of Allegiance and other "early learned set pieces" to the formats for writing in specialized academic fields (p. 4). And each type of automatic discourse is not only experienced in some way, but analyzed as well. Thus the sequence reiteratively moves from experiential to conceptual assignments, resulting in a course that has a recursive as well as linear cohesiveness marked by increasingly deeper and more complex repetitions.

This complex design, manifest to some extent in all of the courses, is intended to serve an interrelated set of instructional purposes. To begin with, it constitutes a strategic way of enacting the idea that writing is a way of learning, for each assignment in a sequence calls upon students to observe something from a different angle, and the shifting point of view in each case yields "a new look, a new experience, a new understanding" (Hubbard, p. 8). The effect of each new observation, in turn, is necessarily incremental. So whatever the subject happens to be—whether it is a type of automatic discourse, a literary work, a problematic pair of abstractions, or a specialized method of observation and analysis—the continually shifting perception of it is intended to yield an increasingly richer knowledge of it and thereby an increasingly more complex understanding of it. This increasing knowledge, understanding, and resourcefulness in a particular subject or activity also makes it possible for students to experience and apprehend the idea that writing *is* a way of learning. In other words, the sequence itself is designed to serve as an emblem and a model that students can apply in other domains. Each sequence of writing assignments, then, is ultimately intended to give students an increased understanding of writing and an increased sense of fluency in some of the ways that writing can be used in any process of inquiry.

Given the commitment of these sequences to writing and learning through experience, they are typically designed to be adaptable to the immediate circumstances of classroom experience. Keith, for example, provides a set of "Extra Assignments" (pp. 36-37) that can be used instead of or in addition to some of the exercises in his already existing set. Hubbard allows for the possibility of "slowdowns" or "loops" at any point in his course that might require "additional exercises...to explore the issues at hand" (p. 5). And Don Maxwell of J. Sargeant Reynolds Community College uses several tactics to insure the adaptability of his sequence. One of his assignments is presented in two different versions (p. 215); another assignment allows students to ignore the task altogether and "write what *you* want to write" (p. 217); yet another invites comments from students that will help him to make mid-course corrections (p. 216); and one subset of assignments can be modified to suit varying campus situations, or it can be replaced entirely by a different subset, as Maxwell discovered when he taught a version of the course in China (p. 212). These assignment sequences, then, are intended to allow for improvisation that will meet the need of classroom situations as they actually arise. They are revised, in other words, not only from term to term, but also possibly from week to week, or day to day, within a term, and thus are by no means static though they might appear to be from their fixed visual appearance in a printed text such as this.

The educational strategy of the Institute courses is based not only on assignment sequences, but also on the centrality of student writing and response to writing in the classroom activity of the courses. In virtually all of these courses, the classroom is regularly transformed, in effect, into a workshop, where student writing is the focus of attention. The workshop, in turn, is flexibly designed to allow for a variety of arrangements, so that student writing is sometimes examined by "the class as a whole, sometimes in small groups, sometimes in pairs" (Dittmar, p. 283). The teacher sometimes guides class discussion, sometimes rotates among the small groups and pairs, at other times works one-on-one with individual students as they request. Responses to writing are sometimes conveyed entirely through discussion, sometimes entirely in writing, sometimes in a combination of forms. The process of responding is sometimes conducted according to highly structured guidelines, sometimes in a relatively open-ended way, as reflected by the "Sample Guidelines for Workshops" that appear in the "Appendix" (p. 281). And the material under consideration sometimes consists of notes and rough outlines, sometimes early drafts, sometimes finished pieces. As these variable arrangements suggest, the workshop is typically adapted to suit a variety of instructive purposes—all of which can be seen as contributing to the goal of writing and learning through experience.

By virtue of repeatedly bringing students together to consider each other's writing, the workshop is intended to develop within the group a community of writers and learners. The community is predicated, to begin with, on the fact that students hold in common the increasingly complex experience of the assignment sequence. Given this common ground of experience, the workshop provides an opportunity for students to learn simply from reading the work of others in the group. Each piece that they read may provide them with new information or a new way of seeing or thinking about the common topic or problem of interest in the sequence. So their perception of the subject at hand may be complicated and deepened not only by the thematic variations in the sequence, but also by the varied knowledge and perspectives that exist within the group.

The workshop, of course, provides an opportunity for students to learn not only from reading the work of others, but also from receiving the comments of others on their own work. Depending on the kind of material that is under consideration, the workshop may help students "decide how to get started on a project and how to proceed," or it may "help solve problems" that arise in the process of drafting or researching a piece, or it may help them "see how others react to what [they] write" (Dittmar, p. 283). So the workshop may be used to help students with crucial aspects of the composing process, from developing and structuring ideas to considering the needs and views of an audience. And so it is that Rebecca Blevins Faery of Hollins College is prompted to tell her students that "you will learn about the whole writing process—not by reading about it, and not by listening to me talk about it, but by writing, by sharing what you've written with me and the rest of the class, by listening to what we say about your writing, and by reading and responding to the writing done by other class members" (p. 282).

Ultimately, the complexly varied activities of the workshop are intended to give students an "experience in the process of reading, thinking, and working together in an intellectual community" (Grindal, p. 76). As Beverly Beem of Walla

Walla College affirms, "They do, after all, come to share a rich body of knowledge about a particular subject that they have investigated separately and in collaboration" (p. 225). Out of such an experience, it is possible for students to develop an increased respect for the views of others and thus to understand the sense in which writing is a profoundly social activity—a way of being in the world.

Given the assumptions about writing that are embodied in the sequences and workshops, it follows that instructors in these courses typically orient their responses not to grammar and mechanics but to the ways that students are using language to shape their sense of reality, to convey information and ideas, to deal with problems and situations, and in general to engage the world of experience. Given the educational assumptions that are embodied in the sequences and workshops, instructors in these courses do not ordinarily cast their responses to an assignment in the form of a judgment or grade, but rather in the form of observations, questions, and reactions that will make it possible for students to experience their writing as an authentic way of learning. So, from assignments to workshops to instructional responses, the courses in this collection embody an intergrated approach to writing and learning through experience.

* * *

The collection includes six groups of courses and programs. Sections I through V contain courses designed primarily for beginning undergraduates. Section VI contains programs for faculty development based on the principles of writing and learning through experience that are embodied in the undergraduate courses.

Each set of courses is focussed on a different topic or problem. Section I centers on language and communication, section II on literary and historical texts, section III on problematic terms and concepts, section IV on perception and problem-solving, and section V on research and writing. These groupings, however, are not air-tight; the topics or problems that dominate in one set are likely to turn up among courses in another set; thus the sections remain unlabelled.

The programs for faculty development are organized to move from material primarily intended for a freshman staff to material primarily intended for faculty across the disciplines. But that organization is also not air-tight; the material designed for one group could easily be adapted for use with the other. In fact, the final program in this set contains several assignment sequences that participating faculty designed for use in their undergraduate courses. So that program may be seen as an emblem of the entire collection—indeed, of the Institute itself.

I

By Design or By Habit

Writing and Learning about Automatic Language

Frank Hubbard

Like the other courses collected here, this one invites students to experience writing as a way of thinking and learning. And like the others it aims to help students learn to write not only for the classroom, but also for the world they will encounter outside of school, where they will have to adapt to changing conditions and changing constraints on their writing. Its distinguishing characteristic is that it seeks to achieve these goals by having students write about language itself, in particular about what I call "automatic language"—the words or phrases or structures or texts that we make routine as ways of accomplishing some limited ends. I chose this subject in part because my students—the students at a large state university campus—bring such widely varying backgrounds, abilities, interests, and values to the classroom that the only thing I can be certain they hold in common is language itself, in particular such automatic language as clichés, jargon, and formulaic writing.[1]

My choice of subject, of course, is ultimately occasioned by a goal that all composition teachers share—to make students thoughtful about language and the choices it offers them as writers. I work towards this goal by asking students questions such as "What is the five-paragraph essay for, and how did it get invented?" or "Given that clichés may cause problems, what are they for, and how do they arise?" or "What is a technical jargon designed to do and what is it not designed to do?" In answering such questions, student writers are compelled to reflect on underlying principles, which are more durable finally than specific formats and thus may help them generate new genres, new formats, and new

---

[1] The first version of this course, which consisted of a sequence of 27 assignments, was designed for California State University at Sacramento where I taught it during the academic years 1979-80, 1980-81. The revised and expanded version published here represents the course as I have been teaching it at the University of Wisconsin—Milwaukee since 1981. At both of these schools, I might add, many of my students have had to work 20 hours a week or more during the graveyard shifts, and then have had to go home to families where they are the primary or only caretaker. For students with such hectic and scattered lives, this course provides an opportunity to make sense of at least some part of their world.

structures to meet whatever conditions they encounter. In this way these assignments have designs on the future.

The underlying subject of the sequence, in fact, is design—the way we use language to reach our ends. In relation to this underlying subject, then, automatic language is only an apparent subject, one meant to stand as a part for the whole. Though the course persistently asks "What are the gains and losses of automatic language?" it is still and always about language and writing. To find this apparent subject, I looked for a question about language whose answer would change with the special area within which it was asked. And the question "What are the benefits and costs of automatic language?" seemed to fit many areas, to allow me to add or subtract segments of the course and to rearrange or expand or shorten what I had.

The grammar of the course, the materials of which it is composed, together with their basic arrangement, is simple. Students encounter a piece of discourse, re-experience it in writing, and analyze the experience, generally also in writing. In the sequence reproduced here, the particular pieces of discourse range from early-learned set pieces such as the Pledge of Allegiance, the National Anthem, and the Lord's Prayer (assignments 1, 2, and 5) to other examples of language use that speakers/writers fall into automatically, such as clichés (3, 14, 15), formulas for organization (18), rote-learned definitions (31), formats for presenting information in different fields (28), and academic modes—narration, description, exposition, argumentation (35-38). In this sequence, re-experiencing such pieces of language frequently involves paraphrasing them. This seemed a particularly appropriate activity to employ with automatic discourse—that is, with language that has been so routinized or memorized that its user finds the language invisible, or nearly so— since the act of paraphrasing helps students focus on the intention, the meaning behind the words, thus helping them reclaim something from its automatic status and restore it to a living and vital form. The analysis of such re-experiences helps students to foreground the text further, and to understand it—sometimes for the first time, sometimes anew. This, I tell my students, is what I mean (in part) by saying that writing can be a way of learning.

This grammar—encountering a stretch of discourse, re-experiencing it in writing, and analyzing the experience—is meant to become familiar, because it represents what I hope students will be able to do by themselves at the end of the course, isolating a writing phenomenon, looking at it closely, and figuring out how it works. By learning this pattern, I hope, students will be able not so much to write tomorrow what they can write today—the five-paragraph essay, for example—but that they be able to learn to write in small groups, write on a word processor, write in unfamiliar formats, even develop new formats. This adaptability is virtually the obsession of the course, as assignments ask over and over for the principles, the guidelines for design, the classification and the explanation for everyone's practice. And everywhere the effect of responding to these assignments in writing is the same: a new look, new experience, new understanding of something like the National Anthem or set phrases or set forms that they have previously taken for granted. But everywhere the learning is different, special, particular in what a given student discovers is gained and lost by making language automatic.

The way the sequence moves from area to area, its logic so to speak, is essentially inductive. Each section contains from one to four tasks and each section asks students to generalize about the area of language experience under consideration (after considering specific examples of it); then we try to find a related area (or areas) of experience and generalize again, across the two. For example, we look first at automatic language in a patriotic context (assignments 1, 2); the suggestion in this unit is that the national texts are acquired very early, and the class begins wondering what else is acquired that way. When more than one student wonders about religious texts, we can pursue that topic, with students writing down, then paraphrasing, a prayer they acquired years before (5). This is followed by a discussion of similarities and differences between automatic language in patriotic and religious contexts, as well as discussions, based on their writings up to this point in the course, about early "learning" and alternatives to it (6).[2] I then work by opposition, asking whether we can deliberately make something automatic. Answering this question requires that students contrast the experience of memorizing something they want to learn with memorizing something they are *told* to learn—in this instance a poem (7, 8)—and of considering what makes poems or any language more or less learnable. The issue of "academic learning" raised by the poem suggests other kinds of academic learning of language, and this leads eventually to consideration of academic formats (18, 27-29), and grammatical forms (31-34). These last two areas are more complicated, so I resist getting into them too early. The sequence begins as it does with the Anthem and Pledge because I expect nearly every student to have considerable success in working with these pieces—in moving from perhaps-thoughtless recitation to understanding the sense and meaning of words; in turning something known "by heart" into something also known by the mind; in arriving at a common ground for discussing the differences between rote-learning and understanding, as well as for discussing the benefits and draw-backs of language and learning that is automatic.

The rhetoric of the sequence casts all members of the class as participants in a serious, and I hope useful, conversation. The voice in the assignments is that of an interested questioner, who does not have the answers to the questions asked, but instead looks to the students for the information and insights which the class as a whole can use. One particularly clear example of this occurs in the assignments on formats (28-29), where students are asked to interview older students in their major area or perhaps graduate students who are already teaching, to find out what the important patterns of writing are in their particular field of interest. From the

---

[2]The course can be slowed down at this point or any other point by introducing additional exercises that will serve to explore the issues at hand. I think of such maneuvers as "loops." The label comes from conceiving of a sequence as a path of experiences heading in a particular direction, which is not necessarily reached most quickly and surely by traversing the shortest distance between two points. Slowdowns are not merely repetitious. They also cover new ground, much as one does in hiking, for example, to visit some outlook or other scenic spot before returning to the trail that is heading where one ultimately wants to go. Often such outlooks can be helpfully orienting or re-orienting.

collected formats brought in by members of the class, students generalize about similarities and differences among formats, and about the various purposes which they serve. I cannot predict what formats will be collected and brought into class for consideration. So of course I cannot predict what their principles of design will be. And this uncertainty is part of the challenge both for me and my students. I tell them that I expect these principles will have something to do with the purposes readers will bring to the texts, but more than that I can scarcely say.

By endowing the assignments with the voice of an interested questioner, I hope that students in turn will recognize the need to take responsibility for their part of the conversation. It was in an effort to make this implied audience more clear that I first included in the sequence the William Perry essay on "Conflicts in the Learning Process" (assignments 11-13), for it provides those of us in the class with a vocabulary for talking about childish and mature ways of approaching learning. So, when a student says, "I can't understand all this. Tell me what you want," I can turn to the Perry essay and say, "Do you see what kind of student you are being when you ask me that?" I remind them that in a serious conversation you don't suddenly stop and say to the other person, "Tell me what you want me to say," but that you instead assume the conversation depends on two sides, with the other person interested in knowing what you think and what you have to contribute. What I expect is that the students will try to make sense of what is going on in the course. What I hope is that they will take responsibility for their own learning. And the class can usually see who is working and who is going through the motions, and some groups have not been kind about students in their midst who did not contribute to the enterprise.

Given the rhetoric of the assignments, the psychology of it is probably obvious enough, but might be clarified by noting that I make three major assumptions. The first is that because all the questions are real and legitimate, the tasks are significant in themselves; these are things I want to know, and generally they are things other people in the class would like to know as well. In other words, nothing is being requested here merely for the sake of something else. My experience with weaker students particularly is that they do not transfer what they have learned when the task of learning seems of no obvious use or interest to them. They develop what I have heard called a "drill set," a frame of mind in which the task has rigidly drawn boundaries beyond which reflection and implication do not go. But when the task is on its face significant or interesting or both, weaker students as well as stronger ones seem to transfer and carry over what they have learned. I have found that teaching the following sequence at the basic or "remedial" level is not much different from teaching it for "regular" freshman sections. I take this effect to be evidence that the assignments do not encourage a drill set, and I draw from this the further conclusion that weaker students may be just the ones who throughout their careers have been unwilling to learn things when they did not understand why they should, while stronger students may be those who have accepted and learned things because someone told them it might have some use eventually. Seen from this point of view, docility in students doesn't look so much like intelligence, but more like an accident of birth. In any case, learning from experience seems to me to mean learning from the inherent meaning of what is going on right now, not learning solely for benefits that may possibly accrue later.

The second assumption I make is that students will improve as writers and will be better able to adjust to future worlds of writing as they become more aware of what they are doing as writers. Because of this assumption, on every assignment I ask writers in my classes to attach a commentary about what it was like to perform the task, what they got out of it, but more to the point, where they had trouble or engaged in activities or thinking which does not show on the page. I invite the attachment of drafts when I don't require them, and I respond to drafts as well as to final pieces and commentaries. In responding I want to do everything I can to make students aware both of the automatic patterns they have used, and of the choices they seem to have made in drafts as well as final pieces. I do so because I do not think that revision can be made otherwise than consciously and deliberately, with an understanding of the reasons. And if the cost is a temporary slowing and lessening of quality for some students, I do not mind. Perhaps it should be that a writing course unsettles the automatic patterns enough to produce such effects, given that it cares far more about long-term changes.

The third assumption behind this sequence is that each student brings to the course things that he or she knows which the rest of us do not, and that the task of the class is to take into account the concerns of as many of the members as possible for the making of secure generalizations and guiding principles of writing. One of the traditional assignments I like and use, the explaining of some technical vocabulary to a general audience (assignment 27), makes a related assumption clear: most of us are not very good at estimating what other people know and don't know, and so to do the assignment well, a person almost has to try it out, go and see whether people know the words or not. And we are even weaker when it comes to knowing what will be a helpful explanation; again, the best way to do the assignment is to try out an explanation and see (assignment 37). For such work, an audience is obviously essential. I also use the class as information gatherers; we can cover far more ground in cooperation than we can in isolation. For some kinds of writing, or with some parts of the writing process, working individually or one-on-one is useful. For other kinds of writing, for other parts of the writing process, the group's range is indispensable. Many of my assignments try to invoke this range, because I believe that good writing is in part making something public, so it requires knowledge of the public, knowledge that is never certain, never available before one has some experience with an audience. The class becomes such an audience for one another, an occasion for testing and refining one's intelligence and judgment with the aid of a group.

As may be inferred from my discussion of it, this sequence takes the authority of experience as the center of knowledge. It follows, then, that throughout the course we do not appeal to authorities for anything that matters, that I as the teacher do not impose answers, and that we do not find it necessary for someone else to replicate results before we accept a finding. We talk about choices rather than rules—about outlining, for example, before and after the fact; about freewriting, used as quarry for main ideas or just as profitably thrown away before the first draft. And we tell each other not to accept any advice about writing that isn't rooted in positive response from an audience and developed out of activities each of us designs to suit himself or herself. So, the course at last depends upon what the students bring and contribute. The content of the course becomes what we tell ourselves and one another as people and as writers. The content is what we find out by interviewing, by reading, by listening to others in the class, and by reflecting on all of this. I want students to formulate for themselves, in terms of experiences they have just had, what the course means, so that they can have similar experiences in the future and formulate again for themselves what the experiences signify; this procedure insures, I hope, that they will understand, rather than memorize before they are able to understand, what it is writers do.

BY DESIGN OR BY HABIT

Prologue: Perhaps you've had an English teacher in the past who had a "hobby horse," some word or phrase that was harped on at length. What was it? What did it mean for the teacher? What did it mean to you at that time? What does it mean to you now? Does it have anything to do with the way you write now?

1. In a career more than twenty years long, a baseball player such as Willie Mays or Henry Aaron probably listened to the Star-Spangled Banner more than 4000 times. If each rendition took two minutes, then these players spent more than 8000 minutes listening to our National Anthem—more than 16 work days of eight hours each. They probably knew the song pretty well before their major league careers began; afterwards…

You may not know the Anthem as well as Mays or Aaron, but you probably know it pretty well. Write out the words to the first verse. Make notes of where you had difficulties.

Now write a paraphrase of the Anthem, putting it into your own words. Again make notes of difficult spots, and at the end make notes of the gains and losses you see in paraphrasing the Anthem. What could you "get"? What couldn't you "get"?

> (To make it clear that I'm not testing memory, I walk around while students write this in class. I suggest using the music to help the memory, and I draw a rampart on the board.)

2. More than twenty years ago, when the Supreme Court made mandatory prayer in public schools illegal, many more classrooms began having a daily Pledge of Allegiance to the Flag. You may not have spent whole days of your life reciting this piece, but you undoubtedly know it pretty well also. Write it down, then paraphrase it, and then go on to answer these questions about it. Please write a connected stretch of words, not just "yes" or "no" or "Number one is such-and-such and number two is…"

— What is the basic act you perform in saying this piece? (I don't mean putting your hand over your heart so much as I mean why we do that in doing something else.)

— Do you perform this act or acts like it anywhere else in your life?

— Think back to the time when you first learned the Pledge. What did it mean to you then? Has it meant anything different to you since that time? And what does it mean to you now, once you have looked at it carefully?

3. You probably know someone (yourself?) who "has a pretty good line," who seems to excel at talking to strangers. Perhaps this person doesn't say very much, but still the conversation keeps going. This person is an expert at what we might call "party talk."

Party talk might be defined as the quick and easy chat people do in brief encounters, over the music, and so on. You have probably had some party talk about going to college, for instance, and maybe even specifically about going to this one instead of another one nearby ("It's cheaper" or "It's closer to home" or whatever). Write down some typical party talk about why you are here. (Because I can't get a job right now? Because I'm afraid I won't be able to get a good job without a college education, and this place is as good as any? Because I'm going to be a _____ and this place has a good program in that? Because I want to become an educated person? Because I want to occupy a certain place in society? Because I was bored, or wanted to change careers? Because I wanted to use my VA benefits?—adapted from Walter Pauk, *How to Study in College*).

But is the party talk accurate? Or hasn't it really been just a way of stopping conversation? Aren't you giving a familiar answer just so no one will be confused? And aren't the real reasons a bit more complicated, at least? (And aren't some of my suggestions rather odd?) Really now, why *are* you going to college? Wouldn't you be better off going right to work, building seniority and doing night classes for just the advanced training you need?

> (This assignment used to be a "loop," with one assignment on party talk, one on changing it into real talk, and one applying the idea of party talk to college, before I asked about "the real thing." But the subtopic must have been too far from things that looked useful, and the weak papers drove me back to a study-skills rationale: work on student motivation before working on skills.)

4. As I threatened, now I want to look at your schedule so that we can see whether it is reasonably adapted to your goals. Give us a time sheet for a typical week; enter your classes first, then your other fixed activities such as work or whatever, then study time (I hope you will leave room for recreation, family and friends).

Did laying out your schedule show you anything? How could your schedule "fit" your goals better? What goals show up here?

5. We have seen two pieces of language you have (more or less!) "by heart," to use a phrase some of you have used. The Star-Spangled Banner turned out to be very complicated, especially in its grammar, and the Pledge of Allegiance turned out to be saying some surprising things about this country. Then we looked at some

language you use which is not exactly like everybody else's, and looked to see what it could tell us about what you are really after, here in college.

Let's consider next an area we mentioned before, religion. Do you have a prayer memorized? Or some other religious language that is deeply engrained? Write it down for us, and then paraphrase it, as before. Then tell us when you learned it, and what it meant to you then. Finally, tell us what it means to you now, once you have had a chance to look at it afresh. What has been the effect of writing it down and writing about it?

> (An important accompaniment of this assignment is a comment by me about "drawing the line" between what student writers want to share and what they want to keep private. "The course cannot draw that line," I say; "it will respect the line where you draw it.")

6. You probably have some other piece of language "by heart." Write it down for us, and paraphrase it as usual. Where and when do you repeat it? Can you separate what it means from what you mean by it? (If you can, try to make the separation as wide as possible for us. If you cannot, what do you think makes the piece different in this respect from what we found for the Pledge and the Anthem?)

In class, we will be talking about the variety of things we learn "by heart"—a puzzling phrase itself, when you look at it closely, because what does the heart have to do with it? Does it make sense to speak of learning a phone number or address "by heart"? A chemistry equation? The multiplication tables? A part in a play?

7. Find something you would like to learn by heart. Learn it, and come to class ready to write or say it. It should be about 50 words long.

In class, you will say what you learned or write it. Then you will write a short piece explaining why you chose this particular item and how you went about learning it. Do you have special tricks to help you remember? Do you know other ways to retain things? How long do you think you will be able to retain this piece? Is there any connection in this exercise between what you learn and how you learn it? What do you think about this kind of learning "by heart"?

8. Learn this piece by next class (Robert Frost's "For Once, Then, Something" or "Design"). When you come to class, you will write it out, paraphrase it, and discuss it.

8A. Write out the poem you have learned "by heart." Paraphrase it in three or four sentences.

The poem is important in itself, and we will talk about it at our next class, but for now we will concentrate on two learning experiences, both having to do with memorization. What similarities and differences do you see between memorizing something you wanted to learn and memorizing something I told you to learn? Did your strategies change? Did the effects change? Will you retain the one you chose a lot longer?

9. The task in this assignment is *definition,* another important academic skill like

paraphrasing. We have just been working with three cases of "learning by heart," a phrase as you'll recall which sounded odd to me a while ago. Write a definition of "learn by heart" in which you clarify whatever might be murky in the understanding of someone not in this course: what has it come to mean to you that an outsider might not be aware of? Add a note in which you step back from the definition to see whether it might *persuade* someone of something. Feel free to cite the examples of "learning by heart" from class.

10. We have just been defining "by heart," which is one of the phrases we have been using for some of our recent experiences with language. But we have had some other, related experiences earlier, which require a broader, more inclusive label, such as "automatic language," "rote language" and "routine language," to mention three candidates.

Choose your own candidate, from this list or elsewhere, for the phenomena we have been working with, and give us an extended definition of it (more than just its general class and distinguishing trait, in other words; more than "chair is piece of furniture for sitting on"). The extended definition should be one that could serve as a statement of what this course is about, say for a student who might be thinking about taking the course next term.

More important even than the definition itself, though that is obviously vital to your making sense of what we're doing, is to note for us the effects of doing the definition *on you*. Has anything happened to you while you did this sorting of experiences and defining of characteristics? Do you see anything now that you did not see before? And what has been left out of this account of our recent experiences, that could not be put into a definition? Can next term's prospective students possibly learn from the definition exactly what you know? Isn't knowledge gained from definition different from knowledge gained by experience? But isn't knowledge knowledge? And what are definitions for, if they can't really impart knowledge?

11. Read the article by William Perry on reserve ("Conflicts in the Learning Process," reprinted in Walker Gibson's *Seeing and Writing*, pp. 88-100). Take notes on the article (another academic skill!) and bring them to class for others to see.

In addition, choose one paragraph from the Perry article that seems absolutely vital to what he is saying. Quote the paragraph (single space, with narrower margins), and then (in regular margins and double spacing) explain what Perry is saying in the paragraph so the rest of us can see why you think *this* paragraph is vital.

12. One of the paragraphs that seems important to many of us who read Perry's article is from page 95, where he is talking about each of us as a mixture of ME and SELF:

The two frames of reference ME and SELF are separate, distinct, and self-contained, but what makes growth into maturity look like a gradual thing is, I think, first that we take the point of view of SELF in one area of life at a time and second, that even in those areas in which we have attained it, it is notoriously unstable. A student, for instance, may attain a mature frame of reference in his social relationships and remain a child in his school work. He may feel and act as an adult away from home, but when he returns to the family that treats him as a child, he will feel like one. It is this jumping back and forth from one frame of reference to another that is the basis, I believe, of the instability of adolescence. Of course it stays with us, to a degree, all our lives.

To what extent is this true of you, that you are both ME and SELF, and what do you think the importance of this point is? To answer this question, must you set up a comparison/contrast structure? Find some areas where you are clearly a ME and others where you are just as clearly a SELF. And give some examples, maybe one good one of each.

Other people in the class will probably want to know more than whether you are a mix, though, right? Think about what you would like to know about others. For example, are they happy with the mix they've got? Or, did they achieve it or did it just grow? Would they like to be more SELF? Do they know or even imitate other people who seem to be SELVES? Does a SELF give up assertiveness? And so on. Try at least to answer the questions you would be curious about in others, and when you read others' papers in class, see how you did at predicting their curiosity.

You may feel that these questions are rather personal, and in a way they are. (Questions like this are asked on many mass-testing kinds of writing exams, because personal experience is the only thing everyone can be assumed to share and know about equally.) If you find yourself beoming uncomfortably personal, I suggest that you shift to the more public aspects of your life. You must simply draw the line where you want it, between the private and the public you.

13. Look back at your earlier writings, especially at the first two and at the questions about how you learn differently when you choose and when I choose what must be learned. What do you think Perry would say about your answers? Can you write his response in something like his voice?

But you have the last word, of course, in your own voice. Can you answer Perry? Isn't it possible that he is missing something? Or are you hopelessly trapped in the adolescent pattern he identifies?

To complete this assignment, you may want to (notice me coercing you?) go back to the reserve room and read the Perry article again in order to notice the places where he seems to have "designs" on you. Were you aware of those designs the first time you read it, or did it seem to be strictly a factual piece? What difference does it make to your reading, once you recognize what he is trying to do? What difference did it make to completing this assignment when you realized what I was trying to get you to do? How can you possibly learn anything with all these attempted influences around you?

14. Another area of language where people often find themselves on "automatic pilot" includes what might be called *set phrases*. As a working definition, let's consider set phrases to be groups of words that are used over and over without changes.

"You shoulda seen me on the court today—I was hot as a pistol!"

"She wouldn't hurt a fly."

"Last but not least,..."

Between now and next class, listen to your family, friends, TV, radio, yourself (!), and write down some of the set phrases you hear. You will need six written down for class on Friday.

(In that class, students in small groups compose stories using all the phrases brought by the members of the group.)

15. Many of the phrases we worked with in class are called "clichés" (klee-SHAZE). Your job this time is to write about clichés.

In addition to giving examples and a definition, you might consider these questions: Why do *you* use clichés? Why do you think other people use them? If you don't use them and don't hear others using them, how would you account for that surprising fact? What does a cliché say, underneath, in addition to its particular meaning (consider the death recently of Valleyspeak, following the release of a record about it)? Do clichés ever get in the way? Are there different types? What do people mean when they speak of "earning a cliché"?

"I've learned a lot in this class. I used to use clichés like they were going out of style, but now I wouldn't touch one with a ten-foot pole" (from Frank and Ernest, 7/8/80). What's supposed to be funny about that?

16. There are many interesting areas of language adjacent to the automatic areas we have been exploring. Proverbs, slang, and advertisements are three, and you can undoubtedly think of others.

Choose one of these areas, or another you believe is closely related, where people are using language on automatic pilot. Give examples from the area you choose, and show what the examples have in common. Is the area important? Why and how? Are there special tricks of language used there?

For our sakes, be sure to make the examples visible, and try not to let the area get too large (like advertising would be). And if you can, surprise us.

17. In our work so far this semester, we have been conducting research into "automatic language." We have looked at several areas that seem to be related. The task now is to draw a line around these areas, and say what is inside and what is outside. This enterprise is related to definition, but it has other uses as well; can you think of one?

Obviously, lots of things are outside. But don't give us just generalities; we can produce those ourselves. Try to find some small, manageable area or example you know about where you can show us, as well as tell us, how the language is working *non*-automatically.

This is one of the more experimental assignments, so please do tell me what went on as you thought and wrote.

18. But even the areas lying outside the line in our last exercise can be reduced to formulae, can't they? And this is what often goes on in textbooks on how to write: the book reduces to a set of rules what someone once discovered as a new way of doing things in language.

Consider a formula for writing that you know. You could use the five-paragraph essay, the T-R-I paragraph, the standard bad-news business letter, or some other. Imagine that you are the inventor or discoverer of this way of writing. What are the selling points? What are the hidden pitfalls? What does the format itself contribute to the message? Does it say anything underneath as clichés do?

19. Let us take a break by collecting some more light-hearted information. Present us with an "emblem" of a time when something went off the track in language. It can be an event, a story, a memory, whatever.

My own emblem is a prayer of my wife's grandfather, a grace he said, which she thought went like this "...And put this food to its ten-and-juice." Later on, of course, she realized that he was saying, "Put this food to its antenna juice." She has never explained what she thought *that* meant. I suppose it had the mystery children often attach to religious language, as we noted in an early assignment.

An emblem of Kenneth Koch's is of how a poem developed from a misprint: somehow a "swarm" of bees became a "swan" of bees on his typewriter, and that gave him the idea for a poem about animals made of animals.

Your story should be a story about language, especially about an accident in language.

20. Walter Erickson, the Canadian architect who designed Simon Fraser University, would teach only first-year students. His first assignment was always the same: "Bring in 7 stones." He gave the students three weeks!

His idea was that his first year students could see things clearly, without preconceptions or prejudices, and that they would design an arrangement of the seven stones which would reveal the principles of design to be found in textbooks.

Are you able to rid your mind of preconceptions and prejudices? Of course you are. So bring in seven words. That's all. Just bring in seven words.

(The lists are read and copied by everyone during the next class; unknown words are spelled and explained.)

21. What were the different grounds on which people chose words? Group the methods into categories.

Suggestion: you may want to try grouping the different principles around a "rhetorical triangle." The rhetorical triangle is a map of a communication situation, with writer, reader, and subject at the corners, and language in the background.

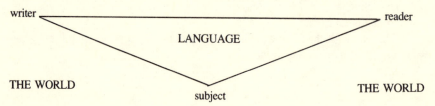

writer — — — — — — — — — — — — — — — — — — reader

LANGUAGE

THE WORLD   subject   THE WORLD

After you have grouped the principles, this way or some other, look at the principles as a set. What do they tell you?

22. The lists of words offer us several different kinds of information. If you see something I don't ask about, please do write about your own insight. Otherwise, choose one or more of the following questions.

   a. Choose the one or two lists that seem to you to make the least sense. What can you do to make sense of them? What does this tell you about how your mind makes sense of things, makes sense of words? How do you think other people might go about making sense of the same strings of words? Same or different? And either way, so what?

   b. Choose three or four lists that make sense in very *different* ways. In what ways do they make sense? Are these ways of making sense fundamental and important to the way we think, or are they just the simplest, quickest, most obvious kinds of arrangements?

   c. Now that you have seen several lists in addition to your own, think again about constructing a list. How many principles of order can you get to operate and be obvious in a single list? Can more than two or three be perceived by a reader? Do you think people ever compose with more than one or two in mind? Why or why not? Is it *better* to have more than one principle working? Now write a new seven.

   d. Choose two or three of the lists that seem to you to reflect a particular kind of person. What kinds of persons? How do you know? What do they think of their readers? What effects do the lists aim at? How do you know that?

23. One of the principles people often choose in making a list of seven "designed" words is the principle of "ultimate" words, words that express absolute values the writer expects the reader to share or at least respect. When you write, apparently, ultimate words could be useful in gaining a reader's assent to the specific argument you are making.

Another basic principle seems to be the taking advantage of some built-in patterns of order. We seem to have a few natural strategies for arranging words or experiences that make them manageable for us and easily grasped by others. When you write, apparently, these simple ordering principles can be useful in getting readers to pick up on what you're doing more easily.

Choose one of these principles and find it working somewhere. You might look at previous papers of yours, at your textbooks, at newspapers, ads, whatever. Present us with a case of the principle's application, and explain enough so that we can't miss it.

24. We have been identifying some of the principles underlying effective written discourse. Let's try them out and see how they work. Let's begin with this school's catalog.

Choose one of the opening statements (pages specified). What was the writer trying to do? To whom was the writer speaking? Who does the writer seem to be? And what is the writer's view of the situation? To what extent, finally, did the writer choose the words and to what extent was the writer more or less forced to do as he or she did? Do you detect any automatic pilot?

25. What you have just been doing to the catalog is called "rhetorical analysis." That means that you have been dissecting a piece of writing for three things, primarily: who seems to be writing it? to whom do they think they are talking? and what is their view of the situation and subject?

Do the same kind of analysis for two advertisements, two as *different* as possible. Choose from different magazines, newspapers or newspaper sections. Please attach the ads or copies of them so others can see what you were working with.

In your analysis, pay special attention to the tip-offs, to the aspects that told you what you found out about audience, persona, and view of the subject. How do you know, in other words, what you say is likely?

26. Analyze a whole magazine in the same way you did the ads in 25. Here again, though, you may find *comparison* helpful, if you can find two magazines treating the same topic. Who is the intended audience, and *how do you know?* Do the writers try to sound like "just one of us," or like insiders or experts? And what is the life-style of the readers, do you think?

The difference between this assignment and the one before is that the audience for your paper will not have the magazines before them. You will have to find some way to address that problem. And there is a significant problem of *"so what?"* here, or *"who cares?"* The content of this writing won't be very new, but the presentation of it may give you some trouble; let me know in a note what you worked on.

27. In your field, as in mine, there is a sub-language you have to know if you want to do well. In one of my fields, linguistics ("the scientific study of language"), you have to know words like "transformation" and "generate" and "derivation" and "innate" and "language-acquisition device" and "universal," just to name a few; each of these words is also in general use, but linguists have given each one a new and *technical* definition. A "universal" is a feature of all languages, for example; the category "verb" is a language universal, but the category "noun," curiously, is not. In addition to these ordinary words used in technical senses, there are other words in linguistics that the man on the street would probably never hear, words like "labio-dental fricative" or "morphophonemic" or "illocutionary." Learning linguistics was partly a matter of learning these special words; having learned them, I now have to be careful in talking to non-linguists in order to remember which words need what kind of explanation.

Your field undoubtedly has words in it which have to be learned and then from time to time explained to outsiders. Give us a short dictionary of examples, four or five of each of the two types described above.

28. Not only is vocabulary special for a special field; paper-writing is usually special too. Particularly if you are a scientist, but also if you are in the humanities or in business, there are these things called "formats" or "style sheets" or "writing manuals." Even if there aren't official documents on how to write in your field, there are strong expectations about how things will be put on paper and about what

you must do to be *"correct."*

You will have to use some judgment in choosing the format or some other aspect of paper-writing in your field, so that you can investigate and report reliably to us. We want to know, as non-specialists, what the format is, but above all *why* it is this way, since we will be trying to make generalizations about all formats and their principles of design. So you must give us a helpful description, but you must also understand the format well enough to tell us how it is meant to work.

Some sources that you might want to try are: official style manuals (like the Associated Press one for media people), textbooks (as on business writing), actual samples of writing from the field (as for papers in the sciences), and opinions (you can and probably should *interview* people in the field). You might want to use this occasion as a kind of introduction to your major, if you are still undecided. This is far from a complete list of sources; I hope you will use some ingenuity.

You will also need to develop the questions to ask and answer, to get for us the information we want. Look especially, I would suggest, for how the piece of writing starts, how one presents evidence (if that is relevant), how one refers to the work of others, how many examples, what kind of development, conclusions, and so on.

29. Now that we have heard about a variety of formats, our task is to see how they operate, what their general principles are, how they are like and unlike each other, how they are related, and so forth. The point (remember we have no textbook in this class!) is to provide for ourselves some general advice about writing that will equip us to work with and even develop new formats in the future.

Within this aim and the data from class, you still have some freedom, the freedom to choose a path through the data that makes sense to you. You should temper this freedom by remembering the audience—not just ourselves, but a wider audience besides, because there is a real chance that you will have something new and useful to say about writing.

Some strategies that you might find useful: sort the formats into types, or arrange them on some sort of continuum or grid, or look for extremes or even contraries.

With this assignment, we begin dealing with the later stages of the writing process. You have done some kind of draft for today, and in class we will have worked on the draft in a workshop. Now you need to develop the next draft, the re-vision, the re-seeing that makes everything crystal clear.

Please turn in both the rough draft and the final version. These should be different! Were there enough clear examples? Do the examples really show what they are supposed to? Are they in the right order? Is the introduction going to interest your colleagues in the class? Do they need the conclusion, or would the general audience need it?

You should also begin compiling your own editing and proofreading sheet. I will ask to have this turned in with some future assignments, and it will be far more accurate then if you start on it now. Such a sheet, by the way, will be indispensable when you start composing your writing on a word processor, if you haven't already; you need to know what kinds of problems to tell the computer to search for. One of mine, luckily, can be spotted pretty easily by a "Search" function; I like to load my sentences with prepositional phrases, and I can give the processor a word list, so that it can tell me whether I've gone overboard on these structures. You should list on yours, for starters, the mechanical problems you've had so far this semester, say the top ten or twelve most frequent, and you should check all final drafts from now on against this sheet.

I am interested to know, in your note this time, not only how you got to your insights about formats, but also whether you found out anything about editing and proofreading.

30. Well, what did you learn about editing and proofreading?

We have said first that there is a distinction between editing and proofreading, which we can draw if we want to: editing can be seen as revising in the pure sense of "re-seeing" or re-thinking an entire subject, from content and approach down to structure and arrangment and format. Proofreading, by contrast, involves matters of punctuation, spelling, getting subjects to agree with verbs, linking potential fragments to whole sentences, using pronouns that agree with antecedents, and so on.

For this assignment, first choose your writing from a previous assignment, one that would really benefit from a fresh approach and another attempt. But rework what is there; do not begin again "out of whole cloth." One of the immediate points of this is to learn the kind of editing that a word-processor can do: shifting material, making insertions and deletions.

Give us three things for the workshop: the original, a photocopy on which you make the changes (edited, in other words), and a final, carefully proofread copy. One of the aims here is to see just how good you can make that final copy; we will get far less out of partial efforts, because we won't know what you are capable of, and you will get lots of advice you don't need.

31. It's time to begin making some more connections between things you have memorized or learned by heart on the one hand and your writing ability on the other.

What is a noun? What is a verb? What is an adjective? An adverb? A preposition? An article? Write down your own definitions, the memorized ones if you recall them and made-up ones if you don't. How many parts of speech are there, and how do you know? Suppose someone told you there are ten; how would that person have to argue?

32. In his autobiography, *Personal Memoirs,* which he finished a few days before his death, Ulysses S. Grant wrote that he had heard "A noun is the name of a thing" repeated so often that eventually he believed it. He went on, "I think I am a verb instead of a personal pronoun. A verb is anything that signifies to be; to do; or to suffer. I signify all three." (Quoted in the *New Republic's* review of William S. McFeely's *Grant: A Biography;* February 28, 1981.)

Grant was dying of throat cancer, in great pain, no little disgrace, deeply in debt, and desperate to recoup through the book enough money for his large family to live on after he was gone. Odd that parts of speech should have occurred to him at such a time.

Parts of speech for us rarely attain such importance as they had for Grant, or for the medieval philosophers who thought that "modes of being" corresponded to the ways words hooked onto the world. Still, parts of speech count for something, and the enterprise here is to see how much they do and should count for in your writing.

1. Choose a paragraph from a paper you've written either for this class or for another. It should be about one hundred words long. It must be all you—no quotes.
2. Re-type the passage, with triple spacing and wide margins.
3. Circle all prepositions, and then underline all prepositional phrases.
4. Put "Subj." above all the subjects of main clauses (either before or after separating off all predicates with //).
5. Put "Verb" above all verbs, main or otherwise.
6. Then answer the following questions in a connected stretch of prose:
   a. Were you aware as you wrote of anything about the grammar of your paragraph? That was a long time ago, perhaps; what about as you typed it?
   b. Do you see any complicated parts now, where you aren't sure what the structure of the sentences is?
   c. Do you see any way that thinking about the grammar of the sentences could have helped you write them? When in your writing process might such thinking be helpful?
   d. Are you aware of the stylistic advice that says you should vary the length of your sentences? Do you do that? And if so, how? Arbitrarily?
   e. Do you see any area where you need to know more about the grammar of what you are writing? Or do you understand pretty well what you are doing in grammatical terms?
   f. How do you account for the importance people attach to using "good grammar"? Why do people think it matters?

(Special assignments can be inserted at this point to focus on specific problems: given a paragraph of fragments, how might it have been written? What would a world be like that was all verbs? I have tried a classical imitation exercise, where students are to fill in blanks labelled only with parts of speech, the pattern derived from some writer.)

33. Write down for us an incident that you recently witnessed; write about one page, and use the present tense; preferably discuss just one event.

34. In class, I will give you someone else's incident. Rewrite it, adding details or explanations if you like, but shift to past tense. Then explain why you like one version or the other better. Does tense have the effects you expected? Would present or past always have the effects they do here?

35. Describe this classroom in such a way that we can know, without your telling us or using emotional words at all, what your feelings about it are.

Now describe this same classroom, using as many of the same details as you can, but in a technical style, being as neutral and as "objective" as you can possibly be.

What does this tell you, that two descriptions of the same object are possible and equally legitimate? Did you have trouble using the same details? Why, do you think?

36. We have written in two of the most common forms recently—*narration* and *description*. We have also uncovered some basic grammatical information and some hints about how words work to represent things. Now let's look at another common form, *explanation,* and in this case a kind of how-to explanation.

Build for us a paper airplane, and bring it, concealed, to class. Write for us a step-by-step account of how to do it.

Attach a note: what were the hard parts of writing this? The easy ones? How would you like to be someone who writes instructions for a living? Where do you think others will have trouble in following your directions?

(In class, of course, we try to follow the directions.)

37. We have just been writing some narration, some description, and some how-to explanation. These are strategies for writing, but they are hardly ever full purposes or reasons for writing. When someone tells you to write description, you naturally want to know, "What for?"

But think about that question for a moment. Why would someone write a description? If you described an object, for instance, it might be so that someone could recognize it (it is stolen, and the police recover it; is it yours?) or work with it. If you described a person, you might want your hearer or reader to value the person as much as you do. If you describe a process, so to speak, you probably want your reader to be able to duplicate the process, to get the right result. In all these cases, you try to make a change in the reader: either the reader comes to believe something or becomes able to do something. These changes amount to being persuaded, and persuasion is our subject now. For next time, write about a time when you were persuaded, either to believe or to do something contrary to what you had believed or done before. Concentrate on the moment of change itself, when you realized or came to believe, and make us understand yourself both before and after, along with the cause of the change in you.

38. More than 2000 years ago, Aristotle described several types of persuasion: by appeal to authority, by reference to agreed-on facts or opinions, by a powerful presentation of one's personality, or by showing how agreed-on goals lead to the desired course of action. Recently, Carl Rogers has pursued the idea about values, saying that no one ever changed anyone else's mind by direct confrontation.

How should a writer go about being persuasive, then? If Rogers is right, it isn't enough to be right and to be direct. But being sneaky probably won't work either, especially if your reader notices.

To answer that question, which is a real one of undying interest on Madison Avenue and elsewhere, please consider and systematize the things that can get members of the class to change their minds. We may not get hired as consultants, but we should be able to get some hints.

Epilogue: Look through your papers from this term. You will probably notice that, although we wandered, we also circled around some of the same things right from the start. What have those things been for you? Have you felt me trying to be persuasive about anything? How do these writing experiences compare with others you have had? What does this course come to for you? If you remember the very first thing you wrote in here, you might note for us what your own "hobby horse" has been through the course. And you might have some ideas about how I could get to the goals of the course better; let me know now or on the confidential evaluation later, as you choose.

"Really Communicating" and Writing

Philip M. Keith

When I began to teach at St. Cloud State University in Minnesota, I was struck by how emphatically my new students valued good communication. At times I had the feeling that "real communication" was an all-inclusive value for them. A relationship was good if one's friend "really communicated." A teacher was good if he or she "really communicated." Parents were good if they "really communicated." These students had little difficulty understanding why they had to put up with the unpleasantness of a course in writing—it would teach them to "really communicate," of course. What was driving me up the wall, however, was how profoundly uncommunicative all this talk about communication was. I never had a clear sense of what "really communicating" was or how it took place. In fact, it seemed that talking about the value of "really communicating" worked for them mainly as a way of getting off the rather painful hook of having to really communicate what they thought and felt, and why they thought and felt as they did.

However, the problem here was not, I knew well, merely a state university problem or a midwest problem. The modern world has an obsession with communication that manifests itself both in serious inquiry in mass-communications, linguistics, sociology, psychology, anthropology, philosophy, and semiotics, and in more popularized forms in business, the media, and the schools. But what too often happens is that an expression of concern with authentic communication—with "being up close and personal," with "telling it like it is," with "really communicating"—becomes a way of evading actual communication, an evasion that is all the more insidious because the glossy, catchy vocabulary obscures with particular effectiveness the fact that the real thing is absent. In a parallel way, the back to the basics movement has declared itself to be intensely concerned with the communication skills of American students, but has translated that concern into a fixation with the surface forms of edited American English—forms that likewise can obscure the fact that no real substance is present in the writing.

As a means of challenging these tendencies, I decided to design a course that would engage my students in a study of rhetoric in I. A. Richards' terms: a study of misunderstanding and its remedies. It would be foolish to presume that the course

22

would cover that subject completely, but it did seem reasonable to have students see that issue in terms of their own writing, and thus to make it a functional subject for them rather than a formal one. I wanted to be working with my students at the point where, in Ann Berthoff's terms, the what and the how of writing are brought into a dynamic interrelationship. They would come to learn something about communication in general from their own activities, and, in turn, they would come to understand some of their own and others' writing problems from what they were learning.

This sequence of assignments, then, is a case study in the problem of defining the idea of effective communication. In a traditional composition course, there is usually a "definition paper" of some kind, but the problem of definition, or of how you know what you know, is so basic that the single chance approach doesn't really provide an adequate opportunity to get into the problem in anything like a substantial way. The overall strategy in this sequence is to have the students first try to say what they mean and why they value effective communication, and then to discover the importance of examples and context in making communication work, and finally to come to a sense of how statements not only express thought, but also relate the communicators in complex ways that can be hard to control.

The assignments are a set of specific problem situations or puzzles that come at the question of understanding how communication works and fails in varied but complementary ways. In the first assignment, the students are asked to display their natural "defining behavior" by saying what they take "effective communication" to mean. As the course proceeds, these initial definitions of communication can be compared by students to other work they do in the course. In this version of this sequence, the students are asked at the end of the course to see how their approach to this question might be different as a way of providing them a measure of how they have changed in the course. But one could have them make this comparison several times during the course to provide a more frequent measure.

Now that we have something to measure improvement by, we move to defining through example. The students are asked in assignments 2, 3, 5 and 6 to describe some communication situations from their own experience and to comment on those situations in some way, saying why communication was working or not, or saying why they found the specimens worth recording. I don't worry over the fact that many of the specimens involve such events as the great meeting of misty eyes at the senior-prom/last game of the season/sister's wedding/death of beloved grandparent or best/other friend and so forth. Class discussions will provide plenty of opportunity for distinguishing between more and less persuasive narratives, and by the end of the quarter the students will have had plenty of opportunities to distinguish between the honest and the canned in their own writing. In my experience with this sequence, much of the best writing it provokes begins as second or third efforts with one of these assignments. In addition, I try to keep the definition problem in the forefront of their minds by asking them in the fourth assignment to summarize some conclusions they have come to as a result of collecting examples of their own and hearing others. This pattern of moving back and forth from examples to conclusions is woven throughout the entire sequence. As the course proceeds, though, the examples deal less with situations drawn from their own experience and more with situations that they confront in reading. By the end of the course, the students have moved from personal writing to analysis of some fairly complex problems in philosophy, politics, psychology and education.

The next concept that we look at as a way of defining is context. Instead of asking simply what people mean, we begin to explore how the context of a statement shapes the way we understand it. This notion is set up by having the students collect some specimens of communication—first from people they know, and then from people they don't know—and then asking them to discuss how having a more substantial context in the first specimens makes what they hear either easier or more difficult to hear and describe. Then, in exercises 8-12, they are given some situations to understand and explain: a typical contest of wills between Lucy and Schroeder from the comic strip *Peanuts*, some cute talking at cross-purposes between children, Salome trying to seduce John the Baptist, a Wordsworthian debate between a teacher and a child on the relation between life and death, and a moment of marital conflict between George and Martha of *Who's Afraid of Virginia Woolf?* Each of these situations is common enough so that the students can at least come up with analogous situations to discuss as a way of explaining what is "going on" in the situations the assignments provide. They also cover a range of situations and topics from the commonplace to the sublime, and from the innocent to the sophisticated, so that any student should find something to "hook into."

Exercises 13 to 15 constitute a kind of mid-point, in which some technical questions about definition are raised. In assignment 13, they are asked to consider how words get defined by a dictionary—not just by a single meaning, but first by a range of meanings, then by relations to other words, by synonyms and by the lines drawn between synonyms, and then by their etymological relations. This gives us a chance to discuss not just the varieties of meaning in the word "communication," but also the overtones that attach to it through its relation to such words as "community" and "common." In exercises 14 and 15, as in exercise 4, the students are asked to give some focus to the diversity of information and conclusions they have collected up to this point by developing a taxonomy, and then by comparing and contrasting their own way of classifying with that of other members of the class. Raising the concept of definition again allows students both to pull together what they have been doing, and to move into the second part of the sequence with some additional awareness of what they are doing with language. When they can read with an active sense of the multiple meaning-relations of words, they can make much more sense of their reading.

Assignments 16 to 25 use the third major concept, the distinction between content and relation. This concept, which borrows from studies in family therapy, assumes that communication takes place on two levels, at the content level or the level of intended statement, and at the relational level or the level of implicit assertions about the relative status of the two communicators. Reading the relational message becomes an important way of understanding what is being said, and since the relational message is somewhat like the style of the message, but not identical, this sort of reading can provide some powerful insights into statements and situations. The students try this out first on the dispute from *Who's Afraid of Virginia Woolf*, and then on the situations from their own experience and the situations they overheard. Two new situations defined in an essay by the environmentalist-poet Wendell Berry and a short discussion of teaching literacy by the radical educator Paulo Freire provide some larger perspectives.

In the final section of the sequence, the students turn their attention to the writing and responding they have been doing during the course. The aim here is to get them to apply their increased understanding of the communication process to the activities of the course itself. The assignments do this by having them examine their own and other students' writing and the reactions to it. We have been doing this from the beginning, of course, in having the class sessions mainly concerned with the writing that the assignments have generated. However, the issue is addressed more systematically beginning with assignment 17, "the writing party." The writing party is a class game in which everyone including the instructor does ten minutes of free-writing on whatever is pleasing or upsetting them. These papers are circulated for others to react to in five minute periods. Usually the students' reactions to the instructor's writing show some "relational stress" that is illuminating. Then in exercises 23-24, each student reads through his or her entire folder and the entire folder of one other student to find where communication has been particularly effective or ineffective. In exercise 25, they are asked to get a graded paper from a student not in this class and to describe and analyze the communication-style of the writer and grader. And in the final paper, they are invited to say something about how what they know and do is or is not different from what they were knowing and doing at the beginning of the course.

Included here are five extra assignments. The first of these options is a revision assignment that provides an opportunity to refine presentational skills by translating an exercise into a more formal paper or essay. The sequence gives heavy emphasis to writing in a problem/solution format rather than in a formal essay format, but the instructor can use this assignment three or four times to give heavier emphasis to the revising and editing skills that are called upon in shaping a formal essay. The second and third extra assignments raise some more sophisticated epistemological problems from Lewis Carroll's *Through the Looking Glass*. The fourth and the fifth take a closer look at the pedagogical activity of responding to student writing as a communication problem through the contrasting vocabularies or methods of William Coles and E. D. Hirsch. When this sequence is used in a multi-section staff format, these tasks can be useful as a staff-development device to help teachers get a clearer grasp of the expectations inherent in problem-solving writing as opposed to formal essay writing.

Despite all the plotting that has gone into this sequence, it is very important that this program be considered as more heuristic or suggestive than rigidly fixed. No exercise sequence, it seems to me, can work very well if its method is not the teacher's own method, and the best way for a prospective user to go about relating the method here to his or her own method is to add or substitute other examples, to reshape the pattern of assignments in part or in whole, and to alter the wording or the overall style of the assignments. So, I would welcome any information or questions about what others do with these materials.

ON COMMUNICATION: SITUATIONS AND CONTEXTS

1. This is a "shakedown cruise" into writing. Let's see what you can do with a given writing problem, how you can work with it. Give yourself two hours in one block to write and revise a paper responding to the question below. After two hours, copy over what you have as a paper into readable form. If you spend less than two hours, indicate how much time you spent at the top of the first page of your final copy. Don't spend more.

Question: We all probably agree that communication is a good thing, that it is good to be able to communicate, that it is bad when we cannot communicate. How and why do you think this is so (or not so)? Obviously you are not going to be able to cover this subject completely. I am interested in knowing what your best reasons now are for valuing or not valuing the ability to communicate. In the process, though, it would probably help if you said what "communicating well" or "really communicating" is, what it means to you.

2. One way of defining a word or expression is through example. You may have used an example or examples in your first paper. If you did, fine. There won't be any harm in doing the same kind of thing several times.

You have probably had an experience where you felt you were really communicating with someone or some group. Describe what happened and how it happened in such a way that your reader will know that "real communication" is what you are describing, and that he or she will not have to rely on your saying it was.

3. Last time you described an experience in which real communication was going on. But many times, when people are trying to communicate, real communication does not take place. Something gets in the way. Choose from your experience an example of bad communication, of communication gone wrong. What happened, and how? Again, try to describe or dramatize the situation so that your reader can see that communication has failed without having to depend on your say-so.

Keep a copy of this paper.

4. Now let's stand back a little and see if we can draw some conclusions about good vs. bad communication on the basis of what you have written on questions 2 and 3. What were the differences between an effective communication situation and an ineffective communication situation? If you think you can say more by using someone else's example or examples, feel free to do so. Finally, remember that we are not looking for the last word on the subject here, just some sensible and useful conclusions. If they seem obvious to you, that is all right too.

5. Now let's go out and listen for some communication. In preparation for this paper, open your ears to conversation going on around you and listen for some

interesting communication between or among people you do not know. (It may also be interesting lack of communication.) It may be in a class, walking across campus, in a dining hall, gym or wherever. You may want to pretend that you are reading or working near a table where strangers are talking. In the next day or so, record as many bits of communication as you can, as completely and accurately as you can, in a journal.

Then, for your paper, copy or reconstruct one or more of the most interesting pieces, filling out the scene enough so that a reader can understand what is going on. Then, in a final paragraph, say something about why you thought that piece or those pieces of conversation were interesting.

6. Now, listen for some successful (or unsuccessful) communication between or among people whom you *do* know. Again, keep reconstructions in your journal, and then, for the paper, copy (and fill out) the most interesting example or examples. Again, add a final paragraph on what you found interesting about it (or them).

Keep a copy of this paper.

7. For the past two assignments, you have been acting as a kind of psycho-socio-linguist, collecting talk and trying to describe why what you collect interests you.

One useful concept for studying conversation in the way we are doing is the idea of *context*. You probably found that recording and discussing the conversation of friends or acquaintances was different (maybe easier or maybe harder) than recording and discussing the conversations of people you didn't know.

Look back over your journals and papers 5 and 6 to see what you might say about the differences that resulted from your having a fuller context for the conversations in paper 6 than you did in paper 5. If, on the other hand, you see no difference, see if you can say why the fact that you know more about the people you were recording in assignment 6 than those you were recording in assignment 5 was not significant.

If indeed you see no significant differences, turn in copies of papers 5 and 6 with this paper. We may be able to workshop some of these problem cases in class.

8. Now we are going to explore some situations in which communication is going wrong.

(At this point I show the students a *Peanuts* cartoon strip which is reproduced on p. 101 of a text also used later in the course: *Pragmatics of Human Communication, A Study of Interactional Patterns, Pathologies and Paradigms,* by Paul Watzlawick, Janet Helmick Beavin and Don Jackson. The cartoon strip is one in which Lucy is characteristically harrassing Schroeder for a compliment, and not getting what she wants.)

a. In a few sentences or a brief paragraph, explain what is going wrong here. How is it going wrong? Why?

b. Now look at your response to the preceding questions and bracket those sentences or phrases that refer to a context outside the particular situation, that is, outside the context defined by the information in this particular comic strip.

c.   How did the context or contexts you brought to your reading of the strip help you or influence you in your reading of the strip?

(Assignments 9, 10, and 11 borrow directly from examples in Kenneth Burke's "Lexicon Rhetoricae," as found on pp. 136-137 of *Counter-Statement* [Berkeley: University of California Press, 1968]. Reprinted by permission of the University of California Press.)

9. Here is another exchange as recalled by an observer:

...we may recall a conversation between two children, a boy and a girl. The boy's mind was on one subject, the girl's turned to many subjects, with the result that the two of them were talking at cross-purposes. Pointing to a field beyond the road, the boy asked: "Whose field is that?" The girl answered: "That is Mr. Murdock's field"—and went on to tell where Mr. Murdock lived, how many children he had, when she had last seen these children, which of them she preferred, but the boy interrupted: "What does he do with the field?" He usually plants the field in rye, she explained; why, only the other day he drove up with a wagon carrying a plough, one of his sons was with him, they left the wagon at the gate, the two of them unloaded the plough, they hitched the—but the boy interrupted severely: "Does the field go all the way over to the brook?"

What conclusions can you draw about what went on here? What reasons might be given for why it happened the way it did? You don't know these people—the characters or the teller—but you may have some context or similar experience to which you can relate it. You may want to tell us about a similar experience in order to make clear why you respond the way you do. On the other hand, if you don't feel you had any significant response, try briefly to explain why.

10. Here is another exchange, this time from a play about Salome by the British playwright, Oscar Wilde. Here Salome is having a conversation with a young Syrian, and Iokanaan, a Hebrew.

SALOME: (to Iokanaan)...Suffer me to kiss thy mouth.
IOKANAAN: Never! daughter of Babylon! Daughter of Sodom! Never!
SALOME: I will kiss thy mouth, Iokanaan...
THE YOUNG SYRIAN: ...Look not at this man, look not at him. I cannot endure it.... Princess, do not speak these things.
    And as the Young Syrian, in despair, slays himself and falls dead at her feet, she continues: "Suffer me to kiss thy mouth, Iokanaan."

What is going wrong (or right) here? Could you identify with any of the characters here? What sense can you make of the communication?

11. Here is a poem, "We Are Seven," by the 19th century English poet, William Wordsworth.

—A SIMPLE Child,
That lightly draws its breath,
And feels its life in every limb,
What should it know of death?

I met a little cottage Girl: 5
She was eight years old, she said;
Her hair was thick with many a curl
That clustered round her head.

She had a rustic, woodland air,
And she was wildly clad: 10
Her eyes were fair, and very fair;
—Her beauty made me glad.

"Sisters and brothers, little Maid,
How many may you be?"
"How many? Seven in all," she said,   15
And wondering looked at me.

"And where are they? I pray you tell."
She answered, "Seven are we;
And two of us at Conway dwell,
And two are gone to sea.   20

"Two of us in the church-yard lie,
My sister and my brother;
And, in the church-yard cottage, I
Dwell near them with my mother."

"You say that two at Conway dwell,   25
And two are gone to sea,
Yet ye are seven! I pray you tell,
Sweet Maid, how this may be."

Then did the little Maid reply,
"Seven boys and girls are we;   30
Two of us in the church-yard lie,
Beneath the church-yard tree."

"You run about, my little Maid,
Your limbs they are alive;
If two are in the church-yard laid,   35
Then ye are only five."

"Their graves are green, they may be seen,"
The little Maid replied,
"Twelve steps or more from my mother's door,
And they are side by side.   40

"My stockings there I often knit,
My kerchief there I hem;
And there upon the ground I sit,
And sing a song to them.

"And often after sun-set, Sir,   45
When it is light and fair,
I take my little porringer,
And eat my supper there.

"The first that died was sister Jane;
In bed she moaning lay,   50
Till God released her of her pain;
And then she went away.

"So in the church-yard she was laid;
And, when the grass was dry,
Together round her grave we played,   55
My brother John and I.

"And when the ground was white with snow.
And I could run and slide,
My brother John was forced to go.
And he lies by her side."   60

"How many are you, then," said I,
"If they two are in heaven?"
Quick was the little Maid's reply.
"O Master! we are seven."

"But they are dead; those two are dead!   65
Their spirits are in heaven!"
'Twas throwing words away; for still
The little Maid would have her will,
And said, "Nay, we are seven!"

For discussion: What is going wrong (or right) here? How? Why? Can you identify with either of the characters in the conversation? What sense can you make of the communication?

Paper Assignment: You have certainly been in situations in which you disagreed with someone. Choose one such situation and write a monologue in which that other person describes the situation from his or her point of view.

12. Here is another piece of communication, this time from Edward Albee's play, *Who's Afraid of Virginia Woolf?* This is a middle-aged married couple talking. What is going wrong (or right) here? How? Why? Can you identify with either of the characters in the conversation? What sense can you make of the communication? (The passage referred to in this assignment appears in Act I of the play, and can be found in Edward Albee, *Who's Afraid of Virginia Woolf?* [New York: Atheneum, 1962], pp. 13-17.)

13. We have been doing a good deal of writing and talking during the last week about communication. Perhaps it is a good time to take a more careful look at just what that word means.

    a.   In your dictionary, look up the words "communicate" and "communication" and write out as many different definitions as you can find. Was there anything here that surprised you?

    b.   Words are defined not only by their definitions, but also by their "place" in the language, by the lines that distinguish one word from synonyms, or words with related meanings. Find five synonyms or related words for either "communication" or "communicate" and for each explain how the lines distinguishing them should be drawn.

    c.   Words are also defined in an even more general sense by their membership in families of words through time. Look up the etymology of "communication" or "communicate" and list five words that this family makes into cousins. Then for each cousin, discuss how the meaning of the cousin applies to the meaning of "communication" or "communicate."

Bring 3 copies of your research into the word to class.

14. In the last few assignments, and earlier, we have been looking at specimens of communication going wrong—at least in part, and in a number of senses.

In this paper, I want you to take a stab at pulling together some of the things you have said, heard and thought about.

    a.   Make a list of the various ways communication has gone wrong or has been seen to go wrong, and relate these ways to specific examples from the exercises.

    b.   Arrange these *ways* in some kind of order that relates similar ways and distinguishes dissimilar ways. This arranged list can be called a *taxonomy*. Your taxonomy will almost certainly not be *complete*, but it should be somewhat *comprehensive*. Furthermore, when we combine the results of everyone's lists, we should have at least an interesting community effort.

    c.   Write a concluding paragraph, explaining what your rationale for it was, why it is in the particular form it is, and perhaps how useful (or good) you think it is (and for what?).

15. You now have two taxonomies, your own and one belonging to another member of the class. Compare the two. In what ways are they different? If they are different in a significant way, can you say why in terms of *context?* If they are not, write why you think this is so.

16. Here is a discussion of communication between people in terms of its systematic "operations." The authors are psychiatric researchers at an institute in California.

    ...a communication not only conveys information, but...at the same time it imposes behavior...these two operations have come to be known as the "report" and "command" aspects, respectively, of any communication.

The report aspect of a message conveys information and is, therefore, synonymous in human communication with the *content* of the message. It may be about anything that is communicable regardless of whether the particular information is true or false, valid, invalid or undecidable. The command aspect, on the other hand, refers to what sort of message it is to be taken as, and, therefore, ultimately to the *relationship* between the communicants. All such relationship statements are about one or several of the following assertions: "This is how I see myself...this is how I see you...this is how I see you seeing me..." and so forth in theoretically infinite regress. Thus, for instance, the messages "It is important to release the clutch gradually and smoothly" and "Just let the clutch go, it'll ruin the transmission in no time" have approximately the same informational content (report aspect), but they obviously define very different relationships. To avoid any misunderstanding about the foregoing, we want to make it clear that relationships are rarely defined deliberately or with full awareness. In fact, it seems that the more spontaneous and "healthy" a relationship, the more the relationship aspect of communication recedes into the background. Conversely, "sick" relationships are characterized by a constant struggle about the nature of the relationship, with the content aspect of communication becoming less and less important. (From Paul Watzlawick, Janet Helmick Beavin and Don Jackson, *Pragmatics of Human Communication, A Study of Interactional Patterns, Pathologies, and Paradoxes* [New York: W.W. Norton and Co., 1967], pp. 51-52. Reprinted by permission of the publisher.)

Write a summary of this passage in your own words. Then, in a second paragraph, apply the distinction between content and relation to an example of a communications snafu in your own expeience to see if it helps explain what went wrong.

Then re-read the passage in assignment 13 from *Who's Afraid of Virginia Woolf?* to see if you can find any moments where you can see a shift in emphasis from *content* to *relationship* aspects. If you can, indicate where and show how this shift is taking place. Then discuss how this distinction helps you to understand what is going on.

17. In Class Assignment

    Day 1: *Writing Party*
a.   Write for 15 minutes on something that is bothering you or exciting you at this time. [Instructor participates in this exercise.]
b.   Circulate papers to the right until the instructor says to stop. Read the paper you have and write a response to the paper for 10 minutes.
c.   Repeat step 2 two or three times more.

(Day 2: Class discussion of two or three student papers and response from the above experience and the instructor's paper and responses. We look at the way different individuals respond differently to the original papers in terms of *content* and *relation*.)

18. Look back at the other four examples of conversation in assignments 9-12. Do you find any moments where the distinction between *content* and *relationship* aspects is useful in understanding what is going on? Choose one and discuss it.

If you find none, say something about why you think this is so.

19. Now look back at the pieces of conversation you discussed in assignments 2, 3, 5, 6 and in your larger journal collection. Can you see any places where the *content-relation* distinction might be useful to explain what is happening in the conversation? Recopy one such example and discuss what is going on and how. You might also want to try to say something about why it is going on.

While you are working with your materials for assignments 2, 3, 5, 6 and the journals, put them together in a folder with a clip or staple and put your name, address and section number on the front of the folder. Bring this folder to class with your paper on this assignment. You will be exchanging folders with another student in class for a later assignment.

20. Read the essay "In Defense of Literacy," pp. 169-173 in Wendell Berry's collection *A Continuous Harmony, Essays Cultural and Agricultural* (New York: Harcourt Brace Jovanovich, 1975).
   a. Summarize the essay in 3-5 sentences in the following way:
      i) In 1-2 sentences, state the thesis and/or main purpose of the essay.
      ii) In 2-3 sentences, show how the writer supports this thesis or main purpose.
   b. What sort of person does the writer sound like? Write a short paragraph answering this question and using specifics from the essay to support your conclusions.
   c. What features in the essay (words, sentences, statements, tones of voice) function as command messages for you? How does the essay define the writer's relation to you? How does it make you feel about yourself in relation to him? Answer these questions in a brief paragraph.
   d. The author of this essay is a writer, farmer, ecologist and college teacher named Wendell Berry. Write him a letter telling him what you think of his essay.

21. In the following passage, the Brazilian educator, Paulo Freire, is discussing his method of teaching illiterate South American peasants the skills of literacy.

> To acquire literacy is more than to psychologically and mechanically dominate reading and writing techniques. It is to dominate these techniques in terms of consciousness; to understand what one reads and to write what one understands; it is to *communicate* graphically. Acquiring literacy does not involve memorizing sentences, words, or syllables—lifeless objects unconnected to an existential universe—but rather an attitude of creation and re-creation, a self-transformation producing a stance of intervention in one's context.
>
> Thus the educator's role is fundamentally to enter into dialogue with the illiterate about concrete situations and simply to offer him the instruments with which he can teach himself to read and write. This teaching cannot be done

from the top down, but only from the inside out, by the illiterate himself, with the collaboration of the educator. That is why we searched for a method which would be the instrument of the learner as well as of the educator, and which, in the lucid observation of a young Brazilian sociologist, "would identify learning *content* with the learning *process*." (From Paulo Freire, *Education for Critical Consciousness* [New York: The Seabury Press, 1973], pp. 48-49. Reprinted by permission of the publisher.)

This selection raises the question of the appropriate approach to teaching writing (and reading). Freire says, "teaching cannot be done from the top down, but only from the inside out, by the illiterate himself, with the collaboration of the educator." In your experience, is this true? Did your English teachers act as collaborators as you learned, or did you have teachers who taught you "from above"? Do you think you would have been better off with the other kind? Why? How? Or does the relation between you and the writing teacher not really matter?

Freire also says that literacy is more than the psychological and mechanical domination of reading and writing techniques. It is, he says, domination of these techniques "in terms of consciousness." What do you think he means by that? You are literate to a degree that Freire's peasants are not. Do you see your literacy as more than a dominance of reading and writing techniques, more a matter of consciousness dominating those techniques? Perhaps you can call up a good example to show how this is or is not true.

But Freire, in the remaining sentence in the first paragraph, translates or transforms those terms into others—to dominate reading and writing techniques in terms of consciousness is "to understand what one reads and to write what one understands; it is to *communicate* graphically," etc. How do these alternative phrasings help you to understand what you are reading here?

Write an essay in which you either use Freire's terms to analyze aspects of your own education in literacy, or use your own educational experiences in literacy to analyze and criticize Freire's discussion.

22. Read through the materials on assignments 2, 3, 5, 6 with the journals that you received from another member of the class. Can you see any places where the *content-relation* distinction might be useful to explain what is happening in the conversation? Copy out a section and discuss what is going on and how. You might want to try to say why too.

23. You will have your papers on assignments 2, 3, 5, 6 back now, and will have shared your responses with your classmates. In this final set of assignments, we will be examining in terms of *context, content* and *relation* some of the communication that has been going on in this course. Probably the most important (but not necessarily) has been the communication that has been going on between you and me. I write an assignment; you write a paper; I write a response to your paper; sometimes you re-write the paper; if you do, I write a response; sometimes classmates write responses. You have all of that in front of you for nineteen assignments.

Read through the entire folder of your papers to date with an eye to the *content* we have been exchanging and the *relationship* we have been establishing. Choose a place where you think something either has or has not been "going on." How? And maybe even, why?

When you turn your entire folder of materials in to me at the end of the term, I will try to write on this question from my point of view. I will also, of administrative necessity, include a grade, though with the hope that you will find that grade trivial beside our written conversations.

When you come to class, bring your entire folder to exchange with another member of the class.

24. Read through the assignments, papers and comments of the classmate with whom you have traded folders, looking at the *content* that is being exchanged and the *relationship* that is being established.

Choose one or more spots where you can see communication "going on" or "not going on." How is it happening? Perhaps you might like to say why.

Choose for your spots some things that you think it would be helpful for your classmate to discuss. There may be much to criticize negatively in any folder, but we want to look for moments or exchanges that we can respond to positively, usefully. This does not mean, of course, that you are to aim at flattery.

Make a copy of your paper so that your classmate can have one copy and you can turn the other in to me.

25. Make a copy of a graded paper that another student from another class has written for another course. Remove the name of the student. Look through the paper and the instructor's response with an eye to *content* and *relationship* aspects. Explain what you see going on here.

Make a copy of your explanation for the student who loaned you the paper.

If you cannot get another student to allow you to use his or her paper, I have some.

26. *Final Paper.* Submit as Preface to your folder.

This is a final summing-up assignment. Look back specifically at your response to the first assignment; review all your papers once again and read through the class anthology. How would you respond to that first assignment now? You might want to begin by writing another two-hour paper to see what you could say now on that assignment.

Then stand back a bit and ask yourself what you have learned about communication, about writing, about you, about me, about students and about teachers.

There are still many problems, of course. Things have gone wrong or not been completed, and I would like you to speak to that. What to your way of thinking still remains for you to do and learn in becoming a really good communicator?

Clip this paper onto the front of your entire course folder and turn the whole thing in.

Extra Assignments

1. Anthology Assignment (to be used 3-4 times during the quarter)

Choose one paper you have written this quarter, excluding papers you have already used for anthology assignments, and revise and develop it for a final graded essay and for possible inclusion in the class anthology.

2. Here is another conversation.

> "I'm sure I didn't mean—" Alice was beginning, but the Red Queen interrupted her impatiently.
>
> "That's just what I complain of! You should have meant! What do you suppose is the use of a child without any meaning? Even a joke should have a meaning—and a child is more important than a joke, I hope. You couldn't deny that, even if you tried with both hands."
>
> "I don't deny things with my hands," Alice objected.
>
> "Nobody said you did," said the Red Queen. "I said you couldn't if you tried."
>
> "She is in that state of mind," said the White Queen, "that she wants to deny something—only she doesn't know what to deny!"
>
> "A nasty, vicious temper," the Red Queen remarked; and then there was an uncomfortable silence for a minute or two.

What is going on? How? What reasons might there be for the characters to be talking in this way? Perhaps you have seen or experienced a similar situation. If so, tell us about it. If not, say something about what makes this scene so unusual.

3. Here is another conversation, a famous one.

> "There's a glory for you!"
>
> "I don't know what you mean by 'glory,' " Alice said.
>
> Humpty Dumpty smiled contemptuously. "Of course you don't—till I tell you. I meant 'there's a nice knock-down argument for you!' "
>
> "But 'glory' doesn't mean 'a nice knock-down argument,' " Alice objected.
>
> "When *I* use a word," Humpty Dumpty said, in a rather scornful tone, "it means just what I choose it to mean — neither more nor less."
>
> "The question is," said Alice, "whether you *can* make words mean so many different things."
>
> "The question is," said Humpty Dumpty, "*which is to be master*—that's all."

Who do you think is right? Why?

Now, think if there are any ways in which that person might be wrong, either in the example or the general conclusion.

4. Here is a paper being marked and revised. Look through the versions paragraph by paragraph to see how communication was "going on" between teacher and

student with an eye to *content* and *relational* aspects. What do you see happening? How? Can you guess as to why?

(For this assignment, I borrow three versions of a paper, with the teacher's accompanying comments, from William E. Coles, Jr., *Teaching Composing* [Rochelle Park, N.J.: Hayden Book Co., 1974], pp. 101-103.)

5. Here is an example of a failure in student-teacher communication.

(I show the class a student's essay at this point, and a teacher's written response to it—a response which does not address the content of the piece and which is not particularly helpful. Such examples are numerous, and can be found in many books about teaching writing. One such example that I have used is reproduced on pp. 157-158 of *The Philosophy of Composition* by E. D. Hirsch, Jr. [Chicago: University of Chicago Press, 1977].)

What is going wrong with this communication situation? Would you say that the remarks the teacher wrote on the paper are helpful? Why or why not?

Do you find that the *content-relationship* distinction can be useful in helping you to understand what is going on between the student and the teacher? Can you see places in the paper and in the comments that seem to be emphasizing *relation* at the expense of *content?*

If you were the writing teacher, what comment would you write in response to this paper?

Language and Reality

An Island Perspective

Ruth Lucas

Frantz Fanon writes of it in *Black Skin, White Masks*—the inferiority complex brought on by the subversion of an individual's native language and culture. A freshman composition student in Hawaii writes of it when recording a grade school experience where a Mainland teacher told children she would answer their questions only if they were asked in "Standard English." And Leialoha Apo Perkins in "Manifesto for Pidgin English" writes of it when describing a young man's new-found self-respect upon discovering the validity of his own dialect. All of these writers had been made to feel inferior because of their first language—an island dialect—and as a consequence they had come to see that language as a handicap. Furthermore, all of them had experienced the damage to self-concept that results when a student must function effectively in an unfamiliar language. In Fanon's example, the Martinique native finds himself a victim of ridicule when he tries to talk to his island friends in academic French rather than the dialect he learned as a child. The Hawaii student, looking back on his third grade experience, remembers that classmates, too ashamed of their English to ask questions, sat silently in their seats throughout each class period. In Perkins' "Manifesto," the narrator, Kaleo, watches in admiration as a pidgin-speaking classmate confronts an English professor obsessed with linguistic "correctness." In all these instances, the writers speak to the confusion and uncertainties students experience when asked to set aside the language of their childhood. Such linguistic disorientation is one of the problems many of our students at Kapiolani Community College have had to face, and so this is one of the central aspects of language that I have sought to address in the freshman course I designed for the College.[1]

The complexity of our students' situations may be seen in a brief review of their

[1]Kapiolani Community College is one of Hawaii's public schools. It operates under an open admissions policy, admitting any person who is a high school graduate, or anyone who is eighteen years of age or older and can profit from the instruction offered. The student population includes recent high school graduates, adults returning to school after years of working, the handicapped, the disadvantaged, early admissions from high school, foreign students and senior citizens.

linguistic backgrounds. More than 95% of Kapiolani's students were born in Hawaii, many into bilingual families, and for many of them their first language is Hawaiian English, also called Island Dialect. A pidgin that has evolved into a creole, Hawaiian English shares many grammatical and syntactical features of the Hawaiian language, with borrowings from the first language of other local ethnic groups (i.e., Japanese, Chinese, Filipino, Samoan, and Caucasian). Since Hawaiian English is widely used for everyday communication, it is of course a language which many of our students use easily and naturally with their friends and family. But it is a language about which they have ambivalent feelings because of the history of attitudes towards it. On the one hand, it is for many of them the language of their youth, and it therefore carries strong emotional connections with early learning and early habits, as well as vague, usually unexamined connections with general cultural experiences. On the other hand, the language has been subverted throughout much of the 20th century by the institutionalized structures of the islands, particularly the educational system,[2] and many parents have come to see it as a barrier to "getting ahead" socially and economically. As a result, many have insisted that their offspring speak only Standard English. Many island-born students thus find themselves in the position of rejecting Hawaiian English, of not valuing their own linguistic background, and of not recognizing the formative role the language has had in their lives. In order to help our students understand and value their complicated linguistic and cultural inheritance, I designed a sequence of assignments for freshmen which focuses upon this heritage and introduces them to the idea that language shapes the world and can be used to lead, mislead, and manipulate people in it.

Generally speaking, this series of writing assignments moves from having students consider the language of personal experience to having them examine the language of public affairs—from looking at nicknames and their influence on character and behavior to investigating weasel words and their purpose in advertising and politics. Throughout the process of writing about their various experiences in and with language, students are gradually led to recognize and understand the relation of language to perception—both to self-perception and perception of the world. This broad framework of linguistic experience and exploration provides the intellectual context within which students are invited to write about situations, stories, and memories that directly raise questions concerning the nature and value of their two English languages, their intimate language of Hawaiian English and the public one of edited American English. The assignments themselves together with commentary on their purposes and interrelationships appear in the following paragraphs.

[2]In 1924, for example, special schools were created for children who spoke "Standard English" as opposed to those who spoke pidgin. This system of segregating children on the basis of the language they spoke persisted until about 1950, and even as recently as the 1960's a student at the University of Hawaii had to pass an English speech test to graduate.

LANGUAGE AND REALITY

(Assignments 1-3 focus on the naming process, how arbitrary it is, how inappropriate it may be, how closely it is tied to cultural considerations. Students first look at their own names, then explore ways they are viewed (labeled) by others. Listing labels (2) is an attempt to make students aware that the labels they pin on themselves may differ from labels given them by others (3). The alternative writing task given in assignment 3 invites students to consider the role labeling plays in prejudice. All three assignments call for narration and development through the use of examples.)

1. The relationship between names and what is named can be exceedingly complex. And if you stop to think about it, the names we use and how we use them can be said to play a large part in what we are and aren't, in what we are able to become or do, and in what we can't become or do. How were your own names (first and middle) chosen? Also, tell us about your nickname, if you have one. How did you acquire it? Tell us in a page or two how people acquire their names, using yourself and your names as an example.

2. We have seen that many names were originally descriptive, as some nicknames are. We've also seen that names have personal meanings in addition to their public ones. So you should not be surprised to learn that titles and labels can serve as names. What titles and labels apply to you? Make a list of at least twenty. Consider your ethnic and religious background, your relationships, achievements, hobbies, jobs and so on. Now select one of these titles or labels and expand it into a letter to a friend, telling about yourself in a role s/he may not realize you play.

3. Titles and labels—especially negative ones—are easy to apply to someone else. Think about some of them, selected because of a person's physical characteristics— Pinhead, Fatso, Shrimp, Blackie, Sharkbait,[3] Turkey Neck. Or their ethnic background—Nigger, Jap, Book-book,[4] Frog Legs, Honky, Kike. Or their religious beliefs—Jesus Freak, Moonie, Holy Roller. Or political beliefs—Commie, Pinko, Red, Mossback. Think of a time when someone pinned a label, perhaps undeserved, on you, judging you before knowing what you really were like. Tell us about it.

   Or, if you'd rather, write about one of your prejudices. Begin by describing it. What do you believe (perhaps unconsciously) about the object of your prejudice? Then try to figure out how you acquired the prejudice (personal experience, peers, parents, teachers, textbooks, TV?). Does the prejudice have a historical basis or explanation? Did you ever have any experience (s) in which reality contradicted the way you prejudged a person, place, thing, or idea? Did your prejudice disappear as a result?

[3]A local term for an untanned swimmer.
[4]A derogatory term for a Filipino.

(In assignments 4-6, students are asked to consider how language affects not only self-perception and perception of their immediate environment but also how it may affect their view of the world. As background for their study of language and perception, students are given a brief description of Benjamin Whorf's theory, and research that seems to support it.[5] They then are asked to gain practice in simple research techniques by reviewing essays about this theory. When they return to class with their notes, they are given a handout illustrating bibliography and footnote format that they are asked to use in writing assignment 5. The "experiment" suggested in that assignment requires that the class be divided into three groups with a leader appointed for each group. Each leader is given a set of the same eight figures and shows them—one by one—for about ten seconds to the group. Then group members are asked to draw the figures—in any order—from memory. In Groups I and II the leaders provide an oral but different clue for each figure. For example, in Group I the clue given for a figure is "kidney bean"; for Group II the same figure is called "canoe." In Group III, no oral clues are given. Students merely observe each figure shown them silently and then attempt to draw it from memory.

After students complete their work, each drawing is rated by the leader— 1, if almost perfect; 2, if slightly distorted but still recognizable; 3, if highly distorted. The purpose of this "experiment," first conducted at Brown University in the 1960's in a strictly controlled environment, is to illustrate how language (in this case, the oral clues) may influence perception. In the Brown experiment, the lowest (best) score was achieved by Group III which received no oral clues. The paper written in class after the introduction to Whorf gives the students practice in using library research, in drawing a conclusion about language and perception and in supporting that conclusion from a text, as well as "hands-on" experience. Assignment 6, taken from a sequence by William Coles, Jr., asks students to look closely at another experiment dealing with language and perception, to assume a role and to write a comparison/contrast essay.)

4. In the last two assignments, we looked at how people perceive us (and we perceive others) according to titles and labels. A linguist named Benjamin Whorf did a great deal of study on the connection between language and perception. He concluded that the two may be closely related.

Spend some time in the library checking out Whorf's theory. What examples can you give to support (or not support) his theory? Keep notes on the references you check.

5. (in class) An experiment relating to Whorf's theory was conducted at Brown University. Participating college students were divided into three groups. The first

[5]A useful reference for students, in addition to Benjamin Whorf's collected writings, is Peter Farb's *Word Play: What Happens When People Talk* (New York: Random House, 1974).

group was asked to draw a series of eight figures, each one named by the examiner as it was displayed. The second group viewed the same figures but was given a different name for each one. The third group repeated the exercise, but this time no oral clues were given to them. Let's try that experiment ourselves.

What can you say about the results? What connection can you see with the Whorfian theory?

6. Another experiment involving world view and language was conducted in the 1960's using as test subjects bilingual Japanese women, living in San Francisco, who had married American servicemen.

The women spoke English to their husbands, children and neighbors, and in most everyday speech situations; they spoke Japanese whenever they came together to gossip, reminisce and discuss the news from home. Each Japanese woman thus inhabited two language worlds.

The experiment consisted of two visits to each woman by a bilingual Japanese interviewer. During the first interview, he chatted with them only in Japanese; during the second, he carried on the same discussion and asked the same questions in English. The results were quite remarkable; they showed that the attitudes of each woman differed markedly, depending upon whether she spoke Japanese or English. Here, for example, is the way the same women completed the same sentences at the two interviews:

"When my wishes conflict with my family's...
    ...it is a time of great unhappiness." (Japanese)
    ...I do what I want." (English)

"Real friends should...
    ...help each other." (Japanese)
    ...be very frank." (English)

Clearly, major variables in the experiment had been eliminated—since the women were interviewed twice by the same person in the location of their homes, and they discussed the same topics—with but one exception. And that sole exception was language. The drastic differences in attitude of the women could be accounted for only by the language world each inhabited when she spoke.

The women in this experiment inhabit what are called different "language worlds," in which they "see" different things, have "drastic differences in attitudes." Write a paper in which you do three things.

First, explain why the women of this study might be seen as fortunate. How might the ability to inhabit two language worlds be seen as an advantage?

Secondly, how might this inhabiting of two language worlds be seen as something that could cause trouble, or be a liability?

Finally, would you yourself want, as these women do, to inhabit two language worlds?

(Before moving into assignments 7-10, which are concerned specifically with Hawaiian English, the students are introduced to the modern history of language interconnections in the islands, a story many of them are unfamiliar with. Most students are aware that the British navigator Capt. James Cook first introduced English to the islands when he stumbled upon them in 1778, and students are also generally aware that English became the official language of the islands somewhat more than 100 years later. But they do not generally know that during those approximately 100 years, English in the islands was being heavily influenced by many Indo-European, Polynesian, and Asiatic languages (all spoken by the many immigrants who swept into the islands to work on the sugar plantations), and that a dialect called *pidgin* (an early form of Hawaiian English) was evolving. The dialect was apparently first developed among Pacific fur traders who carried English to China ports with stop-overs in Hawaii. There, to make bargaining possible, this reduced form of English evolved (with borrowings from Portuguese and Cantonese). The term and the dialect carried considerable prestige at that time because it represented the activity and excitement of contact with the western world, and within only a decade of Cook's landing, pidgin words and phrases were entering the Hawaiian vocabulary, brought back with pride to Hawaii by the young island men who had signed on the trading vessels. In 1820 the first group of New England missionaries arrived in the islands, and from that time on learning English (i.e., Standard English) became a much sought-after accomplishment, with that gradually becoming the preferred language over pidgin (Hawaiian English).[6]

Most students hold a rather low opinion of Hawaiian English, even though it is the "first" language for many of them. After being introduced to the idea that Hawaiian English once enjoyed much prestige, the students are asked to look at the language in ways intended to challenge their low opinion of it: through their own experience, as a language possessing literary merit, and through the eyes of a linguist and the newspaper readers who take issue with him. Assignment 7 asks students to reexamine linguistic labeling by looking at their first language, using narration and description. Assignment 8 presents "Da Beer Can Hat," a story written in Hawaiian English by Darrell H.Y. Lum, the first local Chinese writer to publish a collection of short fiction and drama. Students take turns reading aloud from the selection, replete with such island expressions as "chang-kine (stingy) guys," "no make la' dat" (don't act that way), "bolo head" (bald-headed). The readers and the teacher discuss at length the vocabulary and the implication of Hawaiian English terms that may be unfamiliar to island newcomers. On the following class day, a videotape featuring a Hawaiian language university professor analyzes "Da Beer Can Hat," noting that it is not written in "broken" or "incorrect" English but in a dialect heavily influenced by the Hawaiian language. She also gives students an insight into the non-verbal elements of communication in

[6]Historical references to Hawaiian English in this discussion are from Elizabeth Carr's *Da Kine Talk: From Pidgin to Standard English in Hawaii* (Honolulu: The University of Hawaii Press, 1972).

Hawaiian English. The writing assignments calls for an essay based on comparison and contrast.

Assignment 9 asks students to consider a newspaper account of a university linguist's speech on the value of Hawaiian English and the irate letters it inspires in a Letters to the Editor column. Students, drawing on what they have learned about Hawaiian English in the previous two assignments and what they know about it from their own experiences, argue the validity of Hawaiian English in a letter of their own to the editor.

Assignment 10 has two main purposes: sharpening students' descriptive powers and giving students practice in the use of direct quotations. They read two other selections written in Hawaiian English—"Hadashi, an account of two island boys and their paint-sniffing experience, and "Yahk Fahn, Auntie," a story of an elderly Chinese aunt associated in the writer's mind with memorable dining experiences.)

7. In assignments 3 and 4 you wrote about a label that applied to you or you applied to something or someone else. Sometimes we judge (label) a person because of the language s/he speaks.

For example, in Hawaii, we have two English "languages": Standard English (otherwise known as Edited American English) and Hawaiian English, commonly called "pidgin." On some occasion you certainly have heard someone speak in heavy pidgin or in very "straight" Standard English. What kind of judgment or evaluation did you make of the person? Did you create (or validate) a prejudice about the type of person who speaks in that way? Have you had any experience (s) in which reality contradicted the way you prejudged a person based on his/her use of pidgin or Standard English? Recreate the situation.

(If you are unfamiliar with pidgin, any accent or dialect will be appropriate.)

8. Let's read together "Da Beer Can Hat," written by a University of Hawaii graduate who has composed a number of stories in Hawaiian English.

Select several paragraphs in this story that particularly appeal to you and rewrite them in Edited American English, the kind of English you usually write papers in. What do you see in the first version but not in the second? Does the story change? Do you get a different sense of the characters? What can you say about the language? In what ways does putting "Da Beer Can Hat" into Standard English make it more (or less) powerful? What version appeals to you more? Why?

9. Hawaiian English sometimes gives us a way to get to the point in a hurry. It is a language that makes its users feel comfortable in a social situation. It is the main language used by some kama'ainas (long-time island residents). If Hawaiian English is useful in so many ways, why do you suppose we do not use it to conduct our governmental, educational and business affairs? Read a *Honolulu Advertiser* account of a recent speech given by Professor Richard Day and the response to it in "Letters to the Editor." Then write your own letter to the editor setting forth your opinion of Hawaiian English.

10. Now read "Hadashi," p. 7 in *SUN*. What childhood memory of your own does it recall? Tell us about that memory. Or read "Yahk Fahn, Auntie," p. 38. Is there someone from your own past who has made an impression on your life? Through your writing make him/her come alive as Lum has done with Auntie. No matter which story you choose to tell, try to tell it using the language (dialect and dialogue) that makes the experience or person memorable.

(Assignments 11-16 introduce students to languages that can be used to mislead and manipulate—the languages of advertising and politics. These assignments move students from an exploration of their private language (Hawaiian English), direct and intimate, to a public language characterized by its weasel words. Assignment 12 gives students the experience of writing for four distinctly different audiences, and assignment 13 asks them to pause and reflect on all the audiences they have written for, seeking to explain the rhetorical strategy used for each. For assignments 14-16 students are asked to read Orwell's classic essay, "Politics and the English Language," and then to draw from that essay in analyzing a political speech or interview they find in a newspaper. In assignment 16 students are asked to look back to assignments dealing with the language of advertising and compare that with the language of politics.)

11. You have been getting a chance to look closely at the language of names, language and perception, and Hawaiian English vs. Standard English. Let's change the pace for awhile and look at some of the other kinds of language that powerfully influence our everyday lives. Consider the language of advertising. Certain words sell products. Paul Stevens, a professional writer of television commercials has written a book called *I Can Sell You Anything*. He says he can accomplish this feat by the effective use of weasel words that avoid making a direct statement. Read what he says about them. Then while you are watching TV, list all the weasels you see or hear in the commercials. Bring your list to class.

12. (in groups) Using weasel words, write a commercial for a product that will appeal to 1) a kindergarten pupil, 2) a teenager, 3) a career woman, 4) a retired grandfather. Working with your group, act out the commercial you wrote for the class.

What are the differences in language used in the four different commercials?

13. You've had a chance now to write for a variety of audiences—for your classmates, to an editor, to a friend, and for a television audience. Did you go about writing the same way for each reader/listener? What did you do differently?

14. Just as advertising has its special language, so does politics. Read George Orwell's "Politics and the English Language." Re-read it if you need to. Find a political speech or interview in a magazine or newspaper and bring it to class.

15. (in class) What can you say about Orwell's essay and the political speech?

16. The purpose of advertising is to sell a product. The chief purpose of a political speech is to sell a candidate. Looking back to assignments 11-15, how does the language of politics differ from the language of advertising?

(Assignments 17 through 22 are designed to give students more comprehensive practice in research techniques through the writing of a 3-5 page paper. They are led, step by step, through the proposal of a research topic, compilation of working bibliography and note cards, drafting of a thesis statement, and the writing process. A calendar listing due dates for each of these tasks guides them through the project. For a topic, students are asked to explore any aspect of language that interests them or to research their family history and decide how they are or are not a reflection of a favorite ancestor. The research project (students spend three weeks on it) is viewed as a drawing together of the course content—not as an appendage of the course.

Assignment 23, the final in-class writing assignment, replaces a final exam. Students are asked to reflect on themselves as writers, giving the teacher an opportunity to see how they view their progress in the course.)

17. Here's your chance to test out your ideas about communicating. Using your listening and interviewing skills, find out some facts about your family. What is the oldest memory, handed down from generation to generation in your family? Do you remember a grandparent or an uncle or aunt talking about an ancestor or an incident they remembered or maybe that their parents described to them? Jot down what you know of this ancestor or incident. Then, if possible, interview the members of your family and see what you can learn. Write an account in which you explain as accurately as possible the time, place and people involved in that memory.

18. In this final series of exercises, you will try to use many of the things you have learned about language and writing in this class. You have a choice of two types of research.

Plan A: Focus on one aspect of language that interests you. For example, you already know a great deal about Hawaiian English, but there are questions to explore. Some of them that may interest you: How has Hawaiian English changed in the last twenty years? (Do your parents or grandparents use Hawaiian English expressions that you never use? On the other hand, can they understand all of your Hawaiian Engish?)

What about the effect of different languages upon Hawaiian English? (What words, for example, have the Portuguese contributed, or the Japanese, or the Filipinos?) There is a wealth of unexplored material here.

Perhaps you would rather concentrate on a subject other than Hawaiian English. What about the language used (as a put-down) to refer to women or to minority groups? Or the language (euphemisms) used to make something seem nicer than it is? Or the language of education, government, the courts?

Think of what you would like to know more about and begin there. A first stop will be to browse through the materials about language in the library. Take notes on what interests you and bring them to your next class.

Plan B: Research your genealogy as far back as you can. Begin with your parents. Where did your mother's parents come from? Your father's? Why did they come? What were some of their feelings when they arrived? What kind of work were they engaged in? Were there any problems with the language spoken? What were some of their expectations? What about your great-grandparents? Your great-great-grandparents?

How are you a reflection (or not a reflection) of your parents, grandparents, and great-grandparents?

Document your narrative as closely as you can with references to such things as interviews, letters, family documents, news clippings.

Do some interviewing to see whether you have sufficient information for Plan B. Bring your notes to class.

19. (in class) From what you have read, written, and discussed, what aspect of language do you think you may wish to explore further? What aspect of your family genealogy do you wish to study in more detail? Write an informal proposal for such an exploration. What questions do you have, what sources do you plan to check, and what beliefs about your subject do you hope to support?

20. Do some further reading/interviewing related to your proposal. Take lots of notes.

21. With the information you collected from your additional reading and interviews, state a belief about language or a belief about your family that you now have and say why you hold that belief (three to five pages).

22. Turn in the final draft of your mini-research paper, complete with bibliography cards, note cards, rough draft, bibliography page and footnote page.

23. (to replace a final exam) This exercise serves two purposes: encouraging you to evaluate your own work in this class, and providing me with excellent background materials that I may use in the event you ever want me to write you a letter of reference. Write me a letter about your writing. Think about what I might find convincing. For example, should you concentrate only on your strong points? Think about the adjectives you want to use about yourself that will represent you to the world. You may support your judgment by mentioning some of your papers, if you like. But I am mainly interested in how you see yourself as a writer.

REFERENCES

Carr, Elizabeth. *Da Kine Talk: From Pidgin to Standard English in Hawaii*. Honolulu: The University of Hawaii Press, 1972.

Fanon, Frantz. *Black Skin, White Masks*. Trans. Charles L. Markmann. New York: Grove Press, 1967.

Farb, Peter. *Word Play: What Happens When People Talk*. New York: Random House, 1974.

Lum, Darrell H.Y. "Da Beer Can Hat," *SUN*. Honolulu: Bamboo Ridge Press, 1980.

Perkins, Leialoha. "Manifesto for Pidgin English," *Natural and Other Stories*. Honolulu: Kamelu'uluolele, 1979.

Whorf, Benjamin. *Language, Thought and Reality*. Ed. John B. Carroll. Boston: MIT Press, 1956.

Writing and Regional Experience

A View from the Delta

Jack White

While America becomes progressively more homogeneous with each passing year, still every region of the country retains some of its distinctive cultural patterns. And persons from each of these regions have a special feeling for their part of the country, a sense of place that is reflected with particular clarity in the idioms they use to define themselves and their locale. To this day, for example, I speak of being born in the Delta, not in the town of Greenwood, Mississippi. And long before I could credit the definition to William Alexander Percy, I thought of the Delta as "extending from the lobby of the Peabody Hotel in Memphis to Catfish Row in Vicksburg."

To be from the Delta—indeed, to be from any particular region of the country—inescapably involves a complex and sometimes contradictory set of experiences, values, and styles. My students at Mississippi State University, for example, have a strong feeling for their local culture that is embodied in the fact that they have an enthusiasm for oral traditions, for the details of rural Southern experience, and thus are animated story tellers and eager listeners to stories with local color. But by virtue of being Mississippians, they also have a very strong sense of propriety and civility, a code of manners as strict as the southern code of honor, which strongly colors their attitudes about writing, particularly in a university setting. So, they invariably come to their initial college-level writing course with the assumptions that one must never violate even the most minor convention of usage, and that one must never use the first person pronoun "I" in writing. In effect, they enter university writing classes with the belief that written language must echo in ink-stained phrases the eloquence of oratory or must in some other way be as highly formal and imposing as an ante-bellum mansion. And because their sense of propriety about the written language is so strong, it inevitably leads them not to value, if not to ignore, the rich variety of their personal language experience. The result of these attitudes about language is that they write an exaggerated form of the prose common among freshmen everywhere—prose that is highly stiff, formal, self-conscious, and quite distant from their natural language and experience.

To counteract such artificial prose and the attitudes that give rise to it, I have designed a sequence of assignments that invites students to read, listen to, and write prose that draws heavily on the language of personal experience before facing them with problems in academic discourse. I ask them to observe, describe, and analyze familiar regional experience before they turn to writing about academic material and concepts. In this way, I seek to foster the personal satisfactions of writing that students need to experience as an encouragement for the further development of their abilities. At the same time, I seek to affirm the abilities they bring to the course from their story-telling experience—such as reporting and organizing details—which can in turn be applied to their writing for academic and professional purposes.

As the sequence works its way into assignments that are progressively more academic in orientation, the activities continue to lead students to draw on material related to their regional background. Through this focus, I hope to enhance students' sense of the personal value and cultural significance to be found in the process of acquiring and communicating knowledge. In this way, too, I intend that they recognize that a true command of knowledge and the ability to communicate it involve more than a mere regurgitation of data or a superficial imitation of conventional forms. The sequence consequently serves as a foundation for the research-based writing that students will be asked to carry out not only in their other required writing course, but also in numerous other courses in other disciplines.

As a means of introducing students to the value of their shared regional experience and language, I begin the sequence and the course itself with an in-class exercise that appears on the surface to be merely a mechanical task of filling in the blanks of a descriptive-narrative passage from which various words have been omitted. But once they have supplied words to complete their separate copies of the passage, students share their results in a workshop discussion and discover in the process that they have produced nearly identical versions of the piece. In this way, the exercise serves to reveal to students the cultural cohesiveness and tacit understandings that exist among users of any language. In making and sharing these discoveries about their common regional experience and language, students also discover an important sense in which writing can be a form of knowing. And in making these discoveries through a workshop discussion, they immediately recognize the value in this recurrent aspect of the course.

Following this initial investigation of language and regional experience, the sequence engages students in fifteen assignments that continue to draw on personal and/or southern subject matters. These fifteen are, in turn, organized into five clusters, each of which contains three closely related assingments. As the sequence moves from one cluster to the next, the students are progressively involved in tasks that are primarily expressive (I), primarily explanatory (II, III, IV), and primarily persuasive (V). Within each cluster the three writing tasks (A, B, C) focus on various aspects or elements of language and discourse, beginning with one that stresses some use or feature of diction or syntax, ending ordinarily with one that stresses some larger organizational or rhetorical consideration. This recurrent pattern from cluster to cluster and the increasingly sophisticated tasks that make up each cluster form the spiral movement of the sequence.

The first cluster of assignments, which invites students to remember (IA), to write about (IB), and to rewrite (IC) a past experience, is clearly expressive in orientation and is intended to give students another set of activities which, like the initial in-class exercise, affirms the value of their personal language and experience. In the structure of its three parts, this cluster also introduces students to basic steps in the composing process, by having them begin with some free writing in which they jot down words or phrases from their recollections (IA), then having them write about the experience as if they "were telling someone about it" (IB), and finally having them rewrite it from a different point of view (IC). The final part of this cluster, which invites them to reflect on the effects of their change in point of view, is intended to help them see that a personal perspective, as reflected in first person narration, serves important purposes that are different from but no less important than those served by third person narration.

The second cluster, which calls for description of a campus landmark (IIA), biography of a classmate (IIB), and explanation of personal names (IIC), is clearly explanatory in its emphasis, and is intended to give students an introduction to some of the most essential activities involved in referential writing—gathering information reliably, recording it as objectively as possible, and reporting it accurately in language. As they move from observing a building, to investigating a classmate, to researching themselves, students continue to encounter opportunities in which they can exercise their regional and their personal voices.

The third cluster builds on the preceding one by giving students further opportunities to gather and explain information in writing. In this case, they are called upon to investigate the earlier meanings of words (IIIA), the events that occurred on the date of their birth (IIIB), and the meaning of courtesy titles (IIIC). These less familiar subject matters require them for the first time in the sequence to go beyond observation and interviewing to some basic sources of published information, such as newspapers and dictionaries. These assignments also provide students with academically oriented tasks that call for a less personal voice in their writing. Just the same, each assignment maintains some overt or implicit connection to the personal or regional experience of the students.

The fourth cluster faces students with the most demanding exercises in this sequence that have to do with explanatory writing. Here they translate jargon into familiar terms and then put familiar experience into jargon (IVA), explain a specialized process in familiar language (IVB), and define several common terms for classifying information (IVC). This cluster, thus, gives students experience directly related to academic and professional writing. In showing students some of the perils of jargon and highly technical writing, it also reaffirms the value of familiar language, particularly in discourse for inexperienced or uninformed readers.

The fifth cluster builds on the previous work in the course that has involved students in gathering knowledge and writing. But in this case the assignments are primarily concerned with needs for more persuasive writing. Here, students are asked to write a piece providing material to support a personal conclusion or belief with respect to a particular political issue (VA), to demonstrate to an uninformed reader the southern appeal of a couple of products (VB), and to illustrate for a particular manufacturer the southern appeal of a specific advertisement (VC).

To offer students what I hope will be a satisfying sense of closure in the sequence, I invite them to write either a limited personal geneology or an explanation for the name of a town in which they have lived. This invitation to write a piece based on research into some aspect of their past serves to reinforce for students the fact that their regional experience has been the conceptual center of the course. By echoing some of their previous assignments, this final one invites them to keep in mind the possible ideas about writing and ways of writing that they have discovered through the sequence. Above all, then, it serves to remind them that they can develop a command of language in various kinds of writing if they can transcend their artificial conceptions about writing and thus feel free to draw strength from their regional heritage.

WRITING AND REGIONAL EXPERIENCE

Introduction:

Read through the following passage and supply words that contribute to the sense of the brief writing.

> I remember one hot Sunday afternoon when I sat on the front _____ and looked out across the front _____ where the grass was beginning to turn brown from the constant heat. At a quarter _____ one, the smell of _____ that was frying for lunch lingered in the heavy air, and I could almost hear the grease _____ in the skillet. _____ probably would serve fresh _____ beans from the garden, too. Sunday _____ was always a special meal that we ate later in the day because the _____ sermon usually delayed our getting home until 12:30. I noticed a _____ fly hovering over the puddle of water that had accumulated under the dripping _____ in the side yard. I thought of all of the _____ cakes that I had eaten for breakfast and I got sick _____ my stomach.

> (Most of my students at Mississippi State will fill in the blanks with the following words: *porch; yard; to; chicken; popping* or *sizzling; Mother; green* or *butter; dinner; preacher's; dragon* or *horse; faucet* or *air conditioner; pan; at.* I also give them sample passages that they cannot complete, or that they fill out in quite different ways, so as to confirm the significant influences of their common regional experience, observation, and language.)

I.   A. Go to some place other than where you ordinarily would go to study or write. Sit alone for twenty minutes. Think about an experience in your past. As you remember details from the experience—what happened, where it happened, who was involved, what was said—keep a simple record of your memories by jotting words and phrases that refer to the important details.

B. Later, as you sit at your desk ready to write a piece about this experience, recall the experience again, using the words and phrases that you recorded earlier to jog your memory and to help you think of additional details. Now write about the experience as if you were telling someone about it. Bring this writing to our next class meeting.

C. Select one division or section of your descriptive narration to revise. If you wrote your piece in the first person point of view as a participant in the experience, then revise it by assuming the role of a detached observer. If you wrote in the third person point of view as an observer, then adjust the point of view of the writing through the use of the first person *I*.

As you compare and contrast your original writing and your revision of it, consider these questions:

1. Will a change in technical point of view affect other elements or aspects of the narrative? Do details remain plausible? Do statements of attitudes or feelings remain consistent with point of view? Can an observer make the same statements as a participant? Or *vice versa?* Are there different types of observers?
2. What are the values of using first person narration?
3. What are the values of using third person narration?

II. A. Locate the building that was built in 1901 as the Textile Building. Go there and quickly write your reactions to the building. Return later and attempt to record objectively the sights, sounds, smells, textures, and even tastes that attract your attention.

(The students draw maps on the blackboard as the visual foundation for discussing the influences of perspective, focus, and direction on reporting and communicating detail. Most offer few details and fail to identify directions in their maps. This activity contributes to their recognizing the importance of referential details in their writings, which we discuss on the site as we move to achieve the literal physical vantage point of selected writings before addressing voice, sensory appeals, physical perspectives, and audience.)

B. Interview one of your classmates and write a brief sketch of the person's life. In addition to collecting obvious information—date of birth, hometown, etc.— try to discover something unusual or interesting about the person. Trust your judgments and draw any conclusions that you think are justified.

C. How or why were you given your first and middle names? Offer one of your classmates a brief explanation of your names, including any information that you think is pertinent. After you leave class, investigate the meanings of your given names and your surname in one of the sources that I've suggested. Write a brief "definition" of your name by combining your own knowledge and information from the source.

(We discuss the first writing in a workshop before the students present the paper that synthesizes information.)

III.   A. Read these three passages silently before some of the class members agree to read them aloud.

1. *Metrical Chronicle of Robert of Gloucester* (c. 1300):

    (I include a copy of twelve lines of the medieval text so that the students may respond to usages—eth, thorn, ampersand, capitalization, and syntax.)

2. 1848 Speech of Henry Clay:

    I have heard something said about allegiance to the South. I know no South, no North, no East, no West, to which I own any allegiance. The Union, sir, is my country.

3. The aireon kneads mustment immediately if we are to stay skool.

    A tagmene nores blooply as it gleeps.

    The berkly normant anks dink wevanks that rak woudly.

    Ah ou hungi, ou sweetums? Do ou ike kookie?

    (With minimal guidance, the students are readily able to identify functions and meanings suggested by sound and structure. I supplement the first passage with some glossing and then I offer an overview of the history of English, asking students to look for modern parallels of the major influences of migration, usage, and conquest. The study reinforces the focus upon the South as affected by change.)

The following words had different meanings in the past. Use each word as you understand it in a brief paragraph. After class, investigate the earlier meanings of the words in the *Oxford English Dictionary* (PX/1625/M71/Ref.) and keep a record of your findings for discussion in our next workshop.

   town, wife, meat, liquor, silly, nice, deer, apple, corn, boor, lewd, censure

B. Investigate the events of the day of your birth by reading the front page of a newspaper issued on that date. Consider reported events in a written "analysis" of some possible relationships between one event and your birth.

   (Assignments III A and B encourage the students to see the importance of published sources of information.)

C. List as many courtesy titles and general identifying labels as you can and then select at least two that you recognize and understand well enough to explain to an imaginary reader who has never heard the titles used.

   (Discussion of less ordinary titles such as *saint, the honorable, Jr.,* etc. leads the students to go beyond the familiar *Mr., Mrs., Ms.,* etc.)

   Imagine that you had to explain to your imaginary reader how one might use several different titles and name references (Remember assignment II C?) in different social and professional contexts.

IV.   A. Select a piece of writing other than a textbook in your major academic field or in the profession that you plan to enter. (Consider journal articles, technical manuals or reports or perhaps ask one of your professors for advice.) Identify the specialized words that an average reader might not know or might misinterpret. (Do *you* have some difficulty in determining the meanings of some words?) Rewrite the passage as if it were a transcript of your spoken explanation of the content and then write a second piece in which you explain a common daily experience using some of the specialized words.

B. Each of us has special knowledge and skill. Think about what you can do or make using your hands. Decide upon a specific procedure that you can explain, but try to select some skill that may be unusual or extraordinary for most people. Write a general instruction for an inexperienced or uninformed reader so that the reader may learn how to perform the skill. Bring any physical objects that are needed to perform the skill to our next class meeting.

(I ask individual students to read aloud the instructions thay have written, so that another member of the class may perform the skill. The restrictions are obvious: the process must be safe and must require only those objects that the writer can bring to the classroom. The exercise offers numerous analogies to prescriptive writing and allows peers to assume the role of the evaluator.)

C. Students often hear and read references to facts, judgments, opinions, and expert testimony. What do you think each label means? Write a statement that you think illustrates each of these classifications of information.

(The brevity of the assignment allows time for discussion of the examples and for the assessment of the contributions of different syntactical structures to meaning.)

After our discussion, you may be inclined to believe that one of your example statements is better than the others. Choose your best example as the basis for an essay to be written out of class.

(This traditional academic writing assignment is loaded, because the students respond to the word *essay* and usually exclude opinions from their choices. The writing provides an excellent means of assessing whether the students have transcended the preconceptions of academic writing that they brought to the class.)

V.   A. When, in assignment III C, we discussed courtesy titles, we emphasized the complexities that underlie literal denotations *and* we observed the reflections of different attitudes toward different "labels" in different contexts.

Labels often are used rather loosely in political contexts, too. Terms such as *liberal, conservative, Democrat, Republican, radical, left/right wing, demagogue,* etc. appear in print and in spoken communication so freely that one unfamiliar with the language might assume that they have definite, clearly established meanings. But do they?

Choose a political figure or issue with which you have some familiarity and then *ignore* your selection. I want you to consider someone or something with which you are *not* personally familiar. Be aware from the beginning of your work that you will be collecting information on an unknown subject and therefore working toward developing a knowledge of the subject in which you may be interested but are not conversant.

Collect the information in a structured essay that leads the reader to the conclusion/belief that you support, but don't directly state the stance or contention of the writing until you have presented the detailed information that you have collected.

B. Wander through one of your favorite stores or a store that you frequent. Select two products—perhaps two brands of the same type of product—that you judge to have distinctive appeal for southerners. As you write today, identify specific similarities and differences in the products as you attempt to illustrate the "southern appeal" of these products to a reader who is not aware of the importance or widespread use of the products in the South.

C. We earlier discussed facts, judgments, opinions, and expert testimony. Do you know the meanings of the words *inference* and *implication?* As we consider advertisements that I have clipped from current magazines, let's look for those that we judge might have particular appeal to southerners and those that are directed to more general audiences. Select an advertisement that appeals to you and note why and how it convinces a reader to buy a product. Can you convince the manufacturer of the product that the advertisement succeeds in appealing to an audience?

Closure:

We have considered writing as a "way of knowing" as we have written about experiences that we have understood as individuals and as a group. As a final activity in the class, you may find it interesting to write a personal genealogy or you might like to investigate how a town (or towns) where you have lived gained its name. Such a study may suggest to you that you have found one precise way of explaining or defining a part of the South, or you may find that this idea leads you to see that there are differences that you want to stress.

(I hold individual conferences with each student to review primarily the content that he or she has selected to respond to different activities. I question whether particular ideas and techniques that the individual writer has used in other writings might not be pertinent to this activity, but I do not direct or control the student in making selections.)

II

Literature and Exploratory Writing

Karen Pelz

When I left Dartmouth to take part in the Institute, I knew that whatever course I designed for the College would almost surely attempt to integrate literature and writing. The English faculty at Dartmouth, like that at most colleges and universities throughout the country, is, after all, trained in the field of literature, not specifically in the teaching of writing. So it is not surprising that the freshman course has perennially used literature as the basis for its composition assignments. In deciding to continue this practice, I realized, of course, that I was going against the currently popular separation between literature and writing. Yet I have always felt that the separation is at best artificial, at worst destructive, despite the old abuses that have come from concentrating on literature at the cost of writing.

My goal, as I saw it, was to tap the faculty's interest and enthusiasm for literature, and at the same time to create a course which would be a legitimate freshman composition course, not just a course in which students wrote themes about literature. In order to assure that my course would answer to the needs of students, I chose to use a developmental model based largely on the work of James Britton—giving students experience in expressive discourse and the various kinds of writing that grow out of it. So too I wanted to concentrate on the process of writing rather than on the production of a specified number of themes. Thus I came to settle upon what I call exploratory writing as the foundation for the course.

Exploratory writing, while involving elements of both expressive and transactional writing, is different in its nature and aims from the kind of expository writing done in most composition classes at the college level. Rather than seeking to explain, analyze, or persuade, its main aim is to allow writers to probe their own experience, to reflect upon it, and to experiment, with the intention of discovering and developing their own attitudes, beliefs, feelings, and ideas about the experience, whether that experience be something they have done or witnessed in their own lives, a concept or an idea they have encountered, or a literary text they have read. The audience for such writing is primarily the author of it, as well as trusted friends, classmates, and sympathetic teachers and colleagues who might be in a position to help the writer carry on the exploratory purpose of the writing. Its subject matter, therefore, especially in the early stages of the sequence of assignments, draws heavily on the personal experience and knowledge of the writer, no matter what the nominal topic of the writing might happen to be. Its form is necessarily dictated by the movement of the author's mind in the process of writing, rather than by the organizational conventions that apply to more public forms of writing, such as explanation, analysis and persuasion. Thus its form is typically meditative and associative rather than rigorously topical or categorical. Its style, therefore, is casual, adhering to the natural idiom of the writer rather than to the strict conventions of formal English.

Exploratory writing, then, is a means of discovering and ordering experience, of taking a step back to look at a series of events we have witnessed or been involved in, and asking ourselves questions such as the following: What does it mean? How does it fit into the pattern of my life? Where have I encountered it before? How does it challenge values or beliefs I have held in the past? How does it strengthen my existing values and beliefs? What can I learn from this? How can I use this new information to broaden my knowledge of the subject? What implications does it have for the study I am engaged in? I believe this kind of exploration and inquiry leads to education in the original sense: to bring out of students an awareness of how they make sense of the events and contexts of their lives. Much knowledge comes from within, rather than from without, and exploratory writing is a way to tap those inner resources that lead us from information to knowledge.

An analogy from literature, the ancient genre of the *bildungsroman,* may help to explain my concept of exploratory writing. In such a story, the young protagonist leaves his familiar surroundings, ventures out into the world, makes a close observation of what he sees around him, has his old notions and experiences challenged by events and people who are strange and perhaps even threatening, and finally learns from and is changed by the experience. In American literature one thinks immediately of "Young Goodman Brown," "My Kinsman, Major Molineux," *Moby-Dick,* or *The Adventures of Huckleberry Finn,* just to name a few. Like the protagonist of a *bildungsroman* or an explorer searching for a mountain or the source of a river, student writers begin in known territory, look carefully at the world around them, move by a path that is undefined and offers many possible options, take risks and encounter both obstacles and right directions, and finally reach their goal when they discover at the end something they didn't know at the beginning. Or, like Huck Finn, they leave behind a home of sorts, predictable if not exactly perfect, for a life on the river that takes them on an expedition through danger, excitement, comedy, and tragedy, into worlds at first unknown and then made familiar through experience. And it becomes addictive, this exploration, this wandering life, this *bildungsroman;* even when the comforts of a real home are offered, Huck seeks the life of the explorer, and at the end of the novel he "lights out for the territory," seeking new worlds to explore and investigate and learn from. Only when writers have undergone this process of exploration and discovery can we reasonably expect them to move into interpretation, analysis, exposition, persuasion.

We might say, then, that exploratory writing is an inductive process that begins in familiar territory and moves through a sequence of assignments to less familiar realms. Looking at it another way, we might say that it begins with the particular (personal experience) and moves to the general (the world of ideas). Through language, through internal dialogue, through writing, students begin to explore the world of ideas, and the written expression of those ideas, by starting with that which they know best—the world which they have experienced and can continue to experience directly—and moving into the world of indirect experience through literature. Through exploratory writing students can encounter this world, record their reactions to it, their growing understanding of it, their opinions about it, their analysis of its meaning, and their synthesis of the pieces of information and sensory experience that become their perspective on the world. "Languaging," a word that like "bildungsroman" and "writing" implies process, is, as Britton says in *Language and Learning,* what makes both predictions about the future and memory and interpretation of the past possible. And surely that is at least partly what literature is all about as well.

In the course that follows, exploratory writing is central to the study of two literary texts—*Walden* and *Heart of Darkness.* The set of writings on each text follows a similar pattern, beginning with various kinds of informal, exploratory writing and moving to the more sophisticated forms of exposition and persuasion. The opening assignments of the course, for example, involve students in investigating their immediate environment (much as Thoreau would have done), first writing down their impressions in an essentially expressive piece (1), then gradually interpreting the experience in writings that are exploratory and analytical (2-4). Students begin investigating the text of *Walden* itself in assignments 5-6, exploring several of Thoreau's theories, and then analyzing the implications of these for their own lives. In assignments 7-10, students continue their exploratory reaction to the book, and proceed from here to persuasive writing aimed at a particular audience. When attention is shifted to *Heart of Darkness,* students return to the beginning, as it were, by writing an exploratory personal response to background readings. As they move through the novel itself, students keep a record of ideas and impressions—essentially an exploratory journal, a collection of writings-in-progress. From this journal the students select ideas to develop in the two final course papers, pieces that are explanatory, interpretive, and persuasive. From the beginning of the course to the end, then, the writing and the literary texts work in tandem, the one serving to help the students make sense of the other, the students' explorations being continual throughout.

EXPLORATIONS

1. Spend half an hour this afternoon or tomorrow in one of the more "natural" areas on campus—down by the river, or at Occum Pond, or over in the woods near the Bema. While you are there, write down your observations of the place. You may want to write a description of the whole scene before you, or take a more limited perspective—say a five-foot circle immediately around you, or choose one thing that particularly catches your attention. Or you may want to write about your reactions to

being in the place—whether it reminds you of other places you have been, or whether it is strange to you; whether you like being off by yourself in an isolated part of the campus, or whether it makes you uneasy. Just write for half an hour on whatever occurs to you in these surroundings. Don't feel compelled to turn this into a polished paper; think of it as notes or beginnings towards a paper, or "jottings" like those you might make in a journal. Feel free to illustrate your words with drawings if you like.

2. Sometime this afternoon or evening, go back to the place where you made your original observations. Find some natural object there—a leaf or small branch from a tree, an acorn, a piece of wood, a stone—and take it back to your dormitory room with you. Sit down for ten minutes and write about the object. Write whatever occurs to you—a description, a poem, a dialogue with the object. Do that exercise, spending ten minutes writing about your object, at least four more times over the week-end. What changes do you observe in the object? What changes do you observe in yourself, or in your attitude towards the object? On a third or fourth observation, do you notice anything you haven't noticed before?

3. Now, return one final time to your original place of observation, but this time, go at a different time of the day, perhaps early morning, or just around dusk. What is different about the scene? About your reaction to it? Do you notice things you did not notice before? Take some notes about the place on this second visit, but do not write about it until you return to your room or wherever you do your studying and class preparation. Now reflect back on both visits to the spot. Was the place you observed more interesting at one time of day than another? More beautiful? Different in any way? Write something about the two visits. You don't necessarily have to compare one visit with the other, though that is a possibility.

4. Imagine that the college were not here, and that the area you visited—the river, the pond, the woods—were instead an isolated area two miles' walk from the nearest town. Imagine further that you were going to spend the entire summer there, living in a cabin without electricity, running water, or a vehicle to take you away from the place. How would you feel about such an experience? What problems do you foresee arising? What would be the benefits of living on your own in such a situation?

> (These first assignments are designed to bring the students into *Walden*-like situations—to have the students observe, in a sense to read, the environment around them. The places mentioned in the assignments are quite beautiful in the middle of September when we begin classes, and are places most freshmen have not visited previously. Before they begin reading the text, then, the students begin exploring their surroundings and writing down their observations in the same way Thoreau did. Because I want to allow the early writing in the course to be exploratory in form as well as in content, I engage them in these explorations before asking them to read the text, so they won't feel they have to imitate Thoreau in any way.

These first assignments are also intended to introduce the students to the fact that it is possible to look at the same thing at different times and see it anew each time, that there is no more one right way to describe something than there is one right way to read a book or interpret a piece of literature. If they bring contradictory views or reactions to class, that will lead to a later discussion about the seeming "inconsistencies" in *Walden,* such as Thoreau's criticism of farming and his hoeing up of the weeds to plant a garden, his vegetarianism and his eating of the woodchuck, and his ambivalent feelings about the railroad.

Assignment 4 is specifically intended to get them into the spirit of *Walden,* to help students think of Thoreau's experiment not as something that some weird writer did in the past, but as an adventure any one of them might undertake. The students thus imagine what the experiment might be like for them before they turn in assignment 5 to the book itself, and begin to read what it was like for Thoreau.)

5. Now read the first 27 pages of Chapter 1 of *Walden.* In these pages Thoreau describes the four necessities of life: food, clothing, shelter, and warmth. Which of them seems to present the most problems in your own daily life at Dartmouth? Which seems to take up the most money from your family budget? Are there other necessities of modern life that Thoreau doesn't include? Explore the question of what is necessary for reasonable human existence.

6. Finish reading Chapter 1 of *Walden.* In the remainder of this chapter, Thoreau describes how he built his house and how much it cost him to do it. Pay particular attention to p. 34, where Thoreau relates his experiences building his house at Walden Pond to the idea of education: " 'But,' says one, 'you do not mean that the students would go to work with their hands instead of their heads?' I do not mean that exactly, but I mean something like that; I mean that they should not *play* life, or *study* it merely, while the community supports them at this expensive game, but earnestly *live* it from beginning to end. How could youths better learn to live than by at once trying the experiment of living?" Does Thoreau mean to suggest that students should drop out of college, move to a remote area and build their own houses? What does he mean when he says that students should *live* life, not *play* it or *study* it? Which of those things are you doing here at Dartmouth? What does this have to do with your idea of what your education is all about? Do you think you could educate yourself by living alone in the woods for two years as well as you will be educated at Dartmouth? And will you "be educated" at Dartmouth, or will you educate yourself?

(Assignments 5 and 6 grow out of assignment 4, but also involve the students in the reading and interpretation of the text. Assignment 5 asks students to explore the timelessness of Thoreau's theories and, in a sense, it is also an assignment in definition. Assignment 6 asks students to relate Thoreau's concept of education to the educational experience they are themselves involved in, which demands that they explore their ideas about their own education. These assignments do not ask students to analyze literature as such, but rather to relate significant ideas from the reading to their own lives. Assignments 7 and 8 continue the process of personal exploration of *Walden.)*

7. Read Chapters 2 and 3 of *Walden,* "Where I Lived, and What I Lived For," and "Reading." Find one passage—a sentence or two, perhaps a paragraph—that strikes some chord of response in you. It might be a statement you strongly agree or disagree with, a particular image or example that intrigues you, or a section that you find puzzling. Write the passage at the top of a piece of paper. Then write two or three pages about the passage and your response to it.

8. Read the letter to Thoreau from Daniel Ricketson, found on pp. 257-260 of your text. Now, using the same subject you explored in the last assignment, write a letter to Thoreau in which you agree or take issue with one or more of his ideas or writing techniques. Support and defend your response to what you have read. What argumentative or persuasive strategies will you employ in writing to this particular audience?

> (With assignment 7, the students begin to write papers which may involve argumentation and analysis, but, again, in an exploratory manner based on their own personal reactions to the text and concentrating on their response, whatever it may be, rather than on rigorous logical argumentation. In previous assignments, students have written for the class and teacher; in assignment 8, they change the audience, writing directly to Thoreau, in letter form. This assignment gives them an opportunity to think about the constraints on writing for a particular audience and, of course, it asks them to formulate and defend a thesis, a task that will be required of them in much of the academic writing they do beyond the course.
>
> Assignments 9 and 10 deal with *Walden* as literature.)

9. Read the two chapters about the ponds: "The Ponds" and "The Pond in Winter." In these two chapters, Thoreau uses many metaphors and analogies to talk about the ponds. As you read, make a list of the figurative passages. On page 189, Thoreau says of Walden Pond, "What if all ponds were shallow? Would it not react on the minds of men? I am thankful that this pond was made deep and pure for a symbol." What does the pond symbolize? There is surely no one "right" answer to this question, but keeping in mind the list of metaphors Thoreau used to describe the pond, as well as all that has preceded these chapters in the book, what do you *think* the pond might symbolize—for Thoreau and for his readers?

10. All through the book, Thoreau has talked to us about waking up, about being awake and alive to the world around us. He closes the book with these words: "The light which puts out our eyes is darkness to us. Only that day dawns to which we are awake. There is more day to dawn. The sun is but a morning star." In what ways has reading *Walden* been an awakening to you? Or has the book failed in its purposes?

Please write about your reactions to the book as a whole now that you have finished reading it.

> (In assignment 9, I have asked the students to generate a list of uses of figurative language in the two chapters that describe the ponds, and then to consider how these figures help build towards a symbolic interpretation of the ponds. We spend considerable time in class talking about this process, and emphasizing that the writing is exploratory, that the students are writing about possibilities rather than trying to find "the answer," a simple statement that "Walden Pond symbolizes _____ ." One purpose of this exercise is to give students more practice in making a thesis statement and supporting it with evidence from the text.
>
> Assignment 10 is once again essentially expressive, though for this final paper on *Walden* many students write something that leans towards the persuasive. Some write essays which focus on that final quotation or some other quotation from the book; some write argumentative essays in which they criticize the book negatively; some write about ways the book has changed their lives. A range of responses is possible.
>
> Assignments 11-14, the last four writing assignments of the course, are based on *Heart of Darkness,* although the final assignment involves writing about both books. Because I again want the students to enter the discussion at the personal, exploratory stage, I ask them to write a reaction paper to the background material on colonization in the Belgian Congo. Few of the students have any historical sense of the colonial exploitation of Africa, and while I do not expect them to judge the material for its historical accuracy, I am interested in their reactions to it, the extent to which it supports or contradicts ideas about explorations the students had previously held.)

11. Now on to *Heart of Darkness*. Because we're not so culturally "in tune" with the exploration and colonization of Africa as we are with nineteenth century New England, I'd like you to do some background reading about this subject before you begin reading the novel. So please read pages 85-123 in the Norton edition of the text. When you have finished your reading, write a brief response to what you have read. To what extent, for example, did the readings confirm or contradict your image of explorers? Of the role of Europeans in Africa? Have you ever had a childhood experience like the one Conrad relates as having inspired his interest in African exploration?

12. *Heart of Darkness* is a work that needs to be read carefully and considered as a whole. Therefore, I will give you some extra time to finish the whole work before we begin our discussion. While you are reading the book, your only writing assignment will be to keep a journal of your reading, jotting down questions it raises in your mind, references to passages you don't understand, reactions to the events of the story—whatever occurs to you as you are reading the novel. The purpose of the journal is to aid your understanding of the book, not to convince me you have read it, so don't bother with plot summary unless that is useful to you.

(Assignment 13 is deliberately open-ended. The assignment gives students the experience of refining a very general topic into a specific one, a task frequently required of them in other courses. As with the final paper on *Walden,* the form and mode of this paper are open. Most write an interpretive paper defending a thesis, but some students prefer to write expressive essays.)

13. Now that we have discussed the book, I would like you to go back to your journal. Find a passage where you had questions about the meaning of the book, or a section in which you explored some of the issues in the book. What I'd like you to do is to write a paper about *Heart of Darkness,* using either your journal or class discussion or both as the source for your exploration of the book. You may write any kind of paper you like for this project—analytic, personal response, interpretive— on any topic related to *Heart of Darkness.*

(The final writing assignment asks the students to pull the course together.)

14. Now that we have spent ten weeks doing our own exploring in writing and class discussion of two major literary works about exploration, it's time to attempt a final assessment of what it all means. Exploration implies discovery, if it is successful. Even if a given exploration has been a failure in terms of its original goal, something of importance may have been discovered along the way. In light of your interpretation of *Walden* and *Heart of Darkness,* discuss the discoveries made by Thoreau and Marlow. Were they successes or failures? And in whose terms?

"The American Dream"

A Developmental Course in Writing and Learning

Henry Silverman

The sequence of assignments following this essay is called "The American Dream," because it engages students in reading and responding to historical and literary texts that embody and express American ideals. It is one of a number of courses in the Department of American Thought and Language at Michigan State University which combine the teaching of history and literature with the teaching of writing, and as such it can be seen as reflective of our departmental commitment to fuse the study of American culture with instruction in written communication.[1] While it reflects this fusion of concerns, it does so in a way that is especially attuned to the needs of students in the developmental version of our program.

In the past, our basic writers have often found themselves so burdened by the substantial amount of literary and historical reading in the regular program that they have had difficulty in moving beyond that obstacle to make significant progress in their writing abilities. Thus it seemed important that we design for these students a special version of our year-long program—a version that would reduce the amount of reading so as to provide for an increased amount of writing practice. This special emphasis is reflected in "The American Dream" and its companion courses, which together make up a year-long developmental program that begins by having students

[1] The Department of American Thought and Language has the primary responsibility for offering courses which meet the University's "general education" requirement of nine credits in written communication. Since its beginnings after World War II, the Department has changed approaches to the teaching of writing, as it has changed names. First it functioned as Written and Spoken English, then as Communication Skills, and finally around 1960, as the Department of American Thought and Language. This historical description is important because it makes clear the importance of content material in the Department's writing program. The Department took on, in 1960, not only the responsibility of teaching MSU freshmen how to write but also the task of teaching them about their American heritage. In theory, of course, the two missions were to be complementary. Reading literary, social, and historical documents, mainly primary sources out of the American past, would help students improve their understanding of what it is to be an American and at the same time would help students improve their ability to write and understand the American language.

engage in personal writing as a response to their reading of American autobiography and biography, and that culminates by having them write analytical and critical pieces on cultural issues related to their experience in response to their reading of documents in American cultural criticism. This developmental program, then, is a writing intensive version of our regular program—a version in which the writing is oriented as much as possible to the experience and concerns of contemporary American students.

An overview of "The American Dream" will serve to show the various ways that reading and writing are integrated in our developmental program. This quarter-length course is divided into three main units, each with a central theme: (1) "The Democratic Ideal," (2) "The Pursuit of Success," and (3) "The Land." Reading assignments for each unit provide various perspectives on the particular theme, ranging from historical documents to contemporary statements, from autobiographical accounts to short stories. The writing activities, in turn, call upon students to bring these readings together with their own experiences and observations in three types of assignments: (1) journal entries on individual readings, (2) short pieces on selected topics that pull together a handful of related works, and (3) a major paper at the end of each unit on a challenging question related to the theme of that section. Collectively, these various kinds of writing embody a process approach to learning in that they move students from an early to a more developed understanding and formulation of an idea. And over the course of the unit they keep students moving back and forth from what they read to what they think, provoking them to connect their understanding of ideas from the past to their thinking in the present.

This cumulative integration of reading and writing assignments can be seen from a more detailed review of the thematic units that make up the course. The first unit, "The Democratic Ideal," for example, begins by having students read three major embodiments of the ideal, "The Declaration of Independence," Crevecoeur's "What is an American," and Martin Luther King's "I Have a Dream." Based on these readings, students are then directed to use their journal to record key ideas in each text, to note related ideas among the texts, and to express their own "American Dream." Shortly after this journal writing, students are asked to take some of the ideas from their journal and develop them in a short paper that invites them to see the contemporary relevance of past ideas—"Do you see any of the characteristics Crevecoeur ascribes to the 'new man,' the American, in today's Americans? In King? In you? In your friends? In American society in general?" After this first set of encounters with "The Democratic Ideal," students then turn to reading about the dreams of immigrants. The journal, in turn, becomes a place for students to describe what they perceive in the expectations and feelings of immigrants, and the short paper provokes them to draw connections between immigrant dreams and the dream of Martin Luther King by means of role-playing an immigrant in writing. After engaging the dreams of immigrants, students turn to reading about the experience of minorities and face the problems of prejudice in America, first in their journal, then in the short paper that compels them to take one of the pieces they have read and compare the experience it depicts to the principles in the "Declaration of

Independence." The unit ends with a culminating essay which asks students to bring together their previous reading and writing in answering the question "What does it mean to be an American?" Students are asked here to focus on the expectations of minorities or immigrants and show, with examples from their reading, how these expectations were influenced by the democratic ideal and how the ideal corresponded to the reality of their experiences. This assignment, as can be seen, has been anticipated both by the prior readings and writings. In effect, the series of reading and writing activities in this unit—and in all others—embodies a process of discovering, developing, and refining ideas.

This process can be seen again in the second unit, "The Pursuit of Success," though the intellectual and personal contexts are different. Pursuing success has a particularly important meaning for freshman students, intent as they are on achieving their goals and sure as they are that they will. This unit thus aims to combine the personal experience of students with an awareness of the American success ethic as illustrated by the reading. They read historical documents on the success ethic and short stories that deal with the theme of success and failure. The reading journal and short paper assignments, in turn, call upon students to describe and define the ideas of success and failure they find in the readings and to relate these to their own definitions. Having read and written about particular experiences and ideas of success and failure in America, students then write a final paper for this unit that focusses on "the cost of success in America," on how the ethic of success has influenced the American dream. Here again students are asked to fuse their prior reading and writing in formulating for themselves what success in America means and demands.

The third unit, "The Land," begins by having students read fictional and non-fictional accounts about farm life and small town life in America. The journal writing, in turn, becomes an occasion for students to reflect on the difference between mythical expectations about the land and the actual experience of life on a farm or in a small town. And the first short paper gives students an opportunity to relate their own origins—in a city, small town, or on a farm—to their own ideas about the "land." Following upon this introduction to conflicts between myth and reality about the land, students then engage in a series of readings that points up similar conflicts between myth and reality both about frontier life and the life of the city. Journal writings and short paper topics reiteratively call upon students to explore this conflict from various perspectives. Thus the major paper in this segment invites students to take a position on how they believe the myth and/or the reality of the small town, farm, frontier, or city has shaped American culture.

Having engaged the students in reading and writing about various aspects of the American dream, the course ends by asking students to speculate on what the nature of the American Dream will be in the future, as well as on what major problems will face America in the future. This final paper thus invites students to build on what they have discovered in the previous units of "The American Dream," particularly in their repeated confrontation of the conflict between myth and reality in the American experience. In speculating about the future of American society, students are, in effect, projecting a significant dimension of their own future lives. So this final paper serves for them as a fitting capstone to understanding what the American Dream has meant in both a personal and a broader cultural context.

"The American Dream" and its companion courses have, needless to say, undergone various changes from the time I designed it at the Institute in the spring of 1979 and first offered it in pilot form with a handful of colleagues in the fall of 1979.[2] Still, the basic elements which we believe are most significant in what we are trying to do remain the same. Each course embodies a process approach to writing, seeking to make students aware of the process from the very first and of its importance both to the quality of their writing and the quality of their thinking. In each course, short writing assignments lead directly into longer ones, by way of reading journals, focused paper topics, and major essay assignments. So, for each segment of a course, students find themselves looking at a particular thematic issue from various perspectives, not only in their reading but also in their writing. And the culmination of each course gives students an opportunity to synthesize their earlier writing and thinking in a major essay. By the end of each course, then, students have produced not only an extensively detailed reading journal, but have also written fourteen pieces, including four longer essays. The course, then, is genuinely writing intensive.[3] At the same time, it fuses the reading of literary and historical materials into the writing and thereby keeps up a commitment to the content mission of the Department. It aims specifically at making students aware of their American heritage both through their reading and their writing. As a developmental program, it aims to move students from the personal writing they feel more at ease with to the more academic writing they will be expected to produce throughout the University. To this end the use of American literary and historical materials serves us well, for these give the students a body of ideas and issues to think about and react to—ideas and issues that are not simply part of a historical record but are also able to touch the students personally and significantly once they begin to think and write about them.

---

[2] After being offered in pilot form during 1979, 1980, and 1981, this series of courses became the official developmental program at the University in the Fall of 1982.

[3] As an additional source of writing instruction, all students in this developmental program are enrolled in a two-hour per week writing lab. During their lab hours, students organize into small groups of four or five, each led by a trained undergraduate student, for the purpose of peer editing and draft revision. This allows more time to put the process approach to writing in practice, with students using the sessions for working on their various writing assignments.

THE AMERICAN DREAM

Unit I: The Democratic Ideal (3 weeks)

Reading Assignment: "Declaration of Independence"; "What Is an American?" Jean de Crevecoeur; "I Have a Dream," Martin Luther King, Jr.

Journal Questions: Describe your American Dream. List the five principles of government stated in the "Declaration of Independence." Discuss which of these principles King is referring to in his speech. List the characteristics of an American Crevecoeur discusses in his piece. Discuss how they relate to the American of today.

Short Paper 1: Do you see any of the characteristics Crevecoeur ascribes to the "new man," the American, in today's Americans? In King? In you? In your friends? In American society in general?

Reading Assignment: "Going to America: The Immigrant Experience" (in Leonard Kriegel and Abraham Lass, *Stories of the American Experience* [New York: Mentor, 1973]); "Waves of Immigration," John F. Kennedy.

Journal Questions: What were the expectations of the immigrants who came to America? How did their expectations reflect the principles stated in the "Declaration of Independence"? What contributions did the immigrants make to America?

Reading Assignment: "Seventy Thousand Assyrians," William Saroyan; "Fawn with a Bit of Green," Harvey Swados.

Journal Questions: What was the immigrant dream illustrated in "Seventy Thousand Assyrians"? What did the immigrant have to give up to acquire the dream? What was Kevin's dream in "Fawn with a Bit of Green"? What did he discover about the reality of life in America?

Short Paper 2: What connections do you see between King's dreams and the dreams of the immigrants about whom you have been reading? Choose a character from one of the pieces you have read and have her/him write a letter to King telling him how their dreams are similar or different. Or, have the immigrant write an "I Have a Dream" piece which reflects her/his dream.

Reading Assignment: "Race and Reality," Kriegel and Lass; "Pantaloon in Black," William Faulkner; "The Imaginary Jew," John Berryman; "La Causa," Filipe Ponce, Jr.; "Women in Leadership Roles," Marvin Stone.

Journal Questions: What do these pieces say about prejudice in America? What do they say about the minority experience in America?

Short Paper 3: In the "Declaration of Independence," Jefferson states five basic principles that have become the basis for American democratic philosophy: first, all men are created equal; second, they possess unalienable rights, which he defines as "Life, Liberty, and the pursuit of Happiness"; third, governments are created by men to secure these rights; fourth, government derives its just power from the consent of the governed; and fifth, people have the right to alter or abolish government and establish new government if it becomes "destructive" of its purpose.

Choose one of the pieces from the minority experience and discuss how the author illustrates how one of these principles relates to the minority group discussed.

Reading Assignment: "Why I Left the U.S. and Why I Am Returning," Eldridge Cleaver; "On Discovering America," Pearl Buck.

Journal Questions: What views of America do Cleaver and Buck have? What does being an American mean to them?

Major Paper I: What does it mean to be an American?
This paper should focus on the impact democratic principles have had on the American culture, especially on the experiences of immigrants and minorities. Formulate a thesis in which you deal with the expectations of minorities or immigrants showing how these expectations were influenced by the democratic ideal and how the ideal relates to the reality of their experience. Support your thesis by using material from the readings.

Unit II: The Pursuit of Success (2 weeks)

Reading Assignment: "The Self Made Man in America," Irvin Wyllie; "Frank Is Offered a Position," Horatio Alger.

Journal Questions: What are the qualities of the self-made man cited by Wyllie? How well does Frank fulfill these characteristics?

Reading Assignment: "The Happiest Man on Earth," Albert Maltz; "Cow," Ben Field; "The Girl with the Pimply Face," William Carlos Williams.

Journal Questions: How did each of the main characters of these stories define success? What part of the myth of the self-made man did the dreams relate to? What did success cost each of the main characters?

Short Paper 4: Based on your reading of Wyllie, describe the important characteristics of the success ethic. Discuss how Frank Courtney represents the myth of pursuing success.

Reading Assignment: "Bright and Morning Star," Richard Wright; "Christ in Concrete," Pietro di Donato; "The Man Who Corrupted Hadleyburg," Mark Twain.

Journal Questions: How did each of the main characters of the stories define success? What did achieving success cost each?

Short Paper 5: Choose one character from the short stories and discuss how that character defined success and what he was willing to do to achieve it. How does the character's experience illustrate the reality of pursuing success?

Reading Assignment: "Main Currents in American Thought," Irwin Shaw.

Journal Questions: How does Andrew get trapped by his own success? What does he pay?

Major Paper II: What is the cost of success in America?
The paper should focus on the impact of the success ethic on shaping Americans' dreams of success and on what they are willing to pay to achieve it. Formulate a thesis in which you deal with at least two characters' dreams of success and what they were willing to give to achieve it, and apply their experience to the American experience at large.

Unit III: The Land (3 Weeks)

Reading Assignment: "The Small Town and the Farm," Kriegel and Lass; "Strength of God," Sherwood Anderson.

Journal Questions: What were the expectations about life in the small town? What image do commercials give us of life in small towns and on the farm? How does this compare with reality?

Reading Assignment: "Blackberry Winter," Robert Penn Warren; "Under the Lion's Paw," Hamlin Garland.

Journal Questions: What picture of life on the farm and in the small town do these stories present? How do they compare with the myth?

Short Paper 6: Where do you come from? Small town or farm? City? Write on the ways you think this may have shaped your experience and attitude toward the "land."

Reading Assignment: "The Way West," Kriegel and Lass; "The Frontier in American History," Frederick Jackson Turner.

Journal Questions: How does Turner say the frontier has shaped American life?

Short Paper 7: What is the myth of the quality of life in the small town or farm as illustrated by literature or advertising? What do the pieces you have read say about the reality of the quality of life?

Reading Assignment: "The Blue Hotel," Stephen Crane; "The Luck of Roaring Camp," Bret Hart.

Journal Questions: What myths about the frontier and the West do these stories illustrate?

Reading Assignment: "The Leader of the People," John Steinbeck; "The Frontier," Francis Parkman.

Journal Questions: What realities about the West do these stories illustrate? How do they compare with the myths?

Short Paper 8: Using one of Turner's concepts regarding the frontier or western influence on American life, choose one story and discuss how it illustrates this principle at work.

Reading Assignment: "The City," Kriegel and Lass; "Bartleby," Herman Melville; "How the Devil Came Down Division Street," Nelson Algren.

Journal Questions: What picture of life in the cities do these stories give?

Short Paper 9: Based on your readings of the pieces on the city, what do you see as the lure versus the disillusionment of the city? Use one piece to support your position.

Reading Assignment: "Maggie: A Girl of the Streets," Stephen Crane.

Journal Questions: How does Maggie illustrate the reality of life in the city? The myth?

Reading Assignment: "American Space, Chinese Place," Yo-Fu Tuan.

Major Paper III: What does the "land" mean to Americans?
This paper should focus on how attitudes toward the "land" have shaped contemporary American life and culture. Formulate a thesis in which you focus on one element of the land—the small town or farm, the frontier or the city—and show how the myth and/or the reality of the American experience in this area has shaped American culture. Use at least two pieces to support and develop your position.

Unit IV: Where Do We Go From Here? (2 weeks)

Reading Assignment: "Letter from Birmingham Jail," Martin Luther King; Chief Seattle's address.

Short Paper 10: Which area—the democratic ideal, the pursuit of success, or the land—do you think will have the greatest impact on the future of America?

Major Paper IV: Where do we go from here?
This paper should focus on what you see as a major problem facing America in the future or today. Formulate a thesis in which you state the problem. Support the thesis by referring to sources you consult in the library and from the readings.

Great Texts, Cultural Traditions, and Student Writing

Gracia Grindal

Known as Paideia, the freshman program at Luther College is interdisciplinary in nature, combining practice in writing with the study of both literature and history. So, the following sequence of writing assignments is best understood in terms of the special academic circumstances that govern this program. In keeping with the significance of the ancient Greek word from which the program takes its name, this two-semester course is concerned with the activity of learning and with the cultural traditions produced by centuries of shared learning. To these ends, course material during the first semester is drawn from traditions that constitute the cultural, intellectual, and spiritual roots of the College—the classical Greek, the Christian, and the Scandinavian—and during the second semester from traditions which have come to be part of the expanded intellectual consciousness of late twentieth century American culture—the Black American, the Moslem, and the Maoist Chinese. Given the broad educational mission of the Paideia program, writing instruction must necessarily be attuned to helping students develop their understanding of the texts and contexts that constitute the focus of each course.

Writing instruction in Paideia is also influenced by the fact that the program is taught collaboratively by faculty from the English and history departments. Faculty from these departments typically bring differing intellectual orientations and perspectives to the course, and these disciplinary differences are necessarily reflected in the differing academic purposes for which they want students to develop their writing abilities. The English department, for example, wants students in the course to use writing as a means of exploring and explicating texts and relating them to each other. The history department, on the other hand, wants students to become proficient in reasoning and writing about historical ideas, issues, problems, and sources. And both departments want students to use writing not only as a means of learning but also as a means of coming to understand the nature of an intellectual community, of how they are shaped by such a community, and thus the value of shared knowledge and traditions. The assignment sequence that follows, therefore, represents an effort to serve these multiple purposes in an integrated order.

75

This sequence, which covers the work of the first semester, consists of fifteen writing assignments. These fifteen assignments are, in turn, designed to work in sets of three, each set unified by its focus on one or more literary or historical works. The first and second sets, for example, focus on the *Odyssey*, the third on *The Persians* of Aeschylus and *Histories* of Herodotus, the fourth on "The Inferno" section of *The Divine Comedy*, and the fifth on *The Prince, Julius Caesar*, and Luther's *Address to the German Nobility*. The assignments within each set are intended to be incremental, the first two, in particular, involving various generative activities that prepare students to produce an articulate piece of writing for the third, graded task. Each set, in turn, introduces students to increasingly complex generative activities, as well as calling upon increasingly sophisticated kinds of thinking and writing in the finished pieces.

Within the first set, for example, students work towards a paper on the *Odyssey* by finding areas of the epic that especially interest and intrigue them, which they use as the basis for a brief piece of exploratory writing about their "experience" with *The Odyssey* (assignment 1A). Following a lecture and class discussion, students select one of their questions, explore their reasons for believing it would make a good paper topic, and share their explorations with the class (1B). Then, having found a topic, written down preliminary thoughts about it, and considered reactions to it of their instructors and peers, the students work up this material into their first paper (1C).

The second set follows a similar pattern, with more questions and more class discussion providing a basis for their revision of the piece that culminated the first set. In particular, students read and react to each other's first paper, indicating what they perceive to be strengths as well as areas that need additional work (2A). Using these reactions as a guide, students are then asked to revise one paragraph of their own first papers (2B), and finally to turn a critical eye to their first essay as a whole and revise the entire piece (2C). To this second writing, students necessarily bring a wider vision than they brought to the first, for it encompasses the perceptions of many individuals, and because it is the result of longer and, it is hoped, more critical thought.

The spiral movement of these two sets is intended not only to expose students to the revising process, but also help them see both the centrality of their individual perception and experience of literature, and the importance of modifying and refining their understanding through the process of taking into account the views and perspectives of others. So, when they hand in the second version of their paper on *The Odyssey* (2C), they will not only have learned something about literature, Greek epics, myth, and history, but they will also have had an initial experience in the process of reading, thinking, and working together in an intellectual community.

The process of producing two versions of their paper on *The Odyssey* also provides students with a form of intellectual preparation for the third set which entails them in examining two different versions of the same historical situation, namely the events during and leading up to the battle of Salamis, as described by Herodotus in the *Histories* and by Aeschylus in *The Persians*. For their first writing in this set, students make a chart of the important events as described by each author (3A). From all the incidents in the battle that they discover to have been reported by both authors, students are then asked to select one and to write a brief comparison of the differing presentations (3B). This comparison involves students in the study of motive, of historical explanation, and dramatic presentation. And it prepares them for the final piece of the set, which requires them to explain how the abilities and personalities of important characters at the battle of Salamis influenced its outcome (3C).

Having used the activities of close textual analysis and comparison as the basis for a piece of historical reasoning in the third set, students are called upon within the fourth set to use imitation and impersonation as means of preparing themselves to carry out a piece that blends literary and historical analysis and reasoning about the world view of Dante. In the first piece of this set, for example, students are asked to describe a medieval institution of their choice and to discuss its connection or lack of connection to institutions in the classical world; but in carrying out this description students are specifically directed to model their piece on the techniques of a designated historian; they are, in effect, called upon to imitate the historian (4A). Then in the next piece, they are invited "to be Dante," and to write a new canto that places a classical or contemporary figure within the appropriate place in Hell (4B). Having impersonated Dante, students are then called upon to write a piece which not only explicates the logic and theologic of their canto, but also relates their implied world view to that of Dante (4C). So, this set gives students the complex intellectual experience of entering into Dante's world view and examining that medieval way of viewing the world both in relation to the classical way and to their own.

The fifth and final set of the semester again calls upon students to use impersonation as a means of immersing themselves in an earlier world view, in this instance the world of Renaissance Europe. But in this case, the impersonation entails a complex set of roles based on a complexly related set of works. The first assignment, for example, requires students to play the role of a secret agent to Henry VIII, writing to the king about political developments on the continent by telling him about the possible significance of *The Prince* or "The Address to the German Nobility" (5A). Role playing here is intended to push students towards an appreciation of how these political works might have been perceived and understood in their own time. And it is also intended to prepare students for the world of political intrigue that is dramatized in *Julius Caesar,* the work that is at the center of the remaining two assignments in the set. Students do an initial piece on the play which entails them in analyzing one of its characters or events (5B), and finally students are asked to take the role of either Machiavelli or Luther, and in that role to judge the same character or situation from the play that they had analyzed in the previous assignment. Thus the final assignment involves an extremely complex instance of role playing that draws implicitly upon all the prior historical and literary understandings that students have been developing over the course of the semester— and upon all the writerly abilities they have been developing simultaneously.

So it is that in designing and sequencing the assignments for Paideia, both those for the first semester which are reproduced here, and those for the second semester which are not,[1] we have tried to use writing as a means of teaching literature and history, as well as using literature and history as means of teaching writing. The writing assignments, then, are intended as a way to teach students thinking, to teach them historical method, rhetorical sensitivities, and a self-consciousness about how writing enables people to establish their individual talent by defining themselves in relation to great texts and cultural traditions.

PAIDEIA

1A. You have read *The Odyssey* over the summer and have now arrived at Luther College ready to begin your own *paideia*. You have surely been full of questions as you read the epic, wondering about what exactly it has to do with you as you prepared to leave home to continue your education. Such an event has you wondering, as it did Telemachos, how much one is a child of one's parents, how much one is unique, and how one's choices at this time will have consequences far down the road in ways hardly imaginable now. Telemachos' leaving home is an experience to which you can relate.

The general assignment is to explore on paper what thoughts came to your mind as you were reading the epic. The statements you put on paper might be of two kinds: (1) reactions you have to your readings, especially those reactions which show that you have seen ways in which this story relates to your own experience; (2) questions about things you didn't understand or questions whose answers might open up whole new areas of investigation.

As often as possible suggest some likely answers to your own questions. Don't worry if the answers are "right" or not. And don't worry that your questions will be thought "dumb." You will not be asking dumb questions so long as you are genuinely seeking answers or are really confused about something and not simply filling space on the page.

Glance at the following questions, not in order to answer these specific questions, but simply to get the brain cells working:

With whom do you identify in the story?
What is puzzling or worth noting about the language, word choices, tone?
How realistic, if at all, is the story?
What about the gods and goddesses?
Does anything *annoy* you about *The Odyssey?*
Does anything *please* you about *The Odyssey?*

---

[1]The assignments of the second semester, which include a research project and focus on texts ranging from *Hedda Gabler* to *Ambiguous Adventure* to *From Mao to Mozart*, end with a paper asking students to think about their own education—their paideia, as it were—in the context of all their reading and writing during the course. Thus the final assignment asks them to look back and evaluate their own growth—their growing sense of themselves in the world, their growing sense of limits and powers.

Now put these instructions aside and for the next 15 minutes write as quickly as you can and as much as you can about your experience with *The Odyssey*. This is not an organized essay! You are writing to one another and your teacher.

1B. Some questions can be easily answered, like "What is an oral epic?" Other questions cannot be answered because the answers have vanished, like "Who was the first singer to compose the epic as we have it now?" Other questions have no single answer, but many, like "What does it mean that Helen recognizes Telemachos as the son of Odysseus?" or "What is the significance of Telmachos' remark, 'My mother calls me the son of the man. But I myself/Do not know. No one has ever been certain of his father'?"

To talk about those events in the story intelligently, it helps to know the answers to the first kinds of questions. The more one knows about *The Odyssey*, the more deeply one can interpret it. You can see how the two kinds of questions help us to understand a text more fully. Paideia is built on the notions that one can, and should, ask a variety of questions about texts and ideas to understand them better.

Look back at your first exploratory writing. Examine the questions you asked and see which kind of questions they are and what kind of answers they call for. Decide which questions would be the most interesting topic for an essay. Then in a few paragraphs explain why you think it will be a good topic. You will want to think about what makes a piece of writing interesting, and for whom. Be ready to share your paper with the class.

1C. You and your classmates have now read *The Odyssey*. You have asked a series of questions about it and have evaluated those topics. Actually you know quite a bit about the story. Take the paper you have done in class (1A) and, in the context of class discussions and the lecture on invention, develop your idea into a short paper (350-500 words). You can show how you have come to understand what you did not know before, or how the conversations of your class and others have helped you make a more careful choice of topic. Remember again the lecture on invention and the need to consider that not all questions are equal in importance. The writing process involves refining one's own questions and exploring with one's audience what you are in the process of discovering. You will be a much more effective writer if you admit you do not know everything there is to know on the subject. No one ever can.

2A. In this class we want to develop your skills as best we can, and one of the best ways to do that is to learn how to help each other with our thinking and writing. As you have already heard many times, Luther College values and attempts to nurture the idea of community. One learns to write in a context of other reading and writing. This program can help you with your prewriting and rewriting by giving you thoughtful responses from your instructors and classmates. But the actual writing is something you can do best in the privacy of your own room or library carrel.

By now you have read and heard about various ways of organizing paragraphs and essays, and have been introduced to the concepts of *levels of generality* and *TRI* (topic-restriction-illustration). Such concepts should help you critique your own prose and that of others. Take the papers you have been given by your instructor— responses by your classmates to assignment 1C—and be ready to help your classmates revise them. As you read the papers, perform the following steps:

a.   Look at the paragraphs to see if the writer needs to add more details at a lower level of generality, or perhaps needs to add a more general statement of interpretation over those details. Mark at the bottom of the paper those paragraphs which most need improvement.

b.   Also at the bottom of the paper, or on the back, write a sentence or two identifying and evaluating the idea you think the writer was trying to get across in the paragraphs you chose to critique.

2B. You have seen how others take your words, how they understand and misunderstand what you have written. Take your paper, now that it has been read and analyzed by your professor and by students in the workshop, and look at the comments. Take one of the weak paragraphs that has been pointed out and rework it by following the suggestions that have been given to you. You should concentrate on improving the depth of the paragraph by providing more levels of generality and/or organizing them in a more effective way.

2C. Now that you have gone through the process of improving one paragraph, reread your entire paper looking at the comments on the paper and looking for other spots in the paper that ought to be improved. Improving these portions will be easier after doing both 2A and 2B. Keep reworking the paper by reading it through several times. To revise a paper means more than neatly changing what the red mark said you should. It means re-seeing and re-shaping what you have done before so that others can see what it is that you see and what it is that you think.

The assignment, then, is to rewrite your entire paper, focusing on well-developed paragraphs that keep your ideas connected. This will give your reader a clearer idea of what you think. When you submit your finished paper, you should present it in a form that indicates that you value what you have done.

3A. Based on the accounts by Aeschylus and Herodotus, prepare a chart (or outline) of the important events which constitute the campaign and battle of Salamis. Keep track of your sources so that you can see if they conflict in what they say or do not say. A suggestion is to arrange your information in parallel columns, with references to specific pages in *The Persians* and *The Histories*. Begin your chart in class and finish it for the next discussion.

3B. Choose a specific important incident described by both Aeschylus and Herodotus and note how each answers *who? what? where? when?* for that incident. These are the questions historians use to help in reconstructing the narrative of a past event. Herodotus was a historian, Aeschylus was a dramatist, but their answers to these questions ought to be in agreement. If possible identify what Herodotus and Aeschylus say about the answers to *how?* and *why?* with regard to the same incident. Do their accounts differ? In what ways? Are the differences important? In your judgment, which author has the better sources? Why do you think this is so? Write a paragraph indicating your answers to these questions.

3C. Now that you have a grasp of the framework of the battle and the difference in approach of the two authors, write a paper on the way that human nature or character—whether determined by one's heritage or catalyzed by immediate circumstances—can shape history.

How do the abilities, personalities, and attitudes of characters as portrayed by Aeschylus and/or Herodotus determine the outcome of the battle of Salamis? Your judgment includes deciding who the important characters are.

4A. Using Thomas Greer's *A Brief History of the Western World* as your principal source, select and describe in writing a medieval institution. As you do so, note the way Greer defines and uses terms in context, especially in the section titled "The Emergence of Medieval Institutions" (164 ff.). Some of the institutions he describes include feudalism (knighthood, manorialism, etc.), the medieval town (including guilds and various forms of government), and the Church (including monasticism and the papacy).

In this writing, comment on whether your description represents the largely unchanged continuity of a classical institution, a changed form of a classical institution, or a complete discontinuity from the classical world. Your piece should consist of well-crafted paragraphs. Be sure to footnote the places in Greer where you find your information.

4B. Dante writes an epic poem in the tradition of Homer and Virgil. And, in the same way that they had to know history to tell the epic of their people, Dante had to know his history, both that of the ancient past and that of the times nearer to him. For him the past was as vital as the present because he made it so. Dante is, then, something of an historian. But he does something else with the past. He transforms it and bends it to his own purposes. He sees the ancient world with medieval eyes; his point of view is Christian. We also see the past with our own particular modern focus, conditioned by modern institutions and modern theology. In our Paideia classes we have spent some time trying to understand what it means to be Greek and now we are trying to understand what it means to be medieval.

As a reader of Dante, you can now place any number of sinners in appropriate circles. Imagine yourself to be Dante. Write a short new canto either in Dante's form and style or in another that you feel comfortable with. Assign an appropriate place in Hell to either (a) some figure from classical antiquity, or (b) a well-known figure (historical or fictional) from your own time.

Your discussion leader may wish to direct you toward option (a) or (b).

4C. Now that you have written your canto, write a paper in which you explain in more detail the reasons for your selection and the logic of your placement and punishment. You may wish to explore how the punishment implies a positive value, just as Dante's treatment of a sin suggests a value Dante held to be good. Make your justification as consistent as you can with Dante's classification of sin: the deeper in

Hell you go, the more complex the sin and the greater the treachery involved.

Would your judgment of the severity of the sin correspond to that of Dante? Discuss the ways in which Dante's medieval world view and the presence of medieval institutions conditioned him to think differently from you, if you find any differences.

5A. At this first stage of your paper, you are asked to look at *The Prince* and "Address to the German Nobility" in order to see what they tell us about the political and ethical realities of Renaissance Europe.

Imagine that you are an envoy, or better still, a secret agent from the court of Henry VIII of England around the year 1520. King Henry wants advance intelligence of the latest political developments on the Continent, and you feel it necessary to fill him in on two possibly significant developments:

a. the great stir being created in Florence by a treatise written by one Niccolo Machiavelli which is being circulated in manuscript form among influential people;

b. the likely impact of a letter which has been sent out by a rebellious former monk, named Martin Luther, which is addressed to the German princes and which challenges the authority of the Pope.

Write a letter to Henry in which you estimate the significance of these writings, state whether you find their contents shocking or morally troubling, and warn Henry of the possible course of events in Europe if these documents accomplish what they are intended to do. Your letter will probably be 250-300 words.

5B. In order to move from your discussion in part 5A to the finished paper, 5C, you should focus your attention on a careful analysis of some character or event of the play *Julius Caesar*. Write a paragraph of 100-150 words answering one of the following study questions:

a. Why does Brutus decide to join the conspiracy?
b. Is Brutus right or wrong in opposing the assassination of Antony along with Caesar (see Act II, scene i, 155-183)? Why do you think as you do?
c. Why does Brutus allow Antony to speak at Caesar's funeral?
d. What are the main differences between the speeches of Brutus and Antony at the funeral? Account for the differences in effect.
e. What is the cause of the quarrel between Cassius and Brutus (seen in IV, ii)? What is the result and what does the scene show us about the two men?
f. Why does Brutus take his life? Does he realize his "failure" at the end?
g. Why does Antony call Brutus "the noblest Roman of them all" (V, v, 68)?
h. Describe the character and role of Octavius in the play.

5C. In 5A you looked closely at the writing of Luther and Machiavelli to observe the concerns of their time. In 5B, you briefly looked at a character or action of importance in *Julius Caesar*. In 5C you are to bring these two perspectives together.

Both Luther and Machiavelli were educated in the Christian humanist traditions of rhetoric and logic, as you have been this semester. Based upon your knowledge of them and their ideas, pretend that you are Machiavelli or Luther thinking about the actions and characters portrayed in Shakespeare's *Julius Caesar.* From that perspective, look at a signficant action (or actions) *or* at a character in the play and *judge* it (or the person) according to the point of view you have chosen. Remember that to try to think like Machiavelli or Luther you will need to support your statements with the kind of evidence as well as logic that they would have used. Your first task as Machiavelli, or Luther, will be to generate a thesis about the action(s) or character that you, as that person, can support.

Play and Work

Creativity in Expository Writing

Leone Scanlon

As we know from the testimony of numerous professional writers, the tension between freedom and discipline, between play and work, is at the heart of creativity. But as we know from our experience as teachers, many of our students have never taken themselves seriously or playfully as writers. So we are perennially faced with the challenge of devising activities for our students—occasions for writing—that will enable them to explore the possibilities of freedom and discipline within the artificial compass of a classroom. This kind of exploration is, perhaps, the broadest purpose of the assignment sequence on work and play that I designed for the first-year expository writing course at Clark University.[1] Although play and work are the nominal topics of discourse throughout most of the sequence, the real subject, at last, is expressing, shaping, and revising writing for different audiences and purposes. Play and work thus constitute the field (if all, or even something, goes well) for the playful crafting of language.

A curriculum with a nominal subject necessarily sets some limits on the students' freedom in choosing material for their compositions, but it also helps them

[1]A private university of some 2600 students, located in Worcester, Massachusetts, Clark is both a research university and a small college of some 1900 undergraduates. Expository Writing is one of several courses in Clark's cross-disciplinary Verbal Expression Program, established three years ago as part of a new set of requirements for the first two years. To satisfy the VE requirement students must take a one-semester writing course. Any department or program may offer a VE course, providing that it meets certain guidelines, among which are that it be limited to twenty students and that it require them to write a series of short papers at roughly two-week intervals. All VE courses encourage revision and attention to audience through the use of peer writing groups that review papers before they are given to the teacher. To facilitate these groups the Writing Center provides and trains undergraduate teaching assistants. Among the departments that have offered VE courses are Art, History, Sociology, Philosophy, and the Science, Technology, and Society Program. The English Department offers two VE courses, Introduction to Literature and Expository Writing, both multi-sectioned. Expository Writing, taken annually by some 300 students, differs from the other VE courses in centering on rhetoric and style rather than upon subject matter of a particular discipline. The majority of students who take it perceive themselves as most in need of help in writing—generally a correct perception.

to discover that authentic freedom in writing, as in other activities, does not exist without some kind of discipline. A curriculum of this kind also provides a useful common experience for TA's who teach sections of the course.[2] The sequence of assignments gives them a source of structure, but it leaves them free to develop their own teaching styles. Within the structure established by the sequence, the TA's discover that they have to create and play out their own classroom strategies and exercises, much as the students are running their own personal experience and knowledge through the common topics of the assignments.

Our students' experience in writing, as one might expect, ranges from very little to a background of fairly sophisticated courses.[3] Most have written book reports and term papers, largely by formula. Many distinguish between "creative" writing (e.g., poems or stories) which they enjoy, and school-writing, which they describe as uncertain and unpleasant. (Given many school assignments, these reactions are not surprising.) Here is an informal first-day reflection from Louis:

> I find writing to be both work and play. It depends, of course, on whom I'm writing for and what I'm writing about. Generally, the only time I consider writing play is when I'm writing letters to people. When I write a letter to somebody, I know mainly what I'm going to say. I don't have to sit for hours and think up a lot of bull. That is what I consider work. Work is writing something you know nothing about and really couldn't care less. Of course, I am not that narrow-minded that no topic interests me; there are a few. I like writing on imaginary topics. Making up my own story instead of reporting on a particular occurrence. This to me is fun, not play. Playing is something you enjoy, something you like to do anytime, anywhere.

Given this typical state of mind, my first concern in designing the curriculum for the students was with their alienation from their writing. I wanted them to realize that although the emphasis on the self varies in different types of writing, all writing stems from the self and is shaped inevitably by the writer's point of view, taking life from the writer's spirit. In that sense, most writing is creative.

---

[2]The ten or twelve sections of Expository Writing offered each semester are taught primarily by TA's, candidates for the MA in English, and occasionally by full or part-time members of the English Department. A few of the TA's over the years have had one or two years' teaching experience at the high school level, but most have had no teaching experience whatsoever. Recently, too, many of the TA's have come from foreign countries, such as Great Britain, where composition courses do not exist in the schools. Thus the TA's do not have the training, nor the experience, nor the time to design a curriculum or to frame a coherent sequence of assignments. The TA's and I meet every week to review the course as it unfolds, to discuss problems, to share teaching strategies as well as handouts, and, as it turned out, to revise the sequence each semester.

The following Department members and TA's who taught the course in 1981-82 helped shape the version printed here: Rockie Blunt, Christopher Cartwright, Richard Dean, Valerie Hamilton, Linda Lorenzani, Esha Niyogi, and Roberta Tovey. I am grateful for their criticism and suggestions.

[3]Most Clark students come from the Northeast and have an average SAT of 550. In a typical section of 13 students there will be one or two second-year students; the rest will be first-year. One or two will be from foreign countries.

In the first version of the sequence, all the assignments were on play and work. As the TA's and I taught the course, however, it became clear that the students found spending a semester on one subject restrictive. Thus, to let them tap their own interests, an essential element in their seeing their writing as their own, I modified the curriculum to provide more choice of subject, although not always of genre. Some of the TA's have also made their own changes, the most radical being the assignment of three completely open writings on any subject. Despite this variety, some students still find the curriculum restrictive; many others find ample freedom, as one attested in the course evaluation: "There was a wide variety of assignments that called for different types of thought. It was stimulating to think about some of these topics." For many students, then, I am satisfied that the curriculum has struck an appropriate balance between freedom and structure.

Overall, the curriculum moves through a series of short, recursive spirals, or groups of exercises. At the core is the question: How do words like "play" and "work" mean, or how do they take meaning from personal, social, and historical contexts? The following discussion of a few exercises will explain the goals of the exercises and the recursiveness of the sequence.

Beginning with an invitation to reflect on their experience as writers, the sequence asks the students to tell stories about their experiences working and playing (exercise 2). Despite this request, the exercise frequently results in generalizations or flattened narratives, bare of detail, with sketchy and confused points of view. A few students get the bones and flesh of a story onto paper, and we share these in a class workshop. Exercise 3 asks the students to analyze the focus of their story—or to consider where they might focus the story if they rewrote it. Exercise 4 then gives the students another crack at story-telling. First drafts on these papers are usually read in workshops; the revisions are almost always much more successful than the first narratives, as one would hope after so much preparation. When given the option to revise either of these topics for a grade, most students choose 4.

Near the end of the course the students get a chance to use these early writings, especially 2, 4, and 6, as part of the material for an analysis and reflection on the Quaker statement, "Work is love made visible" (19). That assignment asks the students to reflect upon personal experience as well as upon three published statements on work by a hockey player, a physical therapist, and a writer. To prepare students to read these statements critically, exercise 18 asks them to analyze the point of view of an auto-worker's account of the assembly line (taken, as are several quotations, from Terkel's *Working*) and of Marx's description of factory labor. (The sources of the two quotes are not identified in the text to prevent prejudice from coloring the reading. In fact, taking description for prescription, many students conclude that the writer of the second piece is a manufacturer!)

I hoped that when the students reflected on the accounts of work in exercise 19, they would recall the selection from Marx (identified in discussion after the papers are written). While some students in my class considered only the individual's attitude toward work, others did look at the effect of working conditions upon the worker, although none referred specifically to Marx. Considering the brevity of the selection from *Capital,* this oversight is not surprising. To develop a deeper understanding of the effect of working conditions on the worker, we would have to read economic history and theory. Given the other aims of the course, there is no time for that, unless a student decides to do so in the investigative paper. (No one has.) What is encouraging is that many students refer to their own and other students' narratives on work as well as to the published texts, and most have advanced beyond their earlier simplistic opposition of play and work to understand, for example, that under some circumstances work may be play. In a first draft of her essay (it was too late in the semester to revise), Susan began:

> Work is often thought of as a job that is difficult, tedious, or boring. This is true in many cases, but work can also be a job that someone loves and wants to dedicate his life to.
>
> Many college students take part time and summer jobs solely for the purpose of earning money. There is a limited variety of jobs available, and the factor that decides which job to take, is the amount of money being offered. Most of these jobs are arduous, tedious, and students dread going to work. I worked as a salesgirl, Gary cleaned new cars, and Bruce worked in a lab. None of these jobs are examples of 'love made visible.' Unskilled labor workers who work assembly lines are given long vacations so that they will stay at their jobs. Even high salary professional jobs are not always loved.

An extended reflection on defining, exercise 19 is anticipated by exercise 7, a study of two dictionaries, and by exercise 8, the students' definitions of play and work. Exercise 20 brings these two exercises together, calling for a rhetorical analysis of the lexical definitions and the Quaker definition.

Rhetoric is central to the course. Again and again the sequence returns to the implied question: How do we change our words and literary structures as we write for different purposes to different audiences? The students write narratives, analyses, epigrams, formal letters, editorials, arguments, and reflections to such audiences as the class, the Dean of Students, the Clark community, and me. (See, for example, exercises 9-12.) In my sections there is a strong emphasis on writing to the audience; some of the TA's devote extensive time to writing for oneself through freewriting— to which I want to give more attention. The students need to experience the pleasure of freewriting to balance the hard work of revising and editing. (And, of course, through freewriting they often discover new ideas.)

Just as I try to allow the TA's both freedom and structure, so I try to give the students varying degrees of freedom to choose their subjects within the limits of the sequence. The narrowest exercises are 8—which limits the students to one sentence, gives little choice of subject, and encourages an epigrammatic style—and 18, which requires an analysis of two texts. Exercises such as 2, 4, and 6 delimit a general subject but allow the writers to choose the topics. Where a genre such as argument is stipulated, students are free to choose their own methods of development; no pattern of argument, such as Sheridan Baker's, is prescribed.

For the investigative paper, students may choose their own topics. Since we have a little over a month for this project, we can not allow the students as much time as we would like to explore unpromising topics. In the exploratory exercises, 13 and 14, and in conferences, we help students define topics that they can accomplish in the available time.

The first version of the investigative paper exercise called for students to write on some aspect of play or work at Clark or in Worcester. Students investigated such subjects as Clark's security system and grading policies, the Worcester Consortium of Higher Education, and the struggle between Clark's founder and its first president to establish an undergraduate college or graduate school. The exercise forced students to go beyond one or two secondary sources (the "canned" term paper, all too common in high schools) to interview, to design and administer questionnaires, and to use the Archives. But the plan strained the small staff of the Archives as well as other members of the Clark staff and faculty, who although generous with their time were pursued by too many eager interviewers from Expository Writing. Thus, to relieve my colleagues and to allow students to write on the wider range of subjects that they requested, I decided to let the students choose their own subject. In practice, the teachers encourage students to choose local matters that they can investigate by interviewing and observing as well as by reading, but they always work with the students' interests. That the students do get beyond "canned" papers and that many write on subjects important to them is clear in the course evaluations. Doug, who wrote on the addictive effects of running, reflected: "Usually when writing a paper, I gather a few books and an encyclopedia... In this paper I looked through magazines, books, newspapers, and even talked to other people about the subject." Debbie, whose paper was on the image of women in television commercials, observed:

> This paper was different from other research papers that I've written in that I didn't have a form or outline to follow. Usually the teacher gives some kind of general summary to state what s/he would like in the paper. With this piece of research, it was my decision of what to include, where, edit, why, etc. I learned a great deal about having to think on my own, take complete charge of my work.

Like Debbie's, most of the excerpts of student writing that I have quoted show that the students need considerably more work on their writing. (I want to stress that most of the quotes are from informal, unedited writings.) Nevertheless, Debbie had clearly engaged in the essential act of discovering a form appropriate to her ideas. She had made choices—somewhat informed choices at that. For students like Debbie, just discovering that writers have a wealth of choice is progress. Nancy Sommers has pointed out that unlike experienced writers student writers make lexical but not semantic changes in their work; moreover, they do not have strategies for re-seeing the whole essay.[4] While assigning exercises might seem to deny choice, it can, in fact, increase students' awareness of semantic and rhetorical change, especially when followed by exercises calling for students to reflect on what happened to the text when they altered a major idea, switched the audience or purpose. With a fuller sense of language and greater control of it, students may then see more possibilities for the writing they initiate.

PLAY AND WORK

1. Creation, the creation of a class, a group of people sharing ideas and helping one another to learn; expressing ideas in essays, letters, investigative papers—all of that is what we're about here. For some of you there may have been little creativity in school writing. You may think that only writing poems, stories, and plays is creative. I don't agree that any form of writing is by nature uncreative. Anytime you express what you've learned about the world, you have the chance to be creative.

In or out of school some of you have experienced the pleasure of writing something—a story, a letter, an essay—clearly, powerfully. Was doing it play or work? Or was it both?

Tell me about your experience as a writer. (Remember that I'll need details in order to enter into your world.)

2. Play brings to most of us feelings of satisfaction and delight. But, of course, what is play to one may be misery to another. What is play to you—dancing, playing basketball or chess, solving Rubik's cube, writing poems, making music? And what is it about that activity that satisfies or delights you—winning, problem-solving, mastering a technique, losing yourself, what? Tell the class about a situation that embodies what you enjoy about play so that we can understand and share your experience.

3. The writing you just did (2) was focused on one moment in time. Imagine that I asked you to place a frame around this event, separating it from the flow of time. How did you describe where to place your frame? Did you leave out some aspects of the event? Did you relate the events within the frame in the same order in which they happened? Why or why not? Reflect on these questions.

4. Most of you have held a job, sometimes an unpleasant one that you did just for the money, sometimes a job you enjoyed, at least part of the time. Tell the class a story about a particular experience you have had on a job that embodies what is most difficult and demanding about the job.

Or the opposite, an experience that embodies what is most pleasurable about the job. (Write on *one* topic only.)

If you have not had a work experience, perhaps you can imagine one.

5. You have written two narratives. When you read your last narrative to your group, did the members understand what you were trying to get across? It's always

---

[4]"Revision Strategies of Student Writers and Experienced Adult Writers," *CCC*, XXXI (December 1980), 382-383.

difficult to write so as to enable a reader to understand what you have in mind. In the assignment below we'll consider some ways of communicating clearly and effectively.

(At this point I distribute a supplemental worksheet containing two paragraphs without the authors' names attached. The first is a selection from one of the students' writings in response to either assignment 2 or 4. The second example is a paragraph I make up, as if in response to the same assignment. I design this second paragraph so that it contains several examples of bad writing (i.e., generalizations without supporting details, voiceless or pompous prose, unfocused language) to serve as a contrast with the actual student's paragraph. We briefly discuss the two paragraphs in class, and then I distribute the writing assignment.)

The Writing Assignment: Respond to the questions below in a few paragraphs for the class.

a. Compare and contrast the styles, structures, and ideas of these two paragraphs. Which paragraph is the more successful? How has the writer used style and structure to create a convincing piece of writing?

b. Based on your reading of these two paragraphs, what would you say are some of the techniques writers can use to help their readers understand what they want them to?

c. In what specific ways would you now go about revising one of your narratives?

6. In some of your previous writings you have discussed or implied your interests and values. Now, in an essay for the class, show how those interests and values are embodied in the career you have chosen. If you do not have a particular job in mind, explore what sorts of work your interests and values might lead you to.

7. In some of the writing you have done thus far, you have probably had to define some terms. Perhaps you have assumed that definitions are to be found only in dictionaries. Have you considered that we have been practicing other sorts, for instance, defining by example? The formal definition found in dictionaries is only one type and, in fact, even dictionaries contain several types of definitions.

This exercise invites you to go to the library to explore another sort of dictionary in addition to the standard "word book," which I assume you own. Look up the words "play" and "work" in the *Oxford English Dictionary (O.E.D.)*. Summarize the kinds of information you find in this and in your desk dictionary. (You do not have to copy all the information you find. Classify the various types of information and record a few examples.)

Now pretend that you're a member of next year's committee for freshman orientation. Write a handout for the freshmen describing these dictionaries and their uses. (While the tone may be humorous or serious, the handout should reflect substantial research on the dictionaries.)

8. Not all dictionaries are as ponderous as the *O.E.D.*, or as dry as your desk

dictionary. The nineteenth-century American, Ambrose Bierce, wrote *The Devil's Dictionary,* containing these definitions:

> **abdication, n.** An act whereby a sovereign attests his sense of the high temperature of the throne.
>
> **presidency, n.** The greased pig in the field game of American politics.

In *Women and Economics* (1898) an American, Charlotte Perkins Gilman, caustically observed:

> The labor of women in the house, certainly, enables men to produce more wealth than they otherwise could; and in this way women are economic factors in society. But so are horses.

And the Irishman, George Bernard Shaw, as so often, goaded his contemporaries:

> Democracy substitutes selection by the incompetent many for appointment by the corrupt few.

Now try your devil's hand. Write a one-sentence definition of "play" and another of "work." (If you're stuck on those, try "Expository Writing" and "professor.")

9. Let's turn from meaning to manipulating. Read the account about advertising by John Fortune, a copy chief who was with an advertising agency for eight years.

> (The passage is from Studs Terkel's *Working* [New York, 1974], p. 114. After describing how the sales of a deodorant were increased by changing the advertising rather than the contents, Fortune concludes that a product sells satisfaction, perhaps even a dream.)

Examine an ad in a magazine or newspaper and write an essay for the class, making a case for your view of how the consumer is being persuaded to buy the product. Do you think the copy writer is appealing to the reader's needs or dreams? If so, how? (Please include the ad with your essay, so that your readers may test your analysis of it.)

Some suggestions: You will, of course, have to examine visual images as well as words, but since we are concerned with language, choose an ad that has at least a few words.

You will need to consider the audience for the magazine.

10. Two letters:
   a. Imagine that a friend of yours has been expelled from the University for a serious offense, for example, damaging the film screen in Atwood Hall. As a concerned friend, write a letter to the Dean of Students persuading her to revoke this decision. (Use an actual friend as a model or create a fictional person.)
   b. This time you are the guilty student. Write a letter asking the Dean to reinstate you at the University.

11. Now reflect on the two letters you just wrote. How did you come across in each letter? How did the recipient of the letters affect the way you presented yourself in each? How did you change your arguments? Finally, how did the structure and language of the two letters change as you changed your persona?

12. From writing to an audience of one about a limited matter let's move to a large audience and a broader subject. Select a campus or local issue with which you are concerned, one that you know something about and about which you would like to know more. (This subject may, if you choose, be the topic of a longer investigative paper, which you will write after this.)

Write an editorial for *The Scarlet* [the campus newspaper], expressing your opinion on this subject and trying to persuade your readers to agree with you.

13. With this exercise we will start an extended investigative project upon which we will be working for about one month. You will be required to hand in a paper of 5 to 10 pages, typed, following the MLA's rules for presenting a manuscript.

In the course of our discussions of your editorial you have probably discovered that arguments counter to your own may be made. You may have realized that you don't know how to respond to those arguments, that you need more information.

For our next class (a) Re-state the controlling idea of your editorial as a question. (b) Then draw up a list of questions that you need to explore to answer your main question. Indicate how you might find the answers to those questions. By observing? By interviewing someone? By reading?

Some of you may have decided that you don't want to go any further with the subject of your editorial or that it isn't suitable for a longer paper. In that case, you will have to discover some new possibilities. Perhaps one of your earlier writings has suggested a topic you would like to explore further. You might try freewriting on possible topics, starting with such a statement as "What interests me about this subject is...." Then sum up the freewriting in one assertion or question. When you have decided on your topic, then proceed with the assignment above.

Some of you, especially those who are working from the subject of your editorial, may want to write argumentative papers; others will want to write informative papers. Whatever your choice, work to frame a clear and limited question that you *can* explore in a relatively short time.

Finally, sort out from your list the questions you might answer by reading published materials. Go to the library to see what you can discover, and then bring to class a list of the books, the pamphlets, and the newspaper and journal articles you have decided will be useful to your study. Consult the *MLA Handbook* for the correct form of this bibliography.

14. You have been investigating your subject and working out tentative ideas. Now I would like you to formulate a proposal for your project. In the form of a short essay, state your controlling idea (by now sharply focused) and your purpose. Your audience is the class.

Explain the major controversies or questions about your subject and your plans for informing your readers or proving your thesis. Include a tentative plan for organizing the paper. (By the way, this proposal will be useful later on when you write your introduction.)

If there is anything on which you would like help, jot that down too.

15. Using your organizing plan, construct a draft of the paper. When it is done, write a one-sentence summary of each paragraph. Then number the sentences in outline form. Using this skeleton, check to see whether the paragraphs really do center on the main idea and whether the order of ideas from paragraph to paragraph and section to section makes sense. In the light of this analysis, write a short commentary on how you will revise your draft.

16. Now that you have finished your investigative paper, reflect on your experience. Was it different from previous experiences writing research or term papers? To some extent I have suggested a process to you—freewriting, proposal, post-draft outline. What parts of that process did you find useful? What parts will you discard?

17. Some wit once said, "Love is work made playful." I don't know whether you loved doing this research paper. Many of you worked at it. How about playing with it?

Write a mock set of directions on how to write an investigative paper for next year's freshmen in this course.

18. The two commentaries I've attached to this assignment tell what it's like to work in a factory, something most of us haven't done. In an essay for the class compare and contrast these two views. Consider the writers' purposes (How can we tell what those purposes are?) and how the style of each selection expresses the writer's views.

> (The first commentary is an auto-worker's account of the monotonous and painful work on an assembly line [from Terkel's *Working,* pp. 221-222]. The second is Marx's discussion of how the mindlessness of such work serves capitalists by making the workers less powerful [from *Capital,* IV, XIV, section 5]. Some of the purposes of the assignment are to suggest a larger, theoretical context for personal experience and to provide a focused exercise in close reading.)

19. The Quakers say, "Work is love made visible." Attached to this assignment are three accounts of work to which that statement might be applied.

> (The first two selections are from *Working* [pp. 501-502, 642-646]. In the first a hockey player explains how his love of the game is being destroyed by the owners' exploitation of the players; in the second a physical therapist describes her rebellion against the devaluation of her work. In the third selection, a writer discusses the loneliness and difficulty of her work [Janet Burroway, "Opening Nights: The Opening Days," in *The Writer and Her Work,* Janet Sternburg, ed., New York: W.W. Norton, 1980, pp. 198-199].)

Using these accounts and your own, write an essay in which you consider in what circumstances the Quaker statement might be true, in what false. You might also want to use your classmates' accounts of work, in assignment 2, for example.

20. Go back now to the Quaker definition of work and compare it with one of the dictionary definitions you found. How do the two statements differ? What sort of language do you find in each? Which tells *you* more? In what circumstances might one be appropriate and not the other? Tell us in a short commentary.

21. One last reflection. Think about writing this semester. Does the question, "Was it play or work?" make sense any more? How have you coped with the different sorts of writing we have done? How much have you changed your systems for approaching tasks? What have you accomplished? In what ways does your writing still need work?

Winners and Losers

A Course for Basic Writers

Mary Frew Moldstad

Throughout their lives, many of our students at Ashland College have had winning as a goal, for many come to us as athletes, and they join many of the non-athletes in feeling that "to win" is synonymous with "to succeed," while "to lose" means "to fail." That is to say, they tend to regard these concepts in absolute terms. Because of test scores and lack of experience with writing, many of these students find themselves detoured into our College Writing Improvement Program (English 100), which they must complete before enrolling in the required English 101. Students in this program, athletes or not, frequently have a sense of themselves as "losers," which is intensified by placement in English 100. They carry with them strong, negative attitudes about their writing abilities, and they have little confidence in their written prose. Students in the course may consider themselves winners athletically, but as often as not they consider themselves losers academically.

In developing a sequence of assignments for the College Writing Improvement Program, I was concerned that the course help students gain confidence in their writing abilities, help them feel more positive about their writing, and challenge them to think.[1] I chose to center the course on these two seemingly opposite concepts of winners and losers, which were so familiar to my students, and to use this as the occasion to test their easy definitions and assumptions— specifically of these terms, but by extension of all concepts seen as clear-cut and absolute. I wanted the students to confront the complexities of such concepts, as they saw them at work in their own lives and in the lives of fictional characters. And I wanted to encourage students to develop the habit of questioning their prejudices and preconceptions, as a means of moving them towards one of the goals which the

[1]In designing the sequence, I have tried to observe the ideas of Ashland's Marjorie Dew, whose work at the Institute on Writing was interrupted by her fatal illness. Marjorie had come to believe firmly that when people are challenged to communicate ideas in writing it becomes a matter of pride to do it well. Her work at the Iowa Institute confirmed and strengthened her ideas on how writing can best be learned and taught.

faculty at Ashland College wants its writing program to serve, namely, critical thinking.[2]

The course sequence itself consists of 15 writing assignments, which move students back and forth between personal experience and the experience that comes from observation and reading. Some assignments ask students to write about their own experiences with winning and losing. Some ask them to write about the experiences of others—actual or fictional individuals. And others invite them to define/redefine the basic terms of the course in light of what they have been learning. Each time they return to their own experience it is to consider some new aspect of what constitutes a winner or a loser. As the course progresses, the assignments focus on increasingly more complicated instances of winning or losing, with the terms becoming blurred, the sharp distinctions between them hazy.

The course begins with five assignments which serve students later as markers in gauging changes in their thinking. The first asks them to tell the story of a time they won something, or lost something, that they wanted very much to win. This assignment allows students, who may be feeling very uncomfortable and uncertain about their writing and about their status as newly-arrived freshmen, to recall an occasion when things worked well for them, when they weren't uncomfortable at all (and most do indeed choose to write about a time when some achievement gave them glory, or satisfaction, or a sense of pride). The second assignment asks them to take an altered perspective on the event of assignment 1, and tell others in the class how they should act if faced with the identical experience. This places students in the position of giving advice, but more importantly puts them in the position of imaginatively reconceiving a win or a loss—of making something less of a loss, for example, or more of a win. This introduces to the sequence the idea that there may be degrees involved in winning and losing, and that the terms are not as simple as they first appear.

Assignment 3 asks students to step back from their own experience, to move away from individual situations that involve winning and losing, and instead to define what it is that makes a *person* a winner. Lest students at this point settle for a quick, simple definition, the assignment reminds them that to identify an individual with such a term is to generalize about an entire life, with the implicit suggestion that no one "wins" everything all the time. As in assignment 2, students are faced here with a question of degree, and are asked to take this into consideration when defining the term, and specifically in light of a "winner" they know. The same qualifications hold true in assignment 4, where students are asked to consider what it is that makes a person a loser. Again the assignment suggests that no one "loses" all the time, and that, indeed, in losses there may even be elements of gain—gains in understanding, or in patience, or in compassion, for example.

---

[2]Ashland College is a four-year liberal arts college of 1550 students, with a strong emphasis on career-training. Faculty in such diverse fields as pre-law and TV are concerned that their students' education prepare them to write proficiently in the professional world, and faculty from throughout the college feel that students' writing—on any occasion—should be informed and thoughtful.

Between these early assignments and the concluding one, which asks students to redefine the central terms of the course, the sequence confronts students with nine situations in which losses and wins are ambiguous, in which students must revise and refine their thinking about these concepts. But before introducing these complications, the sequence steps back momentarily from any complexity and asks students to consider some unambiguous presentations of a stereotyped winner or loser. Specifically, in assignment 5, they are asked to discuss ways an advertiser uses the image of a winner or a loser in appealing to potential customers and attempting to sell a product. This temporarily turns attention away from the students' personal experiences and gives them the chance to reflect on how pervasive such images of winners and losers are in the culture. Students may recognize at this point that the ads they select rely upon greatly simplified and unrealistic portrayals of human beings, but even if they do not realize this, the assignments leave them with some extreme examples of "winners" and "losers" against which to consider the more complicated personages and situations they meet in their reading and in their own lives.

A direct consideration of such complicated personages and situations is the concern of assignments 6-14, all of which address variations on the theme of winning and losing. Five of these assignments (6, 7, 8, 9, and 14) center on incidents in which an apparent win turns out to contain elements of loss, or an apparent winner to suffer something of a defeat. In assignment 6, for example, students consider the persona of Orwell's "A Hanging"—whether he is a winner for being one of the survivors and a member of the ruling class, or whether he is a loser for not acting on his beliefs about justice. Using this story or a personal experience as evidence, students discuss what is won and what is lost if a sense of duty dictates to one's sense of right. In assignment 7 students consider another situation, this time from their own lives, in which an experience of winning has contained elements of loss, or an experience of losing has contained elements of gain. In assignment 8 students write about someone they know who "cannot see the forest for the trees," who has won something at close range but has in the process lost something of greater importance for the long run. In assignment 9 they write about a person they had once idealized—had considered a winner—and about the experience of realizing the individual was fallible. And in assignment 14 students investigate through published sources the life of a celebrity, a public winner (like Marilyn Monroe or Howard Hughes), whose accomplishments led, seemingly directly, to despair or defeat.

In addition to considering occasions when winning and losing are not clear-cut, when gain is always paired with loss and loss with gain, students are faced with four other situations in which the nature of winning and losing must be reconceived. Specifically, in assignments 10, 11, 12, and 13, the sequence turns to the subject of altruism, and the tension between altruistic and self-centered actions. The terms "winning" and "losing" do not appear in any of these four assignments—by this point in the course students need a break from them—but the concepts are nonetheless at the heart of this portion of the sequence as well. Since so many of the students in the course have been members of athletic teams, they are generally aware of the concept of working for team glory rather than personal glory. So, in this portion of the sequence they first write about an occasion when they made personal compromises for the sake of a group victory (assignment 10). Then they consider occasions when the desire for personal gain took precedence over a group's needs (assignment 11). Next, using evidence from their own experience and observations, they consider whether the suppression of self-interest is most often evident when the group in question is familial, or if unselfish actions are equally frequent in cases where blood ties are not at issue (assignment 12). And finally students address the situation of going against the wishes of a group close at hand, and write about the gains and losses involved in standing up for beliefs in opposition to a group (13).

By this point in the course students have analyzed so many different experiences which involve so many different senses of winning and losing that they, of course, have become much more agile and thoughtful writers than they were initially. But to insure that they synthesize their experience in the course, I ask them in the last assignment to redefine these central terms of the sequence in light of all the writing and thinking they have put into the previous 14 assignments. Some choose to compare their final definitions to the ones they generated very early in the course. Others discuss the words "winner" and "loser" in light of their writing itself, or in light of their sense of themselves. Having examined the terms from various angles, having considered some of the implications and complexities of the concepts, and having "researched themselves" as well as other sources, the students have throughout the course been building toward informed opinion and more careful thought—towards an awareness, for example, that winning something is not necessarily the last word but may present problems and even losses in its wake. Whatever strategy they use in responding to the final assignment, most of the students thus approach that final definition and discussion with more care than they did the earlier definitions, with specific examples rather than generalizations alone—and with a greater awareness of the mixed quality in their own lives as well as in the lives of others. And by the end of the course, whether we discuss it directly or leave it implicit, we have entertained the idea that to resist hasty and careless thought, to explore more than one aspect of a problem, and to turn analysis upon one's own experiences are all activities that involve winning, with finally much more gain to them than loss.

WINNERS AND LOSERS

1. Think about a time when you won something, or lost something, that you wanted very much to win. Tell us about what happened at the time, and tell us in a way that puts us into your mood. Don't worry about spelling, grammar, or anything except your story.

2. Going back to the win or loss you wrote about in assignment 1, consider what you might have done differently. (Hindsight is always better than foresight!) Now, tell us *exactly* what we should do if we found ourselves in such a situation. If you

lost, maybe you can suggest a way to win; if you won, maybe you can perfect your way of reacting.

3. What is a winner? In the article I've given you on Jon Voight, he is identified as a winner who likes to portray losers in his films. As a successful star, Voight has achieved a fame we might envy. Read through to the end of the article, though, and you will see that Voight cannot be labeled simply a "winner." His private life has not gone as well as his career. The article, in fact, cites Voight's belief that "being a divorced father, going through that trauma in real life…" helped him to have the attitudes and feelings he brought to his part in *Table for Five*. After all, what *is* a winner? You can speak of winning or losing in any given situation, but when you identify a person as a "winner" you are generalizing about a person's whole life. Maybe there *are* winners, but most of us would hesitate to describe ourselves as such. How great and how consistent must a person's success be to be classed as a winner? Write about this, using some winner you know as an example.

4. Maybe it's easier to identify someone as a loser than a winner. We all know "losers." Stories about them have entertained us from time to time. "The born loser" has become a cliché expression, and the idea has even been turned into a comic strip. Let's look at the ending of Frank Norris' *McTeague*, where McTeague and Marcus chase a mule, gone berserk, through Death Valley trying to recover the water canteen and the fortune they are fighting over. Marcus is a loser but McTeague, the winner, is also a ghoulish loser. Write about a loser you know of and about what you think this person has learned from losing.

> (We do not in this assignment read the whole Norris novel, but only the last pages which describe the chase through Death Valley and McTeague's final discovery that he is handcuffed to Marcus' corpse. We usually discuss the geographical aspects of Death Valley as a means of understanding the intensity of his dilemma.)

5. Take one of the magazines I have brought and look for an ad which uses a loser or winner as its central character. Write about how the advertiser uses this character to make the product appeal to potential customers.

6. Was George Orwell, as one of the nervous executioners in "A Hanging," a winner or a loser? As a member of the ruling group, he participated in the event even though he had qualms about its being carried out, and his qualms increased when he noticed the condemned man's sidestepping the puddle and the dog's innocent exuberance give way to silence in the presence of death. He also noticed kindred feelings in the other men as they breakfasted afterwards. Is it winning or losing to let your sense of duty dictate to your sense of right? Discuss this either in terms of "A Hanging" or in terms of some specific personal experience.

7. Sometimes we win even though we've lost, or lose even though we've won. Think of a loss which provided some unexpected bonuses for you, or a win which had its drawbacks. Maybe you didn't get the summer job you wanted most but

found out later that the paychecks weren't regular or the boss was a tyrant. Maybe, on the other hand, you got the date you wanted for the prom but the person really didn't care about you—just wanted to go to the prom! Maybe you were pleased to win an election, only to discover that it meant winning a job with much responsibility and little glory. Write about the experience of realizing somewhat later that your win or loss was not as you had imagined it would be.

8. What does this saying mean: "Win the battle but lose the war"? Can you relate this saying to another popular one: "Can't see the forest for the trees"? We all know people who emphasize details and can't seem to keep themselves aware of bigger goals. Maybe you've seen someone like this during Greek pledging. Maybe you've worried over someone your age who already has a child. Maybe you know an older person who emphasizes details until you think you'll go mad but who won't talk about the final product. Select such a person as your subject. Discuss exactly what it is that causes you to categorize the person in this way.

9. John Wayne, the quintessential hero, found in cancer a foe he couldn't conquer. In her essay, "John Wayne: A Love Song," Joan Didion thinks nostalgically about Wayne's personifying the "Big C" and planning to take it on just as he had thousands of lesser foes. John Wayne's losing this battle perhaps undermines our dream of an unbeatable hero. We can be glad that we still have Superman and Wonder Woman, who can't lose such battles! Write about the day you lost such an illusion, perhaps of one of your parents, who had seemed totally in control of everything when you were small; perhaps of some hero like Superman; perhaps of some mortal hero like John Lennon; perhaps even of yourself. Recall exactly how you realized your hero was not invincible (or *you* were not). Analyze the effects upon you of that realization.

10. Sometimes we surprise ourselves because we find, suddenly, that we are less interested in winning for ourselves than in winning for someone else. Think of some time when you got excited about working for a group victory. The group might be your family, your fraternity, your school, your country, or something else. Write about why you wanted the group to win and about the compromises you made personally for the group.

11. A sociobiologist has noted that where "altruistic restraint was not profitable to individuals...each followed a selfish policy as a result of which all suffered" (David Barash, *Sociobiology and Behavior* [New York: Elsevier Press, 1977], p. 72). For example, we buy cars manufactured in other countries because they are cheap and we like them, as a result of which American companies go out of business and/or lay off workers. By pumping our own gas and stopping at the cheapest stations, we are eliminating the helpful gas station attendant who would start our cars on snowy mornings or do routine mechanical auto jobs. By buying at discount houses, we are homogenizing the merchandise available to us and putting individual merchants out of business. In all three cases we know that our paying more for the merchandise would not make any particular difference to the individual merchant—that it would just cost

us more but not affect the general pattern. When you find yourself in such situations, what do you do? Write about your reasons for choosing the actions you choose. Use particular incidents as your examples.

12. The nature of altruism, acting to help others at some personal cost, has lately been studied quite a bit by sociobiologists. Both in animals and humans—and even in insects—self-sacrifice is common among family members. Altruism of this sort has even been labeled "hard-core"—the opposite of "soft-core" altruism, or an ultimately selfish act for which the person expects some reward (from Edward O. Wilson, *On Human Nature* [Cambridge, Mass.: Harvard University Press, 1978], p. 155). (Humans seem to be the only organisms that practice soft-core altruism.) Experiments with various animal species and observations of human societies show persuasively that preferences among the genetically related are natural and biological. Sociobiologists suggest that altruistic acts without a biological basis of related genes are admired and considered something unusual. For instance, awards given for acts of rescue nearly always go to someone unrelated to the victim. A mother commonly risks her life to save her own child and is perhaps expected to do so. Do you agree that "blood is thicker than water"—that unselfish actions most often support family ties? Argue *for* or *against* this idea, using your own observations as evidence.

13. Shirley Jackson's story "The Lottery" describes a raffle not many of us would care to win. What shocks and repels us about the raffle is not that Tessie, the winner, dies for no good reason. As she screams to be saved, she does not seem cowardly because dying in this way is not brave. The actions of the people in teaching their children to gather stones (the reason for which we understand only later) do not seem humanly valid, and yet they are symbolic of some actions we permit—in war, for example. Tessie is sacrificed to a senseless ritual which seems to continue simply because it is custom. No one supports the ritual with any enthusiasm. Some merely have a business-as-usual attitude, some feel they must continue tradition, some follow rules obediently, while some grumble that the custom should be given up but do nothing. In the characters, we recognize familiar degrees of democratic acceptance, degrees of acceptance we find around us. When did you last decide not to go along with the gang because you didn't like what they were doing? Argue *for* or *against* this issue of whether to follow the crowd. Use down-to-earth examples.

14. For this next-to-last writing project, think of someone who seems to have won everything life has to offer, yet who seems to have been defeated by that very victory. Your "winner" probably won't have been stoned to death, but he or she will certainly be aware that what has been won is a bad honor. Let's think about some situations you might use:

  a. Ingrid Bergman, who died recently, had been idolized in ingénue roles as a young actress. When she deserted her Swedish husband and daughter Pia and ran off with Italian film director Roberto Rossellini, she had to endure great censure, even being condemned on the floor of the United States Senate. She had stones thrown at her largely because she was expected to live up to the image she had projected. "They put me on a pedestal," Bergman said of her public, "and they felt they had been cheated."

b. Howard Hughes became a legend as the richest man in the United States. His very wealth caused him to become a total recluse, so paranoid and paralyzed he couldn't even cut his own fingernails.

c. Marilyn Monroe was a poor child from a broken home who grew up to be a national sex symbol. Somehow she couldn't handle her life and was driven to end it deliberately.

d. Elvis Presley has become a legend as the first successful rock-and-roller. He is remembered with enthusiasm today, but fame didn't bring him happiness.

Choose one of these persons, or think of your own, and do some investigation by looking up your subject in the *New York Times Index,* or some other source at the library. Write a rough draft, taking some clear position about your subject in the form of a thesis idea. We'll discuss these drafts in conferences and class workshops, and then I'll ask you to revise the piece on the basis of these discussions.

15. Look back over all your writing in this course. In light of your reading and your writing in this class, consider again the questions of assignments 3 and 4: What is a winner? a loser? In responding to these questions again, you may want to use portions of your earlier definitions and discussions, perhaps to show how your thinking has become modified. You may want to use examples from your own life, and from your reading, that you have not written about before. You may wish to incorporate in your response examples you *have* used before. You may want to consider what these terms have to do with writing, and what they have to do with you. Whatever you choose, be sure to consider the terms "winner" and "loser" in light of your experiences throughout this course, in light of all our discussions and all your thinking and writing.

Women Writing

Natural and Artificial

Rebecca Blevins Faery

As I worked to design my experimental writing course, the faces of my students at Hollins College hovered always in my mind's eye, making me alert to their situation and that of the College, which was founded in the mid-nineteenth century to give "young women the same thorough and rigid mental training as that afforded to young men." That mission remains the same today, though the role of women has changed dramatically, and so it seemed appropriate that my course be designed in part to help students overcome the intellectual dependence and passivity that many of them have as women been socialized into. Just as they have not dared to think of themselves as "writers," so many of them have feared to confront the issue of what it means to be a woman in our world. So I set about to design a course that would help them begin to develop a strong sense of themselves as women and as writers of increasing awareness and ability, who believed that the world could be interested in what they had to say and who felt confident that they could write to interest, inform, persuade, amuse, enchant their readers.

My aim in the course, then, is a dual one: to confront students with the task of defining themselves as women, and to invite them to become writers in the process. Those two challenges can, I think, be interwoven in an intriguing way, and to this end I use the terms *natural* and *artificial* as the nominal subjects of the assignments for the course. These concepts and the tension between them are at the heart of my students' situation both as young women and as young writers. In the assignments, they are faced, in effect, with a series of problems related to those concepts— problems ranging from broad questions of definition to problems of personal and cultural exploration. What does it mean to feel, or to be, "natural"? What does it mean to feel, or to be, "artificial"? As a woman? As a writer? Is writing for them a "natural" activity? Are the images of women offered to them by popular culture "natural" or "artificial"? How do they locate themselves, and their images of themselves, in relation to popular ideas and images of "natural" and "artificial" behavior? How do their personal conceptions of "natural" and "artificial" influence their reactions to particular places, situations, images, art objects, and verbal

106

expressions? What role do words seem to play in the culture's definition of what it means to be "natural"? To be "artificial"? To be a woman? And most important, what can they themselves do with words—with writing—to define themselves as women and as writers, and to make for themselves a self and a world in which they can live naturally and fully?

Language, of course, is formative, and I want my students to discover this truth and its powerful implications for them as women and as writers. Few, if any, of them have ever considered the possibility that writing might be a significant way of shaping the quality of their lives. Their experiences with writing have for the most part been frustrating or humiliating. They bring with them to college many anxieties about writing, and they believe that while some people are "natural" writers, *they* certainly aren't. Indeed, most of them come into the course because they have experienced serious problems with writing: either they are asked to take the course as first-semester freshmen (usually about ten percent of each entering class) because their test scores and high-school records indicate that they may need some extra help with writing at the beginning of their college careers, or they elect the course after their experience with college writing has led them to feel anxious about it or to despair of succeeding at it. So the course invites them to become more confident writers by using language to explore the place of "natural" and "artificial" activities in writing, as well as by learning experientially how successful writing gets done. And the course invites them to consider their identities as women by considering what the world has to say, and what they themselves have to say, about being a woman, "natural" or "artificial."

Given the prior writing experience of the students and the nominal themes of the sequence, it follows that the rhetorical orientation of my assignments emphasizes expressive writing. I want to help my students overcome the developmental problems that so many young people experience from being called upon to write primarily in what Britton calls the "transactional" mode without receiving adequate preparation. I want to restore some measure of balance by giving my students numerous and thus frequent opportunities to write expressively. Further, even when they move out from expressive language to more transactional or poetic tasks, the expressive element in those pieces is explicitly recognized, encouraged, and validated. So in designing the course I determined to create an array of activities that would acquaint students with expressive writing—with its value in and of itself and with its usefulness as a medium for discovery and exploration, as a starting point for any piece of writing.

This sequence of assignments, then, invites students to do the kind of writing that is closest to them personally, in the kind of language that Britton reminds us is "home base" for all of us, from which we move out to try our hands at more complex or sophisticated kinds of discourse, to which we return recursively to rediscover who and where we are and what we are about. I think this is what teachers mean when they say that an important task for student writers is for them to find their own "voice." Though alienation is, I know, a catch-word of the twentieth century, it is just the same a condition that students too often experience from the writing they are asked to do in school. Helping them to establish an authentic relationship with the words they produce on paper, and to understand the importance of those words in creating a sense of the self, are thus the broadest and most important goals of the sequence.

These broad purposes led me to begin the sequence with several assignments (1-4) that give students the opportunity to write directly about their personal experiences, observations, attitudes, and feelings. Within this context of personal writing, these opening assignments also introduce students to the problem of defining what it means to be "natural." They explore the concept in terms of a situation they have experienced (2), a person they know (3), a lifestyle they have observed (4), as well as in terms of their attitude towards the activity of writing itself (1).

Having given students an initial set of opportunities to see how their experience can be an important basis for understanding a particular concept, I then invite them to approach the concept in a strikingly different way, by means of a formal discovery procedure that entails thinking about an idea in terms of its opposite—i.e., "natural" as opposed to "artificial" (5). This task involves them primarily in a search, both in their own heads and in dictionaries, for words and meanings related to each of these concepts. In this and the other "word search" assignments (11 and 19), my aim is not simply to move students up the conceptual ladder from experiential to intellectual ways of knowing, but also to help them recognize and begin to understand the complicated network of interactions between their experience, language, and their sense of reality. I want them to see, for example, that they make reality for themselves (and for others) in the way that they use words to define experience. And by extension, I want them to see that their sense of reality is likewise being shaped by the way others use language to define experience. I want them, in other words, to experience and reflect on the power that is available to them in and through language.

The influence of language is made especially evident in the next cluster of assignments (6-8), which focus on the use (and abuse) of the term "natural" in various forms of advertising. In the process of evaluating and rewriting individual advertisements, students find themselves faced anew with the challenge of defining what it means to be natural—and of discovering where their definitions and those of the advertising culture diverge as well as converge. Given the numerous products that currently seek to lure women with the appeal of naturalness, this cluster inescapably leads up to the question of what it means to be a natural woman. And I ask them to engage this question first in the context of a popular song of some years back, "A Natural Woman" (9), and then directly in terms of themselves (10).

At this point, another "word search" occurs, but in this case one that centers on "nature" and "artifice." An exploration of this pair of terms serves not only to complicate the previous questions of definition and self-definition, but also to introduce several related themes and topics that figure in the remainder of the sequence. In one sense, the thought of nature immediately suggests a wide range of subjects related to the environment, and these serve as suggested topics for the longest paper in the course, the "search project essay" (12), which students work on over a period of about six weeks. In helping them decide on paper topics, one of my major concerns is that they choose subjects which will take them outside the library for at least part of their work, and thus away from exclusive reliance on secondary material and the artificial research paper behaviors that go hand in hand with it. I want them, in other words, to get experience in some of the more natural ways of searching for information, such as first-hand observation, interviewing, letter-writing, rummaging through public records, and collecting fugitive printed matter. In a similar spirit, I encourage them to preserve their own personal voices from the first through the final drafts of these papers.

While students are working on their long papers, they are also working their way through a group of assignments that face them with some of the most challenging questions that are implicit in the themes of the course. These questions center on the relationship between reality and the symbol systems we use to represent it. Such questions are raised in part by three assignments that call upon them to do pieces about a place "close to nature" (14, 16, and 18), each of which invites them quite self-consciously to use language as a means of recreating the place or the experience of being in it. Alternating with these assignments are two other tasks that call upon them to look at various kinds of visual art and to write about the relation of these works to nature, as well as about the experience of looking at art and writing about it (15 and 17). This group of assignments comes to a climax in the final "word search," which centers on "art" and "nature."

The final "word search" also invites students to review their writing for the course with an eye to identifying which piece they consider most "artful," which most "natural," which most "artificial," and which most "true." To assure that students will have had an opportunity to do some artful writing of their own invention, I provide for two open assignments (13 and 21) during this latter part of the course. In this way, students also have an opportunity to write about something other than "natural" and "artificial" without abandoning the central concern of the course. So, during the final days of the course, it remains only for students to reflect in writing on various aspects of the writing they have done during the semester (20 and 22). My hope, of course, is that by the end of the sequence they will have come to experience and to understand their power to shape reality as women writing.

NATURAL AND ARTIFICIAL

1. The purpose of this course is to help you become a better writer. You are now beginning your college career, beginning a future in which you will be called upon to be a writer. You don't just have a future as a writer, though; you also have a past, a history as a writer, a history of encounters with writing tasks.

But for now, I'm interested in the present. Tell us how you feel *now* about yourself as a writer, how you feel about being in this course. Feel free to draw upon your past writing experiences or to talk about your expectations of the future to explain your present feelings. Does it seem natural to you to express yourself in writing?

Don't worry about grammar, punctuation, spelling; our concern for those things will come later. For now, just get your thoughts and feelings down. We'll talk about these papers in class next time.

2. We have all experienced situations in which we feel comfortable, completely at ease, able to just relax, be ourselves, and act "natural." Tell us about a situation you have experienced in which you felt this way. Be sure to explain what made it possible for you to be your "natural self." What qualities in you were free to be expressed in this situation? If other people were present, how did they react to the self you revealed? Was the reaction of other people important to the degree to which you felt free to act "natural"?

Was the self you revealed in this situation like or different from the self you project in most everyday situations?

What does it mean to be "natural" anyway? How many "natural selves" do you have?

Is there more than one way to be "natural"?

3. Some people seem to be born with a gift, a talent, for doing certain things. We sometimes say that such a person is a "natural" at whatever it is she or he does particularly well—that is, that she or he is a "natural" tennis player, a "natural" musician, a "natural" comedian, a "natural" teacher, a "natural" leader. Tell us about someone you know who is a "natural" at something, and why you think so.

And are you a "natural" at doing something—a sport, a subject in school, an art, a hobby, a personal quality or characteristic? Tell us about something which comes naturally and easily to you. Is your "naturalness" at this like the quality you described in the person you know? How? How is it different?

What does being a "natural" at something really mean, anyhow?

4. Most of us know someone who, in one way or another, pursues what is sometimes called a "natural" lifestyle—with "natural" foods, "natural" fabrics, a "natural" living environment, "natural" cures for illness, and so on. Tell us about someone you know who lives this way. Be sure to describe the way she or he lives so that we understand what you mean by a "natural" lifestyle.

Why do you think the person you wrote about decided to live the way she or he does? Would you want to live this way? Does living in a "natural" way interest you at all? Why or why not?

Would you define a "natural" lifestyle differently now than you would have before you were asked to write this paper?

5. We've been doing a lot of thinking and writing about things called, for one reason or another, "natural." One way of coming to understand something is to think of it in terms of its opposites. One opposite of "natural" is "artificial." Does that make sense to you in light of the thinking you did about the term "natural" for the past exercise?

Right now I'd like you to spend about fifteen minutes in a word search inside your head. Place the words *natural* and *artificial* as the headings for word groups on a piece of paper. Then list all the words you can think of that could belong in either of those two categories. Any kind of words will do—actions, qualities, names of things, descriptive words. Just be sure you can defend your placement of each word in each category.

Before coming to our next class, look up the words *natural* and *artificial* in at least two dictionaries, one being the *Oxford English Dictionary* (O.E.D.) in the library. How are the definitions from the two sources alike? How are they different? What are the origins of both words?

Now look closely at your two word groups resulting from the word search. Are you satisfied that you've placed each word in the right group? Are there changes you'd like to make based on the definitions you read? What words might reasonably be listed in both groups? Do you think everyone would agree with your placement of the words listed?

6. Commercial advertisers have been quick to jump on the "natural" bandwagon, and now we get a daily barrage of advertisements for "natural" or "all natural" products—ice cream, breakfast cereal, vitamins, beer, laxatives, and personal hygiene products, to name just a few.

Choose one particular product which is advertised as "natural" and find out all you can about it. Read labels and advertisements for the product and for its competitors. Check consumer information in the library. If you know someone who uses the product, talk to that person about the product. How does it claim to be "natural"—in its ingredients, its production, the effect it claims to have on the user? What does the product's claim to be "natural" imply about other similar products? Is the implication justified?

For your writing exercise, write a letter to the manufacturer of the product either attacking or defending the product's right to be described as "natural." Remember that this is *not* a commercial or promotion piece for the product; neither is it a condemnation of the product's effectiveness. You are to focus on whether or not the product's being advertised as "natural" is justified. Be sure you have included enough information to make your argument convincing.

7. In order to sell a product, many advertisements base their appeal to potential users on implied effects which have little to do with the product itself—for example, ads which suggest that if you serve the right brand of liquor, the right person will fall in love with you.

Choose an ad which promotes a product in such a way as to distort the real need a person might have for the product. What is the appeal? What is being sold besides the product? How is the message conveyed—in words, or in visual images, or both? Bring the ad with you to our next class.

For your writing exercise, write a new ad for the product, basing your appeal to potential users on benefits which a user might reasonably expect from using the product. Include visual images—drawn or cut-and-pasted—if appropriate. If your ad is for a radio or television spot, write the script and include any other information which will explain how you imagine the ad spot being executed.

Which ad do you judge to be the more effective in selling the product, yours or the original? Why do you think so?

8. Products aimed at women consumers are particularly often described as "natural" or as giving the user the "natural look"—cosmetics, toiletries, hair coloring, and brassieres, to name just a few.

Choose a product designed for women which is advertised in some way as "natural." Find an ad promoting the product. How do you respond to the ad? Does it make you want to buy the product? Why or why not? What kind of person is the ad asking you to be? Does the product itself invite you to be the same kind of person as the *ad* for the product?

For your writing exercise, write a letter to the editor of the publication in which you found the ad, telling how you reacted to the ad and why, and whether you think the ad is honest and effective and should be continued or is misleading (perhaps offensive) and should not appear in the pages of the publication. Don't mail the letter yet; maybe you'll want to do that after our workshop of the letters.

To prepare to do this assignment, you might want to read Nora Ephron's essay "Dealing with the, uh, Problem" in *Crazy Salad* (on reserve in the library).

Be sure to bring both the ad and your letter to class next time.

9. Some years ago Aretha Franklin made a popular recording of a song called "(You Make Me Feel Like) A Natural Woman." (Why might the term "a natural woman" have different meanings for a black woman, like Franklin, than for a white woman? Does it make a difference to you to know that the song was written by a white woman, Carole King, who also recorded it?)

Try to listen to a recording of the song, either by Franklin or King. Listen to it several times, paying particular attention to the words. Read the words through (as they are printed on the jacket of King's "Tapestry" album). What image of a "natural woman" is projected in this song? In other words, what makes her "natural"? Do you agree or disagree with the image? Does it fit your own notion of what a "natural woman" is? Why or why not?

And what *is* a "natural woman," anyhow? That is, how do you define the term?

10. Before writing this paper, read Nikki Giovanni's poem "Dreams" (on reserve in the library).

Are you a "natural woman"? If so, how and why are you? If not, do you want to be? Why or why not?

Where does the concept of "naturalness" fit into your idea of who you are?

11. Let's do another word search, this time looking at the words from which *natural* and *artificial* come: *nature* and *artifice*.

But this time let's reverse the procedure. First look up definitions in at least two dictionaries, one being the *Oxford English Dictionary*. Once again, how are the definitions of each word from the two sources alike? How are they different? What are the origins of the two words?

Now place the words *nature* and *artifice* as the headings for word groups on a piece of paper. Spend about fifteen minutes listing all the words you can think of under those two headings. Scrutinize your list as you did in the last word search. Are you satisfied that each word is in the right column? What words might reasonably be listed in both columns? Do you think everyone would agree with your placement of the words you listed?

What have you learned in doing these word searches, about these particular words or even about words in general?

12. It is time for you to begin work on your search project essay, the longest paper you will write in this course.

We have been talking and writing about nature and artifice, things natural and artificial. Let's try to apply those terms to our environment, to the way we designate the space we live, work, and play in.

How about "nature" areas for recreation? Our country has a vast network of local, state and national parks, ranging from "reclaimed" areas with swimming pools, artificial lakes and beaches, hiking trails, and barbecue grills, to wilderness preserves subject to a minimum of tinkering. Why do we want or need such places? When did the idea of preserving our wilderness capture the American imagination?

Or maybe you are tired of talking and thinking about humankind in a natural setting. Well, what is the opposite of a preserved wilderness area? A shopping mall? An amusement park? Urban renewal? A "planned community"?

You needn't confine your exploration to our own culture, if your interest or inclination leads you in other directions. You might want to explore the history of landscape architecture, the ideal English garden of a specific time, the Oriental garden, the American Indians' concept of the relationship of people to nature. Or, closer to home, the Hollins Outdoor Program, the College's ownership of land peripheral to the campus, the contemporary back-to-the-land movement, organic versus chemical farming.

All of these things, of course, are just suggestions. I want and expect you to develop a topic that interests you and that you are sure of being able to collect information on.

So start searching, and keep a good record of places you encounter information—conversations, interviews with people you know, newspapers, books, magazines, brochures, telephone calls, relevant things that come up in classes or that just pop into your head. Search around a bit before deciding on a specific topic.

In two weeks we'll have a topic workshop, for which you should write a paragraph or two explaining what your topic will be, what you want to accomplish with your paper, and what your sources of information will be.

Later we will have workshops on first and second drafts of your essay, a workshop on documentation, and finally a copyediting workshop for the finished essay.

13. For our next class, we will have a silent reading session: bring in something you have written that you'd like the rest of the class to read and give some response to. Attach two or three blank sheets of paper to the back of your paper so people will have room to write comments. We'll spend the whole class period silently reading and responding in writing to each other's work.

You may write on *any subject* you choose, in *any form* you choose. The only restriction is that what you bring must be something you've written specifically for the session.

14. Choose a place on campus where you can go to feel "close to nature." Spend some time there—at least fifteen minutes—just being passive, receiving impressions. What do you see? Close your eyes for several minutes and experience the place in other ways. What sounds are part of experiencing the place? How about smells, textures, sensations?

After you are through observing, take notes to record your observations and impressions before you leave the spot.

Later, back in your room or in whatever spot you like to write in, *remake* your experience in words for the rest of us to share. (This time you are being an artificer.)

15.   This, therefore, is the praise of Shakespeare, that his drama is the mirror of life.

— Samuel Johnson

It is the spectator and not life that art really mirrors.

— Oscar Wilde

For this exercise, I'd like you to visit the art exhibit in the Art Annex. Spend some time looking at the objects on display. Take time to look at the whole exhibit, and then choose one object to focus your attention on. Describe the object for us. Then describe your response to it.

Was the thing you looked at directly representative of something in nature? Suggestive of something in nature? What else shaped the thing you looked at besides the imitation of things found in nature? What shaped your response?

And finally, what do you make of the quotations above? Do they help you to make sense of your experience of looking at art and writing about it? How?

16. Look back at the writing you did for Exercise 14. In that writing, you were describing your experience of being in a place close to nature. Now I'd like you to revisit the place you chose, and this time I'd like you to *describe exactly what you see* as precisely and as objectively as possible so that someone could draw a representation of what you saw just from reading what you have written.

This piece, then, will be *instructions on how to draw the scene* for someone who hasn't seen it.

(On the day the students bring this paper to class, I bring pencils and paper, pair them up, and ask them to draw the description of the place in their partner's paper, reassuring them that the quality of the drawing is not important, but that following the directions in the piece is.)

17. Here is a passage from Sir Philip Sidney's "The Defense of Poesy":

> Nature never set forth the earth in so rich tapestry as divers poets have done; neither with pleasant rivers, fruitful trees, sweet-smelling flowers, nor whatsoever else may make the too-much-loved earth more lovely; her world is brazen, the poets only deliver a golden.

Go to the library and look at the *Life* and *Smithsonian* articles (on reserve) about the restoration of Monet's garden at Giverny. Look closely at the photographs and paintings, and choose one pair to compare and contrast. How are the two depictions of the scene—photographed and painted—alike? How are they different?

Which version is more "natural"? Which is more "artificial"?

What do you mean by "natural" and "artificial" here?

18. Let's go back once again to exercise 14. This time I'd like you to focus on your own *response* to the place, and to try to capture the essential quality of the response in language.

Of course you may include some description of the physical details, if you want or need to. But in exercise 16, you worked to describe the place *objectively;* this time you are to focus on your *subjective* reactions to the place.

Play with choosing the words, with arranging them. Write a poem, if you like, or a monologue, or a meditation. Try something different, something unusual. Pull out all the stops. You're in charge. How good can you make this?

19. One last word search. Look up the word *art* in at least two dictionaries, one the *Oxford English Dictionary*. How are the two entries alike? How are they different? What is the relationship of the word *art* to the word *artifice?* What is the relationship of *art* to *nature?*

For your writing exercise, look back at the writing in your portfolio that you've done for this course. Which piece do you think is the most "artful"? Which is the most "natural"? Which is the most "artificial"? Which is the most "true"?

20. (In class) You've now finished your search project essay, the biggest and longest writing task of the course.

Right now I'd like you to reflect in writing on your experience of writing that paper. How was writing this paper like writing other papers you've done before? How was it different? What did you find valuable about the experience of writing this paper? What did you learn?

What do you like most about your paper? Do you wish you had done anything differently? If so, what?

How has writing this paper changed your view of yourself as a writer?

21. Open Assignment (same as exercise 13).

22. Now, after all these excursions into writing, tell me how you feel about yourself as a writer.

What have you learned in this course? What have you not learned that you wanted to learn?

Do you feel more *natural* now as a writer than when you began? Are you a more consciously *artful* writer?

IV

Problem Solving and Writing

Patricia Carlson

By virtue of being human, we are all—from birth to death — engaged in an endless round of making and remaking hypotheses about our existence and the nature of our universe. We are forever problem solving. This activity, as defined by cognitive psychologists, involves the assimilation and codification of the world around us into a series of *schemata,* which must then be recognized or confirmed in light of further experience. Throughout these activities, of course, language plays a major role, for it nurtures our thinking, our ability to represent the world, and our ability to manipulate these representations. Our language becomes a means for making our presumptions explicit, for testing their validity, for transforming or amending them based upon our recursive perceptions of "reality."

This connection between language and problem solving is at the center of the Freshman Composition course I have designed for my freshman students at Rose-Hulman Institute of Technology.[1] Specifically, the course is guided by the assumption that writing is both a thinking problem and a strategic act in problem solving.[2] That is, writing is a procedure for uncovering new ideas and for discovering new configurations of old ideas. In writing, we explore new connections and make new combinations. We sift through our schemata—reforming, rearranging, hypothesizing, and testing until we hit upon the answer, the solution to our problem. Writing thus provides us with an integrative mechanism for problem solving.

My approach to the teaching of composition is to isolate some of the basic strategies underlying successful problem solving, and then to apply these techniques to the writing process. By presenting methods for systematic inquiry and means for gathering and ordering information, I intend for the course to help students simultaneously broaden their problem-solving repertoire and improve their writing.

[1]Rose-Hulman Institute of Technology is a 109-year-old college dedicated to a liberal education in science and engineering. This commitment includes an emphasis on oral and written communication in all programs. Graduates of the Institute complete a series of courses intended to develop both technical knowledge and the ability to communicate that knowledge. Almost all courses at Rose-Hulman have a writing component. Assignments are varied and cover a range from the formal lab report in Freshman Chemistry, to short stories and poetry in the elective Creative Writing course.

[2]Linda S. Flower and John R. Hayes, "Problem-Solving Strategies and the Writing Process," *College English,* 30, no. 4 (December 1977), 449.

By periodically asking students to reflect on their growth in writing through problem-solving strategies, I also intend the course to help students gain an awareness of themselves as deliberate users of language.

Ultimately, I am interested in cultivating not only the logical processes of the left hemisphere of the brain, but also the creative activities of the right side of the brain. Mysterious and elusive though they are, right-brain activities evidently influence the language-using process in several important ways. For example, the right side of the brain probably decides upon emotional appropriateness in discourse and thus contributes to the style and tone in which an utterance is cast. Even more important, the right hemisphere is the probable source of intuition, flashes of images, sudden apprehensions, visual mentation, and metaphoric constructions.[3] Clearly, the right side of our brains play a major role in creativity, and language manipulation may be a way of consciously tapping this reservoir of insight. Through language we can shift our frame of reference, hypothesize, fantasize, role-play, and literally create new universes and new perceptions of familiar realms in ways not otherwise possible.

By exposing students to both logical and creative modes of problem solving, I intend the course to provide students with a broad and highly suggestive range of options for approaching the wide variety of writing tasks they are likely to encounter both in college and beyond. But I also believe that students need not only a repertoire of options to draw upon in their thinking and writing, but also a critical awareness of their options. Without such an awareness, after all, their options may be of little use to them. So when faced with particularly difficult problems, they may do no more than write random thoughts, or call upon time-consuming and unproductive composing strategies, or write nothing at all. To help students overcome such problems, I have therefore also designed my course to promote an awareness and self-consciousness of problem solving.

My concern with using problem-solving to cultivate both logical and creative processes as well as to nurture an awareness of this range of options is reflected in the major units of my course design. Unit I, "Self-Awareness" (assignments 1-3), helps students call to consciousness the capabilities they bring to the course. Each of the three writing tasks in this unit is intended to aid students in discovering their own patterns of action, both in problem solving and in composing. Unit II, "Critical Thinking," requires students to apply various *analytical* strategies of problem solving to specific writing situations. Students are asked to identify sets and subsets. among common items (assignment 5), to explore various ways of conceiving such sets and subsets (6), and to examine functional relationships among the parts of a concrete object (7), as well as the parts of a complex situation (8). Unit III, "Creative Play," requires students to apply various strategies for *synthesis* and creation of meaning to writing tasks. In this unit, students examine ways in which the changing of words alters perception (10, 11). They devise instruments for

---

[3]Janet Emig, "Writing as a Mode of Learning," *College Composition and Communication*, 28 (May 1977), 124-125.

"reading" a familiar concept—time—thus creating analogies between concrete and abstract worlds (12). And they conclude these explorations into frames of reference through a flight of fantasy, role-playing something that initially seems impossible in order to reach new insights (13).

Each of these units in the sequence, then, is devoted to examining a specific set of solution-seeking activities. "Meta-assignments" (4, 9, and 14) conclude each of the units. These tasks call upon students to contemplate the various strategies they have employed while trying to resolve the question or problem of the previous assignments and to consolidate the new patterns of behavior they have acquired. The final writing task of the course (15) acts as the culmination for the entire sequence. It asks students both to invent a new transportation system for the future and also to convince a particular audience of its merit. Thus the task requires that students adapt and apply the various strategies—both for writing and problem solving—that they have learned throughout the course.

The following chart provides a picture of the course as a whole.

UNIT I: SELF-AWARENESS
1:           The Process of Problem Solving
2:           Obstructions to Problem Solving
3:           The Problem and The Problem Solver
4:           Reflective Assignment

UNIT II: CRITICAL THINKING: ANALYTICAL STRATEGIES
5:           Identifying Parts
6:           Exploring Parts
7:           Operational Analysis
8:           Causal Analysis
9:           Reflective Assignment

UNIT III: CREATIVE PLAY: STRATEGIES FOR SYNTHESIS
10:          Visual Constructs
11:          Verbal Constructs
12:          Reasoning Analogically
13:          Role-Playing
14:          Reflective Assignment

UNIT IV: CULMINATION
15:          Planning Solutions and Consolidating Gains

Another way of understanding this design is to recognize the theories of problem solving at work in various portions of the course. My approach, let it be admitted, is eclectic, so no single theory of problem solving informs the course. Rather, the various assignments use several basic ideas from cognitive psychology. For example:

Deductive Reasoning—or top-down construction which views thinking as the processing of a mental structure. (This concept is used in assignments 5, 6, 7, and 8, where the writer must identify sets and their subsets.)

Gestalt—or perception psychology which views problem solving as a structuring and restructuring of information. (This approach is evident in assignments 10 and 11, where establishing or changing frames of reference is especially important.)

Constructing Meaning—or cognitive map theory which views thinking as an assimilation of new information into previously existing schemata. (This approach is used in assignments 12 and 13, where imagery and problem representation or definition are central to the writing task.)

Cognitive Development—or maturation which views successful problem solving as influenced primarily by mental "growth." (This approach is used in assignment 15, where experience and self-awareness are central to the writing task.)

Though my course embodies various theories of problem-solving and various kinds of logical and creative tasks, all of the assignments either directly or by implication deal with physical and technical design. That is to say, they are tailored to the particular students at my institution, most of whom plan careers in science and engineering. I have deliberately constructed the sequence in this way so that the students will come to see the activity of freshman composition not as an irrelevant academic requirement but as an essential aspect of the professional work they have come to prepare for at Rose-Hulman. Certainly it is essential to their professional welfare that engineers be able to solve problems and communicate their solutions to one another and to their clients. But it is also essential to the public welfare that our scientists and engineers be able to communicate responsibly with the population at large, which is their ultimate clientele. Sound public policy about such issues as energy resources, national security, space exploration, and urban development (to name just a few) depend, after all, upon the abilities of engineers and scientists to state the choices clearly and to advise the public about the potential benefits and risks of these choices. For engineers and scientists to meet these obligations requires that they be effective problem solvers and writers. It is to such ends, at last, that the following course is addressed.

THE WRITING PROCESS
AND PROBLEM SOLVING

Unit I: Self-Awareness

1: The Process of Problem Solving

Directions: Use the left side of the page as scrap paper for jotting down ideas as you attempt to solve the following three puzzles. Later, I will tell you what to do with the right side of the page.

(After students have solved each puzzle, or reached an impasse, I ask them to use the right side of the page for reflecting on the process of their problem solving. We then discuss various procedures and why some were successful and others not.)

Puzzle A

Eight Rose-Hulman students have to cross the Wabash River and all the bridges are down. The only means of transportation is a little boat in which two small children are playing. However, the craft is constructed so that it can carry at most the two children *or* one Rose-Hulman student. How do the students get across the river?

Puzzle B

This is a game played with five dice and called "Petals around a Rose." There are only two rules for playing the game: (1) the clue to success is in the name of the game; (2) no one ever explains to anyone else how the game is played. The object is to tell how many "petals" there are in any particular cast of the dice. Here are a few examples.

Eight petals

Twelve petals

Two petals

Four petals

Four petals

No petals

Fill in the spots for ten petals

Puzzle C

When I first employed Al, Bert, Charlie, Doug and Ernie in my factory, they used to sit for their many discussions round a circular table to emphasize that in my eyes they were all equal, though naturally as the Managing Director, I sat aloof. In order to make it clear that there was no alphabetical superiority, I insisted that no two men, the initial letters of whose names were next to each other in the alphabet, should be next to each other at the table. Charlie had Ernie's brother sitting on his right. What is the arrangement of the men around the table?

Reflections on Puzzle Solving

Describing the problem-solving process is very difficult since it is almost impossible to be wholly engaged in the activity and to be aware of the process at the same time. Yet you now have at least three rough sketches of how your mind was operating while thinking about the puzzles you worked in class today. Actually, you have two types of records of the process—the left column jottings which were *instruments* in your attempts to find the answer and the right column notations which are *reflections* on your attempts.

Using this information and whatever remembrances of the process come to mind, consider the following set of questions for discussion in class and as an aid in helping you with the written portion of this assignment.

Can you see any common pattern in your efforts to solve all these puzzles? Did you proceed by trial-and-error or did you have a systematic approach? At what point did you formulate an hypothesis (if you did)? At what point did you become frustrated and give up (if you did)? Why were you successful with some of the problems and not with others? What is the difference between the method(s) you used in these problem-solving situations and those you would employ in applying the following equation? (Maybe you do not think there are any differences.)

$$s^2 = \frac{1}{N\text{-}1} \sum_{i=1}^{n} (x_i - \bar{x})^2 \, fi$$

(The preceding questions help prepare for class discussion of the process of inquiry and four categories of problem-solving: (1) random trial and error, (2) rules, (3) strategies, and (4) flash of insight or inspiration.)

Paper 1

Based upon your experiences with the three puzzles and your perception of the process you went through, write a brief account of your activities. Assume that the reader is someone also in the class.

(Before I give the actual writing assignment, which is to be completed for the next class session, I ask students to introduce themselves to someone in the class whom they do not know. I then ask each student to write the paper for this new acquaintance. Giving a sense of specific audience cuts down on the summary and description that most students wander off into and focuses the paper on an analysis of the process.

My purpose in this task is to force the students into some mode—no matter how rudimentary—of self-analysis even at the outset of the course. I want my students to begin to see themselves as problem solvers and as writers, and to understand the complex nature of the process they must go through in order to complete both activities. My feeling is that many students have no appreciation for process because we allow them the luxury of giving up much too easily. When they find they cannot proceed, maybe they owe us—and more importantly, themselves—an explanation of what seemed to work and what did not. The function of this assignment is to make the student self-conscious about process.)

2: Obstructions to Problem Solving

Directions: Assume that a steel pipe is imbedded in the concrete floor of a bare room as shown below. The inside diameter is .06″ larger than the diameter of a ping-pong ball (1.50″) which is resting gently at the bottom of the pipe. You are one of a group of six people in the room, along with the following objects:

100′ of clothesline
A carpenter's hammer
A chisel
A box of Wheaties
A file
A wire coat hanger
A monkey wrench
A light bulb

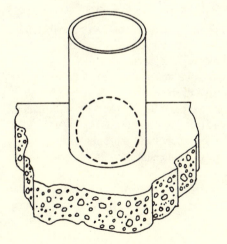
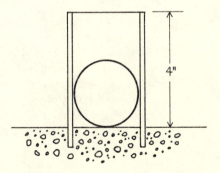

List as many ways you can think of (in five minutes) to get the ball out of the pipe without damaging the ball, tube, or floor.

(Reprinted from *Conceptual Blockbusting: A Guide to Better Ideas,* by James L. Adams, p. 54, with the permission of W. W. Norton and Company, Inc. Copyright © 1974, 1976, 1979 by James L. Adams.)

Look back over the list of solutions you came up with for getting the ball out of the pipe. Did you think of crushing the Wheaties to a powder and stirring the ball to the top of this powder with one end of the filed-in-half coat hanger? Did you think of having all six people urinate in the pipe? Did you think of smashing the light bulb and cutting six people's veins with broken glass in order to draw enough blood to float the ball to the top of the pipe? How about smashing the handle of the hammer with the monkey wrench and digging the ping-pong ball out of the pipe with a splinter of wood—did you think to do that?

And ask yourself, if you didn't think of all such solutions, *why* didn't you think of them? You know that people contain blood and that blood is a liquid and that ping-pong balls float on liquid, don't you? If you didn't think of splintering the handle of the carpenter's hammer, why didn't you think of it? Couldn't you visualize the tools well enough? Were you unaware that a piece of wood, right before your eyes, will splinter if struck hard enough? That a monkey wrench is heavy? And made of sturdy metal? Or what?

Or, to put it all another way (*and here are the questions you are to address in paper 2*), suppose there were someone in our class who came up with all the solutions mentioned above, plus all those you came up with, plus ten more—someone who did this in the same amount of time you spent on the problem. And suppose this were an ability you wanted to praise.

a. How would you explain first of all what the ability here *is* exactly (without resorting to such silly talk as "a quick mind," "smarts," "fast thinking," and so on)?
b. How would you go about explaining that this ability can be developed?
c. Finally, how would you explain that this ability, whatever it is, is valuable for more than getting ping-pong balls out of pipes in sealed rooms?

(The previous assignment made the students aware of process rather than product; this task requires the students to reflect on the nature, potential applications, and value of that process. The accusatory tone in the two paragraphs of questioning is meant to make students aware that they do know more than they realize and thus to make them recognize a basic "problem" of problem solving: very often we do not perceive how to use data, information, or knowledge that we already have. The tone of the instruction is an implicit challenge to the students and serves to engage them more fully in the task.

Each of the three questions in the assignment accomplishes a different purpose. The first asks students to define an abstract concept; in doing this, they will come to terms—in their own words—with the theme of the sequence. By answering question two, students will be doing some planning or self-coaching as well as devising a course of action for themselves. The third question allows students to convince themselves of the usefulness of problem-solving skills.

For this reflective assignment, I am grateful to Professor William E. Coles, Jr., of the University of Pittsburgh.)

3: The Problem and the Problem Solver

Directions: Take a coat hanger and bend it so that the point on the straight side opposite the crook now becomes the farthest point from the crook, as illustrated below.

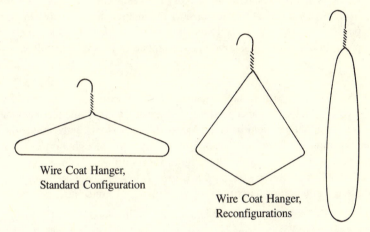

Wire Coat Hanger,
Standard Configuration

Wire Coat Hanger,
Reconfigurations

Next, suspend the coat hanger by the bent end from your index finger. The device will now be parallel to your body and perpendicular to the ground. Now balance a penny on the tip of the crook. Then twirl the entire device so that the coin stays in place while the coat hanger whirls around your finger.

Warning: attempt this feat in a large area that is free from breakable items (especially windows). Also, if you have an audience, please caution them to protect their eyes from flying objects—such as the penny, the coat hanger, your fist.

You have just solved a problem (or, at least, tried to solve it). Now, for *paper 3,* tell the rest of the class what it was like for you, by writing an account of your experience. In doing this, you might consider such things as the following.

How long did it take you? Did you ever want to give up? Where were you during your attempts? Were there distractions? Did this matter? Could you do it again after accomplishing it once? After several unsuccessful attempts, did you try any adjustments in your "style," and reconfigurations of your equipment, any modifications in your surroundings? What was your mental attitude? Did it affect your ability to do the task? Did your attitude change?

What part did concentration and determination play in your success at this task? Do you see any similarities in other tasks you have accomplished in life (for example, learning to ride a two-wheel bike, roller-skating, typing, and the like)? Do you see any similarities between this task and either or both of the two assignments we have done in this class so far?

(The third writing is a medial summary and builds from the experience of the previous assignments. It draws together concepts from the first two assignments, but focuses more directly on the agent, the *problem solver*. In some ways the task is a companion piece to assignment 1; however, this time the problem operates in the domain of motor skills. Assignment 3 is explicit in its invitation for the writer to consider the interrelationship between problem, process, and person. In addition, the writer is asked to look closely at the problem environment and the mental attitude of the problem solver.

4: Reflection

You have now written three papers on the problem solving process. I would like for you to read these papers and see if you can identify some recurrent ideas or comments about the problem-solving process. In other words, how are the thoughts of the papers alike? Then look back and see how the thoughts on the problem-solving process differ. Lastly, by drawing information from all three papers and by reconciling the differences, write a piece (*paper 4*) in which you try to come up with a composite definition or description of your own problem-solving process.

(This first of the "meta-assignments" is intended to give students an opportunity to assess what has gone before and to identify recurrent patterns in planning and performance. This task is built on the familiar rhetorical paradigm of comparison/contrast/synthesis.)

Unit II: Critical Thinking/Analytical Strategies

5: Identifying Parts

We have been talking for the past week about dividing "things" into their components. Analysis (or dividing something down into its parts) is a very powerful device for problem solving—as we saw in the solid geometry problem that we solved in class.

At times, we cannot solve a problem because we are not able to divide the situation into its elemental parts. In this case, we make the problem more difficult than it really is.

Almost everything has parts—even if it appears to be reduced to its lowest level. In fact, there are things that we deal with in our everyday life that we think are reduced to their ultimate constituents but which can still be divided. For example, go into a service station and have *exactly* one gallon of gas put into your car, pay for your purchase to the nearest penny, and then wait for your change. Or—as a second example—we are all used to dealing with conventional clocks or watches, so we tend to think of the smallest measurable unit of time as a second. But is it?

Your assignment for *paper 5* is to write a piece that contains a list of common items that can be divided beyond the state in which we are used to handling them. In collecting your data, you can use any sources you wish—books, personal observation, interviews with professors and students.

The rhetorical problem is how to present your long string of illustrations in connected prose—that is, in sentences and paragraphs. The audience for the paper is the class. However, you may use any *aim* (expressive, referential, persuasive, literary) that you want in writing this assignment.

A *small* prize will be given to the person who is able to give the most illustrations in the most rhetorically graceful form.

(Assignment 5 is the first in a new unit which asks students to practice analytical skills in problem solving and composing. This assignment calls for a relatively simple process of deconstruction of "bunched" concepts or images. Some writers find analysis difficult because they cannot see beyond the surface integrity of an item or idea. They also demonstrate "fixedness" in that they cannot perceive entities functioning in roles outside a well-defined context. "Fixedness" accounts for much of the difficulty in the ping-pong-ball-in-the-pipe problem. Or, as another example, some of us might remember having trouble with so-called "creativity" tests which asked such questions as: "List as many things as you can think of that you can do with a baseball."

Prior to this assignment, I spend some time working with the idea of *deconstruction*. For the most part, I use a deductive or top-down process: I suggest a higher-order generalization or abstraction and ask the students to "unpack" the idea. Through such exercises, the class also develops an appreciation for changing a frame of reference and for the relativity of such terms as *micro* and *macro*.)

6: Exploring Parts

Most problem-solving activity involves a process of inquiry—that is, a series of questions or operations that increases the chances of discovering a workable solution. Such a process serves several functions:

a. Aids the problem-solver in retrieving information stored in the mind.
b. Draws attention to important information that the problem-solver does not possess but can get through supplementary activities.
c. Prepares the problem-solver to discover an ordering principle for the information or to suggest an hypothesis for the solution of the problem.

In *Rhetoric: Discovery and Change,* authors Young, Becker, and Pike liken the process of inquiry to that used by a child:

When a very young child finds something that to him is strange and interesting—a telephone, a transistor radio, or a watch—he sets about trying to understand it. He turns it over in his hands, shakes it, drops it, puts it in his mouth, takes it apart and so on. Whatever adults may think of this, he is actually engaging in the very important activity of rendering the enigmatic world intelligible, and his initial efforts are devoted to accumulating as much relevant information as he can as quickly as possible. *(Rhetoric: Discovery and Change,* p. 121).

As adults, we use a similar procedure to assess a complex problem—but our manipulations are usually mental rather than physical. Through our ability to use language and our ability to shift perspectives deliberately, we can explore problematic data with speed and thoroughness by manipulating linguistic symbols and mental images.

In this exercise, you will practice analyzing a problem by shifting perspectives. Specifically, you will view a unit of experience under three different headings: (1) as a static *particle,* (2) as a dynamic *wave,* and (3) as a *field,* or network of relationships.

Select any handy object—a book, a table, an article of clothing—and for *paper 6* write a description of it first as a particle, next as a wave, and then as a field.

(The purpose of this assignment, "Exploring Parts," is to introduce students to a technique for systematically exploring an issue or entity. The task also continues the emphasis of the entire sequence on flexibility in shifting frames of reference. However, this assignment is much more sophisticated than the previous one because it implicitly requires a combination of analysis and classification.

I have had good results from using the tagmemic paradigm as an invention device. Students are very surprised by the amount of information this heuristic can generate on a given topic. As classroom preparation, I introduce the concept of "heuristic" and we identify some that are used in science, sports, journalism, and computer programming, as well as other areas of problem solving. We also practice using the tagmemic paradigm by analyzing several everyday objects that I bring into the classroom.

This assignment and its conceptual framework are adapted by permission of Richard E. Young from Richard E. Young, Alton L. Becker, and Kenneth L. Pike, *Rhetoric: Discovery and Change* [New York: Harcourt, Brace and World, Inc., 1970], pp. 119-135.)

7: *Operational Analysis*

For *paper 7,* write a short descriptive analysis of the device in the following illustration. First, examine the mechanism according to its parts (main parts and subparts, if any). Then, as a conclusion, turn your attention to the whole by describing how the complete mechanism functions while in use.

For this assignment, assume that your audience is a reasonably intelligent adult who has never seen such an apparatus before and is interested in your giving instructions on how to use it properly.

(In addition to the illustration, I give each student an eraser to examine. An ·operational analysis of it essentially involves an application of the concepts of analysis and classification discussed in the previous two assignments. In preparation for the written work, I introduce inductive logic (or "bottom-up" reasoning). We practice collecting facts and placing them in an interpretive framework. Then I spend part of the class leading a discussion on the implications of the Gestalt concept of the whole being greater than the sum of the parts, using some classic Gestalt demonstrations of perceptual unification such as | | | | ≠ ☐. I close with a quotation from Anatole Rapoport:

> A fact is valuable not for itself but because it can be put to work. All facts are related to other facts—and *it's the relationships that count.* Meaning in its most basic form is the association of one experience with another. (My emphasis)

At the next class session, we look at the variety of perceptions in the papers. What seemed to be a very simple task becomes more complex when students see that there is disagreement on such basic things as the number of major parts to the apparatus. This spurs some very interesting conversation about the nature of perception and writing.)

8: Causal Analysis

One useful technique in problem solving is to establish a cause (or causes) for a certain effect. This is done by examining a body of evidence to find a pattern of events linked closely enough that one can make an hypothesis about its origins.

Although this sounds like a fairly simple procedure, many situations cannot be easily explained. Consider, for example, these hypothetical conditions:

- The rate of unemployment keeps increasing.
- Applications for the freshman class at Rose-Hulman double in one year.
- Pedro Mendoza cannot read.

There are some pitfalls in reasoning that we may fall victim to while formulating hypotheses based on a cause and effect relationship. For example—

- Oversimplification

The rate of unemployment always rises when we have a Republican administration.

- Confusing Temporal Proximity with Causality
  After Rose-Hulman did away with final exams, the number of applications doubled—clear evidence that getting rid of finals attracts students.
- Jumping to Conclusions Based on Inadequate Evidence
  Pedro Mendoza cannot read because he is from a Puerto Rican family.

These and other pitfalls aside, formulating hypotheses about the causes of a certain problem can be a powerful means for suggesting a solution, as you will get a chance to see in the following paper assignment.

For *paper 8,* write a letter to the editor of the Rose-Hulman *Thorn* (the campus newspaper) in which you hypothesize the cause(s) of a particular problem on campus. For example, you might write on one of these topics:

- Increased theft of books from the library.
- Lack of parking space on campus.
- Poor quality and/or quantity of food in the cafeteria.
- Limited access to computer time.
- Boring weekends.
- The basketball team's recent losing streak.

In writing your causal analysis, you may want to include some suggestions for solving the problem. You are free to select whatever "problem" you feel you can best write about, but you *must* select a subject that is of common interest to everyone on campus. In other words, finding a ride home for next weekend is more your problem than it is a shared concern of your classmates.

(This task asks students to identify the parts of a complex situation and to formulate an hypothesis about their relationship. Once again, the assignment is a variation of the classification/analysis principle used in this segment of the sequence—only this time, the application takes place on a higher level of abstraction. "Causal Analysis" is a companion piece to "Operational Analysis" in that the students must "unpack" the *given* and examine the relationship of the parts in order to formulate a meaningful integration.)

9: Reflection

In the four papers from this unit, you have used some methods of analysis and classification to find the functional parts of an entity or situation and the relationship of these parts—both to one another and to the thing as a whole. Select any one of these four pieces and for *paper 9* write an operational analysis of its parts. Use the same set of directions that I gave you for the eraser in assignment 7, namely:

Write a short descriptive analysis of the accompanying device (your paper). First, examine the mechanism according to its parts (main parts and subparts, if any). Then, as a conclusion, turn your attention to the whole by describing how the complete mechanism functions while in use.

(The causal analysis ends the second spiral of the course, and this assignment is intended to help students pull together some of the strategies they have used in the preceding eight writings. The previous meta-assignment (4) required students to analyze themselves as problem solvers. This meta-task invites students to apply analytical techniques to a text viewed as an artifact. By this point in the sequence, I hope to have drawn together by implication and by analogy the dual process of problem solving and composing.)

Unit III: Creative Play/Strategies for Synthesis

10: Visual Constructs

Look carefully at the ink blot for several minutes. What do you see there? Write out your interpretation so that your reader can see what you see.

(Any Rorschach ink blot, such as the one on the cover of Walker Gibson's text, will serve for this exercise.)

Now, for *paper 10,* force yourself to make a different interpretation—a different "reading" of these shapes. Write out your new interpretation as before. (Adapted by permission of Walker Gibson from *Seeing and Writing* [2nd ed.; New York: David McKay Co., 1974], p. 36.)

(This is the first task in a new unit whose theme is that language, because it can shape and create reality, is one of our most powerful devices for changing a frame of reference. In preparing for this assignment, the students and I discuss visualization as a problem-solving mode. I find anecdotes from the scientific world helpful in teaching this concept. For example, the falling apple gave Newton an image with which he could see the relationship among vast bodies in the solar system. Or, Torricelli imagined a sea of air, which allowed him to correct Galileo's concept of the actions of gases. Or, William Harvey worked out the principles of the human circulatory system by visualizing the heart and arteries as a pump, subject to the limitations of any other kind of pump. Or, as a last example, the particle and wave theory from modern optical physics allows the scientist to define *light* as a stream of bullets, but when this image proves inadequate, to redefine *light* as waves. I then lead the conversation to some of the ideas of Benjamin Lee Whorf on how language structures perception.)

11: Verbal Constructs

Reverse logic or applying a new frame of reference to solve a problem is frequently the principle behind the verbal challenge of riddles or anagrams or other more esoteric forms of word play.

Riddles: Riddles serve a useful purpose in reminding us, if we need reminding, that things are not always what they seem.

What wears shoes, but has no feet?
What has four legs and flies?
Which is the strongest day of the week?
Which candles burn longer—wax or tallow?
What can't you say without breaking it?
Why is the Panama Canal like the first U in cucumber?
How many bushel baskets full of earth can you take out of a hole two feet
    square and two feet deep?
What words can be pronounced quicker and shorter by adding another syllable
    to them?
What is it that is always coming but never arrives?
How long will an eight-day clock run without winding?

Puns: Puns involve any kind of play on the meaning of words, as you can see
from "Tom Swifties." Tom Swift's creator, Edward Stratemeyer, died in 1930, yet
Tom's name lives on in the form of "Tom Swifties," or adverbial puns.

"I'm glad I passed my electrocardiogram," said Tom wholeheartedly.
"No, Eve, I won't touch that apple," said Tom adamantly.

Anyone can play. Try your hand at a few.
..., said Tom dryly.
..., said Tom tensely.
..., said Tom infectiously.
..., said Tom intently.
..., said Tom gravely.
..., said Tom transparently.
..., said Tom hospitably.
..., said Tom hoarsely.
..., said Tom figuratively.
..., said Tom weakly.

Anagrams: Anagrams conceal words by scrambling the letters of which they
are made. Here are some scrambled cities of the United States; how many of them
can you get?

1. ccaghio	5. leledncva
2. bnotos	6. ttdrioe
3. aabynl	7. cciiinnnta
4. ttsgrbuihp	8. nulluoho

Rearrange the following groups of letters into words.
1. ganre
2. taril
3. dry oxtail in rear

Now that you've had a chance at making and unscrambling some bits of word
play, it's time to turn your hand to making a more extended verbal construct. Here,

then, is the situation.

You are a "Sand Dolphin," a species of intelligent beings, as yet unknown to people, that live mainly in the South Seas. One day you discover a well-preserved 1974 Volkswagen "Bug" lying in ten feet of water. Of course, you don't know it's a VW. One door is open and swinging slightly in the current. Nothing on the VW is obviously broken. Where did it come from? You don't know and neither does anyone else. Perhaps it fell off a ship transporting it.

The Sand Dolphins have a highly developed culture, complete with an elaborate communication system. It is your responsibility to report the objects you have found to the Ministry of USO (Unidentified Sunken Objects).

The members of the Ministry—like you—look, feel, and (most important) *think* like sea creatures. For instance, their idea of measurement is based upon the dimensions and physiology of a fish. They would never describe any object as being so many "feet" long.

Taking a Sand Dolphin's stance, write (for *paper 11*) a report to the ministry describing *in detail* the object you have found. You may use or ignore the fact that dolphins are mammals.

(From *Strategies of Rhetoric,* 3rd Edition, by A.M. Tibbets and Charlene Tibbets. Copyright © 1979, 1974, 1969 by Scott Foresman. Reprinted by permission. See pp. 33-34.)

(The language games, which we do in class, raise the students' awareness of words—their meaning and their potential. I designed this assignment to show that language itself becomes a lens and that by changing our words we frequently can alter our perception. If time permits, I use a classroom exercise in which each student must select a scientific law, principle, or phenomenon (such as the Second Law of Thermodynamics, or Brownian Motion) and explain it under very rigid language constraints (for example, all simple sentences, or no words over two syllables). We then compare the results and discuss the nature of language as a representation of "reality.")

12: *Reasoning Analogically*

The world is in a constant flux around and in us, but in order to grapple with the floating reality, we create in our thought, or at any rate in our language, certain more or less fixed points, certain averages. Reality never presents us with an average but language does.

—Otto Jespersen

Of course there are a thousand ways to talk *about* time. You can even talk *to* time—"O time, arrest your flight! and you, propitious hours, arrest your course! Let us savor the fleeting delights of our most beautiful days!"—says the poet Lamartine.

The terms available for describing time are practically infinite, and one reason for this may be that you can't see time at all, directly. All you can do is sense it through signs: the alternation of day and night, the regular drips from a faucet, your heart beat, the movement of the sun across the sky, changes of season, the movement of the hands of a clock, phases of the moon, the rotations of the planets, the graying of your hair, the numbers on a desk calendar. In other words, you can interpret certain images that your senses give you, and you call that *time*. Or, to use Otto Jespersen's idea, we create fixed points and regularized measurements in the chaos of reality through image and language(s).

In this exercise you are going to try to "see" time in one particular set of terms—a measurement of numbers that is, perhaps, unlike the scale we are used to "seeing." To see things as numbers, to measure things, is a way of seeing that enjoys enormous prestige in our age, and it suggests all the dramatic improvements of life that have accompanied the growth of science. Whatever else it is that scientists do, one thing they obviously do is measure things, so that the world becomes defined in relation to an organization of statistical language.

How can you express time? You have to have a device, an instrument of some sort, and in the case of measuring the durations and divisions of time, the instrument is called a chronometer. Then you communicate your various readings of this instrument by making use of a scale of measurement.

On reserve are three pieces on the measurement of time—using conventional and unconventional devices and involving conventional and unconventional scales. After you have read these essays, consider ways in which you could measure time if all the "normal" timepieces on earth suddenly disappeared. Think about the natural resources that are available to help you—water, earth, wind, celestial light, and the like. Also, consider the laws of nature (such as gravity) that might aid you in designing a chronometer.

List of articles on library reserve:

J. T. Fraser, "Delightful Early Clockshops: When Time and Life Began," *Science Digest* (June 1980), pp. 70 ff.

Issac Asimov, "Point in Time of No Return," *Science Digest* (July 1980), pp. 64 ff.

David Park, "But What is a Clock," *Science Digest* (August 1980), pp. 38 ff.

Building a Chronometer

Build your own chronometer. Use paper clips, cardboard, pencil stubs, ping-pong balls, whatever your ingenuity can devise. Then run a series of tests with your instrument, using a scale of measurement of your own invention. You may calibrate your timepiece to a conventional scale—but remember that all "clocks" as we know them have disappeared from the face of the earth. During our next meeting, you will present your prototypic timepiece to the class.

Reporting on a Chronometer (paper 12)

After you have designed your chronometer and presented it to the class, modify it according to the advice you received from your classmates. Then run a second series of tests with it—once again using a scale of measurement of your own invention in order to calculate time.

Next, write up your experiment in the form of a lab report. Your report should include an "Introduction," an account of "Materials and Methods," an ordering of "Results," and some "Discussion." Be sure to include in your report a definition of time that arises directly from the method you have devised for reading it.

(Returning to the idea of language and analogy, I present some of the material from J. Robert Oppenheimer's address to the American Psychological Association entitled "The Analogy of Science." I also talk about scientific discoveries that were made through analogical reasoning. For example, Gutenberg combined the techniques of the wine-press and the seal to produce the printing press. And Kepler formulated the role of the sun in planetary movement by drawing a parallel with the role of the Father in the Trinity.

The task of building a chronometer invites the writers to discover new applications of previously known concepts and to perceive the "relatedness" of things in the concrete and abstract worlds. The rhetorical task makes use of a format well-known to the students, but I intend that the novelty of the hands-on experience will cause them to view the formula with new eyes. In addition, much as in assignment 3, this writing task asks students to see connections between experience and rhetoric, between doing and writing.

The tasks of building a chronometer, reporting its measurements, and reflecting on such activities [12 and 13] are adapted by permission of Walker Gibson from his comparable assignments with an anemometer that can be found in "Seeing the Wind" and "Wind as Science," in *Seeing and Writing* [2nd edition; New York: David McKay Co., 1974], pp. 158-173.)

13: Role-Playing

"Lost time is never found again."—Benjamin Franklin

"Dost thou love life? Then do not squander Time, for that's the stuff Life is made of."—Benjamin Franklin

"Backward, turn backward, O Time in your flight, Make me a child again just for tonight."—Elizabeth Akers Allen

"All books are divisible into two classes: the books of the hour, and the books of all time."—John Ruskin

"Time which antiquates, and hath an art of making dust of all things."—Sir Thomas Browne

"Lives of great men all remind us
    We can make our lives sublime
And, departing, leave behind us
    Footprints on the sands of time."—Henry Wadsworth Longfellow

"To every thing there is a season,
And a time to every purpose under the heaven:
A time to be born, and a time to die;
A time to plant, and a time to pluck up that which is planted;
A time to kill, and a time to heal;
A time to break down, and a time to build up;
A time to weep, and a time to laugh;
A time to mourn, and a time to dance;
A time to cast away stones, and a time to gather stones together;
A time to embrace, and a time to refrain from embracing;
A time to get, and a time to lose;
A time to keep, and a time to cast away;
A time to rend, and a time to sew;
A time to keep silence, and a time to speak;
A time to love, and a time to hate;
A time of war, and a time of peace.—Ecclesiastes, 2:24

* * *

A stitch in time...
It was the best of times, it was the worst of times...
Signs of the time
Doing time
Father time
Fountain of time
Making time
Marking time
Time heals all wounds
Time waits for no man
Time flies when you're having fun
Time's a wastin'
The time of your life
Hard times

* * *

Who really knows the time? I mean really know time in the fullest sense of the term? A few days ago you worked on a homemade chronometer and you measured time—after a fashion. But do you really know what time it is? Even now, with your extremely accurate digital wristwatch, do you really know time? Do you know what happened in the past? Where did that time go? What kind of a record did you leave with past time? More importantly, do you know anything about future time?

We can describe time—or at least describe its effects—in ways other than using a chronometer. Harlan Ellison and John Livingston Lowes have written accounts of the effects and measurements of time—and you will find their work on reserve in the library.

But there might be even another way to describe time, and that would be *to become* time. For *paper 13,* then, I want you to write a piece in which you role play time. You can be any measurement you want, from a few seconds, to "billions and billions" of years.

A three-page account of your *timely* experiences is due next week.

(Many times a problem can be more easily solved if imagination and creative play are used. More specifically, sometimes new insights are gained if we shift our frame of reference by adopting—or role-playing—another point of view. This may involve a flight of imagination into the impossible, or at least into the not immediately feasible. However, it is not always easy to slip out of our traditional frame of reference and into the perception of someone or something else. As warm-up exercises for the written work, I use sections from William J. J. Gordon's *Synectics* and excerpts from Edwin A. Abbott's *Flatland.* The material on reserve in the library is Harlan Ellison's " 'Repent, Harlequin!' Said the Ticktockman," and John Livingston Lowes' "Time in the Middle Ages," from *Backgrounds and Horizons of Geoffrey Chaucer,* 1934.)

14: Reflection

For *paper 14,* I'd like you to write a piece that deals with the following questions.

In the four papers from this unit, you have used some techniques of synthesis to create new meanings from old configurations. Read through these papers. How has your *problem-solving awareness* changed as a result of these four assignments? (If you do not think that it has changed, then write from this perspective.)

Now read through these papers again. How has your *composing process* changed as a result of these four assignments? It might be helpful for you to use your papers from assignments 5 through 8 as a basis for comparison. (If you do not think that your writing has changed, then answer from this perspective.)

And last, suggest ways in which you think the composing process and problem solving might be mutually complementary. (If you do not think that they are related, then write from this perspective.)

(This last meta-task is a final attempt to have the students construct a meaningful parallel in their own minds between problem solving and composing. Since the perception of the relationship is really up to the individual author, this assignment is left purposefully vague and open-ended.)

Unit IV: Culmination

15: Planning Solutions and Consolidating Gains

(In preparation for this assignment, the students have read Robert Heinlein's sci-fi short story, "The Roads Must Roll.")

The "problems" and the strategies we have been looking at in the previous eight weeks were all concerned either with past or present situations. However, many times inventors and problem solvers must consider what, if any, long-term effects a particular solution or choice of behavior will have for the future. For example, Robert Heinlein's "The Roads Must Roll," is a depiction of what life would be like in the U.S. if an alternate form of moving people and goods (by conveyor belts) completely dominated our transportation system. In fact, this kind of fictionalized testing of hypotheses is at the heart of much sci-fi literature.

In business and industry, policy makers do not actually write science-fiction in order to visualize the ramifications of their decisions (although some "future studies" come pretty close): Instead, they work out a "scenario." This may be as simple as an account or synopsis of a projected course of action or as elaborate as a motion picture script. Scenarios are not mere flights of fancy; they represent their creators' "best guess." As such, they can be highly sophisticated because they combine the imagination of the poet and the precision of the mathematician.

Let's try our hand at constructing a scenario—on a very limited scale. Here is a hypothetical situation:

> You work for Global Transit, a high-technology corporation which specializes in developing innovative passenger-carrying transportation.
>
> Your R & D unit uses morphological analysis to generate new ideas. That is, you use a "parameters cube" to invent new methods for moving people from one place to another. Three parameters (power source, type of passenger "seating," and the medium in which the vehicle operates) are listed on three axes of the cube (illustrated below).

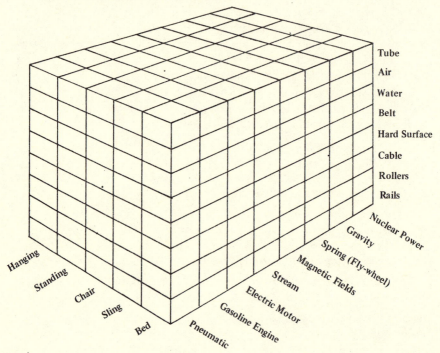

Some combinations have already been fully developed: for example, a steam-driven system that runs on rails and has passengers sitting in chairs. Select one which has not, and work up a rough draft of how it operates. Make sure you consult the list of questions and considerations that accompanies this assignment.

(Reprinted from *Conceptual Blockbusting: A Guide to Better Ideas*, Second Edition, by James L. Adams, with the permission of W.W. Norton and Company, Inc. Copyright © 1974, 1976, 1979 by James L. Adams. See p. 110.)

Following is a list of questions that you should consider carefully in the process of constructing your scenario.

1. What are the technical aspects of your transportation system? Explain them as best you can—certainly to the same degree of sophistication as used in "The Roads Must Roll."
2. How will the ordinary citizen of your society be affected by this new form of transportation? (Like Heinlein, let's not get too carried away by postulating that people—and their lifestyles—are going to be radically different in the future. Let's pretty much stick to the given of past experience and common sense.)
   a. What will be the major concerns about safety? About comfort? About convenience? About cost? (In making evaluations of this kind, even in our "wildest imagination," we need a benchmark—so you will have to implicitly use the world and public as we know them today as your point of comparison.)
   b. What will life-styles be like—that is, work schedules, places of employment, types of employment, family life?
   c. What is your system of distribution of goods and services?
   d. What are the demographic patterns like—that is, city, suburban, and country population figures, age figures, migration rates, etc.?
   e. Are there social classes? What is the distribution of wealth?
   f. Is the fuel for your transportation system a controlled or scarce commodity?
3. How important is transportation in this society? Who will control the use of the system?
4. Is your system saturated during certain times of the day, or is the flow even and predictable?
5. Is this mass transportation or individual vehicles? (You may have *one* primary system. But you could, under special circumstances, have variations on a single principle.)
6. Are there environmental factors which must be taken into consideration?
7. Is your system designed for long distance traveling or for short hauls? Or is it equally effective for both?

By the end of today, you will have worked out a fairly good "scenario" of your new mode of transportation. By then, you will have been able to envision many social, economic, and political benefits deriving from your new system.

But public opinion is the most important factor in determining whether or not your new system is fully used. We all know that the public is very often reluctant to try something new—particularly if the new item is unconventional as well as novel. This was the case with the opening of the Bay Area Rapid Transit (BART) in San Francisco and the METRO in Washington, D.C.—even though neither could be considered a radical mode of transportation. Both the BART and the METRO public relations offices tried to overcome negative opinion by publishing a brochure on the system.

Your new hypothetical situation is this: you have been temporarily transferred to the public relations division of Global Transit to help write a brochure which will convince the public that your new transportation system is safe, comfortable, convenient, and cost-competitive. This brochure, *paper 15,* is your final piece of writing for the course and thus a culmination of all the writing you have done previously in the course.

Bring in a rough draft of your brochure for your group to critique during the next class session.

Following is a list of questions that you should consider carefully in the process of composing your brochure.

1. What persona are you going to adopt? (Engineer, salesman, man on the street, other?)
2. What voice will be most effective?
3. What is your audience like?
4. In what areas of the population are you likely to find the greatest amount of resistance to your transportation system? Why?
5. What are the three most "fearful" things about your new system, as far as the public is concerned?
6. What is your method of distributing this brochure? How does that determine who will read it?
7. What type of information is likely to convince your audience that the system is a good one?
8. Do you need to use some graphics or some art work? What type?
9. How much technical information do you want to include?
10. What kind of sentence structure do you want? Diction? Paragraph length?

(For the first part of this assignment, I set up small groups of three or four students who brainstorm together for two class sessions. The writing of an individual scenario based on these deliberations allows the students to work with a text that considers long-term effects of a particular choice of behavior but, at the same time, is imaginative and fanciful. [Kenneth L. Pike's "Science Fiction as a Test of Axioms Concerning Human Behavior," *Parma Eldalamberon,* 3 (1973), 6-7, is helpful for suggesting ways in which science fiction can be seen as hypothesis-testing scenarios.]

The second half of the assignment requires the writer to convince a particular audience about the merits of a new technology. It is a more formal exercise in that students must attend to the demands of good persuasive writing by considering purpose, audience, and persona. I intend for this paper to be the culmination of all that has gone before.)

Writing, Learning, and Military Training

John Thomson and William McCarron

We tell cadets at the Air Force Academy that while not all officers will fly, all officers will write; and that while the writing produced by Air Force officers consists mostly of technical reports and staff studies, the writing that first-year cadets most need to practice is essentially personal. This paradox, of course, takes them by surprise, for much of their immediately prior experience has led cadets to think of personal writing as having little or nothing to do with their performance in academic and professional situations. Their high school experience, as Emig, Moffett, and others have noted, puts a high premium on performance in formalistic and artificial modes of discourse. As if to confirm the priority of these models, the college catalogues and military announcements that they read before coming to the Academy invariably favor a bureaucratic style. And when they begin taking freshman composition in the fall, they have just completed six weeks of Basic Cadet Training, during which their freedom of speech has been limited to a few formulaic statements signifying obedience to authority. So it is not surprising that cadets often find themselves initially somewhat confused by our stress on personal writing.

By emphasizing personal writing, we seem to many cadets to be telling them the very opposite of what they are being told in military training, where the emphasis is on teamwork and subordination of self to a larger unit. If our teaching seems contradictory or subversive, it is only superficially so. Through practice in personal writing that draws heavily on their experience as cadets, we want our students to develop and clarify their thinking about what it will mean to be a career officer in the Air Force. We want them, for example, to confront the issues that typically arise out of the conflict between an individual's desire for personal expression and the military's need for corporate loyalty. This dilemma is, after all, one that these cadets will struggle with in one form or another, in one situation or another, throughout their professional lives. Ultimately, then, we stress personal writing because we believe it is fundamental to the development of thoughtful—and thereby responsible—military officers. Writing is a way of learning in military life no less than in any other domain.[1]

In keeping with this philosophy, about half of the assignments in our sixteen-exercise sequence have an expressive-exploratory aim, and most of those which are not expressive draw nonetheless on personal experience or observation. The world of military experience figures most prominently in our sequence not only because it is important for young cadets to ponder its implications in writing, but also because cadet life itself is very intense, demanding, and provocative. It is a continuingly fresh and vivid source of material for our students—a common body of experience that they are eager to share in writing. So, our assignments always invite cadets to consider aspects and implications of their life at the Academy. In the present version of the sequence, for example, we ask them to write about Basic Cadet Training, about familiar places at the Academy, about military traditions, and in the research project about military careers. As a counterpoint to this dominant subject matter, we also call upon cadets to write about the experience of art and literature. But whether we are asking our students to write about imaginative experience or about military life, our goal is to have them experience writing as a means both of understanding and of shaping their world.

This goal is immediately evident in the first part of the sequence (1-4), a cluster of topically related assignments that focus on Basic Cadet Training (BCT), the indoctrination to military life that Cadets go through right before the start of their freshman year at the Academy. These four assignments provoke cadets to think about the implications of BCT by having them write about it for various audiences and purposes. The first assignment, for example, which gives them an opportunity to write an expressive piece for their classmates, requires that they do so in terms of a particular time during BCT when they felt the "loss" of their "rights" or when they "enjoyed a privilege" that they had previously considered a right. This focus on freedom and discipline, on rights and privileges, continues in the second assignment, but is complicated by the fact that in this case cadets must write to a skeptical civilian friend, explaining why "the experience of BCT" has led them to "think it was a good decision" to trade their "rights for privileges." Yet another complication is introduced in the third assignment, which calls for cadets to write the squadron commander recommending and making the case for a particular change in BCT, such as a privilege being turned back into a right. And the fourth exercise calls for an entirely new point of view on the experience by directing cadets to consider whether BCT is "merely a rite of passage." This first cluster, then,

---

[1]Like the other courses in this collection, ours is tailored not only to our students but also to the staff members who teach it. The fifteen officer-instructors who make up our freshman composition staff come to us for the most part with little knowledge of discourse theory or the teaching of writing. So, of course, we offer them guidance in summer workshops and in weekly sessions during the semester. So, too, we have adopted for them, as much as for the students, a textbook organized according to the aims of discourse, namely Scholes and Comley, *The Practice of Writing* (New York: St. Martin's Press, 1981). Still, we emphasize to both staff and students that the "real" textbook is the sequence of exercises and responses to them. So, as we continue to teach the sequence, we continue to learn how to teach it, and we continue to shape and refine it based on our experience.

introduces cadets to writing not only as a means of achieving various rhetorical purposes, but also as a way of coming to understand various aspects of experience.

The epistemic dimension of writing is explored in further detail by the second cluster of assignments (5-7), which engages cadets in composing pieces about familiar places and images. The cluster begins, for example, with an assignment that invites them to write a piece describing their "favorite place" at the Academy (5), and typically this place turns out to be their own room, if only because it is a refuge from upperclassmen. As it happens, every freshman cadet's room by regulation is identical, yet their descriptions are often markedly different. And these differences provide a vivid means of demonstrating how feelings color perception and perception, in turn, determines the selection and arrangement of descriptive detail. A similar purpose is served by the next assignment (6), which calls on cadets to describe one of the places in their home town that is personally "important" to them. Here, too, they are faced with an opportunity that builds on the experience of prior exercises (1 and 5) to demonstrate the importance of focusing and detail in composition. Without adequate focus and detail, their classmates will be unable to perceive and to understand their home town place, however important they claim it to be. The complex interplay of perception, thought, feeling, and writing is brought home to cadets in yet another register by the final exercise in this cluster (7), which asks them to look at a painting—in particular a slide of Edward Hopper's "Nighthawks"—and then to write an essay about it, telling what they see in the painting, how it makes them feel, and what they consider to be an appropriate title for the painting. This well-known picture of a late night tavern scene readily provokes very strong, though differing, feelings within students, and lacking a title—a "frame" through which to view and interpret it—they naturally deal with it in terms of their own associations and reactions. So, their interpretations are formed partly by what they see on the canvas and partly by what is in their heads, as they come to recognize by comparing their pieces in class discussion.

The next cluster (8-10) uses literary experience to help students understand how personal reactions—both perceptions and feelings—form the bases of insight and analysis. The cluster begins, for example, by having students write about their reactions to Dylan Thomas' "Do Not Go Gentle into That Good Night." In asking students to tell what the poem makes them feel, this assignment (8) like the one on Hopper's "Nighthawks" is frankly expressive. But in asking them to account for their reactions by focusing on details in the poem, the assignment also has a referential orientation that is intended to build on the descriptive tasks that figure in the previous cluster. (This assignment also entails writing about another work that uses the image of night in a richly metaphoric sense.) Having experienced the complexly varied truth of their own differing perceptions, cadets are then faced in the next assignment (9) with a poem that is self-evidently concerned with the problematic relation of perception and reality—namely Wallace Stevens' "Thirteen Ways of Looking at a Blackbird." And in this assignment, rather than being invited to write about their reactions to the poem, they are asked to enact the truth of the poem itself by writing yet another stanza for it, "a fourteenth way of looking at a

·

blackbird." After entering into the imaginative world of Stevens' poem, cadets are then invited to use imagination in the service of their own point of view and experience, by writing a beast fable "about some aspect of cadet life" (10).

By inviting a fable about cadet life, we intend, of course, for students to draw upon the imaginative experience that has formed their reading and viewing for the immediately preceding assignments (7-9), as well as upon the earlier activities of writing about Basic Cadet Training (1-4). The beast fable also serves as a prelude to the next brief cluster (11-12), which calls on cadets to use their critical imagination in two different kinds of futurist planning with respect to the Academy and the Air Force. In the first case (11), they are asked to write a letter to the superintendent explaining why they believe "intercollegiate athletics at USAFA should be discontinued or maintained." In the next piece (12), they are asked to imagine themselves as offering advice to the planners of a new military academy which will train officers for a new service, the U.S. Aerospace Force.

Futurist thinking, in turn, provides the basis for the research cluster of assignments (13-15). Cadets are naturally curious to know what, besides flying, Air Force officers do, if only because they are curious about what they themselves might do upon graduation from the Academy. So, we have them interview an officer about whose job they want to know more, and from the report of that interview (13) the subject of their final research paper (15) eventually emerges. As an intermediate stage in the research process, we ask them to submit a prospectus (14) in which they can report on their initial findings and look forward to possible conclusions. But as we make clear to students in our lengthy initial commentary on the research cluster, we want them to see it as different from the usual go-to-the-library-and-take-notes-research-paper that so often provides the culminating activity of traditional freshman writing courses. Instead of the usual emphasis on artifacts—on notecards, outlines, and part-to-whole drafts—we focus on the process of inquiry. Our purpose, in other words, is to allow the subject itself and the students' discoveries about it to guide their seeing and thinking about the project. And one of their discoveries, we hope, is that writing, such as they do in 13 and 14, is an important guide to the learning and thinking they embody in their final approach to the paper (15).

In much the same spirit as the research cluster, the final assignment in the course (16), adapted from William Coles' *Teaching Composing,* invites students to assess their own writing—to discover through writing what they have learned about writing, about thinking, and about being in the military world.[2]

WRITING, LEARNING, AND MILITARY TRAINING

1. Well, here you are—the cream of the crop, or what's left of it. Just a few months ago you were seniors in high school. Remember how much freedom you had in those days? Well, the freedoms that in high school you took as rights have now

---

[2]William Coles, *Teaching Composing* (Rochelle Park, N.J.: Hayden Books, 1974), pp. 176–178.

become privileges, haven't they? And the first exposure you had to the loss of freedoms as rights was during BCT.

Was there a time during BCT when your inability to exercise your freedom was especially painful? Tell us about it.

Perhaps, instead, you'd rather write about a freedom you enjoyed during BCT. Was there a time when you especially enjoyed a privilege? Tell us about it.

Whatever the occasion, try to make us feel what it was like to be you.

In all assignments for this course, assume your audience is the rest of the class, unless the assignment tells you otherwise.

2. Remember the day you finally decided that, yes, you were going to attend USAFA? Remember how your family and friends reacted? A few tears, perhaps? Lots of pride, I bet. Maybe your girlfriend or boyfriend choked back a sob and smiled bravely. Through all the adulation, did you notice that there was one person (at least) who didn't understand why you wanted to go to a place like the Academy? Maybe that person thought you were crazy. During BCT you probably had a few moments when you thought you were crazy, too.

For this exercise, try to persuade that person that you made the right decision *for you*. Notice that we're not asking you to try to persuade him or her to join you at the "Blue Zoo." Simply write a personal letter that explains why you traded your rights for privileges and why the experience of BCT makes you think it was a good decision.

Before you write, read the following statement from the official Air Force Academy catalog:

> If you become a cadet, you will be sworn into the Air Force soon after you arrive at the Academy. Your ability to live under military discipline will be tested during the next six weeks when you undergo a rigorous indoctrination to military life. This program called BCT (Basic Cadet Training) is led by upperclass cadets under the supervision of Air Force Officers. The training is highly demanding, mentally and physically. It will continually challenge you and test your endurance, but you can prove equal to the expectations. The cadets who have the least problems are those who are willing to adapt to their new life and put forth their best efforts to succeed. If you successfully complete BCT, you will become a member of the Air Force Cadet Wing and begin the fall semester as a fourth class cadet.
>
> Completing BCT is an accomplishment for which you can be justly proud, yet the requirements for you as an Academy cadet are only beginning. Now you must concentrate your full attention on the education and training which will continue for four years. You must abide by military rules that restrict your personal activities, and you must meet required standards of performance in all phases of the curriculum.

I suppose all college catalogs sound like an institution speaking, but will that sort of "voice" convince your friend?

In response to the obvious question: Yes, I recognize it's possible that BCT did *not* make you think that trading your rights for privileges was a good decision. Your friend, however, wants to know why you're still here.

3. Are you one of those people who said that giving up the right to drink a Coke any time you wanted helped make the world safe for democracy? Were you embarrassed after writing that, when you realized what a fantastic logical leap you'd made? Good. You're about to write a letter to the Commandant of Cadets, and you don't want to embarrass yourself in front of him. It's good you had a chance to practice with your friend.

Did writing the last two exercises bring back memories? (Maybe they didn't—the mind has a wonderful capacity to block out painful ones.) We hope that your creative juices are flowing, for this is another chance to draw on your BCT experiences. Perhaps there's a privilege you ran across during BCT that ought to be a right—or that ought to be abolished. As an ambitious cadet, you decide to try your hand at suggesting a change in the current system. After all, even though the military isn't democratic, the country it's a part of is.

Write an official letter to your squadron commander, your AOC, and the Commandant of Cadets, *in turn,* explaining what aspect of BCT should be changed or eliminated, and why.

4. We've been asking you about the rights and privileges that you live with these days. In Ralph Ellison's "Battle Royal" a young black man is asked to deliver a speech to the local men's club, which is composed of all the prominent white men in his town. Before he's allowed to deliver the speech, though, the young black man, along with a number of his peers, must undergo a series of humiliating initiations for the entertainment of the white men. Although the white men are motivated in part by racial prejudice, the experiences that the young man is required to undergo are similar to the experiences that all young men and young women undergo. For any organization—religious, fraternal, social, or military—that you may wish to join will require you to undergo a ritual initiation, a "rite of passage."

Can you see the main character in "Battle Royal" engaged in a struggle for rights and recognition? Can you see similarities between the experience undergone by the protagonist and the experience you underwent during BCT? Can you describe BCT as an initiation experience? Is BCT merely a rite of passage?

Or, if the parallels between "Battle Royal" and your BCT experience seem remote or strained, try your hand at a personal account of BCT that might replace the "official" version from the Academy Catalogue that we quoted in exercise 2.

5. During the last four exercises we've asked you to examine your experiences during BCT, because personal experience and observation are fundamental sources from which to draw material in writing any kind of paper. As you quickly learned, BCT is an experience you all share, but no two of your accounts were the same. Because you're different people, your perceptions of the world around you are different. Let's take a break from writing about your feelings on rights and privileges

and spend some time examining—examining through writing—your perceptions of the world around us.

    a.   Go to your favorite place at the Academy. Look at it. (Yes, I know you've seen it before, but you've got to see it again. This is the most important part of the exercise. Some of you will be tempted to skip it, but how responsible would that be—to yourself and to us who want to see, in writing, what you have seen?)

    b.   Write down what you see. No seeing can take place except in time and space, so we should be able to tell when you saw it and where you were located when you saw it. The object of this exercise is to get your readers to see what you see, to understand your perceptions.

    c.   Return to your typewriter and write up what you saw, so we can see it.

6. Your view of a place at the Academy, we discovered, is often influenced by your feelings about the Academy. Are you one of the writers who described his or her room, sterile and impersonal as it is, simply because it's a place where you can escape the pressures of upperclassmen, AOC's, and instructors?

In this exercise, write about your home town. Are you homesick? How much of that feeling will color your writing and your perspective? Maybe your home town isn't a place tourists would go out of their way to see. Still, it's important to you, and one or two places in your home town are no doubt especially important to you. Describe one of those places. Since you're the person to whom that place matters, your description ought to let us know why you perceive that place as important, as well as what it looks like.

7. John Updike, an American writer who has twice won the Pulitzer Prize for fiction, has said that a writer is someone who loves the world and wants to describe it. Look back for a moment at the two descriptions you've recently written. Does your writing show a love for the world?

You all know the story of Daedalus and Icarus. Some of you may even have seen a painting by the 16th century Flemish painter Pieter Breughel titled *The Fall of Icarus*. Two 20th century American poets have written poems about this painting, and the painting, as well as the poems, can be found in your text. Can you tell that Breughel loved the world? Isn't it apparent that the two poets understood and shared in Breughel's love of the world as well?

In a few moments you're going to see a slide of another painting. When you do, make some notes to yourself about how the artist who painted this painting sees the world. Does he love the world? What's he describing? What do you see in the painting? And what title does the painting deserve?

Tell us how this painting makes you feel. Use the title you think appropriate for the painting as the title of your essay.

8. Most of you were surprised to learn that the title of the painting you wrote about in the last exercise was *Nighthawks,* by Edward Hopper. Does knowing the title affect the way you see the painting? The title is, after all, a clue to the way the artist

or writer wants the work seen or read. In Dylan Thomas' poem "Do Not Go Gentle into That Good Night" the title doesn't help us much at all, since it's simply the first line of the poem taken as a title. Well, maybe it does help—after all, Thomas could have called the poem anything he wanted, but *chose* to use the first line.

More important for understanding the poem, probably, is the meaning of "night." Does Thomas use the image of night in any way like Hooper uses the image of night? For this exercise write about your reactions to "Do Not Go Gentle...." In writing about your reactions, you don't necessarily have to analyze the poem. It's interesting, for example, to know that the poem is a villanelle, "a strict form with only two rhyming sounds," but is that really primary to the emotional reaction you have to the poem? Can you imagine writing such a poem to your father? your mother? yourself? Under what circumstances? Think about those questions, but when you write your response to this exercise, focus on the poem itself—what it makes you feel, and why.

9. Although the subject of "Do Not Go Gentle into That Good Night" is somber, it is unlikely that many of you found it depressing, for Thomas urges courage in the face of adversity—a very prosaic way of restating "Rage, rage at the dying of the light." That's the trouble with analysis and interpretation—a good one requires as much art as the poet exercised in writing the poem. Ultimately, of course, we value a poem, a story, or any piece of literature not only for its meaning—which is what analysis and interpretation usually try to get at—but for its words. A valuable aspect of art, as Keats says, is that it can be "in midst of other woe...a friend to man." Did you find Thomas' poem to be "a friend to man"?

You may find it a bit more difficult to say how Wallace Stevens' "Thirteen Ways of Looking at a Blackbird" is a friend to man, but start in the same way you did with the Thomas poem. As you read each stanza notice the feelings that Stevens' "ways of looking" evoke in you. In other words, trust your own reactions as you begin to arrive at an understanding of the poem. You'll find the blackbird mentioned in every stanza. Is that fact alone a satisfactory explanation for the title? What does a blackbird have to do with the poem, anyway? Why did Stevens choose a blackbird? Why thirteen ways? Why not four and twenty ways, in memory of the old nursery rhyme about blackbirds being baked in a pie?

Why not fourteen? In fact, what we want you to do for this exercise is write a fourteenth way of looking at a blackbird. With all the magpies at the Academy (and we all know that not every "magpie" here has wings), you have the opportunity to actually look at a blackbird. Choose any form you like for your fourteenth way, but you might be most comfortable sticking with Stevens' free verse pattern.

OK. You've written your fourteenth way of looking at a blackbird. Now tell us why and how you came to that perception. How did you get through Stevens' thirteen ways and into your own fourteenth way? Is your perception of the blackbird consistent in any way with Stevens' perceptions?

(Although not really a difficult poem, "Thirteen Ways" is foreign to most students' experiences with poetry. Still, even unsophisticated readers are able to write successful concluding stanzas, though they are unable to explain how. We surmise that we are observing the difference between two different levels of understanding. The commentaries we ask them to append to their poems require discursive reasoning, while the literary inventions depend on an intuitive comprehension of the tone of the poem. Whether we are correct could perhaps be explained by more research into cognitive psychology.)

10. Well, you've tried your hand at finishing an "unfinished" poem. Now you can take a shot at another kind of creative writing. Are you wondering what creative writing has to do with the other kinds of expository prose you have to write? I hope you are beginning to see that it has everything to do with it.

The brief tales by Aesop in your anthology are examples of an ancient literary genre, the beast fable. Most of you grew up with such fables as "The Tortoise and the Hare" or James Thurber's fables about animals with distinctly human characteristics, as in "The Rabbits Who Caused All the Trouble" or "The Owl Who Was God." Writers and critics generally agree that one of the characteristics that distinguishes the beast fable from other kinds of literature is its explicit or implicit moral.

For this exercise, write a beast fable about some aspect of cadet life using whatever beasts seem appropriate. The meaning or moral of your fable ought to be apparent *without* your having to tell us what it is. Be sure and let us hear the turkeys gobble, the snakes hiss, the bears growl. After all, what's a story without dialogue?

11. The fable has been a part of literature for almost two thousand years. Though each fable writer puts his or her individual stylistic stamp on the fable, the basic form, with its stated or implicit moral, hasn't changed much. So children grow up with these timeless tales, and adults are entertained by them, too. I think we can agree that they're a tradition in literature. By now I expect you're pretty familiar with "traditions," especially the military traditions of the Academy, and I hope you'll agree, tradition should never stand in the way of constructive change. The difficulty is to know when changes are constructive.

General MacArthur refers us to one important tradition of military academies in his well-known analogy between athletic contests and military conflict:

> On the fields of friendly strife are sown the seeds that on other days and other fields will bear the fruits of victory.

Since USAFA was born from the traditions of West Point and Annapolis, our athletic programs are very much like theirs. As *Contrails 1982-83* says of athletics, "the object of the program is to develop traits of courage, aggressiveness, self-confidence, good physical condition, and an intense desire to win, all of which are essential to an officer in the United States Air Force." A cadet receives instruction in three mandatory courses and one elective in physical education each year as part of this program. Furthermore, all cadets who do not compete in intercollegiate sports must participate in "intramurder." And we know from experience that most graduates pursue these habits of physical activity throughout their lives.

But let's examine the present structure of USAFA athletics. Would USAFA's mission accomplishment improve if everyone played intramurals and the Academy did not participate in intercollegiate athletics? Or is the mission best accomplished by exempting many cadets from intramurals so that they can represent the Academy on the intercollegiate level?

Write a military letter to the Superintendent explaining why intercollegiate athletics at USAFA should be discontinued or maintained. Don't mail it, of course; we "staff officers" will read it to see if it merits his attention.

12. In the last exercise, we asked you to consider the tradition of athletics at the Academy. Some of you noted that the Air Force takes great pride in the fact that it is least bound by tradition. In fact, the Air Force has activated a new command; on 1 September 1982, Space Command became a reality. As part of the original proposal for the creation of a Space Command, U.S. Representative Ken Kramer (from Colorado, incidentally) suggested officially renaming us the U.S. Aerospace Force. Well, let's just suppose that happened, and that a few years later a separate Space Command actually broke off by a sort of mitosis, in the same way the Army Air Corps became the Air Force in 1947.

It is now 1990. Five years ago, the year before you graduated, the Air Force was renamed the Aerospace Force, the U.S. Space Command was created, and it was decided that, if we're going to have a Space Command, we'd better have a Space Academy. (Where else would we put all the space cadets?) Most of you are freshly-minted captains, eager for responsibilities and challenges that will assure your promotion to Major. The Space Academy Planning Committee is asking for some new ideas on how to "revise" their Academy. Well, you can be sure that, just as the planners of USAFA adopted much from West Point and Annapolis, the planners of the Space Academy are going to want to examine decades of experience at Colorado Springs.

That's where you come in. Now that you have four years of active duty behind you, you can offer some new ideas to the Space Academy planners. You went to an "earthbound" Academy—how can you adapt your experience to the requirements of space? Explain one thing from your USAFA experience they should avoid, or one thing they should definitely include.

We realize, of course, that you will see this aspect of your cadet experience very differently as a junior captain than you do now that you're going through it. The exercise requires imagination: you've been here only a few months, and yet we're asking you to see those months as you will eight years from now.

Preface to 13-15: The Process of Writing a Paper Supported by Research
Whether or not this course has been different from previous English courses you may have taken, or different from the "typical" freshman English course in other colleges and universities, it is going to conclude with a paper supported by research, a very typical activity for freshman writing courses. This paper will be different from what you've been doing, because up until now every paper has asked you to go

no further than your own experience, your own seeing, your own thinking. But you shouldn't look at this paper, this next series of exercises, as a break with the tradition we've established; rather it is an extension. Once again, the paper you submit (in response to exercise 15, due at lesson 40) should draw on your experience, and it should convey your seeing and thinking. In this case, however, your experience is going to be shaped partly by research you do (and research is not limited to the library), and that research will also influence your thinking and seeing. But please note the words "shape" and "influence" are not equivalent to "control." You, the writer, must remain in control. Don't allow yourself to be intimidated by ideas just because they appear in print. If you will look back at the heading, you will notice that we've very carefully called this, not a research paper, but a paper *supported* by research.

Well, you can no doubt detect the cautionary voice of an English teacher weary of reading lackluster freshman term papers that often seem to be no more than a patchwork coat of quotations and citations snipped out of one or another book, all of them stitched together, often with very obtrusive seams, and the coat worn by the student with an absurd attempt at dignity that is like the antics of a clown, a sad clown with outworn tricks, with only a down-at-the-heels ringmaster for an audience. That usually happens because students find themselves writing about subjects in which they have little interest and of which they have little knowledge. We have designed a sequence of exercises that we hope will help you avoid the first pitfall; the second can easily be filled in by serious, motivated research.

Freshman term papers are often written as though their main purpose was to prove that, yes, the student has been to the library and has shuffled the encyclopedias and periodical indexes around a bit, probably because freshmen are not at home in libraries and, like the farmer with brand-new indoor plumbing, want to draw attention to an aspect of writing that should be less obtrusive. When I come to your house, it's to visit you, not to admire your stainless steel and porcelain appliances and declare over your new hush-flush. Similarly, when I read your paper, it's your ideas I'm interested in. I'll note, of course, that they're admirably supported by knowledgeable experts, but it's what *you* have to say that matters.

The purpose of your paper may be to argue, to persuade, to inform, to classify, to analyze—in short, it may fall under any of the headings listed in your textbook. And since I've mentioned our textbook, let me also mention that the distinction made by authors Scholes and Comley between argument and persuasion is more apparent than real. Argument, they say, is based on facts and figures and logic, while persuasion is a matter of appealing to an audience's emotions. In the "real world" practice of writing, argument may employ, quite legitimately, emotional appeals, and persuasion is, as I hope you admit, quite often accomplished by logical reasoning. Rarely is either found in its "pure" state.

Be wary of writing a paper in response to exercise 15 whose purpose is merely to inform. Such papers usually turn out to be dry, detached affairs suitable for nothing but the encyclopedias from whose volumes their words and ideas are often drawn. If you feel impelled to write such a paper, I urge you to think of it as exercise

14½, submit it at lesson 38, and be prepared for a flurry of suggestions from your instructor as to what you should do for lesson 40. If your purpose seems to be more informative than persuasive or argumentative, ask yourself what, besides duty, is going to cause your reader to read it. Probably if you can give your paper some persuasive edge, you will motivate your audience to read on.

To understand more clearly what I'm getting at, look back at the two preliminary letter-writing exercises you did, 11 and 12. (Ah ha! At last he's making those inter-exercise connections that I've grown so accustomed to.) To the average American, unassociated with the military, issues such as the reorganization and renaming of the Air Force, the formation of a Space Command, and the establishment of a Space Academy would not have the import they have for you, even with your short experience at USAFA. If those ordinary Americans likewise have little contact with the world of education, it probably would not occur to them that there are a myriad of issues to be debated and decided in building such an institution as a Space Academy.

13. In the last exercise you served as an expert consultant, albeit unsolicited. In this one you are going to consult with an expert. In fact, you are going to conduct an interview with an officer assigned to the Air Force Academy about his or her career field, and from your interview your term paper will emerge. Be sure, therefore, to ask questions that will open up the career field to you and will reveal the odd angles and hutments that, with further research, will yield an informative and provocative piece of writing. Your interview, by the way, is your first piece of research, and it needn't take place in the library unless your subject works there.

A special note about the format. Because this is your first piece of research, we want you to get in the habit of documenting outside sources you use in writing. Therefore please provide a note and a bibliography entry for this interview according to the format in the *MLA Handbook*.

Suggestions: Even though 70% of the graduates of USAFA initially go to pilot or navigator training, they all eventually hold other positions in the Air Force—in intelligence, maintenance, personnel, administration, finance, and of course, special duty assignments such as instructor at the Air Force Academy. You can read about these jobs in AFR 36-1, Officer Classification Regulation, and before you volunteer for any of them you should read the reg—at least to make sure you meet the qualifications. But you don't have to read the reg to respond to this exercise. If you really want to find out what it's like to be, say, an Acquisition Contracting Officer, you need to ask someone who has worked in that specialty, someone who holds the 6534 AFSC.

Your instructor has a list of officers assigned to the Air Force Academy by AFSC. Choose an AFSC that you want to know more about, contact one of the officers who holds it, and schedule an interview with him or her. Take notes. Go back to your room and organize your notes into a report of what it's really like to be a missile maintenance officer, a procurement officer, or an interceptor pilot. Note that you need not limit yourself to Academy grads.

If you examine the syllabus you will discover that we're permitting you to proceed somewhat at your own pace with the research. There are deadlines by which you must submit this exercise and the next, but they are just two steps in the process of producing your term paper, the two steps where we have chosen to intervene and offer advice and direction. You may seek advice and direction at any other step, of course, and you may proceed at a faster pace than that outlined by the syllabus. Once again, however, note that the final paper is due at lesson 40.

14. From your report on your interview I have suggested one or more possibilities for further research in periodicals, books, oral histories, films, or more interviews. Before doing any more research, however, you need to look at these topics and try to see which one has the greatest possibilities. Hold a private brainstorming session. The participants will be you, your pen, and some blank sheets of paper. What kind of questions can you formulate about your topic? Write them down. What kind of hypotheses can you suggest as answers? Write them down. Don't censor yourself. (A primary principle of brainstorming is that you never exclude *anything* you think of, no matter how indirect its connection to your subject.) What subtopics occur to you? Write them down.

Now, collect your notecards and pencils and start researching. Depending on your topic, your questions, and your hypotheses, "start researching" may mean get on the telephone and call the Air Force Weapons Laboratory. It may mean return to your interview subject for more information. It may mean a trip to the relevant office in Harmon Hall or down at the Service and Supply Area. It may mean studying the contents of cereal boxes in the Commissary. Or it may mean a trip to the library and an investigation of the card catalog and the periodical indexes. Keep track of where you find what information, because if you use it in your final paper, you'll have to acknowledge your debts.

Now, organize all of this into a research proposal, a prospectus. State the questions and problems as you see them at the beginning of your research, suggest various avenues of pursuit, and suggest what you think are the most likely answers.

By the way, don't be alarmed by the word "prospectus." Sure it's Latin, but it only means something like "forward looking." Prospectuses may take any sort of form that seems appropriate—nothing special is required. Just type it up like all of your other exercises. If you have gone into sufficient depth with your research at this point, your instructor may be able to offer you some real help. But remember, chances are he or she knows less about the subject than you do, unless you happen to be researching in his or her AFSC.

15. The prospectus you wrote includes several topics which will serve as headings (I use the word in its navigational sense) for your research. List the headings in order of priority. This list will serve as a kind of preliminary outline for your paper. Begin with the heading that seems fundamental or most important and research it. Change headings where necessary. It's difficult to chart a trip in writing with much accuracy before you've actually done the writing, so begin your first draft. Revise your outline. Do some more research. Begin a second draft. Consult with your instructor.

As time draws near for the submission of your paper, begin tidying things up. Throw out what doesn't fit. Look for some more information on topics that still have unanswered questions. Revise your latest draft and begin your final approach.

Proofread your final draft and make sure you comply with the format and documentation guidelines of the *MLA Handbook*.

16. From cradle to grave this problem of running order through chaos, direction through space, discipline through freedom, unity through multiplicity, has always been and must always be, the task of education.... The young man himself, the subject of education, is a certain form of energy; the object to be gained is economy of his force; the training is partly the clearing away of obstacles, partly the direct application of effort. Once acquired, the tools and models may be thrown away.

—from *The Education of Henry Adams*

This is your final writing assignment. It requires you to try to run some order through what may seem to you to have been the chaos of English 111, to assess the extent to which economy of your force has been gained in this writing course. The primary model for English 111 is explained in the first two chapters of your textbook. If you wish, you may use it in writing a response to this exercise, or you may take Adams' advice and throw it away.

All writing is to some extent autobiographical, and for that reason this course has frequently asked you to put personal experiences into writing. For this exercise we are asking you to put into writing *your* experience of this course. And it must be *your* experience, because everyone has experienced the course differently. The course includes, after all, not only the 42 sessions that we have spent together, but also the time we spent outside talking, reading, thinking, writing. No one but you knows how it is all linked together. Perhaps not even you. Perhaps writing about it will help you articulate those links.

The primary text for this course was the one we generated together. It consists of the exercises the instructors wrote, the papers you wrote in response to them, my responses to yours, the papers we talked about in class, and other in- and out-of-class assignments that your instructor gave you. Although we generated the text chronologically (we mortals have no other way), now that it is reaching completion you may find that you can make more sense of it by arranging the parts differently; you may discover a spatial order, for example.

Be wary of saying "My writing has improved." When you say that, what do you mean? What constitutes good writing anyhow, and how do you know it when you see it? All semester we have been trying to persuade you that writing is much more an intellectual process than a mechanical one, so it follows that rather than a report on the writing you have done, we would like to see a report on the thinking you have done. Ultimately, though, what we would like to see is an account of *your* experience, and despite the 250 words of instructions you've just received, your instructor can't tell you what to write. In a writing class the teacher is only the guide, the nudger, the shover. I can only work with what you give me to work with. I can't take responsibility for you or your writing.

Experiments in Composing

Sandra Doe

> The American psychologist, George Kelly...takes the scientist as his
> model for man and sees learning, not as a special kind of human
> behaviour, but as behaviour at its most typically human. Man is born a
> predictor, forever framing his hypotheses from past experience,
> submitting them to the test of actuality, and modifying his predictive
> apparatus in the light of what happens.[1]

"Experiments in Composing" is a sequence of learning activities that invites
students to try out various forms of observing, representing, and understanding
experience. Though the activities are not experimental in the strict scientific sense
that entails controlled investigation, they do call on students here at Metropolitan
State College in Denver to explore ways of using language that are likely to be so
unfamiliar or so unusual to them as to be experimental. These urban students, whose
median age is 27.4, are in many instances the first generation of their family to
attend college, and in many instances, too, they are returning to school after several
years of homemaking and some kind of salaried employment. Given this
background and their past school experience, students at Metropolitan State come to
this course in freshman composition with the expectation that it will require them to
write set themes on prescribed topics in stipulated forms, and that their writing will
be marked and graded for its correctness in grammar, punctuation, and usage. They
expect a course that deals with the basics, so they are invariably surprised to
discover that it is designed not according to a prescriptive but an exploratory
paradigm.

This guiding orientation is explained to students in a detailed handout that they
receive on the first day of class, but they can, of course, only come to understand
what it entails when they begin doing the various experiments on which the course is
based. After the first assignment which invites them to record their thoughts in free
writing, and the second which calls on them to draw the Rockies in pen, pencil,

---

[1]James Britton, *et.al.*, *The Development of Writing Abilities (11-18)* (London: Macmillan
Education, 1975), p. 78.

charcoal, pastels, or crayons, they know for sure that this composition course is quite unlike any predictions of it that they might have formulated on the basis of their past experience in English courses.

Those first two assignments, in fact, are emblematic of the sequence as a whole, both in the range of subject matter and in the range of compositional approaches they encompass. Over the course of the semester, for example, students find themselves composing pieces not only about the flow of their thoughts and the shape of the Rockies, but also about the contour of their lives, the behavior of animals, the image in a snapshot, the nature of metaphor, the results of a nationwide test, the design of a scientific experiment, and a host of other problems related to perception and writing. Likewise, they find themselves trying out compositional forms that include not only free writing and representational drawing, but also cumulative sentence-construction, concrete and cubist word-arrangement, role-playing, imaginary dialogue, story telling, letter writing, resumé writing, scientific reporting, and meditation.

By engaging students in so various a set of activities, I intend to expand their sense of the formal and rhetorical options in writing and thus to help them develop a more spacious view of composition as a whole. My hope, of course, is that they will come to see writing not as a narrowly defined body of skills to be acquired and rules to be obeyed, but as a creative means of exploring, translating, shaping, and controlling experience. In other words, my aim is that this array of assignments not only lead students to be more experimental, more adventurous, and more playful in their writing, but also that it provoke them to become more curious, inquiring, and speculative in the way they think about the nature of writing itself. I want them both to try out various ways of composing their experience and to consider various ways of reflecting on what they have composed.

As a means of helping students to develop such an inquiring habit of mind about their writing, I require them to keep a log of their experiments in composition. Much as scientists record what they observe, make notes on their observations, and formulate hypotheses or inferences about the conclusions to be drawn from their experiments, so I intend my students to keep a record of what they have noted in the process of their writing, as well as to reflect on problems and questions related to their experiments. For this reason, almost every experiment in the following sequence is accompanied with a set of questions, called "Log Notes," which raise a set of problems for students to reflect upon once they have done the experiment itself. So, the basic rhythm of the course is that students experiment in writing, then reflect upon what they have written, and thus use writing to explain the world of writing to themselves and to others.

The various questions that appear in the "Log Notes" are designed to raise problems that grow naturally out of the experiments themselves—problems that involve some of the most fundamental and important issues in the world of composition and thus do not admit of easy answers. For example, after students experiment in assignment 2 with various ways of drawing the Rockies, they are asked in the "Log Notes" to reflect on the senses in which their drawings are and are not representations of the Rockies. Then a few experiments later (in 5) students are asked to observe the Rockies once again, but this time to compose a written description of them inspired by a quotation from Fenallosa which asserts that "motion and change are all that we can recognize in [nature]." And after this experiment, they are asked in the "Log Notes" to reflect on whether their description represents the movement of reality and, in turn, whether writing can represent such an aspect of reality. In reflecting on such questions, students are, in effect, exploring the symbolic nature of lines and letters, of colors and words, of visual and verbal composition.

Beyond raising questions about the symbolic nature of language and about the relation of visual and verbal symbols, the "Log Notes" also challenge students to reflect on metaphor and meaning, on writing and knowing, on the significance of self and audience in writing, on the aims and modes of discourse, and on the interaction of form, content, and purpose in writing. So, over the course of the semester, students explore in their logs a broad range of rhetorical issues. Indeed, the issues they explore are not limited only to those which are raised by my questions, for as the students get used to the log they branch out to consider questions of their own devising. The logs thus turn out to be a rich source of inductive learning for all of us throughout the course.

The broad range of issues explored in the logs is, of course, a reflection of the numerous and various problems that are posed by the experiments themselves. The sequence, in fact, consists of fourteen numbered experiments, several of which contain multiple tasks, so that students find themselves doing a total of twenty-four separate compositions, not including the log notes. This array of activities is developmentally structured, so as to take students from expressive and playful experiments in the beginning of the course to analytic and speculative ones at the end.

To achieve this overall process, the sequence of experiments is structured in terms of three main clusters. The first cluster (experiments 1-5) basically invites students to play with language, to maneuver it in ways that go well beyond their conventional notions of form and purpose in writing. So, they not only move words around within the framework of sentences (3C), but they also move them around within the visual space of a page (4), and thus get some sense of the effects and meanings they can achieve from such self-conscious manipulations of form. These concrete operations in language are followed by a much more transactionally oriented use of language in the second cluster of experiments (6-11). This set of activities begins by calling upon students to try their hands at writing for such widely differing audiences as a friend or relative (6A), an eleven-year-old (6B), and a newspaper editor (6C). The cluster then develops by calling upon students to try out various conventional forms for presenting autobiographical information, such as an interview (7), a job resumé (10), and an academic assignment or graduate school application (11). As students write about themselves for these varying purposes and audiences, they also discover how shifting rhetorical intentions can shape their perceptions of experience. In the final cluster of experiments (12-14), students move from writing about personal experience to analyzing and trying out various ways of composing scientific knowledge. Thus they examine the function of metaphor in scientific writing (12A), and they also try their hand at the formal techniques of a conventional scientific report (13B). As a climax to these and the other experiments in the course, the final piece (14) offers students an occasion to speculate on how their shifting compositional perspectives have affected their ideas about the nature of truth.

Methodical though the sequence seems to be from this overview, it may well strike many readers as being quite unconventional or unpredictable at a number of points along the way. Because, of course, it is. Just as the course calls upon students to experiment with language, so my writing assignments are themselves experiments by way of invitation. I've tried to avoid imperatives and directives, to couch my requests in language which has a distinctive and arresting voice, language which addresses the students as compellingly as I possibly can. So, I've tried to craft these invitations to experiment as carefully as a poem, for somewhere in the ice storms and apple blossoms of my experience in Iowa City, I learned that a good writing assignment should be both a teaching device and as nearly as possible a work of art—that it should invite students to gesture in language, allow becoming, produce a richness of difference, and generate (at last) mistakes that teach.

EXPERIMENTS IN COMPOSING

1: Catching Words/Thoughts as They Go By

What you want to do here is to investigate and tap some of the energy transmissions going on in your mind. What I mean to say is that there are thoughts and feelings and images and stories up there in the old brain radio and that your pen or typewriter is a sort of receiver for the messages. You can call this type of writing free association or free writing or interior monologue. In it you attempt to record your thoughts just as they come, and you end up with a sort of transcript of thoughts for that moment of writing, but since thoughts come more quickly than you can catch them, even if you are a fairly fast typist or writer, you won't necessarily catch them all. But you can catch a number of them and such an activity is worthwhile as a kind of image of thinking. It's also a useful way of exploring ideas and feelings, and it's a kind of writing that is, by its nature, not perfect. You write quickly, not paying much attention to correctness, not judging what you write, and you simply try to capture what's going on in your mind. If you get stuck and nothing much seems to be happening up there, write about writing and don't think of this momentary awkwardness as anything but normal for people who write. This kind of writing is concerned with self-expression, and it's a way of warming up. Try three 20-minute transmissions.

(With this assignment I introduce to students the composing process, the concept of the writer's voice, and Peter Elbow's notion of "good bits.")

2: Composing the World

For this experiment you'll need some blank paper (8½ x 11 or larger) and some soft lead pencils, or an India Ink stick pen, or a piece of charcoal. Pastels or crayons are O.K., too, if you've got them around the house. Even ball point pens will do. Take yourself to the open air and face west (perhaps bowing a couple of times in the process!) where you have a good view of the Rocky Mountains. Relax for a few minutes and enjoy the vista. Then, in a single line, draw the Rockies. You can try a couple of these experiments, and you should keep all of your attempts. (Similarly, you should keep all of your writing, all of your drafts, and notes written to yourself on the back of old envelopes or grocery slips or...) And, if one line seems too bare or plain, feel free to experiment by adding shading, color, texture, or detail to successive drawings.

You can investigate this composing in several different ways: you can try to make an exact representation of the range, and you can try drawing it in a kind of contour, keeping your eyes on the mountains and letting your pencil draw the ups and downs of what you see, trying to capture the sense of what you see. "Just draw what you see," an artist once told me. Try erasing and not erasing to see what the different effects are. Try a couple of different pens or pencils, too. (We'll hope for a smog-free day for this experiment; otherwise everybody will bring blank paper to class!)

If the mountains seem too far away, choose another setting to contour (just make sure it's one you can return to, as this "observation" method is one you'll come back to in another experiment).

Write some "process" commentary for yourself while engaging in this assignment, some "transmissions," as in experiment 1. You can record the date, place, time, and your thoughts *before* and *after* being faced with that blank piece of paper and having to make marks on it. You can listen to what you're saying to yourself, record what's going on around you, make a note on the weather condition and on and on. Spend whatever time you need to get into the process of drawing (and writing)—an hour or an hour and a half is about right. Then pack up your kit and stash the drawings away for a while.

Log Notes: Later, get out the drawings, spread them out, and take another look. Then, in log notes (don't forget the date, time, place, and weather conditions) consider what you've made and these questions: Are they a representation of the Rockies? In what way do they not represent the Rocky Mountains? What are the gains and loses of such representation? Bring: a) the log notes, b) your "process" commentary, and c) the signed drawings to class.

3: Lines, Words, and Abstract Thought

(I begin this experiment by showing the film, "The Dot and the Line.")

A. We've been considering the way that lines represent the Rockies, and, in another view, we've been considering reality, the way we compose and frame reality, and the meaning we make out of that composing, framing, and representing. Experiment by playing with lines which represent your thoughts or feelings and see if you can tell a story with lines. (Do you have an idea for a commentary to accompany the lines? If so, jot it down.)

B. The letters which form words, like lines, are really symbols which we use to represent thought. Since we can't see thoughts, we say that thoughts are abstract, that is, considered apart from concrete existence or experience. Just for the experience of inventing, try to draw some shapes which represent abstract thought. Try it. Can you go wrong?

C. Even when we use traditional formal letters to form words, the words which we make are symbols which represent reality. For example, there's nothing about the word COW which represents "cowness"—no horns or hide or mooing comes out of the letters C O W. Each of us has certain associations with COW which we bring to that abstract and general term; but those associations don't come into existence until we *add to* the word COW. If you add the words galloping and purple to cow, you get a different image, as with this verse from my childhood:

> I never saw a purple cow
> I never hope to see one
> but I can tell you anyhow
> I'd rather see than be one

Cook up a list of twenty or so animals, experimenting by adding other words to the animal words. Bring this list of critters to class next time, along with your log notes.

Log Notes: What happened to the original words when you added to them? How did they change? What happened to the thoughts as originally represented? Did any associations surface? What does an aging amorous armadillo look like? Or a pregnant mongoose? Do you dare to decorate your Critterlist with a few drawings? Did Darwin draw? Did Picasso make exact representations? Or daVinci? Why make drawings for a log anyway? (If you have any commentary on the line experiments, throw them into these log notes.)

4: Fragments Arranged for a Class Audience

Return now
>   to Experiment One (or TWO or journal musings)

And consider your
>   Compositions

```
P
U      O
L      U
L      T
```

those sections of the writing
which please you the Most   & arrange them on a blank page

in any order
which you find in$_t$^{e}^{r}e$_s$$_t_i$ng   OR m
>   OR EXCITING ^{e}a
>   n.
>   i
>   n
>   g$_f$
>   u$_l$

You needn't use
(whole sentences) but   you may you can present
>   l$_i$n$_e$s or w$_o$r$_d$s.

Since   you   have   the whole   blank   page
>   can
>   you
>   C O M P O S E
>   the arrangement (???????)

(((this is not
>   to seek
>   perfection
>   but to
>   dr^a^{w} h^{o}n$_e$y out of
>   ALL THINGS)))

Additions +	Prose	S		
subtractions − &	Poetry	P	I	O.K.
deletions	musings	A	S	
are all O.K.	notes…are O.K.	C		
		E		

(I find it useful in connection with this assignment to show students poems by
e.e. cummings or Charles Olson, as a way of letting them see the various
effects that can be achieved by visual arrangements and rearrangements.)

5: *Verbs and Other Additions*

> The verb must be the primary fact of nature, since motion and change are all that we can recognize in her.—Ernest Fenallosa

A. Using your critter list, try creating a list of verbs, words that name some of the actions the critters do. *Add to* these verbs words that *describe* the actions (adverbs and phrases), words which tell *how* they do them. (If your critter "leaps," does it leap "gracefully' or "awkwardly?" "Easily?" "Doubtfully?" Five feet, ten feet, a hundred? Like a rocket, a lead ball exploding out of a canon, a ton of bricks? Over a Mack truck? Through a flaming hoop? As in the critter list, try to picture (in your mind and/or on paper) what your critter is up to.

B. After you've studied Christensen's "Generative Rhetoric of the Sentence," compose a story *from your imagination* about one or more of your critters in action—in a sentence or two or three. Build your sentences up with modifiers.

C. Return to the viewpoint where you observed the Rocky Mountains. Set up your "process commentary" as before, recording the date, time, weather conditions and any other pertinent observations, using an "experiment one" style of writing. Next, concentrate on Fenallosa's quote, noting and listing the verbs *which you observe*. (You have to "frame" your word picture as in experiment 2, but your framing won't be done with lines, shading, or color, but rather with words which represent lines, shading, and color. You might have to alter the framing of your observation to include foreground motion.) Using the list of verbs, then, compose a *description* of what you observe. *You* are the point of reference for this observation. Take this rough draft home and add to it, using modifiers, and bring the description to class.

Log Notes: What differences and/or similarities have you observed between composing from imagination and composing from observation? Did you exclude any details because you assumed that your reader sees what you "see"? What is the root of the word imagination? And, how does that relate to composing? Finally, muse on Picasso's statement: "The picture is not thought out and determined beforehand, rather while it is being made it follows the mobility of thought." Does your description represent the movement of reality? Imagination? Can writing do that? Are there differences between "on the spot" observational writing and "composed additions" to the writing? What are they?

6: *A Question of Audience*

A. In experiment 4, you wrote for a class audience, a group of fellow writers. For this experiment, write to a friend or family member. Your topic? What you've been up to in your composition class. You are the authority on this topic, since you have been in class for some six or seven weeks now, and you have your own observations and composing experiments to draw upon. Your audience, on the other hand, has not had the benefit of your experience, and indeed may have had other kinds of experiences with writing. Your task, then, is to create a context which will allow your audience to understand your present writing experiences, what you perceive as their benefits, liabilities, and purposes. Here you must adapt a voice suitable to your audience, provide context and detail, decide upon your aim as expressive, informational, or persuasive, or a combination of these intentions.

Consider this experiment a mid-term "examination," in the sense of inspecting or scrutinizing this class and your experience in it in detail. Thus, you should observe and/or analyze carefully your work, your interaction with the workshop group, and other elements which have contributed to the flow of your experience to date.

Log Notes: In what way does writing about experience help make sense of it? In what way does language help you "locate" yourself?

B. Take a look at your composed critter sentence, and, considering the nature of your audience, write an expanded version of a critter story for an eleven-year-old child.

Log Notes: What is the world of your audience like? What interests and characteristics must you keep in mind in order to appeal to that audience? Do you think you ought to "write down" to a child? Should you "test" your experiment for audience appeal?

C. Here is a situation: in 1979, the third National Assessment of Writing was conducted. The study asked a random sample of youth, aged 9, 13, and 17, to write short descriptive, narrative, or humorous works. Some of the results: only one-fifth of the 17-year-old young people "usually" enjoy their writing assignments; 37% of those 17-year-olds reported that "little or no time" was spent on writing instruction in their English classes; and, during a six-week period, more than half of the high school seniors wrote less than three papers in all their courses combined.

Using your own writing experience as a base, write a letter to the editor of our local paper commenting on the results of this third National Assessment of Writing. Your letter must consider the audience behind the Editor, and your purpose might be informational, expressive, or persuasive.

Log Notes: What qualities do you think the reader of the newspaper will have? Who reads the "Letters to the Editor?" And, what is the relationship between style and content in your experiment?

7: Contours Leading to Autobiography

A. In experiment 2, you looked at the Rocky Mountains and drew a contour of them, "seeing" them in interpretive perspectives. And in experiment 6, you considered the contour of the class thus far. Now, in order to begin to make a contour of your life, *make a visual interpretation of your life*. (A board game or a map, say?) What landmarks dot the territory? What special trails lead off the main path? Are there detours? Dead ends? What sort of benchmarks, peaks, or valleys can you chart? How can you portray your land formations and weather conditions?

Log Notes: What is a *metaphor* and how does it help you know things that you didn't know before? Does a dictionary definition of metaphor yield the same kind of "knowing" as the experience of metaphor? Have there been many metaphors used to date in this class?

B. Using some of the questions above as a base, *interview* yourself, focusing on one aspect of the map. *Frame one incident, single moment, or important event.* You'll need to invent two voices for this writing, one for the interviewer and one for the person being interviewed. What is the situation, the scene, of the interview?

Log Notes: Is there one true self revealed in writing? Have you framed your interview? Is the framed view seen through the instrument of a microscope or a telescope or some other speculative instrument? (What's a metaphor for?) Did you experiment by using a metaphor in your self-interview?

8: Meditation on a Snapshot

Words, voice, soul work. The breath of being and the energy of dance.
Words, voice, soul work. Writing is. Writing is the act of the instant.
Words, voice, soul work. The freedom of form is way-word. In whatever way.

A piece of writing is a presence saying something from sources. The sources within (and without). Writing is catching the thoughts, jamming with them like jazz.

The monday minor
subdued
blue by fog
Later
R. Creeley
the poet
& Unabashed
Sentimentality

Writing is an act of attention. Writing is an act. Or an action, a process taking place in time, linear time and memory time and non-linear time. Does writing create the world or the world the writer? In writing you have to take the risk and follow the language-lead, trip on with the words to see where they take you. Or follow them as they flow and beguile you on, and you keep on writing to see where they take you. Dangerous because you don't know the territory. Exciting because you might find a key, or a lock, a passage to lead you far away from home and the familiar. Exotic. Unknown. Romantic. Who makes the word-world?

Writing is an act of attention. You can attend to a photograph of yourself (or someone else). A snapshot of static reality. There you are, all fixed in time. And the particle of yourself is stuck on film, some negative, and some piece of paper. Attending to your portrait in that time the world isn't linear anymore. You remember the morning, the moment, the space and time, the place located somewhere which is now, but isn't now. But in the photograph it is and isn't anymore.

The things you attend to tell who you are.

A photograph is an image, a kind of chime of character, a way of seeing the character, a presentation. A meditation on a photograph (or anything else) is a participation in the process. Writing about it gives the feel of it, the experience of it. Maybe.

What I've worked up to here is a suggestion.

(I want the students to choose a special snapshot and meditate upon it, so here I meditate for them on the very act of meditating on a snapshot. Some teachers ask students to write descriptions of the chosen snapshot and then have them write the meditation. Others lead a guided meditation in class, complete with deep breathing and visualization. Most meditations are written in class with crafting completed at home. Students who forget to bring a snapshot to class can write on their driver's license or student I.D. photo.)

9: Choosing a Persona

The Latin word *persona* (plural: *personae*) means mask. A person sitting at a typewriter doesn't literally wear a mask since there is no actual audience to "put on a performance" for. Thus, we use the word in a metaphorical sense, since it is possible for a writer to create a *persona*. The image of the self which a writer creates, intentionally, or unintentionally, is reflected in the writer's use of words and sentences. For this experiment, assume a *persona* for someone or something else: a critter, perhaps, or an actor in some other scene.

That is, for this experiment you will have to invent the *actors,* the *scene,* the *purpose* for your writing. Indeed, the idea is to act out a character in language, to assume a role. Does this require a shift in your frame of reference?

Log Notes: Can a writer enact the person that he or she is choosing to become? That is, can a writer project a *persona* that he or she would like to assume? And, if this is possible, how is writing related to becoming?

10: The Vitae of Your Life

Consider, once again, the experience of your life: the "Travel Guide" or "Board Game" or other visualization which you used to make up the pre-writing contour to your autobiography in experiment 7. Review, too, your self interview. But now cast your experience in the form of a *vita*, a Latin word which means life. Vitas detailing a person's life are sent to prospective employers or graduate schools, and they provide another sort of picture of a person's life. An obituary could be considered a vita, or, perhaps since it is after the fact of vital existence, you might call it a post-vita. For this experiment, write a vita (or resumé), a one page snapshot of your life. (And, if you care to, you could try to write an obituary notice describing the accomplishments of your life as you envision them.)

Log Notes: Imagine the specific audience for your resumé. Who is that audience? What do you know about him or her? What can you find out? How old? What kind of educational background? What kind of life experience? Is a vita informative, persuasive, or both? In the case of an obituary, do you need to summon an audience by virtue of your life?

11: An Academic Autobiography

Sometime in your college career you may be asked to write an autobiography. You may take a "credit for life experience" course, or you may enter a program which asks you to relate your personal experience to your course of study, or you may apply to a graduate school. In each of these cases, the readers of your autobiographical statement are interested in the connections which you map out in language, in the voice of the speaker and writer, and in his or her ability to communicate expressively, informatively, and persuasively to the intended audience.

So as a spectator on your life and your writing, look back over experiment 7 again, attending to the contour which might be created or is created. Frame your experience in language, this time in the form of an autobiography. What part of your life will you select and arrange to create a presentation of yourself? Is there any one moment you'd like to frame? Can you find a metaphor to translate an aspect of experience? Do you wish to persuade your audience (the class members) about some aspect of yourself? Considering these questions, and the question of purpose or intention, create an autobiographical contour with words.

Log Notes: Is the persona in this piece different from the persona answering and asking the questions in experiment 7? Is there one true self which is revealed in writing?

12: Metaphor, Science, Literature

A. John Wiley is a science writer for the *Smithsonian* magazine. Annie Dillard is a writer of literature who includes scientific concepts in her work. Both use metaphor to explain the complexities of quantum physics. For this experiment, isolate and examine the metaphors which each writer uses to explain the present scientific "world view." Pull out those metaphors and write about them: their implications, their ramifications. Can you separate the metaphors into categories? What sorts of classifications can you find about the uses of metaphoric language by these writers? Discuss your findings and speculations with your workshop group.

B. Next analyze and write about each writer's use of voice, style, and the kind of audience which each envisions. Share your findings with your workshop group.

C. Now that you've experimented with seeing what you can see, talked about your observations, and speculated about these preliminary inquiries, write an essay, using Dillard and Wiley as examples, based on this quote from Albert Einstein:

> Most of the fundamental ideas of science are essentially simple, and may, as a rule, be expressed in a language comprehensible to everyone.

Or, you might want to use this quote from Werner Heisenberg:

> Even for the physicist the description in plain language will be a criterion of the degree of understanding that has been reached.

In any event, you should remember that the word "essay" means to try. Usually an essay opens, closes, and elaborates on an idea in the middle. Essayists (like Wiley and Dillard) write in their own voices, cite their ideas as a *hypothesis,* and bring *evidence* to bear on that hypothesis (sometimes known as a thesis). So, remember to provide a context for your readers to supply evidence in the form of comparisons, contrasts, analyses, and examples.

Log Notes: What problems did you encounter in this experiment? How did you solve them? And, despite the extensive use of the "contours" metaphor in this class, do you still think of that Rocky Mountain image as a usable metaphor—a representation of contemporary reality? Why or why not? If you were to choose another metaphor, what would it be?

> (For this assignment I put on library reserve the following titles: John P. Wiley, Jr., "Phenomena, Comment and Notes," *Smithsonian,* February, 1981, pp. 30-38; Annie Dillard, *Pilgrim at Tinker Creek* [New York: Bantam Books, 1975]. But any science writing that relies heavily on metaphor will do.)

13: Life Experiments and Scientific Reports

A. All of us experiment in order to understand the world. We experiment and solve problems for the purpose of knowing something about the world, for the purpose of integrating some experience or some piece of knowledge into our own knowing. Sometimes our experiments are conscious; sometimes they are unconscious. Reflect on the experiments you have made in your life—social experiments, scientific experiments, literary experiments, technical experiments. What hypothesis guided your "laboratory" work? What questions did you ask? Did your results verify your hypothesis? Or did you have to restate your hypothesis? Restate your question(s)? After these general reflections on your life experiments, choose one experiment which typifies your personal use of the "scientific method" and write an essay describing your use of the experimental method. Present your description as a rhetorical argument so that your audience can judge the validity of your conclusions.

Log Notes: In what way is scientific writing rhetorical? Who are the speakers in science? To whom do they speak? Does scientific writing use argument? Is a research situation a rhetorical situation?

B. To be "scientific" an experiment must be replicable, that is, capable of being reproduced by some other experimenter. The one you will find on library reserve obviously is. Study this account, discuss it with your workshop group, and rewrite it in the form of a laboratory report. Do you need any more information to reproduce this experiment? If so, what kind?

(For this experiment, I put a copy of the following article on library reserve: Hung-Hsiang Chou, "Chinese Oracle Bones," *Scientific American,* April 1979, pp. 134–149, but any essayistic account of a scientific investigation will do.)

Log Notes: For experiment's sake, what does "wrestling with a question" look like? A drawing, perhaps? And, what is the relationship of the question to the answer?

14: Complementary Contradictions

Two seemingly incompatible conceptions can each represent an aspect of the truth...they may serve in turn to represent the facts without ever entering into direct conflict.

Louis de Broglie, *Dialectica,* II, 326

As you leave this class, you'll be a writer, encountering various subject matters—chemistry, anthropology, physics, literature, art, nursing, space technology. You'll work toward the perception of subject matter, toward drawing relationships with other subject matters; as a writer you'll consider various frames of reference, explore, hypothesize, test, and verify or disprove your speculative questions.

For this final experiment, sum up your composing experience in this class in light of the statement above. In what way do your experiments represent different aspects of the truth? Of yourself? How does frame of reference or point of view affect perception? Is reality "static" or "in flux"? And what about you? A solid or a flow? Your voice in words——fixed or moving?

Log Notes: How does the framing of the question predict its answer?

V

"Writing to Think and Learn"

An Interdisciplinary Research Course

Trudy Dittmar

"Writing to Think and Learn" is an interdisciplinary course that I conceived as a way of both improving and promoting writing across the curriculum at Brookdale Community College.[1] The version of it presented here is the first of several that have since been developed with Brookdale students and Brookdale's resources in mind. In the process of explaining the underlying structure of this course and how it came to be developed, I hope it will also become evident that "Writing to Think and Learn" embodies policies and practices that are adaptable to the needs and resources of other schools.

As an interdisciplinary course, it uses subject matters from a variety of disciplines to serve as contexts for activities and experience in writing. To complete the course, students must carry out five search-research projects, each related to a different subject. The sequence presented here, for example, consists of projects in Anthropology, Dance, Law, Natural Science, and Human Sexuality. The project for each subject consists, in turn, of a developmentally structured series of writing/ learning activities. The majority of these are journal assignments which engage students in exploratory or reflective writing. Some journal assignments are distinctive to a specific project and are intended to guide the student in writing to explore the particular subject matter of that project. Other journal assignments are so broadly related to the processes of thinking, learning, and writing that they are used in the same form project after project. Such "universal" journal assignments are

---

[1] Brookdale Community College, a two-year open admissions institution founded in 1969, serves Monmouth County in central New Jersey. Courses offered at the main campus in Lincroft, the satellite campus in Long Branch, and the several extension centers scattered around the county are attended by over 10,000 full- and part-time students, aged 18 and up, from the wide range of social, economic, ethnic, and educational backgrounds (from high school drop-outs to college graduates) that reflects the county's diverse population. Many register for isolated courses, but most enroll in a degree program, and a good number of these transfer to four-year institutions once they have received an associates degree. The college is committed to providing programs that meet the very varied requisites and aspirations of its heterogeneous student body.

intended to guide students in writing to reflect upon how they go about researching, thinking about, and writing about a topic or problem. In addition to journal assignments, each project usually contains one paper assignment, intended to guide students in a transactional writing task—that is, in writing a paper to inform (and sometimes persuade) an outside audience of some aspect or point about the subject they have explored. The following set of numbered paragraphs outlines the kinds of assignments that typically make up a search-research cluster and the pattern in which they are arranged, illustrating each step in the pattern with the corresponding assignment from the project on Law.

1. **Systematic Search Activity** (Journal Assignment). Each project assumes that most students have had little or no experience with its subject. Accordingly, this first assignment sets up a situation intended to provide students some direct experience with the subject, usually requiring them to do some sort of observation as a means of introducing them to it. Although it is true that students could usually gain such an introduction through reading, it is also the case that direct experience helps to stimulate their personal involvement and disposes them to engage the subject, to think about it, rather than simply to take in information passively. The search assignment for the Law project, for example, directs students to visit one of three kinds of local courts, to interview one of the courtroom personnel, and then to sit in on a session while cases are being heard. In the interview, students gather background information on the nature of that particular court and on the general purposes of sessions held there. During the session, they select a case that interests them and gather information about it. This assignment is intended to give students some rudimentary sense of the subject and to provide them with a mental stance from which to explore it further.

A component of each search assignment is a procedure called "Creating Heuristics." This procedure sets up a systematic method of generating questions to guide students in approaching the situation set up by the search assignment. It is intended to help them gather information and—to some extent—to analyze and order that information. In the Law project this procedure helps students devise two sets of questions, one to use in conducting the interview and one to guide them in listening to the case that interests them most. Once students have finished the search activity, they are usually directed to freewrite in their journals about the experience, jotting down their reactions to it, their sense of what they have learned from it, and their questions about it. Using this journal piece as a guide, students then discuss their experiences, comparing reactions and questions, adding to one another's information and answering one another's questions whenever possible. This activity is intended to help students review what they have found out on their own, to broaden their knowledge and views of the subject, and to stimulate further thought about the ideas they have formed up to this point in the project.

2. **Identification of Point of View** (Journal Assignment). Once students have had a chance to reflect upon the search experience in writing and to compare their reflections with those of others in the class, this assignment asks them to try to place themselves in relation to the subject matter of the project. Reflecting in writing

upon the questions asked here should help them to examine the extent of their experience with the subject at this point and to identify their present ideas and attitudes about it. This activity is intended to provide students with a vantage point from which to begin research on the subject, to suggest to them some avenue of investigation—a theme to explore, perhaps, or an attitude or idea to test.

3. **Research** (Journal Assignment). This assignment guides students in beginning their research. It provides them with instructions and information (varying in degree of specificity according to the project) on where to find or how to look for information on the subject, and usually includes some suggestions or guidelines on taking notes. In the Law project, for example, the assignment directs students to specific legal reference works and instructs them to find out as much information as they can from these sources about the issue involved in the case they observed and took notes on in court.

4. **Review of the Research Process** (Journal Assignment). After students have begun their research but before they have completed it, this assignment asks them to reflect in writing on their research experience thus far, articulating for themselves the procedures they have followed, identifying which were fruitful and which were not, pinpointing their confusions, and jotting down the questions they have at this point. This activity is intended to make them conscious of habits they have formed or are beginning to form, to make them aware of what procedures they follow that work well and what aspects of doing research they might need help with. In the class discussion that follows this writing, students compare methods and problems. The purpose of this discussion is to reinforce successful approaches, to suggest to students methods they may not have tried, as well as to answer their questions and solve their problems if possible. The repetition of this assignment in each of the projects is intended to help students develop their own set of purposeful research procedures and thus to establish an approach to research that works well for them. After students have shared their reflections in class discussion, they then go on to finish researching their chosen topic.

5. **Synthesis of Search and Research** (Journal Assignment). Following completion of the research, this assignment guides students in comparing the information they have gained from the different sources and procedures they have used in doing the project. In directing them to find areas where their information coincides and diverges, overlaps and contradicts, this writing activity is intended to help them review all the information they have gathered, to analyze and evaluate it, to order it, and possibly to reach new conclusions about the subject under investigation. In the process of doing this activity, students often develop ideas for organizing and presenting their information.

6. **Paper Assignment.** This task sets up a rhetorical situation to which the students must respond by using the experience and information they have gathered on the subject of the project. It sets a writing task, designating both the purpose students should try to accomplish in their papers and the audience to whom they should be writing. In the Law project, for example, students are called upon to demonstrate to an expert in the field what they have learned about some aspect of the

law. The assignment makes suggestions about some of the points that students should probably cover in a paper of this kind.

7. **Workshop Questions** (Journal Assignment). A basic list of questions guides students in writing an evaluation of one or more papers submitted for the project. Depending on the instructor's decision, students work in groups or individually, sometimes examining the papers of other students and sometimes their own, trying in each case to assess how the paper accomplishes its given purpose for its given audience, where it succeeds and where it might be improved. This writing session is often followed by a discussion session in which author(s) and respondent(s) confer with each other. This activity is intended to stimulate students to think further about their papers, and to suggest alternate approaches they might have taken in writing it. Repeated workshop projects after each paper provide students with several opportunities to work on the process of improving their writing.

Additional journal reflections and explorations—sometimes near the beginning of a project, sometimes near the mid-point; sometimes focused on prior knowledge and belief, sometimes on earlier writings—round out the assignments in a given project. Each project incorporates a linear structure of assignments (as reflected in the preceding outline), but the overall sequence of projects embodies a spiral structure. That is, at the start of each new project the sequence loops back to a search activity, working its way through the same kinds of activities that made up the preceding project, and in each new project these assignments are progressively more demanding, more complex. The increasing sophistication of tasks can be seen, for example, in the paper assignments which cover a broad scale of complexity, ranging from a personal speculation written for the class in the case of the anthropology project to an argumentative piece for a public audience in the case of the human sexuality project. The spiral structure of the sequence can be seen in the following overview of the several projects.

1. **Anthropology.** This project is the first and the simplest, containing only three basic tasks: the search activity, the paper assignment, and the workshop questions.

2. **Dance.** The full range of eight assignments outlined above is introduced in this project. Specialized tasks, however, are kept at a relatively simple level. In the research assignment, for example, students are directed to read a specific book on reserve in the library and told which pages to read.

3. **Law.** The full range of tasks is repeated in this project, but the information gathering activities become more complex. The search assignment, for example, now contains two parts rather than one, calling upon students both to conduct an interview and to engage in observation. The research assignment is also more demanding by virtue of the fact that it requires students to consult multi-volume reference works that incorporate a special format which must be mastered in order to locate the necessary information.

4. **Natural Science.** This project also contains the full range of activities but is more complex in that it involves two kinds of research material (the first a pair of

films, the second a wide variety of printed matter) and two paper assignments rather than one.

   5. **Human Sexuality.** This project is the most difficult of all because it requires students to assume a substantial share of the responsibility themselves for devising search procedures, for identifying and selecting research materials, and for defining their paper topics.

   The various projects and assignments discussed above, when combined, result in the following course outline:

PROJECT I: ANTHROPOLOGY
   1. Systematic Search Activity
   2. Further Exploration
   3. Paper I
   4. Workshop Questions

PROJECT II: DANCE
   1. Initial Exploration
   2. Systematic Search Activity
   3. Reflection
   4. Identification of Point of View
   5. Research
   6. Review of the Research Process
   7. Synthesis of Search and Research Findings
   8. Paper II
   9. Workshop Questions

PROJECT III: LAW
   1. Systematic Search Activity
   2. Further Exploration
   3. Identification of Point of View
   4. Research
   5. Review of the Research Process
   6. Synthesis of Search and Research Findings
   7. Paper III
   8. Workshop Questions

PROJECT IV: NATURAL SCIENCE
   1. Systematic Search Activity
   2. Further Exploration
   3. Identification of Point of View
   4. Research, Part A
   5. Reflection
   6. Paper IV A
   7. Research, Part B
   8. Synthesis of Search and Research Findings

9. Paper IV B
10. Workshop Questions

PROJECT V: HUMAN SEXUALITY

1. Systematic Search Activity
2. Identification of Point of View
3. Research
4. Review of the Research Process
5. Synthesis of Search and Research Findings
6. Paper V
7. Workshop Questions

The overall design of this course is intended to serve two basic goals for the students. One, naturally, is to prepare them to write papers for the variety of courses they will take in college, by developing their ability to gather knowledge in various areas and to convey in writing what they have learned from their research. The other goal—one that is less traditional, but, I believe, of prior importance for college freshmen—is to reveal to students the valuable role that writing can play in every aspect of their academic activity and intellectual development. It is for this reason that the course does not simply confine itself to having students write papers on a variety of subjects, but calls upon them to use writing as a means of confronting and researching each new subject, as a means of ordering and making sense of new information, as a means even of reflecting upon papers once they have been written, and thus as a means of discovering how the presentation itself might be improved. As students repeatedly engage in this range of writing activities, they come to see the various ways that writing can help them to learn as well as to present their learning to others. So, in a variety of ways the course is intended to serve the goals of writing and learning across the curriculum.

The goals of writing and learning across the curriculum are served not only by the course itself, but also by the process of designing it, for a course such as this is inevitably the creation not of a single individual but of several colleagues representing the various subjects of study that are combined in the course. When, for example, I designed the initial version of this course at the Institute, I was able to envision its deep structure and to sketch it out in skeleton form. But I was not able to elaborate its surface structure, its particular assignments, for I was not knowledge-able enough to determine the content for assignments in a number of fields. So, I necessarily found myself compelled to solicit the help of colleagues in other fields. A brief record of my work with these colleagues will serve to indicate how designing such a course can also promote the long range needs of writing across the curriculum within an institution.[2]

[2]For their valuable assistance in the creation of this sequence, I would like to thank the following faculty at Brookdale Community College: Dick Cole (Natural Sciences), Lori DeShaw (Dance), Charlotte Engleman (Para-Legal Technology), Lillian Frantin-Edwards (Art), Richard Masluk (Sociology/Anthropology), Tom Shostak (Interdisciplinary Studies), Sherri West (World Cultures).

In order to attract the interest of colleagues in my project, I began by writing a description of the course, outlining its basic structure, and summarizing its purpose for students and its potential value for all areas of the College. To illustrate the kind of project assignments I envisioned for the course, as well as to indicate the kind of assistance I needed from colleagues, I prepared a sample assignment cluster for a project in art history (the one subject I felt I knew enough about to develop on my own). I then sent all of these materials along with a memo to colleagues in other academic areas of the College asking them to help me write similar clusters that might represent their disciplines in the new course. In the memo, I made clear my expectation that our working together would require relatively little work or time from them other than three brief meetings during the course of a semester, and I closed by letting them know that I would call in a week to learn their decisions and make appointments if they were agreeable to collaborating. As it turned out, everyone agreed to meet with me once, and nearly everyone I met with agreed to collaborate with me.

In the first meeting I elaborated on my plans for the course, explaining the rhetorical and educational theory behind the specific assignments and the rationale for their arrangement, emphasizing the importance of writing in helping students to learn. In this connection, I outlined some of the ways that instructors in any discipline might use writing assignments to help teach their subjects. At the end of each individual conference, I asked my colleague whether he or she would be willing to imagine a search assignment and a follow-up research assignment that I might incorporate into a project in that person's field of specialization, assuring each colleague a generous amount of time to do so.

Six to eight weeks later I called each volunteer and made an appointment to talk once again, to learn what ideas the colleague had developed for assignments. At this meeting my colleague did most of the talking, explaining ideas for assignments, and I confined myself to taking notes and asking questions for purposes of clarification. I then put the ideas and suggestions of my colleague into the form of written assignments which I incorporated into a search-research project in that person's field, and sent a copy of the material to my colleague for approval or for suggested revisions. I met with each colleague one more time, to hear comments on my proposed assignment cluster—criticisms, suggested additions or modifications—and then, if necessary, rewrote the assignments. Once I had a colleague's approval, I incorporated the assignments into the overall sequence for the course.

This method of working with colleagues in a number of other disciplines not only helped me create a course that I did not have the breadth of knowledge to develop on my own, but it also served as a stepping stone toward promoting greater understanding between staff members in writing and faculty in other areas of the College. Once I had not only established the deep structure, but also elaborated the surface structure in this particular version, it readily became a model that other members of the writing staff might draw on in creating other versions of the course. Some members of the writing staff have already written new projects for different versions of the course, and as they have done so new contacts have proliferated between the writing staff and colleagues in other fields. The next step in using this course as a vehicle for writing across the curriculum at Brookdale will be to hold a workshop to be attended by the writing staff and by colleagues from all other areas whose disciplines have been represented in one or another version of the course. In this workshop, persons who have taught the course can present the results of the various project assignments as a springboard for discussing the role that writing can play in any course. Such a dialogue between writing instructors and instructors from other disciplines will lead, I hope, to integrating writing more significantly with learning throughout the curriculum at Brookdale.

WRITING TO THINK AND LEARN

Project I: Anthropology

1. Systematic Search Activity

What images come to mind when you hear the word *anthropology?* Tribal dances and old bones? Is that what anthropology is about? What does an anthropologist do?

The first subject you are going to think, write, talk, and learn about is anthropology. As you engage in the following activities, you will not only discover something about anthropology, but you will also begin to get some ideas about how to approach a new subject. *And* you will learn something about writing, as well.

I imagine you are expecting as a first step that I'll try to get you to absorb some information about anthropology. You may be thinking that I'll feed you the information in class, in a lecture, or you may be thinking I'll give you a reading assignment. Not so. I am not going to give you information to absorb; you are going to go out and find it. And you won't be looking for it in books. Instead, you'll be looking in an everyday sort of place—in a bar, a bus station, or a sporting goods store. And—another surprise—the information you gather won't be "about anthropology." Not directly anyway. But that information, information you find *yourself,* should eventually enable you to make some worthwhile discoveries about anthropology.

Here's the assignment in general terms:

Go to a place you're not very familiar with, a place generally frequented by a group of people you don't belong to. Observe and take generous notes on the setting and on the activities and actions going on in the setting, trying to discover some patterns of behavior. The patterns you discern should enable you to hypothesize about the significance of this place and the actions that go on there in the lives of the people you have observed.

Don't panic. Stated this way—generally—the assignment probably sounds terrifying, impossible. But it's not. It just seems that way because you're faced with new territory, and it's always scary to venture into the unknown. But I think you'll find that if you venture a bit at a time and acclimate yourself gradually, the territory won't seem so frightening or so impossible to cross.

So let's break the assignment (the trip through the territory) into parts and take it one step at a time. As you proceed through most of the steps, you'll use writing to help you make sense of the unknown, to help you think and make the kinds of discoveries necessary to complete the assignment.

Essentially what you need to do is 1) choose an appropriate place to do your observation, 2) decide on how to take your notes, and 3) figure out a way to analyze your information once you have it. You'll receive help in each of these areas, in this assignment and following ones.

1. First of all, I'll help by limiting the kinds of places you might go to:
    a. some kind of a bar (a disco bar, a gay bar, a fishermen's bar, a "go-go" bar, a young executives' bar, a fancy New York bar, etc.)
    b. some kind of store (a sporting goods store, a sexy lingerie store, an adult book store, a head shop, a women's fashion store, an ethnic grocery store, etc.)
    c. some kind of transportation station (a train, bus, or subway station; an airport or heliport)
    d. some kind of restaurant (fast food, ethnic, seafood, etc.)
    e. some kind of theatre lobby (movie, opera, rock concert hall, Broadway theatre, non-Broadway live theatre)

Stick to one of these five categories of places. Then from that category be sure to pick a kind of place that you're not too familiar with, that you have never or rarely gone to, a kind of place frequented by a group you don't belong to. This may be a different ethnic group, a different socio-economic group, a different professional group, a different interest group, etc. For example, if you want to gather information in a bar and you generally go to disco bars, this time go to a fishermen's bar.

2. What might worry you next is how to decide what to observe once you get there, what kinds of notes to take. We can help each other with this problem right now by deciding as a group what we should look for. Together, as a class, we can create a *heuristic,* a device for helping one to discover or learn. I'll start things going and then, using the sheet entitled "Creating Heuristics," everyone will contribute ideas about how to learn from the search experience. Here's my contribution: When you go to the bar or subway station or pet store, you'll be observing a social situation. A social situation consists of three components: a place, people, and action(s). So, the three main things you want to find out are:

    a. What is the place?
    b. Who is in it?
    c. What are they doing in it?

Starting with these three basic questions, we can create a heuristic together. Turn to "Creating Heuristics" to see how. Once the heuristic has been devised, be sure to copy it in your journal, so you will have it to guide you when you do your observation. Use it to take thorough notes, for the more notes you have, the easier it should be to make sense out of your observation later on. Take all notes in your journal.

Creating Heuristics

A heuristic is a device for helping you to discover or learn. It is a method or procedure you can follow when setting out to learn about a subject you know little or nothing about. When you are engaging in a new activity, a task you've never tackled before, a heuristic can help you make sense of what you're doing. It will help you direct your activity purposefully. Since in this course you'll be engaging in activities you've never engaged in before and learning about subjects you don't know much about, heuristics will be very helpful to you.

What does that all mean? Probably not much yet. It's an abstract definition. Usually an abstract definition is just about meaningless to someone who has not been exposed to any of the concrete objects or situations that the definition applies or refers to. After doing only part of the first project in this course, though, you'll understand that definition. By the end of the course you will know by heart what a heuristic is, and more important, you'll also know not only how to devise a kind of heuristic yourself, but also how to use one to help you learn.

Although heuristics can take many forms, in this course a heuristic will always be a set of questions. You will ask yourself questions which will help you know what to look for as you do your search and research activities. If you were to seek information without the aid of the questions, your notes might end up a hodgepodge of confusing details. Without the questions it might be hard to decide which details were of major and which of minor importance. It might be hard to see the relationships between the details. The questions will help you see which details deserve more attention and which less. They will help you find relationships between the details. In short, they will help you decide what information to take note of and how to interpret and understand that information.

Each time we tackle a new subject in this course, we will create a new heuristic to help us learn about it. At first the class will do this together, as a joint effort. Later, once you've had practice, you'll be able to do it on your own. Below are the steps we'll follow in creating heuristics together, as a class:

A. *Instructor:* I will give you a few starter questions, the most basic questions we'll need to answer in order to learn about the subject. (For example, in our first project—on anthropology—I suggest that the three main things we need to find out are 1) What is the place you are observing? 2) Who is in this place? and 3) What are they doing in this place?)

B. *Individual Student:* You will write each starter question at the top of a separate sheet in your journal. Under each one you will write as many related, but more specific, questions as you can. (For example, in the anthropology assignment under #1 you might begin by asking What kind of place is this? and What is its name? Under #2 you might begin by asking how many people are here? and What age groups are represented? Under #3 you might begin by asking What kinds of talk are going on? and What kinds of gestures are people using?)

C. *Small Group:* Once you've written as many sub-questions as you can under each starter question, I'll ask you to divide into groups. People in the group should pool their sub-questions under starter question #1 to form one list. They should repeat this procedure for each of the remaining starter questions.

D. *Large Group:* Someone from each group will read me the list of questions under starter question #1 so I can write a master list on the board for all to see. When all groups have reported their questions, I'll add to the list any questions I've thought of that haven't been covered. We will repeat this procedure for each starter question.

E. *Everyone:* Copy all the lists of questions (the heuristic) into your journal, and take it with you when you do your search and/or research activity.

As you use a heuristic for the first time you will probably find that you can't answer all the questions. That's to be expected, so don't worry. Just be sure to try to cover as many areas as possible. In doing your investigation you may also discover information not covered by the questions. If it seems at all pertinent, take it down. The more notes you take, the easier it should be to make sense of your topic later on. Take all your notes in your journal.

When the time comes to create a heuristic on your own, the assignment will help you to do so.

KEEP THIS SHEET. You will use it at some point during almost every project required in this course.

2. Further Exploration

Now that you've taken your notes—done your field work, as anthropologists would say—you can study that information, seeking some meaning in it. A good way to try to discover meanings is to look for relationships or connections among details which may initially appear to be unrelated. For example, can you notice similarities in the ways several people were dressed, in the things they said, in the way they talked, in their gestures? Do you perceive that certain actions always (or frequently) led to the same kinds of responses or results? Can you fit people, things or actions you observed into categories? In other words, what *patterns* can you discover in the details you've jotted down?

In your journal, list as many patterns (categories, similarities, causes-and-effects) as you can find. Spend at least 15 minutes doing this, and write with the intent to share what you put down with someone else in the class. Since you will have an audience, even though an informal one, try to express your ideas clearly. Then pair up with someone and discuss the relationships you've found.

Once you've done this, write in your journal the answer to this question: What do you perceive as the significance of this place and the kinds of behavior that go on there in the lives of the people who frequent the place?

We will discuss many of the answers in class.

3. Paper I

Are you wondering what happened to anthropology? As you should soon discover, it's been here all the time. For what you have just done is essentially what an anthropologist does, although you, of course, have done it on a very small scale. Now that you know this, what conclusions can you draw about what an anthropologist does?

Using the experience you've just had as evidence, support, and illustration, write a paper to explain what you think an anthropologist does. Write it with this class in mind as audience. This means that you'll be writing to people who are in the same boat with you—people who are not experts on anthropology, who are a bit shaky in this situation themselves, people who aren't threatening to you, who can't judge you and say you're wrong. Your opinion is as good as theirs.

Also keep in mind that one of the reasons you're writing this paper is to explore your ideas, to articulate and consolidate them. In a sense, you're writing as much to *learn* for yourself what you think as to *communicate* what you think to others. So don't be afraid to take a few risks. Say what you suspect, even if you're not sure about it. Just be sure to back up what you say with evidence from your search experience.

The following questions should help you direct and organize your thoughts:

a.   What does an anthropologist do? That is, what kinds of activities does an anthropologist engage in?

b.   What are the anthropologist's assumptions (or expectations, or *hopes*) while engaging in these activities?

c.   What are some of the diffculties involved in doing what an anthropologist does?

d.   Why do you suppose the anthropologist bothers? In other words, once the job is done, what has been accomplished for the anthropologist? For others?

4. Workshop Questions

Now that you have completed the paper assignment for this project, write an evaluation of the particular paper you have just been given. Use the following questions to guide your thinking and writing:

a.   What points does the paper make?

b.   What evidence substantiates each point? What is the source of each bit of evidence? How do you know?

c.   What questions would you need to have answered in order to understand the paper more thoroughly?

d.   What evidence, if any, seems unnecessary or irrelevant? Why?

e.   In what ways does the paper accomplish its purpose? How might it do so even more thoroughly?

f.   In what ways is the paper suited to its audience? In what ways might the writer make it even more suitable for its audience?

Project II: Dance

1. Initial Exploration

In your first assignment you engaged in a search activity as a way of exploring a new subject, to help you get an idea of what that subject was about. You used writing to help you think and learn about it. Now you will use writing again, not only to help you explore a new subject through a search experience, but through research as well.

What is dance? Do you think you know? You've probably seen people do it. You may even have done it yourself. Most likely you have had some experience with dance, either as an observer or a participant, that has led you to form some opinions about what dance is. Even if you have not formulated any opinions, your experience has probably given you the basis for doing so.

Freewrite in your journal for fifteen minutes or so about dance. Try to explain to yourself what *you* think it is, what *your* ideas about it are and how *you* think you got them. You will not have to share this piece of writing with anyone. Since it is just for you, since you are doing it just to get in touch with your ideas, you do not have to worry about form, about grammar or spelling or ordering your ideas logically. Just get down as many ideas as you can, to make your explanation/definition as full as possible.

2. Systematic Search Activity

You have done some thinking on paper about what dance is. You have sat in a classroom—away from dancers and dancing—and written about it off the top of your head. I wonder whether the thoughts you've jotted down are definitive for you. I wonder whether you might modify them somewhat if you were to write about dance again after a more direct exposure to dancers and dancing than you were able to get by sitting in a classroom trying to draw on only memories of dance.

Now that you have your journal piece as a starting point, I would like you to engage in an activity that will further expose you to dance. Through this exposure you will probably discover more about dance; as a result, you will probably expand or modify your present explanation/definition. Further exposure to dance may be gained in one of the following ways:

Doing: If you're adventurous enough, or curious enough, or if you've always had a secret desire to try dancing, you could learn more about dance by doing it. That is, you could participate—for free—in a dance lesson. Here's how:

You may take a dance lesson by participating in a dance class at Brookdale. The instructor, Lori DeShaw, is willing to have you participate in any one of her classes. Even if you have no idea of what a dance class is like, she guarantees she can easily incorporate you into a class at any point in her learning program.

Lori's classes meet every Monday and Wednesday from 8:30 until 11:30 A.M. All you have to do to have your "lesson" is show up at one of her classes about ten minutes early and tell Lori that you're from English 126 and have come to participate in her class.

As for dress, if you have dance clothing—tights and leotard—fine. If not, that's fine too. Sweat pants and a T-shirt or even a jogging suit will do.

Observing: If you don't feel adventuresome enough to try to learn more about dance by doing it, you could try to learn more by watching it. Here are two possibilities:

a. You may observe non-dancers learning about dance in a Brookdale course. Even if you don't wish to participate, Lori will welcome you as a spectator in one of her classes. If you decide to choose this option, see *Doing*, above, for meeting times and location of classes.

b. You may observe professional dancers performing on film. Your instructor will give you a list of the films available and tell you the procedures for viewing them.

The reason for doing or observing dance in one of these ways is to help you learn more about what it is and what goes into it, and also maybe to discover what you feel about it—what your attitudes are. Writing about whichever activity you choose will help you explore, articulate, clarify, structure, and examine whatever ideas you get from engaging in the activity. Therefore, I ask you to write in your journal about whatever activity you do. If you choose the *Doing* activity, then write about it in your journal as soon after doing it as possible, so as not to forget what you did or lose your immediate impressions. If you choose an *Observing* activity, do your writing on the spot, while observing.

Remember, this piece of writing is to help you think. You are doing it for yourself. You will not be required to share it with anyone else.

Again, as in the first project, we will create a heuristic to guide you in thinking and writing about your search experience. We will use the following starter questions and "Creating Heuristics" to do so.

(For "Creating Heuristics," see pp. 184-185.)

Starter Questions for the Doing activity:

a. What were you doing with your body?
b. What were you doing with your mind?
c. How did the experience help you to know more about dance?

Starter Questions for the Observing activity:

a. What are you seeing?
b. What are you thinking and feeling as you watch?
c. How does watching help you to know more about dance?

Be sure to record the heuristic in your journal and take the journal with you when you go to do your search activity. Use it to help you write about your search experience.

3. Reflection

Once you have written about your search experience in your journal, go back and read your first journal piece in this project. Compare the two. Do both pieces express the same ideas and attitudes about dance? Why do you think they do or do not, as the case may be?

In your journal write a brief comparison of the two. This piece will be shared with other members of the class.

4. Identification of Point of View

Now that you have had the chance to discuss your search experience and to hear about the search experiences of others, write a brief piece in your journal explaining for yourself your frame of reference and your point of view regarding the subject matter you've searched. The following questions will help:

What was the extent of your experience with and knowledge about this subject before you did the search activity? Before the class discussion? What is it now? What were your ideas and attitudes about this subject before your search experience? Before the class discussion? What are they now?

We will discuss frame of reference and point of view in class after you do this piece of writing.

5. Research

You have engaged in an activity to help you think and learn something about dance. You have thought on paper about your experience and have written some personal explanations/definitions of dance. You have shared and discussed these with other members of the class. Now let's see where your thoughts and observations, your explanations and definitions, coincide with those of "experts." By expert, I mean someone who has devoted time to studying dance (either by doing it or observing it extensively) and to thinking and writing about it.

You will do your research in the book *The Dancer Prepares,* which is on reserve. Although this book focuses on modern dance, most of what it says applies to any form of artistic dance. You will not need to read the entire book, although it is very short and you could do so easily if you should be especially interested. You should, however, read all sections that are pertinent to the search activity you engaged in.

As you read, you should take notes in your journal. The following questions should help with your note-taking:

What ideas and information in the book are related in some ways to ideas and information in your notes—that is, to ideas and information you got, or started to get, as you did your search activity? What ideas and information are totally new?

Does the book give or suggest a definition of dance? If so, what is it? If it doesn't, why do you think it doesn't?

Does the book explain what some of the elements of dance are?

Do you think it would have been better to have read the book before doing the search activity? If so, why? In what specific ways would it have been better? If no, why not? In what specific ways is it better to do the reading after the activity?

Why do you think the assignment asks you to do the activity first and then do the reading?

6. Review of the Research Process

Now write in your journal a brief account of your research experience so far. What research have you done? Where did you do it? How did you go about it? How did you feel as you did it? Were you confused at any point? Did you need help? How did you get it? What procedures or steps did you follow in doing your research? How did you arrive at those procedures? Did you invent them yourself? If so, do you know how? Or did you learn them? How? How did you keep track of your information as you got it? How many sources did you look at? How many of the ones you looked at did you actually use? What problems are you having with your research? What questions do you have?

7. Synthesis of Search and Research Findings

Now that you have completed your research, look back and compare your research notes with your search notes. Reflect on what you learned through the direct experience of your search project and what you learned from someone else's experiences—from the reading you did in your research. Where do the information and ideas gained from each of these methods of inquiry coincide or overlap? Where do they diverge? Does the information in the research notes ever contradict information in the search notes? What kinds of things did you learn from doing research that you never could have learned from doing the search project only? What did you gain from the search project that you could not have gotten by doing only the research portion? Do the similiarities and/or differences in the knowledge gained in these two ways lead you to any new conclusions about the subject you explored in this project? Do they lead you to any new conclusions about knowledge and learning?

8. Paper II

Now that you have explored dance in two ways, firsthand through your search activity and secondhand through your reading, you should have a better basis for explaining it to someone else than you did before you began the project. Whereas up until now most of the writing you have done for this project has been for yourself, to help you *think and sort out* ideas, your next and final piece of writing about dance will be for someone else, to *communicate* your ideas.

Thinking of me as your audience, write a paper explaining what dance is and what your attitude toward artistic dance is. Remember that I am someone who has done a search-research project on dance along with you, but I am also someone who knew the whole sequence of assignments for the project ahead of time, as you did not. This means two things. First of all, it means that I, like you, am not an expert on dance, that I learned something about dance along with you. It also means, however, that I am a bit of an expert on writing—that I knew how the project was designed to help you learn more about writing. Therefore, although I am not in a position to pass judgment on your ideas and attitudes about dance, I can judge how clearly and convincingly you present the ideas and attitudes. What this all means, in turn, is that you have a good chance of teaching me something about dance and of influencing the way I think about it, but you will have to do so through good writing—by presenting effective details and examples from both your search and research activities to illustrate your points *and* by ordering those points, details and examples clearly and logically.

Or, stated more simply, you may find that the key to appealing to this audience lies in how well you say what you have to say.

9. Workshop Questions

Now that you have completed the paper assignment for this project, write an evaluation of the particular paper you have just been given. Use the following questions to guide your thinking and writing:

a. What points does the paper make?
b. What evidence substantiates each point? What is the source of each bit of evidence? How do you know?
c. What questions would you need to have answered in order to understand the paper more thoroughly?
d. What evidence, if any, seems unnecessary or irrelevant? Why?
e. In what ways does the paper accomplish its purpose? How might it do so even more thoroughly?
f. In what ways is the paper suited to its audience? In what ways might the writer make it even more suitable for its audience?

Project III: Law

1. Systematic Search Activity

In this search-research project you will use writing to help you explore and learn something about law. The search portion of your project will entail visiting a court and doing some interviewing and/or observing there. The research portion of your project will entail reading about what you observed firsthand in court. Your final paper will synthesize what you have learned in both portions, presenting along with the facts your attitudes and speculations about some aspect of law.

Your main purpose in visiting a court will be to hear cases with a view to choosing one to explore in depth. Hopefully during the session you attend a number of different kinds of cases will be presented, because this will both make the session more interesting for you and give you a greater range of possibilities from which to choose "your case." Needless to say, you will have to watch and listen closely to the case and to keep pretty thorough notes in your journal of what the cases involve, because when it comes time to work with the case of your choice you will want to have as much information about it as you can.

One way to try to ensure that you will understand what's going on as cases are being heard is to get an overview of how a session in this particular court works—to understand, that is, the procedures followed and how a session is structured. Although you will not have anyone to summarize and interpret cases for you—meaning that you will therefore have to rely on your own direct observation for your understanding of them—you may be able to get someone to help you understand the workings of the court. So, if possible, you should probably seek an interview—however informal and brief—with some court personnel (the judge, the prosecutor, the clerk, the judge's secretary) to get an explanation of how sessions in this court work. If you understand the context in which the cases are heard, you may better understand the cases.

Before thinking any further about how to conduct your observation, you might like to know more specifically where you can go to do it. You have a choice of three kinds of courts, listed below along with some information about their locations and the kinds of cases heard in them.

a.   *Municipal courts*. These are the courts with the most local flavor, for they are the local courts, the court of the town, city, or township, you live in. Municipal courts hold hearings and trials, and cases are usually quasi-criminal, involving offenses like traffic violations or the passing of bad checks. (Sometimes, however, the preliminary hearings for serious offenses are held here.)

Since defendants frequently do not bring lawyers to municipal court, these hearings and trials are often not very formal.

One advantage of choosing to attend a municipal court is that they hold night sessions. Another is that it is probably a bit easier to get to talk to court personnel here, due to the relatively informal nature of the sessions.

If you decide to visit a municipal court, call ahead of time to find out when sessions are held. Also, when you call, be sure to ask how you might go about getting an interview with court personnel before or after the session.

b. *County District Court.* There are two branches of District Court in Monmouth County, one in Long Branch and one in Asbury Park. These courts hold trials dealing exclusively with civil cases, involving things like people suing other people for money. (Suits handled in County District Court, however, do not exceed $3,000. If you want "heavier stuff" you'll have to go higher.)

These courts are in session five days a week, but again you should call for the precise schedule. Clerks should be helpful in letting you know how to get to talk with court personnel.

c. *Superior Court.* This is the highest court in the county, located in the county seat, Freehold. Here you can see and hear full-scale trials, for both civil and criminal cases. All trials are open to the public, except for juvenile cases.

Again, it would be wise to call to find out when and where what kinds of sessions are held and to try to make arrangements to talk with court personnel.

Once you have decided on where to go and found out how to get to talk to court personnel, you'll want to think about what you need to find out during your visit. I suggest that you might feel more comfortable and do a better job if you have a plan for conducting your interview. Using the basic "starter" questions below and the steps outlined in "Creating Heuristics," we can devise a master set of questions from which you can choose those appropriate to your interview. The basic questions to use as starting points are:

a. What are the general purposes (goals) of a session in this court?
b. What are the procedures followed in a session?
c. How is a session structured?

Be sure to copy the heuristic we devise into your journal. Before making your court visit, pinpoint which questions you want to use in *your* interview.

(For "Creating Heuristics," see pp. 184-185.)

It will probably also be helpful to have some guidelines for taking notes on the cases. What should you look and listen for? Again, beginning with the basic "starter" questions below, we can create a heuristic to help you discover the important points in each case:

a. Why are these people in court?
b. What are the issues involved?
c. How is the case conducted?
d. What are your reactions to the case and the way it is conducted?

Again, be sure to copy the heuristic in your journal so you can use it when you take notes on the case. And remember the following pointers.

- As you listen to each case, be sure to make a separate list of any terms you don't understand.

- As you listen and take notes on cases, be looking to single out one case to explore further later on. Choose a case that particularly interests you. For example, is there a case you identify with for some reason (*any* reason)? Is there one that stands out for you because it strikes you as being handled particularly well or particularly unfairly? Is there a case that stands out because you are puzzled by how it is being handled and would like to clear up your confusion?

- Be sure to take all notes in your journal for future use.

2. Further Exploration

Once you have left the court, freewrite in your journal about the case you found most interesting. What did it involve? Why did it grab your interest? We will discuss these choices in class, so even though you are writing informally, try to keep an outside audience in mind.

3. Identification of Point of View

Now that you have had the chance to discuss your search experience and to hear about the search experiences of others, write a brief piece in your journal explaining for yourself your frame of reference and your point of view regarding the subject matter you've searched. The following questions will help:

What was the extent of your experience with and knowledge about this subject before you did the search activity? Before the class discussion? What is it now? What were your ideas and attitudes about this subject before your search experience? Before the class discussion? What are they now?

We will discuss frame of reference and point of view in class after you do this piece of writing.

4. Research

You have seen the law in action and have chosen an aspect of the law that seems interesting enough to explore a bit more thoroughly. Furthermore, you have thought a bit about how much you know about some matters related to law and how you feel about these matters. This all serves as useful background for doing some research about law.

You will do your research in order to understand more about the case you have chosen—to learn more about the offense or issue involved, the action taken on the case, and how this particular case relates to and reveals something about law in general. I suggest you use the following books, all available in the LRC: the legal dictionaries, the green books entitled *NJSA (New Jersey Statutes Annotated)*, and the legal encyclopedias entitled *American Jurisprudence* and *Corpus Juris Secundum*.

You should go first to a legal dictionary, to look up and write down the definitions of any legal terminology that you heard in court and did not understand.

The next book you choose will depend on your case. If you chose a criminal case, then you will probably do your research in *NJSA*. If you chose a civil case, you will probably find one of the legal encyclopedias more helpful. (Of the two, *American Jurisprudence* is probably more readable.) The *NJSA* and the legal encyclopedias will give you a definition of the offense or issue your chosen case involves. In addition, the encyclopedias will give examples, history, and other background related to the offense.

Read to learn as much as you can about the offense or issue and the kinds of actions taken for it. Take notes as you go, not only on what the books say, but also on any thoughts you have about your chosen case in relation to what the books say.

5. Review of the Research Process

Now write in your journal a brief account of your research experience so far. What research have you done? Where did you do it? How did you go about it? How did you feel as you did it? Were you confused at any point? Did you need help? How did you get it? What procedures or steps did you follow in doing your research? How did you arrive at those procedures? Did you invent them yourself? If so, do you know how? Or did you learn them? How? How did you keep track of your information as you got it? How many sources did you look at? How many of the ones you looked at did you actually use? What problems are you having with your research? What questions do you have?

6. Synthesis of Search and Research Findings

Now that you have completed your research, look back and compare your research notes with your search notes for this project. Reflect on what you learned through the direct experience of your search project and what you learned from some else's experiences—from the reading you did in your research. Where do the information and ideas gained from each of these methods of inquiry coincide or overlap? Where do they diverge? Does the information in the research notes ever contradict information in the search notes? What kinds of things did you learn from doing research that you never could have learned from doing the search project only? What did you gain from the search project that you could not have gotten by doing only the research portion? Do the similiarities and/or differences in the knowledge gained in these two ways lead you to any new conclusions about the subject you explored in this project? Do they lead you to any new conclusions about knowledge and learning?

7. Paper III

You have searched and researched an aspect of law—an offense or issue heard at some level of our county court system. Now write a paper to show someone who is knowledgeable about law—an instructor, a lawyer, someone connected with the legal system in some way—what you have learned.

In doing so, there are a few basic areas that you will probably want to cover. You will want to explain the case you observed and how you reacted to it. You will want to give the professional definition of the offense or issue involved and to relate your case to this definition. You will also want to discuss why you think the decision went the way it did and how you felt about it. Use plenty of specific evidence from both your search and research experiences to help you make your points.

Also, be sure to document all evidence gathered through research.

8. Workshop Questions

Now that you have completed the paper assignment for this project, write an evaluation of the particular paper you have just been given. Use the following questions to guide your thinking and writing:

a.   What points does the paper make?
b.   What evidence substantiates each point? What is the source of each bit of evidence? How do you know?
c.   What questions would you need to have answered in order to understand the paper more thoroughly?
d.   What evidence, if any, seems unnecessary or irrelevant? Why?
e.   In what ways does the paper accomplish its purpose? How might it do so even more thoroughly?
f.   In what ways is the paper suited to its audience? In what ways might the writer make it even more suitable for its audience?

Project IV: Natural Science

1. Systematic Search Activity

Most people associate the study of science with test tubes, laboratories, and tightly controlled experiments. But few think of scientists as writers. Few would imagine that there is a connection between writing and doing science. For many scientists, however, writing is an important tool. They use it to help them sort out, clarify, examine—in short, to think about—information and ideas they have gathered in their experiments. They use it to explain what they've observed—to themselves first, and then to others. In your next project—on natural science—you should gain an awareness of how writing can be as useful to scientists as to people working and learning in other disciplines.

Living as we do in a state and county bounded on one side by the Atlantic Ocean, we are close to an area that is under constant study by natural scientists: the shore. In this search-research project you will investigate a problem that faces many beachfront areas in New Jersey and other coastal states, the problem of beach stabilization and erosion control.

You might expect that the logical way to begin the assignment would be for me to explain these terms and give you a clear, concise definition of the problem.

Since I believe, however, that any definition I give you will have less meaning for you than one you arrive at yourself, I am not going to do this. Instead I will ask you to engage in a few activities. In doing so, you should arrive at your own understanding of these terms and begin to develop your own definition of this problem.

As the search portion of your project you will visit a beach. Your reaction to this might be, Hey, I don't have to do this—I've been to the beach a million times before. But I'd guess that you've never experienced the beach in quite the same way as you'll experience it this time, and for this reason, doing this portion of the assignment is crucial. It will give you a steady grip—a firm starting point and a clear frame of reference—which will make the rest of the project easier to understand and much more interesting.

You may choose any beach in the county. I would especially recommend the oceanfront beach at Sandy Hook, the beach in Asbury Park, or one of the beaches in Sea Bright or Long Branch backed by a seawall or bulkheads.

Take your journal with you and be prepared to do some roaming around. Don't just view the beach from a boardwalk (or any other *single* point). Walk along the beach; cover at least a mile. As you roam the beach, make note of the following characteristics: natural elements or characteristics and artificial elements or characteristics of the beach. What parts of the beach are natural—put there by nature? What parts of the beach are artificial—put there by man? You might jot down notes as you walk.

2. Further Exploration

When you've finished your search, sit down and freewrite for fifteen or twenty minutes about the natural and artificial elements and characteristics of the beach. Reflect on their meaning. You can do so by trying to answer these questions:

> On the basis of what you've observed, what do you think is the reason for the presence of artificial elements on this beach? In other words, when humans intervened to alter the natural beach in some way, why did they do so? What were their intentions?

And a harder question, but one worth speculation:

> What are the effects of human intervention on this beach?

> We will discuss your reflections and speculations in class.

3. Identification of Point of View

Now that you have had the chance to discuss your search experience and to hear about the search experiences of others, write a brief piece in your journal explaining for yourself your frame of reference and your point of view regarding the subject matter you've searched. The following questions will help:

> What was the extent of your experience with and knowledge about this subject

before you did the search activity? Before the class discussion? What is it now? What were your ideas and attitudes about this subject before your search experience? Before the class discussion? What are they now?

We will discuss frame of reference and point of view in class after you do this piece of writing.

4. Research, Part A

Now that you have examined the beach and looked at and thought about the differences between natural and man-made elements and characteristics of beaches, we will view two films about these two aspects of beaches. The first film, "The Beach: A River of Sand," explains something about how beaches are formed and how their formation can be distorted or impeded. The second, "The New Jersey Shoreline," explains something about how beaches are destroyed and introduces some of the methods used to prevent or remedy that destruction.

You may want to take notes in your journal as you watch each film. After you view each film, you will have fifteen minutes or so to reflect in your journal upon what you've seen.

5. Reflection

You have examined some natural and artificial aspects of beaches firsthand, and you have seen two films prepared by scientists who have studied and drawn some conclusions about these aspects of beaches. Look back at your journal and compare the notes on your search experience with those on your research experience of viewing the films. Reflect in writing on what you learned through the direct experience of your search activity and what you learned from someone else's experiences—condensed and presented to you in the films. Where do the information and ideas gained in each of these ways coincide or overlap? Where do they diverge? What kinds of things did you learn from your research (the films) that you never could have learned from doing the search activity only? What did you gain from the search project that you could not have gotten by doing only the research? Do the similarities and/or differences in the knowledge gained in these two ways lead you to any new conclusions about your subject? Do they lead you to any new conclusions about knowledge and learning?

6. Paper IV A

You were told at the beginning of this project that you would investigate the problem of beach stabilization and erosion control, that you were to discover for yourself what these terms meant and that you were to develop your own definition—your own explanation—of this problem. At this point you should be able to define the terms and formulate a working definition of the problem.

Write a brief paper doing just that. Consider as your audience new students in a natural science course—that is, people who (like yourself before you began this project) may think they understand the terms and the problem but really have a good deal to learn before they have an informed understanding.

These papers will be discussed in our classroom workshop.

7. Research, Part B

You now have an informed understanding of the problem we are investigating. But is the problem as simple as it seems? Probably not. Sometimes the deeper you look into a problem, the more thoroughly you examine it, the more complex and difficult it reveals itself to be. Is beach stabilization and erosion control such a problem? Do a little more research before you attempt to answer.

In the LRC you will find several articles and publications which deal with this problem in more detail. Read at least two, at least one dealing with natural methods of resolving the problem, and at least one dealing with artificial methods. (If you wish, you might contact the American Littoral Society for extra information.)

As you read, you will of course find it helpful to have an idea of what you're looking for. Essentially you will want to see 1) how your definition of the problem holds up against more information and 2) how *you* think the problem can be resolved. We can transform these two points into starter questions, and you can use them in conjunction with "Creating Heuristics" to devise a set of questions to guide you in your reading.

Be sure to copy the heuristic in your journal and have it with you to help when you do your research.

(For "Creating Heuristics," see pp. 184-185.)

8. Synthesis of Search and Research Findings

Now that you have completed your research, look back and compare your research notes with your search notes from this project. Reflect on what you learned through the direct experience of your search project and what you learned from someone else's experiences—from the reading you did in your research. Where do the information and ideas gained from each of these methods of inquiry coincide or overlap? Where do they diverge? Does the information in the research notes ever contradict information in the search notes? What kinds of things did you learn from doing research that you never could have learned from doing the search project only? What did you gain from the search project that you could not have gotten by doing only the research portion? Do the similarities and/or differences in the knowledge gained in these two ways lead you to any new conclusions about the subject you explored in this project? Do they lead you to any new conclusions about knowledge and learning?

9. Paper IV B

You have searched, researched as a class, and then researched again individually the problem of beach stabilization and erosion control. Now write a paper about what you have learned. Consider as your audience a natural science instructor, someone knowledgeable about the problems that face our beachfronts. Write to show your audience what you know about the problem you have investigated and what *you* personally feel its solutions are and why. Use as evidence, support, and illustration a combination of the most vivid, valid, and convincing details and facts you gathered in doing your search and research. Remember that your audience is a professional who will expect that you document any facts and ideas you gained from your research. These papers will be discussed in class.

10. Workshop Questions

Now that you have completed the paper assignment for this project, write an evaluation of the particular paper you have just been given. Use the following questions to guide your thinking and writing:

a. What points does the paper make?
b. What evidence substantiates each point? What is the source of each bit of evidence? How do you know?
c. What questions would you need to have answered in order to understand the paper more thoroughly?
d. What evidence, if any, seems unnecessary or irrelevant? Why?
e. In what ways does the paper accomplish its purpose? How might it do so even more thoroughly?
f. In what ways is the paper suited to its audience? In what ways might the writer make it even more suitable for its audience?

Project V: Human Sexuality

1. Systematic Search Activity

In your final search-research project you will think/write/learn about some aspect of sexuality in our culture. If you think about it for only a few minutes, it will probably strike you that *sexuality* is a word which requires a very broad definition. (Think of the hodgepodge of terms one can associate with sexuality—words like *repression, monogamy, sublimation, love, homosexuality, eroticism, prostitution, rape, taboo....*) Not only does sexuality encompass a wide range of behaviors and attitudes, but the study of it involves a diversity of disciplines, from sociology to psychology to biology to history to law to....We could go on, but you've probably got the point.

The point of beginning with this point is to introduce you to how this project will be different from the others you've done so far. Certainly each subject you've investigated has been a broad one. But for each of the previous projects you've done, the assignments have focused on one aspect of that subject; they have, to a great extent, restricted the topic for you. This time the assignment will not focus on one aspect of the subject. Instead it will present you with a variety of aspects of the subject—a variety suggestive of the wide range of behaviors and attitudes the subject covers—and ask you to determine the aspect you would most like to investigate. You may explore any aspect of human sexuality, from individual roles and relationships to social attitudes and issues.

In providing you with a greater range of choice, however, this assignment also imposes upon you greater responsibility. You will have to make more decisions on your own about how to conduct both the search and research portions of your project.

The search portion of your project will involve some kind of interview or observation. Below is a list of possible search activities, each accompanied by two or three questions suggesting the goal(s) or purpose(s) of the activity.

1) Interview a teacher or administrator in a local elementary, junior high, or high school about that school's sex education program. Why do they have such a program, and what is it like? If they don't have a sex education program, why not?

2) Visit a birth control clinic. What kinds of services does it offer and why? What kind of population does it serve?

3) Look through a variety of magazines (including some directed at different kinds of audiences—e.g., *Field and Stream* and *Family Circle*) to discover how sex is used to sell products. What are the motives of the advertisers? How and why does the use of sex in advertising differ from one magazine to the next?

4) Visit an adult book store. What kinds of products does it offer? What kind of clientele does it serve?

5) See an X-rated movie. What is the difference between an X and R rating? Why are people attracted to an X-rated movie?

6) Go to a performance or presentation featuring the work of people who belong to an alternate sexual culture (a culture in which sexual relationships take a form other than heterosexual monogamy). You might, for example, go hear a lesbian poetry reading or go see a transvestite show. Compare the performance to one featuring the work of people in the heterosexual-monogamous culture. What role does sexuality play in each of the two performances? What does each reveal about the sexuality of the people who created it? Are there any essential differences between the two?

7) Interview a lawyer or judge about the issue of child custody. Why do women usually get custody in a divorce case?

8) Go to a police station and interview police about sex crimes. How are rape cases handled? Why are women reluctant to report rape? What does an examination of the victim consist of?

9) Interview someone in an alternate sexual relationship—one other than heterosexual monogamy. You might choose to talk to someone involved in a homosexual relationship, a "group" marriage or communal relationship, or you might interview someone who has chosen to live alone, a "confirmed bachelor," for example. What is the structure of this relationship? What role

does sex play in it, or what are the sexual roles? How is it different from the traditional heterosexual monogamy?

Once you've decided on a topic to explore, you'll need an approach to help you discover and learn about it. Since you are working more independently in this project, you'll be responsible for devising your own heuristic to guide you in your interview or observation. Along with "Creating Heuristics," use as starter questions the questions which accompany your activity (see list above), and in your journal write as many more questions as you can. When you are finished you might pair up with someone and exchange questions. Even if you've both chosen different topics, you can react to each other's set of questions and perhaps suggest additional ones to each other.

Be sure to record notes on your interview or observation in your journal.

After you have completed your search activity, you will be grouped according to general areas that topics fit into: sexual roles, sexual relationships, social issues. You will share your findings before going on to the next journal writing.

(For "Creating Heuristics," see pp. 184-185.)

2. Identification of Point of View

Now that you have had the chance to discuss your search experience and to hear about the search experiences of others, write a brief piece in your journal explaining for yourself your frame of reference and your point of view regarding the subject matter you've searched. The following questions will help:

What was the extent of your experience with and knowledge about this subject before you did the search activity? Before the class discussion? What is it now? What were your ideas and attitudes about this subject before your search experience? Before the class discussion? What are they now?

We will discuss frame of reference and point of view in class after you do this piece of writing.

3. Research

You have gathered some information about an aspect of sexuality in our culture, and you have formed some opinions about it. That is to say, the search experience has become part of your frame of reference and has perhaps influenced your point of view about an aspect of human sexuality. Now you can go on to expand your knowledge and perhaps even alter your point of view through doing some research on the area you have begun to explore.

Again, you will be working more independently this time, with less guidance from the assignment. This time you will be responsible for locating your own sources of information. Go to a library (the LRC, the Monmouth County Library) and check for books and articles on your topic. Librarians will help you. In addition, Tom Shostak, who teaches the Human Sexuality course here at Brookdale, has offered to give you suggestions on research sources. You can find him during his office hours at his desk in the Interdisciplinary Studies area on the main floor of the Human Affairs Institute.

Once you have selected books and articles related to your topic, you can use the heuristic you devised for your search activity to guide you in your reading and note-taking. You have found the answers to many of those questions through interviewing and/or observing. Now, read to see how the "experts" (or simply other researchers) have answered the same questions.

Obviously in your search project you visited a specific place on our list—such as the Thompson School in Middletown (1) or Planned Parenthood of Monmouth County (2)—or one specific person—a particular lawyer (7) or a particular policeman (8)—and it is unlikely that you will find information on that specific place or person. What you will be looking for will be information on sex education (1) or birth control clinics (2) or procedures for the investigation of rape charges (8). You will be doing general research on the aspect of sexuality you began to explore through a specific case. After you have completed the research you can see how general information on the topic compares with the information you discovered in a specific case, or—to reverse the order—you can see how the place you visited or the person you interviewed fits in with other places or people in the same category, i.e., other schools (1), other birth control clinics (2), other lawyers (7), etc.

4. Review of the Research Process

Now write in your journal a brief account of your research experience so far. What research have you done? Where did you do it? How did you go about it? How did you feel as you did it? Were you confused at any point? Did you need help? How did you get it? What procedures or steps did you follow in doing your research? How did you arrive at those procedures? Did you invent them yourself? If so, do you know how? Or did you learn them? How? How did you keep track of your information as you got it? How many sources did you look at? How many of the ones you looked at did you actually use? What problems are you having with your research? What questions do you have?

5. Synthesis of Search and Research Findings

Now that you have completed your research, look back and compare your research notes with your search notes for this project. Reflect on what you learned through the direct experience of your search project and what you learned from someone else's experiences—from the reading you did in your research. Where do the information and ideas gained from each of these methods of inquiry coincide or overlap? Where do they diverge? Does the information in the research notes ever contradict information in the search notes? What kinds of things did you learn from doing research that you never could have learned from doing the search project only? What did you gain from the search project that you could not have gotten by doing only the research portion? Do the similarities and/or differences in the knowledge gained in these two ways lead you to any new conclusions about the subject you explored in this project? Do they lead you to any new conclusions about knowledge and learning?

6. Paper V

You have now searched and researched an aspect of sexuality in our culture. In doing so you have established or clarified for yourself an attitude toward the topic you explored.

As you probably recognized long before you did this exploration, human sexuality is the kind of subject that people have strong opinions about. It is a controversial subject. As an aspect of human sexuality, whatever topic you have explored is probably the object of some controversy. Whatever opinion you have formed about your topic, it is likely that there is a group of people who feel quite differently about it.

You are to consider such a group the audience for your paper on human sexuality. Using the most appropriate, most forceful details and examples from both your search and research findings, write to promote your opinions on the topic. Write to try to persuade those who feel differently to see things your way. If possible, go even further and write to try to convince someone to take action on your idea. For example, if you chose option 1, you may feel that all schools in your community should have sex education programs. In this case, you could write a piece directed at parents, at the school board, at any or everyone who might be able to make this happen if you could persuade them to accept your opinion. Your piece could be written as a letter to a discrete group (e.g., the board of education), as a letter for general circulation to a larger group (parents), or it could be in the form of a letter to the editor of your local paper. The specific audience and the form you choose to write in are up to you.

Remember, when you are trying to convince someone to do something, they will want reasons why and evidence to support your claims. Use facts and observations from your search and research notes and journal entries to provide these. Give further weight to your argument by documenting your sources.

7. Workshop Questions

Now that you have completed the paper assignment for this project, write an evaluation of the particular paper you have just been given. Use the following questions to guide your thinking and writing:

a. What points does the paper make?

b. What evidence substantiates each point? What is the source of each bit of evidence? How do you know?

c. What questions would you need to have answered in order to understand the paper more thoroughly?

d. What evidence, if any, seems unnecessary or irrelevant? Why?

e. In what ways does the paper accomplish its purpose? How might it do so even more thoroughly?

f. In what ways is the paper suited to its audience? In what ways might the writer make it even more suitable for its audience?

Places and Persons

A Course in Personal Writing and Research

Donald Maxwell

This course, like others in this book, works by the inductive method, a procedure I found necessary to explain to my students in the People's Republic of China where I taught for a year using a modified version of the course. Since original thinking and inductive reasoning are even less encouraged there than in the United States, my students were wondering why I was asking them to do the things I was. One student evidently got my explanation a bit confused, however, as I discovered when I overheard him trying to tell someone from another class about what he called "Maxwell's *seductive* teaching method."

I was amused by the student's verbal slip, especially because it caused me to know what I had sensed about the course all along—that it should seduce students into writing thoughtfully and well. Originally, however, I had simply designed it as an alternative to the "conventional" freshman composition course at J. Sargeant Reynolds Community College in Richmond, Virginia. That conventional course had required a research paper and six regular papers, all in a 10-week quarter, and the kill-ratio in the course was high—nearly 30% dropped out—even for a school in which most of the students have been identified as "non-traditional" and "high-risk." My hope with this alternative course was to realize several of the goals for which the conventional course had been designed: to give students plenty of writing experience; to prepare students for the second and third quarter composition courses, which are dominated by the study of literary genres; and to insure that students be able to handle the formal research papers they were likely to encounter in other courses. But I also wanted to keep the students in class. And I decided that if I were to accomplish that, the students would need to see their writing in the course as real writing, and satisfying in itself, rather than as an abstract school exercise, written solely because it was assigned.

I designed the course, then, to deal with many of the kinds of writing traditionally associated with composition courses, but I didn't approach the activity of writing in traditional ways. For one thing, the subject matter was different. I decided that one way of making the writing real was to keep students at the center of it, having them write about what they knew, from where they were, as the cliché

205

goes. And I took that cliché both literally and figuratively. So this course includes assignments that invite students to look at neighbors, at neighborhoods, at their own homes and favorite places, and at their emotional conflicts and relationships with other people. These assignments, while encouraging students to write about and examine their own experiences and their own lives—something I believe valuable in its own right—also invite real-world examples of certain aspects of literature— character, setting, point of view, and conflict—so they lead right into the literature courses that at my school follow this one. And because they involve interviewing, searching government records, and exploring other relevant periodicals and books, they constitute serious research writing as well.

My intent in the course was also to give students experience with various forms of writing, so I designed assignments that would elicit pieces approximating the "traditional modes." Because my intention was to have students discover the forms for themselves, rather than to teach them directly, the various forms arise out of the writing situations rather than being imposed on the students from the start. So you will find assignments here which, without addressing the forms or strategies directly, invite narratives (as in 3, 13, 14, 18, 19), pieces heavily reliant on description (as in 5, 6, 7, 12), persuasion and argumentation (12, 17, 20), and such expository strategies as comparison and contrast (9, 10), definition (12), division and classification (12), and cause-and-effect analysis (15).

I also wanted the students in the course to write often—and they do. In addition to the twenty assignments, which are spread evenly across the ten weeks of the course, I usually ask them to complete three entries a week in a log of unassigned free-writings. And I ask them to write about their writing, sometimes about a single assignment (as with the individual commentaries that begin with assignment 3), sometimes in connection with their work to date (as with the mid-term and end-of-course self-evaluation). That's a lot of writing—too much for some students. If, after a couple of weeks, several students are having trouble keeping up, I sometimes cancel the log requirement or make it optional. I think it's important for students to write every day; but it's much more important that they feel *successful*, and that means being able to keep up with the pace of the assignments.

A casual look at many writing sequences might not show clearly all of the ways the assignments are interrelated. I hope that's true of this sequence, because I believe that too obvious a mechanism, while it may be very clear, tends to inhibit a student's analogical, holistic, and intuitive thinking processes. In this, a good sequence works like a good story or poem because even though it can be understood as a structure, its main power resides in what it does for the non-systematic areas of one's mind. In a sequence, as in a story or poem, much of the fun and excitement comes from discovering what is there and from participating in the creative process along with its author. So while these opening comments and my others that are spread throughout the assignments will point to the major inter-connections and development of the sequence, some connections will only be suggested, and others, which I have not seen, will remain to be discovered by you.

An additional word. The assignments in this sequence, simply because they are published in this book, may seem to be finished and complete. To me, however, they're the *hearts* of assignments, and in using them with actual classes I often add reflections on class discussions, explanatory comments, or anything else that personalizes the assignments or improves communication between me and those particular students. The purpose, at last, is to draw the students in—draw them into discoveries, into research, into consideration of the common elements in literature and their own lives, into self-evaluation, and into the power which writing gives and makes possible. And so if everything works right, my Chinese student's slip about the "seductive method" really *does* describe the course accurately.

PLACES AND PERSONS

1. You've probably been writing, in one way or another, since you were in the first grade, and you're probably pretty good at it by now. (Most people think they're *not* good at writing, so don't be surprised if you think that about yourself. But you might try to figure out why you have that opinion.) But here you are, sitting in yet another English class—this could be the thirteenth straight year of writing instruction for you. If this is your first experience in college, you may be a bit scared and a bit excited by the idea that this course just might be different from all those in your past. If you've already taken other college courses, you might be a bit disillusioned by now—or not, depending on who you are and how lucky you've been. (If you've already tried this particular course before—well, what can I say that you'll believe? Courage!)

So what are you feeling right now? You're sitting here, in this classroom, pen or pencil in hand, a blank piece of paper in front of you. You're beginning this writing course. How do you feel about it? How do you feel about writing and about having to take a writing course?

A FEW ASSURANCES BEFORE YOU BEGIN: I won't grade your writing. I won't use it to embarrass you. I don't care how long or short it is, only that you write what you feel and that you try to write truth. I don't care about your spelling, or your grammar, or your punctuation, or your handwriting. I'm interested only in what's on your mind, in what you want me to know. I'll probably use a few samples of good writing from this batch of writings in class next time, so if for some reason you don't want your writing shared with the class, just write "Don't use in class" on the top of your paper.

2. (As with assignment 1, this assignment invites students to express themselves, but this time in the form of a story.)

J. Sargeant Reynolds Community College is still pretty new to you (or new for this quarter, if you've been enrolled here before), and your first impression of the place is probably still clear to you. Before that first impression gets away from you, try to capture it on paper. Write down what you felt and noticed the first time you came here. You might like to try writing it in the form of a story.

3.   (This provides yet another opportunity to tell a story, but this time the students
        have to select a specific incident further in the past.)

In assignment 1, you tried to capture and communicate your feelings at the
time you were writing. (That's called "expressive writing," by the way, because you
were expressing yourself.) In assignment 2, you tried to tell a story (narration)
giving your first impression of a place, including what you felt and what you
noticed. (That was a combination of expression and observation.) In those two
assignments you've written about the immediate and about the recent past. For
assignment 3, I'd like you to think back over your years as a student and find some
memorable experience, either good or bad, that you had in school. Tell us in the
form of a story what happened. (To tell a story means—obviously—that you have to
have a story to tell. Be careful not to confuse telling a story with describing a
condition. There are all kinds of stories, but they all have in common that *something
happens*.)

There's a second part to this assignment. Attach a note to me telling me what
you did in writing this assignment that was different from what you did last time.
This gets you to focus on the writing process itself, after you've finished working
through it. Please do this for all future assignments too. Let me know what you tried
out, what you think worked well, what gave you trouble, and so on. Otherwise, I
might miss it or misinterpret something. Address me in the note; but in your
response to the actual assignment address the entire class.

Also, please title your writings from now on. And to keep us from getting
confused about which writing is which, please number them in accord with the
assignment number.

About manuscript preparation for the assigned writing: do *at least* two drafts,
period. The second one you can think of as a clean copy, if you like, but don't be
afraid to make changes as you copy. I almost always need three or four drafts to get a
thing right. And for the final copy, please type it or write it in dark ink on paper
without a ragged edge. (Try to turn a pile of ragged-edge papers into a stack, and
you'll see why I'm asking you to do that.)

For the freewritings, don't worry about getting each one right. Practice is
practice. Maybe you can think of the freewritings as practice and the assigned
writings as performance.

(Beginning with this assignment, and continuing until the end of the course, I
ask students to reflect upon each of their assigned writings. This activity is
new to most students, and is probably the most difficult aspect of the course
for many of them, especially for those who are accustomed to hiding their
weaknesses from the teacher. It takes these students quite some time to realize
that I am not keeping secret grades on them, though most of them eventually
seem to understand that I'm not out to get them. However difficult these
writings are for them, I still believe this activity is one of the most valuable
aspects of the course, because it really does help most students to get outside
the immediate experience of *doing* writing. Eventually, most of them become
able to see their own writing more or less objectively, something I specifically

ask them to do in their self-assessments and grade recommendations at later points in the course.)

4. For assignment 3 you told the story of a memorable experience that had something to do with school. Now try to make a statement *about* that experience. What was it that made the experience memorable for you? And just exactly what would you like us to understand about it?

(This is the first time I specifically ask students to abstract from experience. The questions suggest two levels of abstraction, the first closely connected to the student's personal experience, and the second—a bridge—aimed at communicating with the audience. I've found that these particular questions are especially helpful to students not accustomed to thinking in formal abstractions, students who, without such questions, have difficulty making coherent statements about their experience.

I sometimes have students do this assignment in class, even though that allows little time for reflection. There's a certain value in writing under pressure, especially when it's a follow-up exercise like this, and the pressure seems to help some of the less fluent writers accomplish the abstracting I ask for.)

5. (This begins a sequence of assignments dealing with place. The focus of assignment 5 is the place where each student writes. The assignment serves two main functions. First, it provides a bridge between the previous writings about the student's school experiences (1-4) and the writings to come (7-12) which are about the place the student lives. Second, it provides an opportunity for students to discuss their own study habits. This is especially helpful for the so-called "high-risk" students, who may never have thought about what conditions are conducive to study. In every class discussion of this assignment, I hear students offering each other gentle advice about where and how to study.)

When you write for this class or for other occasions, such as writing letters, paying bills, or studying for other courses, where do you do it? Where do you feel like writing? Maybe, like me, you write in different places. But all the places I write have some things in common, so I think I can say that "writing place," for me, means "type of place," or "conditions for writing." Maybe you do all kinds of writing in the same place, or maybe you do different kinds of writing in different places. Or maybe you haven't settled on a "writing place" yet. If that's so, then you probably should try out a few places to see what your "place" is like.

A friend of mine in college used to write in the bathroom. He said it was private and well-lit. After a while he turned the bathroom into a darkroom and became a photographer, so maybe the place affected him in some way that neither of us anticipated.

For several years Ernest Hemingway wrote in sidewalk cafes, in Paris. In winter he rented a one-room apartment only for writing and lived a few kilometers away from his wife and kid. He wrote in the morning, read in the afternoon, and talked with people in the evening. Later in his life he composed in pencil and typed standing at the mantle. Virginia Woolf wrote standing up at a tall table placed smack in the center of her workroom. George Orwell used to write at night and slept all morning. Another friend of mine likes to find a study carrel in a far corner of the library. One summer I wrote on the flat roof of a house on a hill in central Mexico, with farms on one side and the village on the other, and a mountain beyond. Finally, I had to go and climb the mountain.

And your place? What's it like? What makes it different from other places? If you write in more than one place, what do those places have in common? In what places *can't* you write? How is your writing place related to its surroundings—to the building it's in, or whatever?

P.S. Assignment 5 is the beginning of a sequence of writings designed to help you with certain types of analytical writing. In them you'll need to observe certain things, analyze them in certain ways, and communicate to the rest of us what you observed and analyzed. You can think of the assignments as being both independent of each other and interconnected. If you want to get another perspective on this sort of writing practice, look up the word "synergy" in a good dictionary.

(You may recognize the questions for this assignment as derived from tagmemics, the procedure for discovery developed by Young, Becker, and Pike. Although many students aren't ready for this kind of analytical thinking, this heuristic procedure helps them develop their analytical thinking skills without their being aware of what's happening. Many of them simply answer the questions directly, which makes for a somewhat mechanical piece of writing. On the other hand, it enables them to see something about organization—again, without that being the subject of formal discussion. The more skilled students usually go on to write rather sophisticated analyses in which the method of inquiry is invisible.)

6. ˙ (This is an exercise in direct observation, not only of a place, but also of the way being in that place causes the observer to feel. In that regard, it's a much more sophisticated version of the expressive writing requested in assignments 1, 2, and 3.)

Your first four pieces of writing for this course were mainly about your feelings and experiences as a student. In assignment 5 you wrote about the place where you write, and I invited you to think about that place as a thing by itself, as one of a type of similar places, and as a part of a larger structure or system. Now I'd like you to combine the focuses of those writings: write about your favorite place around here, the one place where you usually feel good. It might or might not be the place where you write; it might be in your home, or it might be up a tree or in some public place. What's important is that you feel good there. (If you have trouble identifying a single place, make a list of several and go try them out. Write about the one that feels best to you at the time.)

Go get yourself into the place and feel it out for a few minutes. How does it affect you? Try to identify what it is about the place that causes you to feel good. How does the place differ from other places almost, but not quite, like it? In what ways do you feel different in that place than you feel just a little distance away from it? How big is the place for you? How far can you move from the center of it and still feel the same way? Is there any way to predict where you're likely to feel good?

At first glance, this assignment might seem a lot like the previous one. One difference is that this time I'm inviting you to think about your *feelings,* as they're related to a place. But there are other hidden differences, as well, and one of the things you might mention in your note to me this time is what differences you discover in the process of writing this assignment.

I have one caution for you. This is not a memory exploration; it's an exercise in direct observation, so you absolutely *MUST* BE IN YOUR PLACE WHILE YOU WRITE THE FIRST DRAFT. Otherwise, you'll never know how it affects you directly, and you'll write only what you *think* is true and not what *is.*

(Despite my cautionary notes, several students in every class try to write this from memory or from their imagination. But in almost every case, the others can tell those jobs from the real thing, and so everyone learns a lot about both observation and writing.)

7. (There are two parts to this assignment. One is the writing assignment itself, and the other is a reading assignment—an excerpt from a book on deciding what part of one's home to use for an office or study. The excerpt is meant to follow up on assignment 5, whose writings the class will have discussed by this point. The excerpt provides an approach to writing assignment 5 that probably no student used, and it provides an inconspicuous model for one of the options for assignment 12.

    The writing portion of assignment 7 is an expansion of assignments 5 and 6. It asks the students to observe their own neighborhoods and try to see how their sense of place—of neighborhood, in this case—is related to their own personality and to their own view of the world.)

We've been concerned with "place" lately, and one of the ways we've looked at places is in how they affect us—how they influence us, maybe without our even being consciously aware of it. Before we go on to the next assignment, you might be interested in seeing one person's suggestions for choosing a place in your home to use as a study or office. Stephanie Winston is an expert in helping people and businesses get themselves organized, and her book *Getting Organized* contains many suggestions that people have found useful. Before our next class meeting, read pages 54-59 of the book so we can discuss them in class.

Now I'd like you to examine the neighborhood you live in. How does it differ from other neighborhoods or "places" you know about—especially from other places you have been or have lived in? How big is it? Are its borders clear-cut, or are they indeterminate? How do you *feel* about your neighborhood? And how do you feel when you're there?

One of the things you'll have to consider for this job is what you mean when you think "neighborhood." Your writing probably ought to demonstrate what you mean by that term—or what that term means to you. Another thing I might mention is that this is another exercise in observation, something like what you did in 6, only on a much larger scale. In 6, by the way, you probably recognized that you were investigating the interrelationship between place and personality. But in order to do that you had to observe carefully both your surroundings and yourself. You had to see what was really *there*. That's never easy.

Before you go out and do assignment 7, I'd like you to try a brief experiment in observation right now. Get out a penny. Study it. LOOK at it. Write what you see. We'll compare what we see in a few minutes.

(This little exercise in observation at the end of assignment 7, observing and describing a penny, may at first seem elementary. If so, try it yourself, and I think you'll soon see how complicated it really is. I've found it to be very helpful, here in the middle of several assignments requiring direct observation of more complex subjects, in clarifying many students' conceptions of observation.

I should say right here that assignment 7 and several of the succeeding assignments are designed for students who live off campus. [At my college, all students commute.] However, these assignments can easily be modified to suit the situation of dormitory students.

[In China, I decided to omit assignments 7-12 altogether, because I didn't want to appear to be prying into matters that didn't concern me. In its place, I put a series of rather didactic assignments that provided models of several kinds of writing—business letters, Aristotelian arguments, Rogerian "arguments," and so on. The students were happy to have the models, as Chinese education demands careful imitation, and at first they thought I was really *teaching*. Later on, however, I learned that many of them had decided they preferred the inductive style of learning that the rest of the assignments supported, that even though the didactic method was familiar to them, it made them nervous.])

8.   (This assignment expands the observation to include another person's view of a place and begins a series of writings in which the students are exploring not only places but persons as well. This is an indirect means of inviting the students to consider certain elements of fiction—setting, character, point of view, and [beginning with assignment 13] conflict.

Assignment 8 also gives the students some experience in interviewing and note-taking. It begins a sequence of assignments [8-12] that taken together amount to a formal research project including the personal interview, a search of government records, library research, comparing and contrasting different opinions, and the like. The research portion of the course can be expanded or contracted, or made more or less formal, to suit the needs of the particular students.)

So far I've been inviting you to write from your own perspective, sometimes about your immediate feelings, sometimes about events stored in your memory, and sometimes about what you see in front of you and about how what you see is related to your emotions. (For a freewriting sometime soon, you might try to sum up what you've learned or observed about writing so far in the course.) Now I'd like you to explore a few other perspectives on your world. I think you'll learn some surprising things (and not only things about writing).

Last time you wrote about your own neighborhood as you see it. This time, get another person's view of it. Find someone else who lives there, preferably someone whose experience of the place is likely to be different from your own—a long-term resident, if you're a recent arrival, say, or maybe a man if you're a woman, or an old person if you're young. You know that no two persons can ever see things exactly the same way, so find out what your informant's view of the neighborhood is and how it differs from your own view. In other words, explore your neighbor's neighborhood.

Report what you learn from your informant, using indirect quotations and summaries. If your informant says something that is worded in such a way that you'd like us to know the exact words, give us a direct quotation.

Does this assignment make you nervous? Well, if it does—tough! Do it anyway. It may change your life. Who knows?

In your note to me for this assignment, you might mention something about your interviewing process—what worked for you, for example, and what didn't—and its relationship to the writing-up part of the assignment.

9. First you wrote about your neighborhood from your own perspective, and then you gave us the perspective of one of your neighbors. The two of you probably agreed on some points, but you almost certainly saw some things differently—not only because you see the place from two different locations, but because you're two different persons. In what ways do your views differ?

> (This assignment is a standard "compare and contrast" essay in disguise. Within this course, it invites the students to take stock of what they've been doing lately, and it prepares them for later assignments that will ask them to analyze a conflict between themselves and someone else.)

10. (This assignment involves a trip to unknown territory. It is an expansion of the interview, with the addition of yet another point of view on the familiar neighborhood. It also involves predicting what might turn up and analyzing the results of the job. And it's a second opportunity for the students to experiment with taking notes.)

Up to now you've been examining your neighborhood through your own eyes and through those of a neighbor. In other words, you've been gathering personal impressions of the place. But your neighborhood has been described in another way, in one or more public documents that are on file in a city or county government building. One easy way to gain access to this sort of information is to look up the deed to the property you dwell on and the tax records for it. You should be able to find lots more information as well—maybe even an aerial photograph of the place. These records should be available to you even if you live in a multiple-family dwelling, because they're a matter of public record.

For next time, I'd like you to explore the public record of your neighborhood. You might be nervous about this job, but overcoming that nervousness will be part of the benefit of the assignment. I think you'll find it interesting and maybe even fun.

Before you go, make a list of what you expect to find. Then while you are there make notes on what you discover. Afterwards, make notes on anything that surprised or puzzled you. We'll compare notes in class next time. (It would be a good idea to organize them a bit before you get here.)

(By this point in the course some students actually feel a little cheated if I don't ask them to *write* something for each class meeting. They aren't satisfied by the part of assignment 10 that asks them to compare notes orally with their classmates. Therefore, I sometimes add to the assignment one or both of the following invitations.)

a)   Write about the public view of your neighborhood. How does it differ from your own view and that of the neighbor you interviewed?

b)   Write a statement both expressing how you felt while you were in the government center and describing the ambiance of the place (taking into account the demeanor of the officials you encountered there).

(This assignment would be awkward for dormitory students. They could, of course, go to the college housing office, or look up the public record of the college itself. But the officials in either place would probably get crabby after the first few identical inquiries.

At a residential college, I would simply ask the students to scout around the city and find one or two residences or other buildings that interested them. [Perhaps one each from poor, middle, and rich neighborhoods.] Then the students could look up the public records on those places.)

11.   In assignment 10, I asked you to go to an unfamiliar place and to explore the public records of your neighborhood. Now I'd like you to go to another public place and explore it, while getting still another view of neighborhood. Go to a library. Almost any one will do, and in fact a public library might be as good for this job as an academic library. Find a periodical article and a book, each on some aspect of neighborhood planning. (What *is* "neighborhood planning"? You may not find such a heading in a card catalogue or periodical index.) Make notes on whatever seems interesting to you, especially if it pertains in some way to your own neighborhood. You can almost certainly do that without checking anything out of the library if you allow yourself enough time—a couple of hours, say. Then get your notes organized enough so that other people can make some sense of them and bring them to class next time. We'll compare library research strategies and the specific information you turned up.

Before you begin, you might take a few minutes to review whatever you've already learned about taking notes. You may have taken notes in interviewing your neighbor, and you almost certainly did at the government center. And you've probably been exposed to some kind of note-taking instruction (whether good or bad) in school. In your real life, what seems to work best for you? In what situations? And how can you take notes *fast?*

12.   (I have included two versions of assignment 12, the first more "academically oriented," the second more "practical." Because my department has recently moved away from insisting that the first-quarter composition course include a full-blown research paper, I've moved in the direction of version 2.)

Version 1: You've studied your neighborhood in some detail, and from several different perspectives. Now it's time for you to generalize about the place in a somewhat larger piece of writing that accounts for what you've learned in doing all of those previous writings about "place."

For this writing, then, I'd like you to characterize your neighborhood, drawing on all the information you've gathered about it. You'll be considering the relationship of the physical neighborhood, the official or legal neighborhood, and the social neighborhood of the people who reside there. Even if you don't plan to answer it directly, you might keep in mind the following question: "What does the world look like from your neighborhood?"

Version 2: We've been exploring the reality of realty lately—both in terms of our own real neighborhoods and in terms of the concept "neighborhood." Now I'd like you to do one more piece of writing on the subject, one that I hope will prove practical even when this course is over.

There are two steps to this assignment; please be sure to keep them separate from each other, and do the first one first.

Step 1. Develop a set of criteria for yourself for choosing a place to live. What is important to you? The neighbors? The physical layout of the streets and so on? The appearance of the buildings? The population density? The ownership of the properties? The—? Write down your criteria, so they won't vanish from your view. Probably a brief list will be sufficient.

Step 2. Now think about how you'd give advice to someone else who is looking for a new place to live. Write up your advice in the form of a guide to finding a new place to live. You might want to consider these questions: Who is your probable audience? What format will you use? Will you simply make a list? Or will you need to explain or discuss each of the criteria, in order to be sure that the user of your guide can really use it effectively? What will you call your guide?

Before you start, you might take another look at the excerpt I gave you (as part of assignment 7) from Stephanie Winston's book on organizing your household, to see how she did what she did. You might look at a few other "how-to" guides, too—not that I think you should imitate someone else, but it never hurts to see how other people do things.

(Version 1 can be a fairly complete research report, including notes and bibliography, or it can be merely a review of the previous few assignments, or something in between.

Version 2, on the other hand, is more prospective. It uses the information and insights gained in the previous assignments to develop a system or set of criteria for choosing a place to live. When the students finish this writing they have both a set of personal criteria and a pamphlet that others might use. And they have explored point of view and audience in a very practical way.)

* * *

Midcourse Correction. This course is a little more than half over now, and I think this is a good time for you to see where you are and where you're heading. Please write me a note in which you assess your own writing so far in this course. Here are some things you might consider: What aspects of your writing are you most pleased with? In what ways has it most improved? What aspects of it do you feel least comfortable about? Please feel free to write anything else you feel appropriate, too. This assignment is partly for your benefit and partly for mine, so anything you might tell me about my part of the course will help both of us.

(In requesting that the students assess their own writing, I'm not only asking them to take stock of their progress so far, I'm also giving them a chance to practice what they will be doing for the final writing assignment of the course. And I'm reminding them that they really are responsible for their own progress in the class.)

* * *

13.   (The section of the course represented by assignments 5-12 focuses on place [though it is also generally concerned with persons]. The next section of the course, assignments 13-19, focuses more directly on persons [though it is also about place]. The more significant difference between these two sections is the increased emphasis in the second on point of view and audience. You'll see that in regard to the types of writing I request this section mirrors a previous movement in the course, beginning with expressive writing, in the form of a story, and then moving on to more analytical tasks.)

Think of the person you know whose existence troubles you most. (It has to be someone you actually know—not Hitler or some other well-known person you've never met. Those persons are essentially abstractions; we want real, live, flesh and blood here.) But instead of trying to write *about* that person, tell us the story of an incident that will enable us to *see* that person troubling you. You'll probably feel the need to get in some dialogue, even though you can't remember exactly what the persons involved actually said. Don't let that bother you—just try to make each person sound true to life, and don't apologize for any possible misquoting.

By the way, I specified "real, live, flesh and blood" and used the word "see" because you can *see* flesh and blood—and smell it, hear it, feel it, taste it. You can believe it. ("Seeing is believing.") Try to describe an abstraction sometime, and you'll see what I'm getting at. Be sure to think up a title for your story.

P.S. Because there will be other assignments about this same subject, I'd better caution you not to write about yourself. That would make at least one of the coming assignments awkward. Oh, and by the way, you might write about someone you *love* for this assignment.

(Most students seem to like this assignment best of all. It's very similar, of course, to assignment 3, which invited them to write about a school experience. But school evidently is more painful [or more boring] than personal relationships, however troubling they might be, and so this is the clear favorite for nearly everyone.

There are some students who at first are afraid of this assignment. They usually say that they can't think of anyone to write about, that no one "troubles" them. Often, however, these same students end up writing the more subtle pieces about personal relationships, although I suspect they have to do quite a lot of soul-searching, and many of them have seemed to be profoundly affected by the experience.)

14. Take another look at the story you told us last time. But this time write a newspaper version of it. Be sure to use the journalists' heuristic (who? what? where? when? why? how?—though not necessarily in that order). Before you begin to write your piece, you might read a few professionally-written news stories to see how they were done. How are they organized? What is the point of view? What is the tone of voice in them? How are they titled?

In your note to me this time, you might consider how this piece—when it's finished—differs from the piece you wrote in assignment 13. In other words, you might at this point focus on the finished products rather than on the processes of writing.

(In this assignment I am deliberately asking the students to step outside themselves for a time, to be reporters, rather than students. I also have this assignment in the course because it enables me to address the matters of attribution, form, and mechanics in a much more natural way than if this were a conventional composition course. By this point in the course, these are no longer much of a psychological problem for most students—simply because I have largely ignored them—and so I can impersonate an editor without causing the students to feel defensive.)

* * *

Retrospective Option. This is a semi-optional assignment. If you don't want to write it, then write what you *do* want to write. Here it is: Mull over that song of Malvina Reynolds', "Little Boxes," and write about whatever it cooks up in your brain.

(I added this assignment only very recently, after it occurred to me to play to the class Malvina Reynolds' recording of this song—a song that presents a cynical view of self-perpetuating suburban life, where people are as similar as the houses, with everything very constraining and predictable. Although the song is obviously related to the neighborhood assignments, it seems to work well at this point in the course, after the students think they're finished with looking at their neighborhoods. To put it in the middle of the "neighborhood writings" might influence their observations unduly.)

* * *

15.   (This is an analytical task that leads most students to revise drastically their ideas about the person they've shown us in assignments 13 and 14.)

You've shown us a person troubling you, from two different points of view. Now describe the person, but this time without telling a story. Try to say just what it is about this person that troubles you, and why. By the way, you've probably already noticed that at least *two* persons are involved in this trouble, so you'll probably have to decide whether you're writing about a person or a relationship.

In your note to me this time, you might consider your response to this assignment in the light of what you did for assignments 13 and 14. You might think about form (that is, structure, or organization) and the voice you used, and what you were trying to accomplish in each of them.

(In my suggestion for the note I have tried to turn the students' attention toward matters of form. These matters inevitably come up earlier in the course, but almost always because students ask questions, rather than because of my initiative. But now, nearly at the end of the course, I can direct them to study the form of their own writing without inhibiting them, because they have already discovered for themselves the importance of form in communicating with their classmates.)

16.   (This is another experiment in point of view, but it catches most students by surprise.)

You've examined a troubling relationship in three ways. Now let's explore the point of view of the person who troubles you. How would that person have responded to assignments 13 and 15? For assignment 16, combine 13 and 15 into one piece of writing that both tells the story and gives an opinion. But this time, write it as if you were the person who troubles you.

* * *

A Reflection on Structure

(One of the reasons I include the following essay on structure in the course is that I can't count on being with these particular students for the second-quarter course, and so I need to insure that they will be prepared to write conventional academic papers. With the essay, then, I try to both make that transition and also help the students with assignment 17.)

In most of the writing assignments so far you've been operating inductively. That is, you've been doing concrete writing first, and then later you've been trying to derive general principles or understandings about writing. And a lot of that deriving has probably been unconscious, happening even though you may not have been consciously aware of it.

In discussing the news stories you wrote for assignment 14, however, we operated more or less deductively. We discussed the formulaic structure of most news stories, and I insisted that the structure of your news story adhere to the formula. There are a few other types of writing situations that generally call for formally structured writing. The inter-office memorandum is one, the scientific lab report is another. And the academic essay is a third. (I don't mean to suggest, by the way, that the *contents* of any of these types of writings ought to be formulaic: on the contrary. But it's often easier to see what is original when it is presented in a standard structure.)

Now that I've said that much, I want to back off and try a somewhat different tack.

One of the oldest and most highly developed writing forms is often called *argument*. That word generally suggests a fight of some kind, and that's just what formal argument usually turns out to be—a fight to the death in which you try to smash your opponent. A lot of academic writing takes the form of argument, so I'm going to describe the standard structure right now, and suggest an alternative structure that in many real-life situations is much more effective.

The argument as a form has been around for more than 3,000 years. There are many variations, but a synthesis of them can be stated like this: 1) state your thesis or position; 2) state the other party's position correctly and completely; 3) show what is wrong with the other party's position; 4) state your own case, giving clear and objective evidence to support it.

There may also be an introduction and a conclusion. (An introduction introduces the audience to the thesis, and the conclusion returns the audience to their own lives ready to apply or use the thesis.)

This argument form works fine if you're trying to demolish someone. But Carl Rogers, a clinical psychologist interested in helping people get along with one another peacefully and productively, has developed a gentle variation that we should all pay attention to. Rogers says that you're not likely to convince anyone by logic alone (or by deceit, either, for that matter). You might be "right," but you'll never "win" an argument. The best you can hope for, he says, is to show that you're reasonable and that you have a valid point of view. If you can do that, then you may be able to convince the other party to modify their position somewhat, even though you probably won't ever get them to change their mind completely. Your intention, in this Rogerian argument, is not to polarize yourself and the other party, but to improve communication between the two of you by *establishing a goal you both share*.

Rogers' main idea is to state the other party's position first. This has the double function of making the case clear and showing that you have taken the trouble to understand the other party's position. Rogers had in mind face-to-face discussions, but his idea works just as well in most other argument situations.

You might try it and see if it works for you.

(I wrote that essay in China, when I was trying to adapt the inductive teaching method to the Chinese educational system, in which even now the students memorize and imitate the models of their elders. [This is due in part to the writing system, in which each word is essentially a picture that must be memorized perfectly. It takes most Chinese about four years to become literate in their own language.] I used this essay to explain to the students why I was requiring them to do certain things, as well as to give them some information about English-language formal thought patterns, which are quite different from the traditional Chinese patterns.

The essay has turned out to be as useful in America as it was in China, especially for the way it helps students get ready for the final writing assignments of the course, so I have included it here.)

* * *

17. To round out this series of writings, let's put everything together. Write a letter to the person who troubles you, explaining your view of the troubled relationship and what you believe to be that person's view of it, and trying to suggest some way for you two to deal with it.

Just to give you another perspective on this sort of task, here's a poem by William Blake about troubled relationships. [I distribute copies of "A Poison Tree" to the students at this point.]

18. (Now it's time to turn the students' attention to something affirmative.)

Tell us of an important moment that you shared with someone else. What happened? What made it important to you? What do you want us to understand about it?

(I've found it helpful to continue supplying a few questions even this late in the course for students who still seem to need that guidance. You'll see that in assignment 19, which is in essence very similar to 18, the students are on their own.)

19. Write of a painful or pleasurable moment that you experienced in this course.

(This assignment is reminiscent of the first few assignments of the course, and its main function is to turn the students' attention back toward the course itself and to help them gain some objectivity about it, so as to help them get ready for assignment 20.)

20. The course is just about over now. You've written at least nineteen compositions so far, and there's only one to go. In it I'd like you to assess your own writing during this course.

If you feel uncomfortable writing about yourself, you might try acting as a ghost writer for me, writing the assignment in the third person, as if I were writing about you. But whichever way you do it, your assessment should be such that I can either agree with it or disagree with specific parts of it.

Before starting this job, you should review the grading criteria that I gave you at the beginning of the course and that we will use in determining your grade. Your assessment in this piece should reflect those criteria, and somewhere in this piece you should also say what you think your course grade ought to be.

Instead of commenting on your work paper by paper, you might try to analyze what you tried to do with your writing in the course and how successful you were at each thing you tried. You'll want to emphasize successes, of course, but for the sake of credibility you'll need to account for any non-successes as well.

Please give me two copies of the assessment (one for my records and one that I'll return to you) along with your portfolio of writings from the course. I'll meet with you next week to return your work with my own written comments and a grade for the course, and to discuss with you whatever seems appropriate.

Writing about a Historic Place

A Course in Research and Learning

Beverly Beem

Almost every community has a building or place that stands as a reminder of past times, times that helped shape the character of the present. An old church or mill or home or inn or courthouse or school, for example, holds the memory of the people who built it and the times associated with it. A historic site, then, is not merely a physical structure or place, but also an emblem of the events that occurred there. Seen in this light, a historic place becomes something like a literary text, rich with meaning that can be investigated and interpreted from a variety of perspectives. So, like a variously significant text, it offers students the opportunity for intellectual growth through exploration and discovery. For these and other reasons that will become clear in the following discussion, a historic site can be a useful focus for a course in research writing. At Walla Walla College, the nearby Whitman Mission has served as such a focus.[1] Although the course described here is designed specifically for the Whitman Mission, the assignments, as will be seen, embody principles that can be adapted to any historically important site.[2]

The Mission, built in 1836 by Marcus and Narcissa Whitman, was originally designed to serve the Cayuse Indians, but it became increasingly important as a stop-over place for travellers on the Oregon Trail. The flood of emigrants to the Pacific Northwest in the 1840's brought increasing tensions between the two cultures, climaxed in 1847 by a conflict that led to the death of the Whitmans and the destruction of the Mission. This event has come to be regarded as a crucial one in ending the power of the Cayuse and moving Congress to establish the Oregon Territory. Today, the Whitman Mission is a national historic site, commemorating the

---

[1] By the time students take this research course, they have already taken two quarters of freshman writing and have gained experience in writing for different purposes and audiences. This course builds on these two quarters of writing. I want to thank my collaborators in teaching pilot sections of these courses: Terrie Dopp Aamodt, Marilyn Glaim, Jon Glenn, Peggy-Joyce Grable, Dale Hepker, Dan Lamberton, Irene Lottman, Sylvia Nosworthy, Carolyn Stevens, and our chairman, Gary Wiss.

[2] Sandy Doe at Metropolitan State College in Denver has adapted this course to the early Denver sites located on the Auraria Campus.

story of the Whitmans and the Columbia Plateau Indians as a part of the greater story of America's westward expansion.[3] The Whitman Mission is thus an especially promising site for research because it is a starting place for exploring many historical and cultural aspects of the Northwest.

The assignments in this course are designed to give students the opportunity to explore the Mission for themselves, but before beginning this exploration (in assignment 3), students carry out two writing activities (in assignments 1 and 2) that are intended to help them see and think about the relationships between systematic research projects and the ordinary learning that they acquire from the daily experience of their lives. Assignment 1, for example, invites them to think and write about how they ordinarily acquire knowledge "day by day," and subsequent discussion of their responses is intended to broaden their conception of research so that they come to see it as including not only reading and investigation of what others have written, but also their own observing, exploring, categorizing, and interpreting of experience. This expanded concept is then put into practice in assignment 2 which invites the students to write up and to share their prior impressions and knowledge, if any, of the Mission. Most students turn out to have visited the Mission, so the assignment naturally prompts them to review those experiences and to reflect upon their significance. But most importantly, this assignment comes to serve as a major point of reference throughout the course, since it constitutes for the group an initial inventory of their knowledge about the Mission. Thus the class is able to look back to this point, comparing what they have learned with what they knew at the beginning.

This preliminary stock-taking provides a base for exploration, which begins immediately in assignment 3. Within the first few days of class, students are told to explore the Whitman Mission to make their own personal acquaintance with it. That is, before they study what happened in the past, they become acquainted with the site as it exists in the present, observing it first-hand, absorbing it with their senses, and taking note of what they learn. When students bring their notes back to class, they discover from their discussion and questions that different people observing the same site may see different aspects of it. This variability of observation helps them to see the importance of an individual perspective in research. It also enables them to realize that whatever they learn from secondary sources must be checked against what is actually at the site. Thus, instead of working entirely from information provided by other scholars, they observe for themselves from primary sources and evaluate the contributions of others by what they have seen first hand. So, in a pattern which will be repeated throughout the course, they observe, record, form preliminary conclusions, and ask questions for further study. This procedure offers students opportunity for personal discovery and gives them an original perspective for writing.

[3]Thanks to David Maxon, the chief of interpretive services and resource management at the Whitman Mission National Historic Site. He and his staff have been hospitable and helpful to the class in our visits to the site.

After their first systematic study of the Mission, students return to the site and continue their observation (in assignment 5), looking at it not from the perspective of the present, but from the perspective of the past, as it is interpreted for them by the Park Service. Assignment 5 thus calls upon students to develop a sense of historical imagination, to see the place not only as it is but as it was. By trying to do so, they discover that direct observation is not enough, that they need other sources of information. In this way, assignment 5 provides a lead-in to the next three assignments which invite students to engage in various kinds of historical role-playing: first with respect to the site itself, by making archaeological field notes on the various artifacts to be found at the Mission (assignment 6); then with respect to their own rooms, by writing a field report and an interpretation of what they find for an imagined future audience (assignment 7); and finally with respect to the site once again, by describing the Mission from the point of view of someone who would have been there during the time of its operation in the 19th century (assignment 8).

Historical imagination, however, must be disciplined by historical verification, so in assignment 9 students look back at their descriptions and for each bit of detail they answer the question, "How do you know?" This assignment requires them to document their observations. The more technical aspects of documentation are introduced in this context of the need to substantiate their observations. Throughout the course, the mechanics of research writing are dealt with on this need-to-know basis. For instance, in assignment 4, when students are confronted with a mass of accumulating material, they see the need to develop a note-taking system. Later, in their search for library materials, they must develop a system for a working bibliography. This approach enables students to see research conventions not as ends in themselves but as tools for achieving their goals in writing.

Though assignments 2-9 have engaged the students in extensive observation and investigation of the Mission, they need to recognize that there are still many things that they do not yet know about it. So, in assignment 10 they are invited to formulate a series of questions about the Mission that they think would bear further study. Then, after pooling their questions in class discussion, they expand upon this activity in assignment 11 by exploring the kinds of questions that might be asked about the Mission by specialists in various academic disciplines. This activity, of course, helps to make students aware of the diversity of fields in liberal education. More importantly in the context of the course, it is intended to help them realize that different fields of study involve not only different subject matters but also different frames of reference and procedures for research, which in turn yield different kinds of knowledge and understanding.

In assignments 12-16, students take part in the process of research as it is carried on in the professional academic community by writing and seeking publication for the results of their investigation into a specific question. Since the story of the Mission touches many aspects in the history of the Northwest, these questions may take students beyond the boundaries of the site itself. They may consider, for example, some aspect of Indian culture or travel on the Oregon Trail. But even though they may shift the focus, their research on the Mission has given them the background and the questions they need for further study. After finding a focus for this last paper (assignment 12), students then research the available library resources (assignment 13), investigate various publication formats (assignment 14), prepare a letter of proposal to a hypothetical journal editor (assignment 15), and, finally, write the paper itself (assignment 16).

Most freshmen, of course, are not ready to prepare scholarly papers for a highly specialized audience, but role-playing the crucial steps involved in the preparation of such a paper helps them to experience research as a process involving not only the investigation of specific problems, but also the sharing of results with a community of specialized readers. Indeed, as the students develop their own special questions, interests, and lines of investigation, each bringing to class the knowledge gained from his or her continuing study, they find themselves developing something very much like a community of scholars. They do, after all, come to share a rich body of knowledge about a particular subject that they have investigated separately and in collaboration, and this shared knowledge enables them to understand the special obligations that scholars must fulfill in their writing.

Having experienced research in something like a scholarly community, students need to be reminded, as they had been in the first assignment, of its connection to everyday life. Thus in the final assignment (17) students are given a task that calls upon them to apply what they have learned about research by explaining to newcomers in a community how to go about exploring the history and culture of their new surroundings. This assignment is intended to encourage students to look back over all the thinking and writing they have done during the quarter to form some general principles about how one comes to know. By applying these principles to a new situation, students are encouraged to see that research is not only an academic activity, but is also a habit of life, a habit motivated by natural human curiosity, a means of becoming more aware of the world in which they live.

A research course that focuses on a historic site thus makes it possible to help students see the activity of seeking knowledge and communicating it to others in the most spacious context. It takes students out of the classroom and involves them in asking questions and seeking answers about a place important to the community. It enables them to learn about the history of their own region and at the same time study the ways they have learned it. By writing the results of their study to their fellow researchers, they form for themselves a community of scholars and complete a course in freshman writing which opens the way for the writing they will do in their own academic disciplines.

WRITING ABOUT A HISTORIC PLACE

1. Just to loosen up your writing muscles, think for a few moments on paper how you go about finding out things. You probably know more today than you did yesterday and certainly more than you did last week or last year. Yet you don't likely start each morning with the noble resolution to learn something new that day. So,

how does it happen that you keep adding day by day to your knowledge of the world around you? If you can recall a specific incident where you learned something you didn't know before, tell us about it. These accounts will be the subject of our discussion next class period.

2. Though the real subject of our study is writing and researching, the topic of our writing this quarter will be the Whitman Mission. Let's take a few minutes of class time to brainstorm on what we know about the Whitman Mission. Maybe you are new to the area and don't know more than the name of the place. Maybe you have lived here for some time and have accumulated a fair amount of knowledge about the Mission and its history. No matter. Let's write down and pool our information to see what we know already about the Whitman Mission.

3. Before the next class meeting, go to the Whitman Mission and make your own personal acquaintance with it. Don't go into the visitor center yet or worry about the interpretative markers. Instead, take some time when you aren't hurried to walk over the grounds and see what you can see. Then find a comfortable spot that gives you a comprehensive view of the place and sit for a while and look and listen. What is going on at the site? Who is there? What are they doing? What natural things do you see? What man-made things do you see? In a notebook write as fully as you can a description of what your senses tell you about the Mission. Write what you see, what you hear, what you feel, and what you smell.

Even though the Whitman Mission is important for what it meant in the past, it is also important for what it means in the present. As you write your observations, note also what you can tell about the current significance that this place has for the community and the people who visit it. Then, before you leave, make note of any questions that have occurred to you in your looking at the Mission.

4. During the next few weeks you will be acquiring a great deal of information from a wide variety of sources. In order to make good use of this accumulating material, you will need to devise a system of recording and organizing it. You will want to be able to find the information you need quickly and easily and keep track of its source. If you have not already done so, develop a system of note-taking that you find easy to work with and write an explanation to the class. We will divide up into small groups and look at the characteristics of the different methods and decide what qualities of good note-taking are a part of all systems and what qualities are unique and individual.

5. Go back to the Whitman Mission to get another first-hand look, this time seeing the place not only as it exists today, but also as it was. For this you will need some help. The Park Service has developed several interpretative activities to help visitors understand what the place meant to the many different people who lived at or visited the Mission. Don't worry yet about taking notes on the particular facts you are learning. That will come later when you know what specific aspect you want to explore. For now, scout out the land and find out what kinds of information are available.

To do this, read the markers and listen to the tapes along the trail. Go inside the visitor center and watch the film and look at the displays in the museum. Examine the artifacts preserved in the museum and any living history displays that might be there. Look over the books and pamphlets available in the lobby. Note especially those written by the people who lived or visited there at the time of the Whitmans. Feel free to talk to any of the Park Service personnel and ask them questions. Make a list of all the different sources of information, both primary and secondary, you can find on the site itself.

6. One of the most important sources of information about a historic site is the material people leave behind. These artifacts, often broken and fragmented, are evidences of the activities that went on at the site. What can you learn about the Whitman Mission and the people who lived or visited there from the artifacts you saw displayed in the museum? Suppose you were an archaeologist who uncovered these objects in a desert mound. What questions would you have about them? What could you tell from these objects about the site, the people living there, and the nature and purpose of the settlement?

Choose five artifacts and write up a complete set of notes in which you describe the items you have found, categorize them into manageable units, and draw preliminary conclusions about their significance to an understanding of the Whitman Mission.

7. Now that you have had experience thinking and taking notes like an archaeologist, suppose you were an archaeologist who uncovered the materials in your own room. What questions would you have about these artifacts? What could you tell about the site, the people living there, and the nature and purpose of the room? Write a report to an archaeological journal of some future century describing your findings and explaining their significance to an understanding of college life in the late twentieth century.

8. In assignment 3 you described the Mission on the basis of your own observation. Now, after the thinking and writing you have done about the site as it was in the past, describe the Whitman Mission from the viewpoint of someone who was there during the Whitman's time: Narcissa or Marcus, one of the Sager children, an Indian, a traveller on the Oregon Trail, or someone else. Describe what this person would see there. For instance, what things would be significant to an Indian woman, or what would be memorable to a pioneer traveller? Be sure that the elements in your description have a basis in fact that you can trace and document.

Then, in a separate paragraph write your observations on the following questions: What differences do you find between the description you just wrote and one you would expect to find in an encyclopedia article or other history? How do you explain these differences?

9. Look back at the description of the Mission that you just wrote from the viewpoint of someone who was there during the Whitman's time. How true or accurate was your account? How did you know the information that you included in

your description? What were your sources of information? Go back through your paper and document it, providing the notes and bibliographic references needed to acknowledge your sources and support your observations. As you do this, check to see if any aspect of your description may now be considered questionable. Is there anything you wish to add or delete or modify? Make any necessary revisions in your description as you document it.

10. You have learned a great deal about the Whitman Mission and the people connected with it, and this information has come mostly from the site itself. Now, look back over the thinking and observation and discussion of the past few weeks and formulate some questions that you think would bear further study. These questions may be about any aspect of the Mission or a related topic stemming from it. We will talk about these questions in class next time and plan some strategies for answering them.

11. The kinds of questions we ask about a subject determine to a large extent what we learn about it. The major you choose in college teaches you not only a particular subject, but also a particular way of asking questions. Imagine, for instance, a biologist and a historian walking side by side across the Mission grounds. What kinds of questions would each be asking? Or how would an artist look at the Mission? Or a home economist? An anthropologist? A linguist? A literary critic? A sociologist? An economist? An industrial technologist? A physicist? A geologist? A theologian? An engineer? A novelist? A physician or a nurse? A psychologist? An archaeologist?

Look at the Whitman Mission from the perspective of your particular discipline or major. If you are undecided, just choose one that interests you. Develop a series of questions which someone from your discipline might ask concerning the Whitman Mission. Then interview a specialist in this discipline to find out how he or she would go about exploring the Mission and finding answers to these questions. What techniques and resources would such a specialist use? What other questions might he or she ask? Make notes during your interview, and write up a report of your findings for the class. Be sure that you record clearly the specific questions that specialists in your discipline would ask and the tools and resources they would use to explore the Mission. We will discuss these interviews in class next time.

12. We have looked at the Whitman Mission from many perspectives. We have searched it with our own senses to see what it can tell us directly. We have looked at it from the perspectives of different people who have been a part of the Mission's history. And we have examined it from the perspectives of various disciplines, each with different questions and different ways of answering these questions. Now, it is time for you to choose a specialty.

Choose some aspect of the Whitman Mission that particularly intrigues you. Over the next few assignments, pursue this topic as fully as you can and present the results of your research to the class in a paper of about 6-8 pages. To do this, it is necessary to focus your attention on one question or one specific aspect of the

Mission and its relationship with the history and culture of the Northwest. For now, compose a focusing question that can guide you in your coming research. Also, explain the reasons for your interest in this particular question and the strategies you plan to use in answering this question.

13. Before you decide on a topic for research, you need to determine if there is enough information available here to sustain your inquiry. You know what the Mission itself has to offer. All its resources are available to you in your study. But you may need more than the material offered by the site and the Park Service. Survey the library holdings on your particular topic. Find some systematic way of doing this, both to make sure that you don't overlook something and to make the project manageable. Look through the book catalogs, the periodical indexes, and the vertical file, and any other library resources. Compile from your search a working bibliography of sources available to you on your topic. Include both library materials and the resources from the Mission. We will discuss in class both the materials you found and your method of finding them.

14. One of the obligations of specialists in any discipline is to convey their findings to their colleagues and to interested laymen. How would specialists in your discipline go about doing this? If they were writing to their colleagues, where might they publish their work? One way to answer this question is to browse through the library's periodical shelves. Go to the library and survey the journals in your area.

Then pick one with a subject range that includes your topic and has a general style and format that is congenial to you. In order to write for this journal, you will need to understand its editorial requirements. Examine a few recent issues of your journal to find out as much as you can about its style, readers, format, and editorial policies.

After making notes of your general observations, demonstrate the validity of these observations by writing an analysis of one article, showing how these general principles are applied.

15. Before editors will publish an article in their journal, they must be convinced that it will interest their readers and add to readers' understanding of the subject. Write a letter of proposal to the editors of a journal that you hope will be interested in your work. In your letter, convince them that your article would be appropriate for their journal.

In order to do this, describe the main purpose of your paper and summarize the main points. Explain the background work that led you to investigate this topic. Show the editors how it interested you and will interest their readers. Then describe what other research has been done in your area, possibly even referring to previous articles in their journal, and show how your paper will contribute to what has already been written. Finally, survey the resources that are available and that you intend to use in your research. Attach a tentative bibliography to your letter.

16. You have written a letter of proposal to your publishers to explain the purpose of your project and to convince them that it would be appropriate for their journal.

Now, bring your letter of proposal to class and we will divide into small workshop groups. Each group will serve as the Editorial Board of a journal. Bring also your stylistic analysis of your journal to show the workshop group the expectations of your audience. Your workshop group will then write you a letter of acceptance or of deferral, explaining the reasons for their decision and offering any editorial suggestions they may have. If your proposal is accepted, note any suggestions or recommendations your group has made and proceed to write your article. If your proposal is deferred, note the reasons for the decision. Then, rewrite and resubmit your proposal accordingly, before you write your article.

17. In the thinking and writing, searching and researching, that you have done this quarter, you have learned a great deal about a place significant to the history and culture of this area. Though we have studied the Whitman Mission intensively, the real subject of our study has been *writing* and *different ways of coming to know*. Look back at the thinking and writing you have done this quarter. Where have you found the information needed to write so extensively on the Whitman Mission? What have you learned about searching for information and ways of knowing? What advice would you give to newcomers to a community who want to find out about the history and culture of their new home? Write a letter to someone in this position explaining how one comes to know a place.

VI

Writing as a Way of Learning to Teach

A Program for Teaching Assistants

Timothy R. Donovan

> It's strange to have people regard you as being a teacher after years of being a student.

It would be strange, of course, for any new teacher to feel differently from the teaching assistant who recently made this remark to me. Indeed, it would be especially strange for a *new* teaching assistant to feel differently, since most TA's, like ours at Northeastern, come directly into their new positions soon after taking their B.A. degree. A few, to be sure, are returning to school after raising a family or after several years of work in some other field, but most are in their early- to mid-twenties, have had little or no teaching experience, and almost certainly have no formal training in the teaching of writing. They may not even have taken a writing course in college. Their future professional plans are unsettled, and their uncertainty is exacerbated by the depressed job market for high school or college teachers of English. Their only academic certainty is, indeed, that of "being a student," especially since they are still in that role in their graduate classes. Thus it is hardly surprising that they are an anxious group of newcomers to teaching, somewhat like the students they are about to teach.

This anxiety is a besetting condition of any program for TA's in writing, as is the fundamental problem that gives rise to it, namely that such TA's are expected to teach something they are just learning to teach. Though they are called teaching assistants, they do not, in fact, assist anyone, as would be the case in a lecture-discussion course. They do not move gradually into the full set of responsibilities connected with teaching. Instead, the typical TA in freshman composition prepares and conducts class sessions, devises reading and writing assignments, holds student conferences, responds to and evaluates papers, and awards final grades. The new teaching assistant in writing is thus expected to assume overall responsibility for the affairs of the course, without any prior experience in having done so.

Given this troubling state of affairs, it is hardly surprising that many schools have tried to alleviate it by giving TA's the sense of security that derives from having

233

in hand a pedagogical overview of the course, a sample syllabus, a standard set of texts with instructor manuals, and a detailed explication of these materials. A detailed road map, after all, is the only sure way of completing so long and complicated a trip. And so it is that most of us in the profession learned to make our way through our first experience in teaching freshman composition. We walked through a route that had already been mapped for us, and after a few trips through we had it memorized. We became expert in the materials that had been designed by others, but not in the teaching of composition.

So when the course was revised, or the textbooks changed, or we moved on to our first full-time position, we faced the task of having to learn an entirely new course and new set of materials. Our initial sense of security and our gradually developing sense of mastery turned out to be illusory. Is it any wonder, then, that so many earlier members of the profession tended to regard the teaching of writing as a tedious chore rather than an intellectual challenge—as a mechanical activity without guiding principles and practices?

Nowadays, to be sure, there is no reason to regard the teaching of writing as an activity without substantial intellectual foundation, what with the extensive body of research and theory that has developed over the past fifteen years. So, of course, some programs have required their TA's to read in the burgeoning literature on rhetoric and pedagogy. Most TA's are probably more richly informed now about the teaching of writing than their predecessors. Indeed, the knowledge they acquire will almost certainly be of more enduring value than the mastery of a particular course plan, as in the past. But here, too, there are limitations, even dangers, however wisely the readings are chosen. TA's may accept the wisdom of scholars and veteran teachers too readily—or misapply it. They may also have difficulty working new ideas into their own style of teaching or may tend to revert to what "they had to do" when they were undergraduates. Finally, they, like many of us, may not really be influenced by experiences other than their own. In short, reading is always second-hand information.

While citing these problems, I am not, of course, suggesting that TA's shouldn't have some course structure upon which to rely. That would be unfair to the beginner. Nor am I devaluing the usefulness of scholarly literature, for teachers of writing, like any serious professionals, should consult the important books and journals in the field as often as possible. What I am getting at is that these are only partial solutions at best and at worst merely the expedient response to the pressure of getting TA's into and on with the course. What is missing is experience. Over a period of time, a dedicated teacher can interpret theory in light of practice, and vice versa; instruction becomes less mechanical, more intuitive, and, of course, more professional. With enough time, TA's too could make better sense of the theory in the readings and the practice in the course outline, while assimilating both into their teaching.

A few universities do provide the time for TA's to gain experience. They request that they first observe composition classes, possibly assist or teach a class, perhaps tutor in a writing lab, while taking courses in composition, rhetoric or pedagogy. This approach is certainly sensible. However, at most institutions TA's arrive in the fall, shortly before classes start, and their experience begins when they begin the freshman course. At Northeastern, TA's arrive about a week before they are to teach. Yet the training program I am describing here attempts nevertheless to provide them with a broad range of preparation for teaching writing—theory, practice, and experience—before they enter the classroom.

My assumption is that the teacher of almost any subject has to be knowledgeable about three concepts: the nature of the subject, how it is learned, and how it may be taught. While the concepts seem neat and direct, when applied to writing they generate questions in profusion, most of which the TA's have never had the occasion to ask, much less ponder:

I. The Nature of Writing

How does a writer choose a subject?
How does a writer develop information?
When does a writer consider form?
What is the role of purpose and audience?
How does writing change through revision?
How does a writer know when to finish?
How important is publication?
How does a writer work through the series of difficulties, decisions, and accidents that have come to be known as the composing process?

II. Learning to Write

How does a writer improve by writing?
What does a writer gain from direct instruction about writing?
What does a writer learn from reading the writing of others?
How is the quality of writing affected by the motivation of the writer?
What does the writer take from the commentary about his/her writing?
How is the writer affected by grades? Success? Failure?
What stages, patterns, or progress can be noted in the development of writing ability?

III. Teaching Writing

Why should students write?
What is the most effective use of class time?
What assignments, if any, are most helpful?
How much writing should be required?
What kinds of comments on student writing are most effective?
What can be accomplished in a student conference?
When and how should writing be formally evaluated?
What satisfaction is there in the job of teaching writing?

This is a lot of ground to cover with TA's, and these seem merely the basic questions. True, there is now some conventional wisdom, even clichés, which may serve to answer them, but convenient packages of information won't suffice. For instance, in a writing course we don't "cover" material for students, but, in a sense, coax it out of them. They create their own work, and they go about it in many different ways. Thus in any given class, students provide about twenty-five different answers to these questions every time they write. Teachers, too, experienced or not, provide their own answers as they deal with the idiosyncrasies of writing and writers.

So it seems to me that the *most* direct route to understanding writing, and how it is taught and learned, is through writing itself. In other words, the TA's need to enact these three concepts in order to know if we have the right questions, not to mention the right answers. In this way they cannot escape drawing inferences or arriving at conclusions that will inform their teaching not just the next day or week, but during the year and years to follow.

We begin the program, then, not with syllabi or reading, but with writing. We undertake various composing activities, looking to analyze the process by which writing, including our own, comes into being. We share the progress of our writing through various drafts. We receive and respond to comments about our writing in conferences, small groups, on the papers themselves. We develop ways of seeing writing, talking about writing, handling writing. In short, we start to become teachers of writing by teaching ourselves about writing. To be sure, there is reading beyond that of our own writing, but it is assigned *after* the related activity, when TA's can make the best sense of it.

Although we take up pedagogical questions as they naturally arise, they tend to be downplayed until later in the week. By that time TA's can see that they have, to a surprising extent, created the course within themselves. They can ask students for writing because they have asked it from themselves. They can give criticism of papers because they have received it on their own. They can conduct conferences and small groups because they have been part of each before. They can demand hard work from their students because they have worked hard themselves. They have authenticated the course in a way, it seems to me, that would be difficult to achieve in any other way in so short a time.

An experiential program of this sort demands considerable patience and trust from everybody, but this is an advantage since these two qualities, after all, are also needed in the classroom and in the office, where TA's work together as colleagues, sharing problems and successes. Another advantage of the experiential program is that the nature of the course is revealed to TA's without their ever having taught it. Certainly they refine their techniques in time, but this program allows them to see the essentials early on. A final advantage is that TA's can be given sufficient latitude to initiate their own teaching strategies. By starting out the course with a decent understanding of writing, they can develop their own teaching style more quickly. A testament to this kind of independence is our curriculum guide, developed by second-year TA's who collated and edited the course logs required of all TA's.

Once the course begins, the TA's meet with me weekly for about two hours in what has evolved into a formal graduate course in the teaching of writing. In these meetings we review the progress of the freshman course, plan classes, discuss important books and articles on composition, share problems, work on solutions. Although these meetings are a vital part of the support we give TA's, in the outline that follows I have refrained from elaborating this part of the program, for, once TA's are teaching an assigned course, the options for maintaining a program depend upon the institution.

As for the portion of the program I present here, while it did grow out of the particular needs of a particular program at a particular university, it can be—and has been—modified, expanded, or curtailed to suit other forms of faculty development at other institutions. Its applicability is extensive, and its focus is not on any particular course. Even at Northeastern, its primary purpose is not simply to prepare TA's to enter a specific freshman composition class, but to provide them with a structured set of experiences in writing and responding to writing that will serve them in any writing course they might teach.

AN ORIENTATION PROGRAM FOR TEACHING ASSISTANTS

First Meeting

1. TA's pair off and interview one another for about fifteen minutes each. They then introduce each other to the large group, the assignment being to "make the person interesting." This is an ice-breaker and the first step in the group's becoming a teaching and writing community. It is also a composing exercise in its requiring the development and shaping of information for an audience according to some purpose.
2. TA's are engaged in a constrained writing activity; that is, they are assigned a rather ordinary topic to be addressed within a brief time limit. This procedure mimics the least effective, but all too frequent, kind of writing and writing instruction. They *should* feel constrained.
3. For contrast, we write through an expanded composing process, using five index cards, to illustrate a model of the process—from discovering to focusing to exploring to drafting to revising. These stages typically involve the following kinds of activities:
    a. Discovering—listing a number of words or topics of interest on the first card;
    b. Focusing—selecting two or more of those words or topics and, on the second card, elaborating each of them;
    c. Exploring—listing on the third card further thoughts, details, impressions about one of the topics selected in b;
    d. Drafting—organizing these thoughts/details/impressions into a paragraph;
    e. Revising—rewriting the paragraph after evaluating its purpose, weaknesses, and strengths.

We all read our cards at each stage. Other variations with the cards are possible.

First Assignment:

- Write a rough draft of non-fiction prose on any subject
- Make some notes describing the process (i.e. various decisions and problem-solving) of writing the draft
- Begin a notebook of daily writing containing reflections on the orientation, writing, teaching, or other TA's (Daily writing is required of the freshman.)
- Reading: William Irmscher, "Lore and Folklore about Writing," *Teaching Expository Writing*. New York: Holt, Rinehart and Winston, 1980.

Second Meeting

1. The rough drafts are shared in a "silent" reading session, a relatively non-threatening activity in which the diversity of writing styles, interests, and abilities in the group can be observed by all.
2. The TA's respond in writing to three or four of the drafts according to specific questions, such as:
   a. What is the purpose of the paper?
   b. How is that purpose achieved? not achieved?
   c. What parts of the paper are most successful, and why?
3. We discuss our composing notes, trying to discover different styles of composing and isolating the variables involved in writing, including settling on a subject, generating information, evaluating content, preparing for an audience, stylistic mannerisms, idiosyncracies, and so on.
4. Discussion of assigned reading.

Second Assignment:

- Revise first draft of paper
- Daily writing
- Reading: Donald Murray, "The Writer's Seven Skills," in *A Writer Teaches Writing*. Boston: Houghton Mifflin, 1968.

Third Meeting

1. The TA's are divided into groups of three or four and they share copies of their revisions. They are given guidelines as to how to discuss papers. I am indebted to Stephen Tchudi of Michigan State University for some of these:

   FOR READERS
   - Look for highlights and tell why they work for you.
   - Respond, don't critique.
   - Suggest alternatives, rather than THE solution.

   FOR WRITERS
   - Help out the readers with specific questions.
   - Test out alternatives on your readers.
   - Don't argue with your readers' perceptions.

2. Following the small group work, there is large group discussion about the reactions to receiving comments on their writing. We also discuss group dynamics, possibly comparing how individuals meshed in the groups, what papers presented problems, what kinds of responses were helpful, whether writers felt they benefitted from the groups.

3. The TA's are assembled in small groups to brainstorm the topic, "Why Write?" With the TA's having already done some writing—and having begun to think of themselves as teachers assigning writing—this seems to me to be an elemental question that should be addressed. They usually develop a score or more of reasons, and we discuss the philosophical and pedagogical implications of their response.

4. Discussion of assigned reading.

Third Assignment:
• Revise paper again
• Review samples of student writing
• Daily writing
• Reading: excerpts from Thom Hawkins, *Group Inquiry Techniques in Teaching Writing*. Urbana, Illinois: NCTE, 1976.

Fourth Meeting

1. The TA's pair off in order to conduct one-on-one conferences about their revised papers, exchanging the roles of teacher and student. The process is repeated in a different pairing. As with the small group work, TA's are given some guidelines which should make the conferences effective:
   • Let the writer explain the composing process of the paper.
   • Ask the writer what the purpose of the paper is.
   • Find out which part of the paper is giving the writer trouble.
   • Isolate the most significant or solvable problem.
   • Be sure the writer leaves with a definite plan for improving the paper.
   • Listen, listen, listen.

2. In a large group we discuss the nature and value of these conferences. We also look ahead to the usefulness of teacher-student conferences in the writing course, and we try to affirm or expand on guidelines for conducting conferences.

3. We break into small groups to compare general impressions of the sample student papers. We note the various levels of quality and range of topics, imagining the authors of these papers as our students.

4. We reconvene in a large group to address specific pedagogical questions:
   a. How would you describe this paper?
   b. What are the strengths and weaknesses?
   c. What would you say to the *student* about the paper?
   d. What strategies would you develop to help the student improve the paper and his or her writing ability?

5. Discussion of assigned reading

Fourth Assignment:
- Begin reading the curriculum guide for teaching Freshman Writing
- Write a draft of an introduction to the course for your students
- Daily writing
- Reading: Dwight Burton, "Evaluation: A Monologue or Dialogue," in *Teaching English Today,* Dwight Burton, *et al.* (Boston: Houghton Mifflin, 1975); Donald Murray, "The Listening Eye: Reflections on the Writing Conference," *College English,* Vol. 41, No. 1 (September 1979), 13-18.

Fifth Meeting

1. We share course introductions, noting the various concepts and tone they embody regarding writing. We also consider the likely success of certain requirements and expectations, such as number of papers, length, format, class attendance, grading, etc.
2. We begin planning the first week of class, covering administrative procedures, diagnostic essays, initial assignments, and classroom practices.
3. Discussion of assigned reading.

Fifth Assignment:
- Continue reading of curriculum guide
- Revise course introductions for first class
- Write notes or lesson plan for first three class sessions

Writing Across the Disciplines

A Memo to Colleagues

Priscilla Davidson

> I want to know why this student turned in such a lousy research paper in *my* course when he passed *your* freshman composition course last semester. Wasn't that course supposed to teach him how to write a term paper?

The logical response to that kind of question is likely to run something like this one from a memo distributed to all of our faculty at Roosevelt University:

> The fact that a student has satisfactorily completed a research paper in English 102 cannot certify that he or she is therefore able to handle the variety of similar projects assigned in other disciplines. Nor should it be assumed that a passing grade in any freshman composition course certifies that a student has nothing more to learn about the composing process and the complex issues involved in each fresh rhetorical challenge he or she will encounter in, and outside of, school.

But once an English department has conveyed that essential message to faculty in other departments and other colleges—then what? And once professors in other fields acknowledge that the task of advancing student literacy must be a university-wide responsibility—then what? For instance, what might we say to this?

> I'm not trained in English; my field is history [or biology, or psychology, or whatever]. And even though I can recognize most mechanical errors and some structural weaknesses when I see them in a student's paper, I can't offer much help toward correcting them or showing students how to avoid those same mistakes in the future. I've forgotten most of the rhetorical terms and grammatical rules I once learned. Besides, the semester is just too short for me to deal with everyone's writing problems! And as for teaching research writing from the bottom up, that's just too unrealistic an order. Of course, I want my students to improve, and of course I'm willing to do whatever I can, but....

Dealing with such legitimate—and typical—concerns is by no means an easy matter, especially not at places like Roosevelt University which are urban-based,[1] with a widely-dispersed faculty.[2] Among our faculty there is intense concern about student literacy, and by now most of the seasoned members have discovered that one or two or even three semesters of freshman composition cannot make finished writers of our students.[3] The need to provide constant opportunities for writing experience across the curriculum has, in fact, long been clear at Roosevelt. Perhaps because of this awareness, many of the professors, including even the most enthusiastic ones, have raised those typical questions about how the writing commitment can be fulfilled at the classroom level by faculty not professionally trained to teach rhetoric, nor even to deal with individual student writing problems as they arise. At many schools, I realize, it has been possible to answer such questions through a series of colloquia, or forums, or other kinds of meetings in which faculty come together to discuss cross-curricular issues in writing and to develop practical approaches to using writing purposefully in their courses. But at Roosevelt, as at many other urban schools, the faculty is so dispersed, and so many instructors have schedules which keep them isolated from others in the university community, that it is extremely difficult if not impossible for them to participate in cross-disciplinary conferences and meetings.

Given these circumstances, it seemed to me that the only way to discuss these issues with everyone in all five colleges of our university was to prepare and circulate a series of written memos. As director of a scattered composition staff, I had grown accustomed to the memo method of addressing colleagues whose paths might not cross mine—or each other's—more than two or three times in an entire semester. Indeed, faculty throughout Roosevelt have long relied on housemail as a

[1]Our students are mostly city people, mostly educated at public city schools, and often on city streets. Anxious to get out of school as swiftly as possible to take up careers in business, computer science or the helping professions, many are poorly prepared for the writing tasks they will be asked to perform in their coursework and in their future jobs. About three-quarters of the student body are transfers, primarily from metropolitan junior colleges. At least sixty percent of these students fail the two-hour English Qualifying Examination essay upon entering Roosevelt, and the test, it should be noted, is given only to those who have already passed English 101 and 102 with grades of C or better at their former schools.

[2]Out of a total faculty of approximately 450, about two-thirds are part-time instructors who are only on campus long enough to teach one or two classes and to hold a weekly office hour before they depart for other commitments at opposite ends of the city. (Part-time instructors teach most of our freshman composition sections, for example. Since a part-timer is allowed only two sections per semester, most of them must teach elsewhere as well, and thus cannot remain on campus to participate fully in the life of the university.) Even full-time faculty are not likely to be regularly on hand throughout each week, for many are on two- or three-day schedules, or divide their time between the downtown Chicago campus and the two suburban satellites.

[3]All 4000 undergraduates at Roosevelt must satisfy the University Writing Requirement in order to graduate. This means that they must pass a semester each of Composition 101 and 102, or, if they are transfer students, Composition 103. There is also a remedial course, English 100, that student can take prior to Composition 101.

major means of disseminating crucial information, so I could be reasonably assured that my messages would not be ignored. The collected memos were published in-house under the title *A Brief Theoretical and Practical Guide to Writing in All Disciplines at Roosevelt University,* and were distributed to every dean and faculty member in the University.

This set of four memos was designed to achieve the following purposes:

1. to reiterate the University's concern for and commitment to student literacy—defined as the capacity for using language to control one's environment and oneself in relation to it;

2. to provide a group portrait of our students as writers and learners, and to outline their special needs as language users;

3. to explain the scope—and limitations—of the freshman composition program in meeting these needs; and

4. to present concrete suggestions for using writing as a purposeful way of learning in all academic areas of the University.

As is evident from this list, the first three purposes were essentially a prelude to my main purpose in the fourth. So, too, the first three memos were intended to establish a sense of the collegiality and inter-departmental understandings that are fundamental to a successful cross-curricular program.

The final memo in the series—the one reproduced here—follows naturally from the first three. As you will see, this memo takes up a variety of issues related to writing across the curriculum. The first part, "The Teacher's Role," for example, discusses the various ways that instructors can respond to student writing—as examiners, guides, or learners. The second, "A Little about Reading," shows some of the ways that writing can be used to help students develop their reading abilities in general and in particular disciplines of study. The third, "The Uses of Informal Writing," discusses the benefits of encouraging a range of writing tasks in any course, and the particular value of pre-writing assignments and informal journal writings designed as aids to thought.

The fourth part, which is by far the longest portion of this memo, "Assignments in Research and Research Writing," takes up the process of research through a series of ten interrelated writing and research tasks. My discussions over some twenty years with Roosevelt faculty and students have frequently revealed that many instructors routinely assign the conventional 10 to 30 page research paper due at the end of a term, and then leave students altogether on their own to deal with the project as best they can. That approach to research and writing evidently puts most of its emphasis upon end products. With the memo reproduced here, by contrast, my aim has been to draw the attention of my colleagues to the equally important *process* of research and the role writing can play in that, as well as to the benefits and even pleasures that can be derived from the unfolding discovery and exploratory activities possible in any investigation. I think of the assignments here not as "ten sure, handy ways to do research writing," but rather as possibilities, as ideas that instructors can tailor to their own academic disciplines, subject matters, course designs, and teaching styles. In the same spirit, of course, I think of the entire memo not as "a sure way to bring about writing across the curriculum," but rather as embodying a possible approach that writing directors and instructors at urban-based schools might adapt in communicating with their widely-dispersed colleagues in other disciplines.

A MEMO TO COLLEAGUES

I. The Teacher's Role

By nature, we are always to some extent in the process of changing our attitudes and perspectives. But adopting different methods and styles of teaching is not so natural, and it is never easy. I don't therefore presume to recommend that anyone on this faculty abandon any of the techniques or styles that have been carefully developed and successfully employed through years of experience. I can only suggest some postures teachers might assume in implementing writing in courses in all disciplines.

To begin with, it is not necessary to feature ourselves as examiners every time we ask students to put something on paper and turn it in. The teacher-as-examiner model in its most extreme form fosters, and indeed sanctions, the very phenomenon many of us wish we did not have to reckon with: the emphasis on grades. Grades seem likely to figure prominently in academic settings for some time to come. But not every product a student produces needs to be graded, and the removal of inhibitions about grades can induce a greater willingness in students to take risks in expression—to test their own ideas on paper. Sometimes the effects are magical. Freed from prospects of penalty, students may outdo themselves by advancing points they would not have hazarded at all otherwise. We may learn more about the ways our students are thinking and operating if we occasionally give them the chance simply to write out what's going on inside their heads about the subject matter, rather than to attempt duplication of what they imagine to be going on inside ours. In the next sections of this memo, I will make concrete suggestions for several types of such ungraded assignments.

Secondly, students are interested in us not only as mentors but also as fellow learners, and we can make use of this curiosity in our teaching. Students appreciate finding out about our own research, our own writing. When it is possible to share stories and documents, the time spent in class for it is well taken. Furthermore, in order to demonstrate our awareness of the pitfalls of academic toil, we might describe our experiences in composing and the perils and triumphs we have encountered in our search for material.

Finally, there are the matters of assignments we make and the ways the assignments are used. In the earliest days of my own teaching, a student who had just learned what the next writing assignment would be for my class exclaimed, "Good grief. I'll betcha the only person in the world who'd ever want to do an assignment like that is *you!*" He was only partly correct. I couldn't have stood it either. In the following sections, I'll suggest some assignments you and your students *might* like to try.

II. Class Activities: A Little about Reading

I will remark on reading first by declaring that it ought to be the function of all beginning courses in the university to help college students to read. Formal reading instruction of the kind most of us know little or nothing about seems necessary in some degree these days, but those of us who lack knowledge of how to handle poor readers' problems with fundamental skills may still be very useful in assisting students at lower- and middle-range ability levels to read the texts in our courses. Here, ungraded writing can be an ally in our efforts. Those new to a subject area will encounter new terms, for instance, and these may or may not be adequately defined in the textbooks. An entire chapter devoted to a new term might seem simple and clear enough to students as they read it, but many of them, when asked to report on what the key words mean, are embarrassed to realize they are not quite sure after all. Moreover, terms pile upon terms at the early stages in the study of anything, and it is difficult to grasp them all at once. Reading and understanding with one's head bent over a text is not necessarily grasping meaning. Can the reader then articulate the meaning with the book closed? ten minutes afterwards? a day later? the next week? Writing is a help in articulation. Readers confronting the task of putting the material into their own words in writing, whether by composing one- or two-sentence explanations of terms, or by describing more complicated concepts in a paragraph, often discover the difference between the *illusion of understanding*, which they experience as they read, and *genuine understanding*.

Giving students a chance to tell us, on paper, what they think they are learning, and to then tell them, by our responding comments, where and how they are missing some point or misconstruing the whole, is a profitable exercise for them. Writing in this way arrests and focuses attention, as recitation does not. Writing, after all, is a lonely business—but therein lies one of its chief uses: writing forces us to encounter our own language, our own thinking, alone. A ten-minute exercise on the text material might be included daily, the papers returned on the following day. Better than objective quizzes, such writing gets students to choose their own expression, and the time spent in looking over their work is no longer than that required for grading quizzes. Nor is there any need to bother about the mechanics of writing at this point. These will probably interfere at the beginning of a course, but that is to be expected, as part of the struggle for understanding. (If problems in writing seem consistently severe for a particular student, remember the English Department and its fine services!)

Another way in which teachers can help students to read is by describing the features of the discourse—the language—most likely to be encountered in typical documents in the field. The discourse in a report on a chemistry laboratory experiment will obviously differ from that in a piece of literary criticism. Call students' attention to how materials are arranged on a page in a report, book, article;

point out the conventions of form and style, and whatever else distinguishes works in the discipline. In discussing a given piece, ask students to pay attention to the rhetorical situation of it. What reading audience is addressed? What are the author's frame of reference, point of reference, point of view, authoritative status? How do the frame and point of reference define and limit the author's view of the subject? What are the peculiarities of the language, form, style? It is sometimes overwhelmingly difficult for students to decode forms of discourse they have not previously encountered, so we can help by pointing out to them such things as arrangement, assumptions, the handling of terms, the use of graphic symbols and the like, all of which may be so familiar to us that we forget they are potentially baffling to new students. Again, student writing can be useful in helping students determine, for their own benefit, whether or not they are getting at and into the text. Short-answer questions like "Is this book written for sophisticated practitioners or novices in the field—and how do you know?" can be revelational. (For instance, the simple realization that the beginner is not being addressed can supply that modicum of confidence students need when they discover they are not "supposed to" know and to grasp everything in a text.) Further, the writing assignments teach the instructor where students are having problems with the reading. Dozens of other questions which ask about a work's rhetorical situation (writer, audience, reality, language) can be framed, and having students write their responses assures that they will be placed in that solitary state which throws them back upon their own conceptualizing resources.

III. Class Activities: The Uses of Informal Writing

Informal, ungraded writing of the kind already suggested has many uses. It allows students an opportunity for exploration and for making the mistakes that can be called to their attention before graded exercises are required; it also frees the teacher from having to focus attention on finer points of discourse which are considered in more formal assignments; and, even more than that, regular ungraded writing allows an instructor to see how the class is progressing. I would urge you to invite what Lou Kelly, the Writing Lab Director at the University of Iowa, calls "talking on paper," by calling for notes, outlines, even questions which would ordinarily be asked aloud. (Framing questions on paper is a very useful exercise— sometimes so difficult that it cannot be done well at first, and sometimes so easy that the mere act of framing itself yields the answers.) Other informal writing might include an occasional exercise which asks students to "talk" in writing about how materials for the class relate to their own experience. This, indeed, is what learning is all about.

I suggest that students be asked to keep spiral notebook "journals" for the course. Not to be confused with diaries or logs, the journals could become the books in which informal, personal exercises for the class are kept. Exercises already recommended would belong there, along with notes and questions encountered as each student reads or writes at home. Encourage students to show you their journals and to address you directly in them whenever they are having problems or are thinking of questions. Encourage them—if it would be helpful—to write summaries of passages and to let you look them over. Outlines of textbook and other materials can also be included in the journals; if students elect to outline, however, look their work over and discuss their system(s) with them in an effort to make sure it works efficiently. Sometimes outlines made as students read are not useful, other than at the time the student has contact with the book. Some people, for instance, merely copy the definitions of terms directly from the text, but later, when asked to give meanings, cannot do so. And whereas individuals should be left to their own outline forms, their own shorthand, their own species of notes and memos to themselves, these do not always prove helpful in the long run to them as writers, even though the time and effort spent in outlining give the illusion that a lot is being accomplished. To point out that such work may be mere busywork is to do the student a real favor. From there, an instructor may demonstrate a better way for reporting material for oneself. Whether we collect journals periodically or invite students to submit entries they particularly want us to see, we would do well to insure that the writing is returned to students promptly, to encourage more of such communication. And when responding to journal entries, or answering a student's written question, we might consider writing those responses, as this will further underscore how much we value what we are asking students to do.

Of course not everyone's teaching style is congenial to all of the methods I have recommended here, but I would also like to assure you that these activities are not as time-consuming as they look. The students become largely responsible for their own learning when writing accompanies reading and discussion. The more we get students to write for us, the more we reinforce writing as enacting cognition. There is a term for the kind of informal personal prose which will emerge as students go through the exercises suggested here: *expressive*. The term should not arouse suspicion; it doesn't refer to anything of the touchy-feely school. Expressive writing is here meant as a form of verbalizing consciousness, as a way of trying to get at understanding—however slowly and painfully—by telling the self what it knows or thinks it knows or needs to know.

Another term for the writing activities I have mentioned is *pre-writing*—prose expression that is preliminary to formal audience-directed discourse. In pre-writing exercises, students sometimes write to themselves, sometimes to the instructor, who reads journals and exercises and first drafts when that is desirable. If we are offered, or ask to see, writing at this stage, we may well respond as a trusted adult—operating, that is, more in the spirit of a friend than of a judge and examiner, even as we make the necessary judgments on whether or not students are getting at the ideas they are trying to state. For students, pre-writing is different from composing essays and other forms of prose for "regular," graded assignments. These latter are more difficult, surely, more time-consuming, and more demanding of awareness of the serious final evaluation to come. The next section of the memo will treat such formal assignments, but at this point I shall make what I hope will be my most forceful plea, *that writing in expressive forms become an ongoing activity in any course at any level in any department.* Pre-writing is a way of knowing. So are the more formal kinds of discourse—variously called *transactional, expository, persuasive,* etc. But pre-writing—if a great deal of work in it can be done—inevitably has an astonishing effect upon students' more public, audience-directed prose—and that includes an effect upon grammar. Often the inability to construct a grammatical sentence is really an inability to clarify one's thoughts to oneself. Syntax, or sentence structure, is a species of ordering; composing a sentence, then, is a way of telling ourselves about relationships. Pre-writing, in the expressive mode, encourages students to do this. And struggles with note-taking and preparing early experimental drafts demonstrate the value of this activity, and pave the way for recognition and correction of error, and for direct attention to detail. Pre-writing is a means of achieving higher literacy.

IV. Class Activities: Assignments in Research and Research Writing

A. Overview

My aim in this section is admittedly an ambitious one: to present a sequence of research writing assignments that may be adopted in—and adapted appropriately to—any beginning course in any department here. As I have noted previously, students need to practice and make use of the skills they learn in freshman composition classes, for even those who write fluently and well will encounter, throughout the remainder of their lives as writers and as learners, fresh and often unique problems in every new rhetorical situation, and will have to invent their own solutions as they go. Humans learn to write mainly by writing—and learn to write effectively only over time. Freshmen at Roosevelt—and certainly this includes transfer students who are still at the freshman level in their writing—need all the reinforcement they can get. If guided writing—especially research writing—ends with the composition course, we should not be surprised if, by the time these people are seniors, they appear to have been poorly trained and virtually as inexperienced as they seemed a couple of years before.

The sequence I will offer here is pitched to the student who is still relatively new to guided research and to writing about it, but it can be altered and parts of it borrowed for students at any level. It is not recommended for students who have had no composition; and students who have not completed remedial courses may have difficulties. Furthermore, the assignments do not work toward the production of a *long* research paper, since we may not assume that all students are ready for that in their 100- and even some 200-level courses. What these assignments *do* do is promote continuous research and practice, allowing students time to give attention to each task in the process. Each assignment takes the class close to the materials in the field under study; together the assignments expose students to a variety of the available texts.

No one need be trained in teaching writing in order to take students through this sequence. The finished products that will emerge from it may, in fact, in a few cases, seem somewhat unpolished in spots, however much the instructor will insist

(I hope!) on quality work generally. But it is not total mastery that is expected here, for that is impossible; it is the opportunity to work with unfamiliar or only slightly-known forms in order that they be *ultimately* mastered.

Each of the early assignments (1-4) focuses on one or two skills, and requires little or no grading and only minimal teacher comment. Assignment 5 asks students to work on a simple short paper which, like the two assignments preceding it, is based on library reference materials related to current classroom concerns, and on practice in more complicated fundamental skills. Since assignments 6, 7, and 8 deal with the mechanics of paraphrasing, summarizing, and handling direct quotations, it may be argued by some readers that those assignments belong more properly to English courses. Whereas these assignments are indeed optional, it should be considered that the person most competent to evaluate the effectiveness of paraphrases and summaries is one who can make the most precise judgments on a student's handling of the subtleties in the language of the texts in that discipline. Assignment 9, which calls for more of the work done for assignment 5, may seem redundant at first glance, but it introduces new skills on a short, "semi-formal" paper that precedes the longer one to be done for assignment 10.

That assignment, the last in the sequence, has many steps and is carried on across time—probably the remainder of the semester. At first sight, it will appear formidable and complicated perhaps, and, in certain places, tedious; but users will discover that the previous assignments in the sequence have done much to prepare students for those parts which are generally most onerous in research writing: those having to do with documentation. Assignment 10, part D, "Writing the Paper," shows rather than prescribes several ways in which to approach organization. Composition textbooks—including the one(s) students will own for the course—ordinarily insist upon only one technique for organizing, and this technique is often difficult and unnatural to work with, as many students will testify.

Finally, let me address the issue of correctness in grammar, mechanics, and form. The responsibility for consistent correctness rests on all our shoulders; students' exposure to these aspects of writing in composition classes may be plentiful indeed, but the comp class must not be the only one in the university where accurate prose is demanded. Unless the English Department and its charges receive the needed reinforcement, our work counts for less than it might if students were provided practice outside of our courses. Yet, even though I realize it is unrealistic to ask that professors in disciplines outside of English become experts in explaining skills, there are some things they can do. Indeed, equipped with a handbook, such as the *Harbrace College Handbook,* which is widely used here at Roosevelt University, professors in other departments can check on particular problems and make suggestions as they feel comfortable; or they may refer students to appropriate sections of the text. Furthermore, the English Department staff, the Director of ELP, the Director of the Writing Laboratory and of course myself are ready to cooperate as consultants with all colleagues. The exercises I propose here for use are primarily designed to give students chances to enhance their thinking—their cognitive development, and hence their true literacy. So, if a teacher will give care and time, insist on proofreading, refuse to accept slovenly work, understand that students are striving *toward* literacy, and that the process cannot be completed overnight—if, that is, the teacher will temper judgment with patience, then the issue of correctness will be addressed as well as it can be.

There are many forms of research and many sources to be used. Lab experiments, interviews, field observations, surveys, statistical studies, and more, are all areas for investigation; ideally college students should have experience in all of them. Since it would be impossible to treat them all here, I will focus on the library as the chief source of materials—again assuming that modifications and adaptations will be made where necessary.

B. Preparation and Materials

1. Make a date for early in the second week of the semester to have a library orientation session for your class. The Reference Librarian or one of the assistants will acquaint students with the facilities and holdings in your field. A tour requires one class period, and appointments must be made in advance.

2. Use your own bibliography as you will, but read the sequence of assignments here first; it may persuade you not to distribute your bibliography at the beginning of the course.

3. Recommend that students purchase a text that explains the operations involved in research paper writing. Many students have such texts already, so if this is the case you may want them to use their own, since uniformity is not crucial. Many Roosevelt students own *The Harbrace College Handbook* in one of its many editions; others have copies, or you can order copies, of one of the following: Willis, *Writing Term Papers* (Harcourt); Lester, *Writing Research Papers* (Scott, Foresman); or Campbell and Ballou, *Theses, Reports, and Term Papers* (Houghton Mifflin). (Note: Hereafter I shall refer to books in this category as HBs.)

4. Since most HBs will contain descriptions and illustrations of bibliographic and footnote forms, it may not be necessary that students also own a style sheet, such as those published by MLA and the University of Chicago. The English Department has its own style sheet—a two-page mimeographed summary of most points of documentary form which may or may not be useful in other departments. If you would like to see it, request a copy from the English Department secretary, and have enough of them duplicated for distribution to your students if it seems suitable.

5. Some students will find notecards uncongenial to their ways of working, nor will these be necessary for the early assignments. Purchase of notecards should be optional, then; students may take notes in notebooks or their "journals" (as described in an earlier section of this memo).

6. Recommend that students purchase a collegiate desk dictionary, if they do not already have easy access to one.

C. The Assignments

1: Introduction to the Library. Library orientation day: one class period devoted to a lecture and tour by the Reference Librarian. Encourage students to remain after the session to examine some of the holdings.

2: A Search for Material. Shortly or immediately after the library visit, ask students to make some small use of the reference materials to find information on bibliographies and/or points being encountered in the lectures and reading for the course: the definition of a term, a short biography of a significant figure, a statistic, a date, etc., to get students acquainted with the "feel" of researching. (Consider this: Purchased course texts deprive students of the opportunity to find materials for themselves. This is not to suggest that texts are not necessary, since time in a course is not forever. But sometimes research in library sources can easily be substituted for a chapter or so of textbook reading; the benefits are obvious when this can be done.)

    This assignment should not be presented as a testing device; in fact, students could do it in pairs, helping each other on several short problems which would get them to handle a variety of reference materials and to note their locations. What they should bring back to class are their own notes, probably recorded in their journals—not as a written "paper"—to be shared with the class. This is the stage at which they should be told about bibliographical citations and the proper form for them in the field. If form is optional, have students consult their HBs. Tell students they'll be using the same form throughout the semester.

    There is nothing to grade here. The assignment can be repeated indefinitely—perhaps daily at the beginning of the semester, or as is appropriate given the number of reference texts the instructor wishes students to be familiar with.

3: A Reading Assignment. Have students look over the materials in the chapters or whole texts of the HBs—especially the introductory materials—in order to acquaint themselves with the writing of research papers. College handbooks, like the *Harbrace*, have whole sections on research papers.

4: Finding Bibliographic Materials. When students are ready for it, perhaps still in the second or during the third week of the semester, have them return to the library to compile a brief bibliography of articles in periodicals on a topic being currently studied in class. A few people could work at once on the project. (This is not a test.) The finished list of articles, with citations in correct form, could be presented to the class for ancillary reading; a master bibliography could be made from the collected materials.

    This assignment could be repeated for other types of sources. There is little, probably, for the teacher to check here.

5: Reporting on a Journal Article and Getting the Sense of the Function of Research Writing. Individuals are on their own for this first prose-writing assignment. Each will go to the library to find an article (or it could be another type of *short* piece) related to current study; then each student will write, simply, a report/summary on the content of the work read. Do not ask for any complex rhetorical maneuvers, like comparing and contrasting two authors' views on a subject, or arguing a point, since the focus in this assignment is on general *form*. Require only that students convey information accurately. A brief summary is all that is called for, but tell students they must use at least one direct quotation.

The function of this assignment is to get students to employ common sense in addressing the needs of an *audience* in a documented paper. Once a consciousness of audience is created, many of the other rhetorical concerns will be addressed and the problems of handling them will be almost automatically solved.

Correctness of technical form in relation to some style sheet or HB specifications is not at issue here, and must not be insisted on. The point is that students recognize a need for footnotes in the first place, and that quoted material be incorporated smoothly and effectively. This paper probably should not be graded, but rather only commented upon briefly to tell whether or not students have met the demands noted in the instructions (below). Make it clear that students do not have to use their HBs or stylesheets for this assignment; it would be preferable that they did not.

* * *

To Students.

You will be writing a brief report to summarize the content of _____. Assume you are preparing the report for the other members of this class; they will, in fact, actually read it. Consider first the needs of your audience: How much do they already know about the field and the topic of your article? What sorts of things would be valuable to them at this point? What sorts of things might be used in their studies of the subject in the future? Assume that they would like to know what you are saying, but that they do not have access to the article (or whatever) you are reporting on, although they may be able to locate it sooner or later—so they'll need the bibliographical reference.

Bearing these readers in mind, write a short summary report on your article for them, with explanations, where necessary, of terms, etc. Since you must use one direct quotation at least, include it in your own text and make a footnote for it; you are free to use a few quotations, but try to have no more than three. If you paraphrase by sticking *very* close to the author's own words, you must include a footnote for that also.

Your concern is not that footnote form be "correct" as specified by a stylesheet, but that it be easy to use, that it contain all the information your audience would need to know—especially if the audience wanted to check your accuracy or to read more in the work you are referring to. Finally be sure you put it in what you think is the right place on the page. YOU are inventing the form for this paper. Keep your readers in mind and you'll have no trouble.

* * *

The instructor's comments on the paper should only address matters specified in the instructions to students above. Look at the way quotations are incorporated in the text to be certain that a reader knows where the student's and the author's words are. A follow-up discussion in class would center on such things as use of paraphrase, summary, footnotes—*their uses, not their forms* at this point. Many questions arise here about the writer's relationship to the audience, about *when* paraphrase and quotation are needed—especially about what paraphrase is and how it works. Students may have learned this before, but paraphrase is so tricky and the potential for unintentional plagiarism so certain, that it is a good idea to discuss paraphrases over and over again with students. That is why I have included the next group of exercises.

Reports done for this one could be collected and "published" for class distribution, or they could be otherwise exchanged. The assignment is excellent for diagnostic purposes of several kinds.

6-8: Practice in Paraphrasing, Using Direct Quotations, Summarizing. I will just provide a model for the three assignments here, using the assignment in paraphrasing, the more difficult of the three skills. The model may then be adapted for use with the other two forms of documenting/reporting materials from sources.

Begin this assignment with a reminder of the hazards of unintentional plagiarism.

Paraphrase: An assignment which has the whole class paraphrasing a portion of a common text (perhaps the class textbook or a handout, with the material read in advance) makes accuracy and subtlety easy for instructors to evaluate. This might even be done in class with everyone working at once on the same passage. I guarantee that the effect of seeing different versions is very revealing to students— and teachers. From this assignment we can learn as much about how students read and interpret what they read as we can learn about their ability to paraphrase, so this assignment has tremendous diagnostic value. The writing might be done in the first half of the class, and the finished versions discussed in the second half, when problems should be brought into focus. Usually there are fairly extensive entries in HBs on the perils and techniques of paraphrase, as well as the mechanics involved in incorporating direct quotations in students' own texts.

Direct Quotations: Also a revelational assignment for the teacher, this one tests accuracy in simply copying information. Surprisingly, many students may produce misspellings of words they are presumably looking at directly; they may omit portions and make other errors on the shortest pieces, as well as on long ones. Thus it is a good idea to stress precise focus on the texts, and to point out the care and attention that must be given to fine matters, such as commas and the like.

But students should not only copy what the book says. Have them incorporate quotations in sentences of their own which introduce them, and in sentences of their own which begin with the quoted material. And now is the time to call their attention to the HB sections on the uses of *sic.*, ellipses, and square brackets.

Summaries: You might talk about occasions when summaries are needed—in what kinds of contexts; when a précis is desirable, and what a précis is; techniques for ascertaining which portions of a text are not relevant in summaries, etc.; and conventions for use of summaries in your field.

9: A Short Documented Report. This assignment should take a five-day or seven-day week to finish, and it is drawn along the same lines as assignment 5. By now, students should be ready for reports on short pieces of material such as articles, chapters in books, pamphlets, entries in reference texts, and the like; and they may be asked to include more of their own comments in response to what they read. Again, the audience should be the other members of the class; refer students to the instructions included for assignment 5.

The point here is to have students practice quotation and paraphrase, and to follow a specific form of footnotes and arrangement of the finished manuscript. No more than two sources should be required, and the importance of taking careful notes should be stressed. The stylesheet, or style pages in the HBs, should be used. It is not necessary, however, that all students follow the same form, though that is probably desirable. Consistency of whatever footnote form is chosen is most important here. If a student's first note has a comma after the author's name, that same convention should be used in the successive notes, etc.

Now is the time to call attention to those sections in the HBs which explain citations for second references to the same book, use of the abbreviations *ibid.*, and (if used) *op. cit.*, and the like. Students new to these mechanics will need to be reminded of them at later stages also. Grade these papers, if necessary, but it may be better to call this an experiment.

10: The Short, Complete Research Paper in Several Steps. It is to be hoped that by now students have had enough practice in the rudimentary techniques that they may begin work on the longer 5-7 page paper to be done in guided steps, perhaps throughout the remainder of the semester. If students do not seem ready—that is, if assignment 9 posed too many problems for too many people—either 9 could be repeated or the problems corrected on an individual basis. Assignment 10 may be followed in the order suggested, and repeated in fewer steps later, if it seems desirable to have students do more than one short paper. Better still, a final short paper (perhaps a kind of take-home examination at the end of the semester) could be done without guidance.

    a.   *Selecting a Topic.* It is impossible for me in this document to prescribe generally for the entire faculty the best means of selecting topics. They may grow out of students' reading interests; they may be directly assigned by the instructor (plagiarism will not be much of a problem on this project, since students are taken through steps and are handing in materials before the final paper is due); or sometimes topics may be pulled out of the blue as a result of sudden "inspiration." In any case, have students read materials on topic selection in their HBs, and be sure to check each student's choice for suitability and workability: these are short papers, after all. Sections in HBs are helpful in describing how to narrow topics to realistic size. Many students tend to select subjects that are too broad, so the teacher's judgment may be the only guide they have to the appropriateness of topic size.

        Nor should topics be too complicated, since students are still sharpening skills and are likely to be overwhelmed by all of the processes they anticipate for this project. If we make this assignment too difficult, we run more than one risk. First of all, we cannot follow their progress closely enough when there is too much material to handle. Secondly, if the search for material becomes too lengthy or prodigious, students may be tempted to resort to shortcuts and to get a little too much "outside help." Whatever can be done to ensure students' personal success should be done. At the same time there should be sufficient challenge to ensure that the process is not overly simple.

b. *The Preliminary Bibliography.* Up until now, students have not had to consult the Card Catalog to any great extent. (If they need a review of it, the HBs will help; so will a trip to the library. Nor should they be diffident about asking a librarian's assistance.) Perhaps they will use the card catalog here in hunting for new types of sources—pamphlets, monographs, abstracts, nonreference books, as well as reference works and periodicals they have not had occasion to use yet. The HBs will give help on things to consider in compiling tentative, or working, bibliographies; just refer students to appropriate sections, and of course supplement them with your own advice. In general, the number of works used should be kept down: 3-5 is reasonable, but the figure may vary, depending on length and depth of materials, and on the instructor's special requirements for types of texts, etc.

  Whether or not students choose to use notecards for bibliographies (and notetaking) should be left up to them. Many of us find the business of keeping together and shuffling notecards a real bother; nor is it really necessary. (Cards probably do provide the most efficient means of storing and organizing materials for *longer* papers.)

  Instructors should check on preliminary bibliographies for suitability of texts and so on, so students should hand these in.

c. *Notetaking.* All the HBs, as I have noted, will have materials on notetaking techniques which students should study carefully before they begin: paying particular attention to the pitfalls of inaccurately quoting a source; forgetting to include bibliographical data on each note or notecard; failing to copy page numbers; not making distinctions between page numbers where a given quote begins and ends; using inadequate subject heading identification on each notecard or notesheet; forgetting to indicate whether a note contains paraphrase, quotations, or the student's own words, etc. Reading HBs on footnoting itself would not be premature at this stage, especially as it would help students get down their notes in forms most convenient to transfer to footnote citations when the papers themselves are being written and documented.

  If students elect (as some will) to use pages in a spiral or looseleaf notebook for notetaking, suggest that pairs of facing pages contain the same subject- or topic-heading; notes can then be organized in patterns that will not be hard to decipher at the actual writing stage. If notecards are used, students will find plenty of instruction in their HBs on how to manage them—usually including graphic examples.

Other students might devise entirely different systems of note keeping. Stress only that, whatever method is chosen, it must be systematically organized and suited to each student's own way of operating—not to someone else's. A short speech on the kinds of problems that could be encountered if notes were scattered, incomplete, left without page number references, topic headings, etc., or were messy and unreadable, etc., should help prevent some small disasters. If *you* have devised some personally useful and efficient method of your own, share it with your students. Sharing the tale of a disaster will probably be quite helpful too.

Set a deadline on which notetaking should be finished, but, before that, ask to see cards or notebooks, making spot checks for things students might be doing—or not doing—that could cause confusion during the writing stage. Neatness and readability are obviously important for good reason; a word to the wise about having to make an extra trip to the library because of some indecipherable notes could certainly be helpful, just as it is a good idea in general to remind students that the day of reckoning approaches—the day when the notes will be there and the books and other reference materials won't.

d.   *Writing the Paper*

i. Audience. Before students write, tell them that they will be each other's audience; after all, written research is generally meant for someone else to read. Papers should be written with readers besides the teacher in mind, and the class audience is a congenial and sensible choice. Follow through with finished papers, then; if students know they will have their work read, they will hand it in before the very end of the semester so the exchange can be made with others in the class.

ii. Organizing in Advance: A Word about Outlining—and Not Outlining. Most HBs urge students to outline their papers, and include elaborate examples of outlines, sometimes of two or three different types, one more impressive-looking and detailed than the next. For a short assignment, like the current paper, an outline may be necessary for some students, in which case there is no reason to discourage them from making one. But you might tell students that if their notecards and notesheets have been kept in orderly fashion under topic headings, the simple arrangement of these in sequence can serve essentially the same function as an outline would. Individual points can then be arranged according to their headings in an order based on the logic of the material and common sense.

Studies in the composing process, and the personal experience of most English teachers, and indeed of anyone who does regular research, demonstrate that people instinctively plan and write papers in the ways best suited to their temperaments, work habits, and orders of mind. To insist therefore that the person who cannot abide outlining and would never voluntarily do it be forced to plot his or her paper in that fashion is to go against nature, as it were, and to create confusion and frustration, even, perhaps, to court failure. (Proof of this is the testimony of dozens of students who confess they write papers first and then trick up outlines after they have finished—just to fulfill a teacher's requirement that an outline be submitted.) By the time many students have taken notes and been attentive to where those notes are leading, they are ready to start writing. Others, more diffident about the task in general, or the adequacy of their notes, feel better if they sketch out some sort of rough or detailed plan. Still others write quick rough drafts and then spend as much or more time revising and shaping them. Let students discover and use their own methods, however unlike your own they may be.

When students are worried about planning, it is occasionally because the job ahead seems so monumental that they cannot bring themselves to focus on it "just yet." And when students are genuinely baffled and really do not have any notion of where or how to begin, you might offer assistance in getting started at least. It is best not to flood the Writing Lab with people who have to write term papers; if your students know you are available for conferences at this stage, you can probably get the neediest ones going in a one half-hour interview—especially because you have checked their progress at other steps along the way.

iii. Writing Sections of the Paper. Generally students should be encouraged to present finished papers in three conventional parts or sections: an introduction which states the purpose and thesis and provides a little background information on the subject; the body paragraphs, which illustrate and support the thesis; and a conclusion, however brief or elaborate, which draws everything together at the end. Again, the HBs are full of hints and instructions for writing; sections with titles like, "Getting Started," "Writing the Paper," "Making a First Draft," "Beginning to Write," etc., can be used if students feel the need for such elaborations.

But composing does not always move according to neat categories, with the Introduction being completed first, and so on. Indeed, many writers move inductively through the work—or in mysterious directions for various reasons not necessarily "bad"—and may go through a series of body paragraphs, and/or the conclusion itself before learning what needs to be covered in an introduction. We often discover *as* we write, and it is the discovery that is important, not the filling of a prescription for the universally "correct" steps.

iv. Uses of Pre-Writing Techniques: Handling Problems Encountered. "Pre-Writing," defined in an earlier section of this *Guide* under "The Uses of Informal Writing," can be very helpful to both those students who can't get started, and those who are stuck somewhere along the line. Such people should be told to take out their journals and write freely to themselves without regard to mechanics and the like. Peter Elbow's book, *Writing Without Teachers,* could profitably be consulted here by students (and even their teachers, *as writers.*) Elbow describes a variety of unconventional-sounding, but remarkably sound and useful, techniques for dealing with blocks and other problems in progress. Free-writing about problematical portions of papers, and letting ideas "cook" (in Elbow's term) as one writes associatively about them, have long been helpful techniques for both professionals and amateurs. Sometimes it is well even to leave writing aside for a while after having spent a great deal of time belaboring a point in one's own text—we all know that; some students do not.

Even teachers of English are hard-pressed sometimes to help students write certain pieces they are struggling over. But if students have been through at least one semester of freshman English before your course, they will already have been introduced to several kinds of discourse and should be able to determine the best way to proceed at the composing stage of this relatively short paper. The HBs can be a help, but there is nothing amiss in encouraging students to help each other along the way. If class time can be taken, they may exchange partial drafts and discuss them. Small groups are especially good for this—after all, each paper's audience is the class as a whole, so the exchange is a form of audience-testing. Do give students plenty of time to write—checking progress by letting them consult each other as often as possible. To rush them through by setting an early deadline is to defeat the purpose of the activity. Understanding about snags and writer's blocks and a sudden necessity to revise a section, or to add a paragraph or two, is essential.

v. Multiple Drafts and Revisions. Allow time, too, for papers to go through as many drafts as students' needs dictate. While it is natural to wish to set a reasonable ultimate time for handing things in, and to ask students to meet it, allowances should be made where conscientious writers, because of various snags, cannot do so. If such writers are pressed to finish when they would do better with more time, they should be given that time. It is time in which they are learning about the composing process—having to make adjustments, choices, and the like—and such activity is exceedingly valuable to each writer.

vi. Footnotes. Fortunately students have already had experience with incorporating paraphrase and quotation, and with footnoting papers. The HB sections on footnoting should be read here also, to reinforce what students already know, and to explain the form which should be followed. Specify such things as where notes should be placed—at the bottom of each page or on a separate page; and call attention in the HBs to sections that explain such things as *ibid.,* short forms for second and successive references, etc.

vii. The Bibliography. If a paper is so short, a bibliography is probably not necessary, unless it is conventional to include one, or the instructor wants it. If so, the form should be prescribed, and the HB and/or stylesheets consulted. Students have already done considerable work with bibliography, so creating a list should pose no difficulties.

viii. The Final Draft. Typing a finished paper of the sort described here is easy for some people, and it is certainly gratifying for writer and reader alike to behold a clean copy of the finished product. For others, typing a paper is worse than composing its most difficult paragraphs, and the final copy is often distressing enough to make an instructor want to exact some penalty for it. Insist on neatness and corrected, proofread copy, but I would advise not to insist on typing. Typing footnotes is very hard for inexperienced typists; handwriting allows for better focus on detail, page proportions, margins, and other aspects of the physical manuscript. Handwriting is easier to read, and there is more room for instructor's comments and notes if the manuscript is doublespaced, as typed pages should also be.

Be certain that students know the specifications for the form of the final manuscript before they begin their final copies.

e. *Evaluating and Exchanging Papers.* Students for whom this is the first experience in writing documented papers should not be too harshly judged on finished products that are less than perfect. If they have tried conscientiously and learned well, this is the most important benefit to come from the activity. In fact, I would rather see them judged on their handling of the process than on the final product, but your grading methods are your own affair, of course. I do suggest, however, that since the class was the audience for these papers, they be given the opportunity to exchange finished papers before the teacher grades them. Students might write comments on separate sheets for each paper they read.

Writing Across the Disciplines

A Faculty Development Program

Elizabeth Ciner

The program I offer here is one designed not for students but for faculty—specifically for faculty who are concerned about their students' writing (or willing to learn why they should be concerned about it), and interested in using writing more effectively in their classes. Unlike other programs in this volume, this one does not come with an elaborate sequence of assignments. In fact, as you will see, it includes only one writing task, an assignment that was used to open the week-long faculty writing seminars at the center of this cross-disciplinary program. These seminars—there have been three, offered in three successive Augusts at St. Olaf College in Northfield, Minnesota—led participants through a series of activities designed to help them think about the role of writing in their courses—to consider both what they *were* doing with writing and what they *could* be doing with it. Participants came from all departments of the institution; they applied to be part of a seminar, and in two of the three years those selected received a small stipend for attending. Across the three summers, a total of 60 faculty members took part.[1] Our main goal in these seminars was to spread responsibility for the teaching of writing, not by consolidating authority traditionally invested in English departments, but by providing occasions in which faculty from a range of disciplines could be empowered to make informed and creative decisions of their own about writing. Our hope was to foster a sense of community among those who cared deeply about writing, and then to nurture this community with a variety of follow-up activities, in the hope that it would lead to improved writing instruction not only in specific classes but throughout the institution as a whole.

The seminars were jointly designed and directed by me and by Paul Diehl, a cross-curricular specialist from the University of Iowa. We intended the seminars to

[1]Funding for the first seminar and a portion of the second was provided by the Eli Lilly Foundation as part of a Critical Skills Grant to strengthen math and writing instruction at the college. The third seminar was funded in part by grants from the Bush Foundation and the Northwest Area Foundation. Remaining expenses were covered by the college, and by the Keay Gift to the Department of English.

be opportunities for participating faculty to examine their attitudes toward writing and language, to consider why they had students write, to explore why certain problems occurred in students' papers, and to think about what connections existed between, on the one hand, their assignments and the students' writing, and, on the other hand, their responses and the papers students subsequently wrote. The faculty who took part in these seminars were not very different from those one might find at any college or university today, which is to say they were people whose sense of language ranged from the sophisticated to the suspicious; of faculty who were themselves writers, if not of published articles and books then at least of memoranda, recommendations, course descriptions, assignments and syllabi; and of teachers many of whom already used writing effectively in their courses. Most of these participants, though, came to the seminars looking to the English Department for definitive answers to specific questions about what they should and should not do and about what they should tell their students to do and not do. And many were concerned that participation in a writing program required a kind of technical expertise in grammar. Paul and I did not have many definitive answers for participants (no handbooks nor handouts which could guarantee good results), but we could reassure them that biologists and art historians would not have to "become" English teachers.

In keeping with this assurance, the seminars followed an experiential rather than an authority-based model. That is to say, they were designed to draw upon the experiences and understandings the participants brought with them—as specialists and teachers in their fields, as writers, as makers of assignments, as readers of student writing, and as responders to that writing—and to take them through further experiences with writing and responding from which discussions about these matters could emerge. To this end, each participant was asked a month or so before the seminar to submit to us the following materials: (1) their response to a single writing assignment (which you will find reproduced at the end of this essay), and (2) any two pieces of student writing that they wished to have discussed, together with the assignment(s) which elicited the writings. These documents—the participants' writing, the student writings, and the assignments that had prompted them—were duplicated and distributed to all participants prior to the seminar. These were the assigned readings for the week, and the basis for our discussions throughout the five days.

Broadly speaking, our attention throughout each week-long seminar moved from exposing attitudes about writing (day 1), to examining the effects of assignments on students' writings (days 2-3), to considering the effects of an instructor's responses on student writing later received (day 4), to seeing the discussions and discoveries of the seminar in connection to future plans and cross-curricular writing activities (day 5). As for the conduct of the sessions, there were no lectures but a series of discussions instead. We met as a group 3-4 hours each day, and, in addition, set aside time each late afternoon for individual conferences.

The seminar writing task served as the basis of our first day's discussion, and was a focus of recurring consideration throughout the week. Even before the seminar began, this writing assignment had served a number of purposes. Its opening lines had been designed to channel the participants' attention to their motives for assigning writing to students, and to the range of their requests:

> To give a common starting point for our discussions, please spend some time in the next few weeks thinking and writing about the kinds of writing assignments you make in your classes. A few of the questions you may want to consider are as follows: Why do you expect and demand that your students write? Or, if you don't have your own students write, why do you think you (or anyone) ought to require writing at all? What kinds of writing do you ask your students to do? What different writing situations do you ask them to enter into and why?

These questions encouraged faculty members to examine their own assignments with a critical eye, and to think about how they functioned, in themselves and within the context of a particular course (reflections faculty otherwise, as a rule, rarely have the time for). The first paragraph of the assignment ended, however, by turning faculty members back to themselves as writers:

> …what about yourself as a writer? Do you write regularly? Why? Or, do you dread writing? Why might that be? How do you feel about the writing assignment we've just given you? What kinds of problems does it produce for you?

This double focus—on faculty members as elicitors of writing and as writers themselves—made possible a comparison of their own practices with what they advocated. Moreover, the assignment put faculty members in the role of students— writing on demand, on a subject not of their own choosing, for an audience they might suspect knew more about the subject than they did. (The week before the assignment was due, it was not uncommon for participants to call and ask me, "What do you want?" The week following the due date, colleagues whose responses I had not yet received avoided me on campus!) Thus participants began the seminar having recently examined some of their own instructional expectations and practices and having experienced something of what it feels like to be student writers. By the time of our opening discussion, participants had also had the opportunity to compare their own responses with those of their colleagues. And because we specifically asked them to be prepared to address these concerns, they had also considered what common or contradictory assumptions about writing seemed to be at work in the responses.

Needless to say, our discussions about the assignment, about the experience of doing the assignment, and about the collected responses to the assignment contributed to an understanding of the nature and purposes of writing, an understanding which became increasingly clarified throughout the week. While the following realizations which emerged during the week may not look extraordinary in themselves (and may go without saying for many of us), they constituted new understandings for many seminar participants:

1. Writing, especially professional writing, comes easily to almost no one; anxiety about some kinds of writing is almost universal.
2. Writing is not a monolithic activity, one thing done in one way, with a single format. People write for a variety of reasons.
3. Given the various reasons for writing, and given the differences among individuals, the very processes of writing may change, from one purpose to another, from one writer to another.
4. Faculty ask their students to write for a variety of reasons. A chemist, for example, assigns writing because "it is important to describe experimental work clearly enough for the experiments to be repeated by other researchers," while an economist assigns writing because "most of the important questions economists raise are those for which there is no single answer," so that what becomes important is not so much the answer obtained but the process of reasoning that leads to it.
5. Writing is an important way of knowing and an important tool for learning. Language is the medium through which we categorize, sort out, and make sense of the world. We find out what we know *through* language, and in written language we find it in a form we can examine.

Taken together, the seminar writing assignment and our first day's discussion asked faculty to think about writing, in effect, as a subject interesting in and of itself, to articulate for themselves the reasons they believed writing important, to confront the question of why they had students write, to note the gap between their ideals and the reality of their students' writing, and to consider what it was they were asking students to do when they assigned writing. Important questions inevitably arose out of the assignment and the discussion: Is anxiety salutory or damaging? Do we in fact ask our students to write in a variety of forms and for a variety of reasons? Do our assignments nurture learning in our students? Do our students know why we have them write? Why is it that for many students writing is seen as nothing more than a substitute for an examination, a way of demonstrating comprehension of set assigned material? What effects does this misunderstanding about what writing is good for have on our students?

As a means of addressing some of these questions, and of exploring solutions to some of the implicit problems, we devoted most of the remainder of the week to analyzing actual assignments, student writing, and the range of possible responses to student writing. For at least two of the five days, we examined the connection between the sample student papers submitted by the participants and the assignments which elicited them. Generally, we would move from a question such as "How would you describe what is going on in this paper?" to "Why do you think the student is writing this way?" These discussions, in effect, moved between identifying the problems students were having and identifying the part the assignments had in those problems. For example, one group of seminar participants considered a short paper written by a basic writing student near the beginning of the term. It was unclear, given the opening of the paper, what the student thought he was up to. His first paragraph was as follows:

> Dear High School Senior,
>
> Hi! You are having a hell of a lot better time than I am right now. I've got midterms coming up and I've been very uptight lately. There are many differences between high school and college. Two differences that I'll tell you about are study time and social life.

After the group had discussed the paragraph, and identified the problem—the strange mixture of the genuine (this student "getting into the spirit" of letter writing) and the fake (the capricious use of contractions, the lack of connection between feeling "uptight" and "there are many differences")—we asked what could have produced this curious combination. An answer to that became clear when we looked at the assignment, for it had asked students to "write a letter to a high school senior who is considering going to college next fall," and then added the following admonition: "Although there are many types of differences about which you might write, narrow your letter to one or two aspects of college living, social and/or academic, which have been most important in your own adjustment here." The assignment, the seminar participants concluded, did not *force* the student to write poorly (and, in fact, someone added, one way to distinguish between "good" and "poor" students may be that the good students somehow overcome the handicaps imposed on them by an assignment). But the assignment did seem to create a situation where the writer had to struggle between writing naturally ("a hell of a lot better time") and doing what he had been told ("narrow your letter"). As one participant argued, it would be highly unlikely that someone who genuinely wanted to say something to someone else would decide ahead of time to narrow a letter "to one or two aspects of college living."

A better writing assignment might not have helped the writer of that letter, but the seminar group concluded that this assignment, while designed to be helpful, had not really been of much assistance itself. That assignment might have been dismissed as a peculiar case, since the instructor was clearly trying to engage students in a sort of role playing. But assignments like it, equally well meaning but not well-conceived, showed up a number of times in the collection, from a number of courses—and not just those in the department of English. The following, for example, was submitted by a participant who had given it to his students in a religious thought class, "Interpreting the Bible":

> Geography is important in the Scriptures, so this essay deals with a place or a geographical feature (e.g., a river) which has come up in the readings and which interests you. Describe the location of the place; use several maps from atlases and biblical dictionaries, etc., and tell what you learned from the various maps and descriptions. What was helpful or not from these resources? Then using a concordance or your memory, select and study two passages from our readings (e.g., a battle or journey) which deal with the place. Describe how the physical features or location of the place played a role in the passage. Three to five pages.

At first glance, this assignment seemed promising, giving students clear enough directives, encouraging them to write on subjects which interested them. In this particular case, however, the instructor reported to us that the papers were poorer than he had expected them to be; the paper which seminar participants examined was typical, he said—overall organization was weak, sentences did not connect very well one to the next, and by the middle of the second page the writer seemed to be wandering aimlessly in the topic. Questions the seminar group explored included the following: To what extent is the assignment to blame? Could picking a place or a geographical feature "which interests you" simply lead you to a dead end? Does following the assignment necessarily result in something which can be turned into "an essay"?

The student whose paper we looked at had done what the instructor had asked, but had failed to produce a coherent essay demonstrating insights into the importance of geography in biblical study. In our discussions, the group concluded that the assignment might actually have encouraged the poor writing—prompting students to force paragraphs which were not about the same thing into some form which pretended they were all related. If part of the purpose of the religion assignment was to get students into the library, as it seemed to have been, an essay assignment might not have been the best approach. And if part of the purpose was to evoke lists from students, a short answer test might have been more appropriate.

In discussing the inter-connections between assignments and student writing, we sometimes began with the student's writing alone, asking participants to infer the assignment from that particular response to it. Other times we looked at an assignment alone, and talked about what it apparently expected from students. In this context, the seminar writing assignment again came into play, this time not as an *instrument* for eliciting attitudes and for putting faculty into the role of students, but as a *model,* embodying as it did different approaches to assignment making, and providing a contrast to the assignments of most faculty members. We discussed, among other things, its tone and its design: the opening paragraph of fifteen questions intended to elicit quantities of information; its second paragraph collapsing the fifteen questions into one, encouraging participants to some kind of synthesis; and its third paragraph addressing the question of form, inviting participants to use any form of response they saw fit, be it an essay, a letter, a narrative, or something else entirely.

A number of assignments submitted to the seminar also served as possible models for the participants. One of these, written by an instructor in Economics for an upper level class on Public Finance, appears after the seminar writing assignment at the end of this essay. The assignment, the instructor explained, was the first—and the most detailed—in a series of three. He noted that everything the students needed in order to fulfill the assignment was contained in the instructions, and that the students could use the information and form of this assignment as a guide when approaching the later two papers, where they would have more liberty, being able to choose both their subject and their specific approach. This detailed assignment implicitly dealt with issues of purpose and audience, and suggested procedures to consider in fulfilling the task. By extension, it also addressed the kind of language a student should use—in this case the language appropriate to a consultant hired by the Policy Analysis Division of the Minnesota state legislature. In clearly establishing the rhetorical demands of the situation, in suggesting a logical and connected pattern of organization, and in presenting students with a means of analyzing the problem, this was a model assignment which encouraged students to learn by doing, an assignment which in its form taught students something about making their way through such problems.

In choosing papers and assignments to be discussed, Paul and I usually began with writing material from the hard sciences—where issues are more generally perceived to be clear, where the objects of attention are more or less concrete, and where the purpose is often something as specific as making it possible for someone else to replicate an experiment—and then moved to sampling assignments and pieces of student writing from the social sciences, and finally the humanities. For any given day, we chose pieces which would reinforce a sense of common problems and purposes. We looked for papers displaying a range of problems, including papers which displayed problems the group might already have encountered but which were appearing in different forms. Among the subjects of our discussions, which always grew out of the sample pieces we had before us, were the following: the relationship between a use of jargon or inflated language and fuzzy thinking; problems in diction, paragraphing, overall organization, spelling, and general appearance; effective and appropriate use of charts and graphs; plagiarism; proper citation form. (Most of the students' papers we looked at had problems typical of a good student body at a fairly select institution, so errors of grammar and usage were infrequent.) Although we generally focused on problems in student writing, we always included one or two first-rate papers in the discussions to give participants an opportunity to articulate what was going right in a paper and to remind us all that the outstanding writers as well as those that are floundering are entitled to our considered (and considerate) response.

Having asked participants to examine a student's writing with an eye to understanding what might have given rise to any problems in it, the next question followed naturally: "What can we tell the student which will help him or her to improve this piece or the next one?" Here, as before, we kept particular pieces in mind. For example, we asked participants to respond to a single piece by saturating it with red marks, noting everything they could could possibly find to say, everything they could possibly find to correct. Then, after distributing clean copies of the same paper, we asked them to read the piece again, and this time to limit their response to a single thoughtful end-comment. We considered the possible effect upon students of first the one form of response and then the other, and compared the messages each of these two approaches gave. This inevitably led into discussions of how the form and content of our responses indicate the role(s) we see ourselves in, and want students to see us in: perhaps as examiners, noting what is going wrong; perhaps as editors, indicating to students what we think they should have done; perhaps as one speaker in a written dialogue, encouraging a writer to pursue an idea further; perhaps as a teacher, suggesting alternative strategies that might make future writings of the same kind more effective. We also discussed how the form and content of our response suggests what we value in writing and, by extension, want our students to value: perhaps rhetorical abilities, the degree to which the writer handles the major demands of the task; perhaps style, tone, and point of view; perhaps mechanical abilities, the student's control of surface features and conventional forms; perhaps the ideas, and the degree to which they provoke us to further thought.

A number of questions inevitably arose as we continued to analyze the messages implicit in our responses, and to explore the ways our response can affect what we later get from students. Was it more appropriate to focus on one weakness in a paper or several? Might we at times implicitly ask students to pay attention to too many concerns, thereby running the risk of discouraging them? Did the values implicit in our responses reflect the attitudes about writing we thought we held? Would the kinds of responses we wrote to students be the kinds of responses that would help us were we the ones receiving them? Did our responses imply that we expected our students to already be accomplished writers and performers, or that we expected them to be learners, practicing to become better? At different points in the course, should the form of our response be different? At different points in the course, should our role(s) in responding vary?

Given all these questions and concerns, we could only begin to address them in the closing days of the seminar, and during the final meeting we talked about ways of continuing our discussions throughout the year, of pursuing the subjects in meetings with one another and with colleagues who had not been part of the group. We discussed the format for follow-up meetings, gatherings of faculty who would come together during the school year. (And these gatherings took place, and continue to, and have usually been similar in spirit and form to the seminar: people coming together to "workshop" an assignment, a student paper, a response, a faculty member's own writing.)

The seminars, then, were a starting point, a means of beginning to build a community of understanding about writing and its role in the classroom. Moving from assignments to student writing to responses, the seminars served to remind participants, among other things, of the influences of their own writing on their students' writing. They served to emphasize, then, how powerful the language of assignments and responses can be, and to give faculty time to consider how they were using and could be using writing in their own courses. Such seminars as these cannot guarantee that the quality of students' writing will improve. But they do offer good reasons to hope that the quality of writing instruction will improve. While we cannot provide formulas to fit every occasion, we can provide a solid conceptual and practical framework with which to deepen awareness of the nature and purposes of student writing, and of the role an instructor can play in that writing.

SAMPLE ASSIGNMENTS

Seminar Writing Assignment

To give a common starting point for our discussions, please spend some time in the next few weeks thinking and writing about the kinds of writing assignments you make in your classes. A few of the questions you may want to consider are as follows: Why do you expect and demand that your students write? Or, if you don't have your own students write, why do you think you (or anyone) ought to require writing at all? What kinds of writing do you ask your students to do? What different writing situations do you ask them to enter into and why? How do you treat that student writing? What role do you place yourself in as you read your students' papers? What role do the students perceive you to be in as you read their papers? Have you been satisfied with the writing of your students? One more question— what about yourself as a writer? Do you write regularly? Why? Or, do you dread writing? Why might that be? How do you feel about the writing assignment we've just given you? What kinds of problems does it produce for you?

Or, these questions might be collapsed to this: why do you ask your students to write—from the viewpoint of a liberal arts education, from the viewpoint of your own discipline, from the viewpoint of your own experience?

We do not know the most congenial form for each of you to use in conveying your responses to us. We're open to essays, letters, narratives, or whatever other form suits you best. But we do hope that each of you will respond in some form. It is not only that your writing will help acquaint us with the concerns and problems of the group, but also it is from the discoveries you make by confronting these concerns that we will structure the workshop and establish the beginning points. In addition, this writing will allow us all to share with each other the things we hold about writing and learning. To this end, we will run off copies of each of your papers; they will become the first items on our brief reading list.

Assignment from an upper level Economics course on Public Finance
David Schodt

Consider the following information:

This year both the federal government and the Minnesota state government passed legislation which increased the tax per gallon of gasoline. Minnesota raised the state tax on gasoline and diesel fuel from 13 to 17 cents. Justification for this tax increase was somewhat different at the different levels of government but both indicated that the additional tax revenue would be used for transportation projects, either highway repair or mass transit. Minnesota argued that the increased tax would also encourage the production of ethanol in the state. Minnesota's gasoline tax is exceeded only by Michigan's, which is 17.8 cents per gallon.

Assume that you have been hired as a consultant by the Policy Analysis

Division of the Minnesota state legislature. Although most legislators agree that additional revenues must be raised to pay for needed transportation projects, many are unconvinced that an increase in the gasoline tax is the best way to do this. Your task is to evaluate the gasoline tax increase so that legislators can compare the economic effects of this tax with that of other possible sources of revenue. Since other economists have been hired to work on this project, you have your choice of analyzing either the efficiency or equity of the gasoline tax increase.

Begin your analysis by defining an efficiency or an equity question which you feel would be helpful for evaluating this policy. For example, an efficiency question might seek to determine the welfare cost of this tax; an equity question might investigate the burden of this tax by income class or occupational group.

Once you have decided on an efficiency or an equity question, you will need to develop an economic model which you can use to construct an answer to the question you have raised. Your model may be graphical or mathematical but in either case you must specify very clearly the assumptions on which it is based. For example, the model of supply and demand may be useful. It rests heavily on the assumption of perfect competition. Remember that whatever approach you decide to take to this, you will have to address the question of tax shifting at some point.

Once you have specified your model fully, you should use it to discuss those factors which are likely to determine an answer to the question you began with. For example, if you are interested in the burden of this tax on the poor, a supply and demand model would suggest that your answer would depend on the elasticity of demand for gasoline by income class, among other things.

Finally, *without* consulting any of the empirical literature, or doing your own empirical test, explain what data you would need to answer your questions *and* indicate clearly what would be reasonable sources for finding these data. (The Policy Analysis Division should be able to find the data it would need to complete your study from these sources.) Then indicate what answer you would consider most plausible and explain your reasons for this choice. Do not compute a quantitative answer to your question; the Policy Analysis Division would like to examine your economic analysis before committing themselves to paying you to undertake the computations.

Your paper should be approximately three pages in length. It should contain a clear statement of your question, careful development of the model, and as precise an answer to your question as you are able to determine without undertaking any calculations.

Writing Across the Disciplines

A Program for Curricular Development

Lana Silverthorn

Virtually all writing specialists would affirm that we learn to write by writing and that students, therefore, need continuous practice and guidance in writing throughout their college careers. In much the same spirit of unanimity, composition specialists would affirm that writing is a fundamental mode of learning in all disciplines, and that for this crucial reason as well students should be called upon to write throughout their college careers. It is one matter, of course, to affirm these truths, another to put them into practice on a campus such as the University of South Alabama, which includes a variety of colleges and programs, ranging from traditional subjects of study in the liberal arts to newly emerging technical and applied fields in engineering and nursing. In such institutions, it is especially important to honor the delicate balance that must be sustained in all cross-curricular programs between the needs of the academic community as a whole and the professional integrity and distinctiveness of each discipline in particular. To achieve this balance requires the development of policies that serve the entire community, as well as a practical means of implementing them that can be applied by each discipline as it sees fit.

At South Alabama, we are working towards this goal by means of a university-wide program that aims to make writing an integral part of the work in all upper-level courses for undergraduates. This overall program, we believe, will assure that our students receive continuous practice in writing, and that the writing they do meets the needs of each discipline, since the writing will have been assigned and assessed by faculty members in each field, rather than by members of an English department or a separately constituted writing staff. A nursing professor, after all, is likely to be the best judge of form and content in a medical log or a clinical report, much as a professor of engineering is likely to be the best judge of a proposed engineering project.

Knowledgable though they are about the specialized forms of writing in their fields, professors in all disciplines are, often by their own admission, quite uninformed about how writing might be used as a way of learning in their fields.

Few instructors in any area, after all, can be expected to have a working familiarity with the concepts of language and learning. So, not surprisingly, they generally tend to regard writing primarily, or even exclusively, as a means of communicating knowledge, and in turn assign writing as a means of testing their students' knowledge and their ability to communicate it in appropriately specialized forms. At South Alabama, therefore, we have been offering week-long seminar-workshops to familiarize faculty in all disciplines with the idea of writing as a mode of learning, and to show them methods of putting this idea into practice in their own courses. From their inception in 1981, these workshops have been the most important element in the development of our cross-curricular writing program.[1]

The workshop, which takes place each year shortly before the fall quarter, provides an uninterrupted oportunity for me and our outside consultant—David Hamilton of Iowa—to work closely with a group of 20-25 faculty. In planning these workshops, David and I decided that our major goals would be to show faculty how to prepare a sequence of writing assignments and how to respond to student writing so as to integrate writing and learning in their courses. We have each colleague prepare a sequence, because we want to encourage the use of relatively short writing assignments spread across a course—continuous writing, as it were—rather than the one-shot, lengthy term paper that is currently so widespread a phenomenon in upper-division courses everywhere. We also work on sequenced assignments, because we want to be sure that multiple writing tasks are not simply added on to a course in hit or miss fashion, but are purposefully designed and arranged so as to be integrated into the course and to help students conceptualize particular topics or problems that figure in the course. Ultimately, we focus on sequencing and response, because we want faculty to leave the workshop with tangible materials and methods that they can immediately use to strengthen the quality of writing and learning in their courses.

Given the classroom orientation of these goals, we have designed the workshop itself to grow out of the faculty's classroom experience with writing. In particular, we ask them to bring an essay to the first session, describing the kind of writing assignments that they typically make and the purpose that writing typically serves in their courses. These essays stimulate faculty to think deliberately and self-consciously about the way they use writing in their courses. Their initial thinking and writing on this issue serves, in turn, as a springboard for our first day of discussion, which begins with a consideration of the basic rhetorical purposes that writing generally serves, and within this context the purposes that writing typically serves in the classroom. The challenge of having to write an essay for this first day of the workshop also provides faculty with an experience upon which they readily draw in talking about the various problems and satisfactions that are connected with

---

[1] Workshops in 1981, 1982, and 1983 were funded by the University of South Alabama. Funding for additional workshops and related cross-curricular activities in 1984 and 1985 will be provided by a grant from the National Endowment for the Humanities.

writing. So, the experience of doing the essay enables them to see how a writing assignment can be a form of learning, as well as of testing. Overall, then, the first day of the workshop is designed to begin the process of reorienting the way that faculty think about writing in higher education, and thus to provide a general basis for their subsequent work on sequencing and response.

To provide a more specific academic context for our work, we turn our attention at the beginning of the second day to scientific writing and use it as a paradigm for understanding the nature and function of writing in other academic disciplines and courses. The practical demands of scientific writing are likely to be closer to the concerns of the group as a whole than any other kind of writing, so it serves as a good testing ground for our approach. We look, in particular, at the conventional format of scientific reporting (the abstract, review of prior research, description of methods and materials, presentation of data, analysis of results, and conclusions), and note that this structure embodies basic elements of organization to be found in other forms of writing (thesis, background, development, conclusion). Yet we also acknowledge that the form of scientific reporting disseminates knowledge in a way that is distinctive of scientific research and learning, much as any other such specialized form is a distinctive way of embodying knowledge. Given the significant implications of each particular form, it becomes evident to faculty that students in upper-division science courses, for example, might do such a report as a means of coming to understand the nature of scientific research itself. At the same time, we suggest that faculty in the sciences would do well to design assignments that enable students to work toward a full report, doing the parts separately and then combining them. In this way, students would be led to understand the makeup of each part, its relationship to the other parts, and its bearing upon the report as a whole. This example of leading students by stages to the production of a full-scale scientific report also provides a convenient introduction to the instructional value of carefully sequenced writing assignments.

Having introduced the topic of sequenced assignments, we then distribute and discuss sample sequences, so that faculty can get a detailed illustration and understanding of the method before turning to work on a sequence of 4-6 assignments for one of their own upper-level courses. One of the model sequences that we examine, David Hamilton's "Reading the Wind," is reproduced immediately following this essay, together with David's parenthetical remarks on his intentions at several important points in the sequence. As is evident from the assignments and his remarks, the sequence embodies an inductive approach to learning. So, his assignments are designed and arranged to engage student writers in progressively more systematized and scientifically disciplined methods of observing, reporting on, and defining the wind. And throughout the sequence, he calls upon students to try out each other's methods of observing and reporting, so that they serve in something like the role of an audience of scientific peers, much as the sequence itself is intended by David as a "serious parody" of the activities involved in scientific observing and writing.[2] Having discussed a few model sequences, we leave faculty free during the afternoons to work on their sequences and to consult with both of us for response to draft versions of their sequences. But we continue to discuss various approaches to sequencing during the morning session of the third day, considering in particular the idea of a sequence that is intended to carry students through the stages of the composing process in drafting a particular piece of writing. Throughout this discussion and the individual consultation, we encourage faculty to keep the purposes of their courses clearly in mind in planning their sequences. Most of all, we stress the importance of designing writing tasks that will guide students through complex ideas and activities that are central to the course.

Once the faculty are clearly well along in drafting their sequences, we turn our attention during the fourth morning session to methods of responding to student writing. As a focus for this discussion, we look at sample student papers that faculty members have received in their courses and submitted earlier on in the workshop as representing the range of student writing they have encountered. In looking at particular pieces, we take special note of where the writing seems to be particularly effective, where it seems to be particularly flawed or out of control, and what seems to account for the distinctive quality in each case. As papers are examined in progressively closer detail, we usually discover that genuinely effective writing and a sound understanding of concepts go hand in hand, much as truly flawed writing is usually in some important sense the reflection of imperfectly worked out ideas, as if it were the case that the mind in the process of struggling on one level also struggles on others. Given these observations, it becomes clear to faculty that in responding to student writing, they should concern themselves primarily, if not exclusively with helping their students to develop a surer grasp of important concepts. Needless to say, this discussion raises the question of what faculty members should do about careless editing or unintelligible writing. Giving no credit for a piece of writing that is very carelessly edited goes a long way, we assure them, toward motivating students to be more careful. Likewise, we advise that giving no credit for unintelligible writing serves as a strong motivation for students to seek assistance at the writing lab.

By the final day of the workshop, faculty usually find themselves so intensely engaged by the overall experience that they want to go on record about various aspects of a university wide writing program and the role of writing in the curriculum as a whole. In fact, the written reports from the first two workshops led

---

[2] David's sequence, it should also be noted, is purposefully longer and more elaborately worked out than the sequences we expect participants to produce over the relatively brief period of the workshop. We intend the contrast to put participants at ease by having them see that what they are preparing is a draft sequence to be refined over successive offerings of their course.

the University to adopt an advanced writing requirement for graduation.[3] Still, the most significant outcomes of the workshop, according to the testimony of both faculty and students, have been the distinctive sequences of writing assignments. Thus immediately following David Hamilton's sequence, I have included a few sequences developed at our most recent workshop to illustrate what we are doing at South Alabama to improve writing and learning across the curriculum.

SAMPLE SEQUENCES

Reading the Wind[4]
David Hamilton

1. While remaining behind a window, describe what you see that gives you reason to believe in something you are willing to call the wind.

2. Take a walk in the wind. Report on what you see and feel.

3. Interview three persons and ask them about the wind. What makes one of your interviewees a better informant than another? Can you, at this point, make a summary statement about what the wind is?

> (These first three assignments are obviously introductory, allowing us all to get a better feel for the subject and work our way into it. They are in the main descriptive/representational tasks. There is overlap enough from the first to the second assignment that a latecomer in the course can, probably, step right in, no small practical consideration in itself. And by the time of the third assignment, which may come as soon as the end of the second week of the course, questions of evidence, of point of view, and of our movement from detail to generalization will be making themselves felt as practical considerations. With this third assignment, furthermore, a teacher had best offer additional directions. It could yield three distinct sections, or one section, say the trial definition of the wind, could subordinate the other tasks to itself. Neither is a necessary strategy, so far as I can see; but the array of tasks will cause some anxiety for the student, and quite possibly for the teacher, unless plans have been agreed upon beforehand, or at least unless one's openness to a variety of strategies has been made clear.)

---

[3] All undergraduates at the University of South Alabama are now required to take two upper level writing component courses, with at least one course chosen from their major or minor. Writing credit courses have been defined as content courses in a major or minor field which include a designated writing component. No limit has been set on the number of writing credit courses a department can offer nor on the number of faculty who can apply to add such credit to their courses. The University Writing Committee has been asked to formulate and distribute a general list of criteria for writing credit, based on the reports from all the faculty who attended the pilot seminars.

[4] Inspired by two exercises on the wind in Walker Gibson's *Seeing and Writing*.

4. Look for something the wind did, something like limbs fallen from a tree, milkweed blooming on a slope, or paper pushed up against a chainlink fence. What sense does it make to say, "The wind did it"?

5. Write a brief story or report in which the wind figures prominently. Invent to suit yourself or take suggestion from what you witness around you.

6. Your reports, so far, have been highly personal, even idiosyncratic. Imagine yourself going on the radio with such a report. How might you alter it for that occasion? Write a script for a two-minute radio report called "Today's Wind." Add a comment on what you looked for as evidence this time and how that may have changed from the occasions of your earlier reports. In particular, did you want to do more than give a descriptive picture of the wind?

> (The point of these assignments is twofold. First it is to extend and to allow for some growing complexity in the direction first taken, of essentially descriptive/ narrative reports. In addition I want to introduce the attraction of a less subjective stance toward our subject. Not that we will move far in that direction in these assignments. But at least there will begin some brainstorming toward such possibilities, and that effort will prove useful. For now we wish to accelerate the scientific urge toward quantification and toward the abstraction necessary for a scientific report. Assignment 6 should invite movement in that direction; with it we enter the middle section of the course.)

7. In hopes of offering more standardized reports on the wind in the future, design an instrument, an anemometer, that might assist you in making those reports.

> (After this assignment the class will select four or five proposals that seem the most promising and divide into as many groups for pursuing them. The next few assignments, then, will be group projects.)

8. With your group, construct an anemometer that can be assembled and disassembled. Devise a scale of measurement for it and write a set of instructions for its assembly and operation.

9. Exchange your disassembled anemometers and your written instructions for their operation with another group of experimenters. Set up and test the one you have received. Write a critique of the anemometer and of the directions you have tried to follow.

10. Using the critiques you have received, or ignoring them if you find them worthless, revise your anemometer and its written instructions; prepare to demonstrate both in class.

> (This is obviously a crucial group of assignments. The nature of the case encourages parody and a spirit of play. The wind is too hard "to get" and the materials and methods too hard to master otherwise. But this is all to the good. Invention is freed more if the students feel challenged to improvise, not to compete with the airport or the weather station. All sorts of adequate

anemometers can be made from cardboard, dowelling, ping pong balls, styrofoam cups, mascara brushes, water, tin cans, and other ready-to-hand things. Furthermore, as they will learn by doing and by seeing others do, their attention can be quite exactly focused on even the most homemade instrument. It is not the degree to which they capture the real wind, whatever that is, that matters; it is the degree to which they examine what they have made and allow it to calibrate some further knowledge for them. "I am a handicap to my anemometer," a student remarked once; "the accuracy of the readings corresponds to the exactness with which I counted revolutions."

Revision is also built into this series of assignments, and it is enacted in its most literal sense. The critique of one group can startle another toward new understanding. At least two levels of revision come into play, that of the persons making the critique and that of the original group responding to it. Both are managed in an arena that probably compels a more impressive degree of re-vision than one usually summons from a student alone with less tangible material. Here, for example, is evidence of re-thinking, highlighted by a useful piece of jargon, constructed for the occasion.

> Another thing that put a limit to the effectiveness of our anemometer was the need for an "effector breeze" that was strong enough to set the pen in motion. The friction caused by the touching of the pen to the paper made it stay put until such a breeze came along. The friction was necessary due to another shortcoming of our apparatus.
>
> The curvature of the arc that the swinging pen made was not taken into consideration in the construction. This caused an inaccuracy because of the fact that for the pen to make a mark at a distance far away from the center, it had to be set at a point such that it touched the paper and caused friction. On the other hand, if the pen was set correctly for the center markings, it would not make a mark for the strong winds....

An additional challenge through this series of assignments, of course, is to give clear instructions to other workers. That is a fundamental task for writers, just as replication is a fundamental process of laboratory science.)

11. Write a report on your instrument in which you advocate either its mass production, because of its commercial advantages, or its continued development because of other advantages it has.

12. Write a second report in which you define the wind as your anemometer has enabled you to know it.

(I would make the first of these assignments the last in the series of group projects and return to individual work with the second. That movement could come with assignment 11 if you prefer. In either case, 11 is something like a term paper, a research project. But in this case the notecards come from the stages of group work and from the critiques of colleagues rather than from the library. It has the further advantage of having grown under the students' hands all semester—we could be just beyond the midpoint of the course—and not arising now as a separate obstacle. Thus we avoid having to say, in effect, "Now we come to the research paper. Go out and learn enough about something to write a longer, documented, information-laden paper."

The second assignment in this series is a most challenging follow-up to the longer report. The point here—a sophisticated one from the point of view of scientific inquiry and of the intellectual life generally—is that the wind is that which their anemometers make known to them; exactly and only that. For the purpose of this assignment, the wind doesn't exist one millimeter to the side of their instrument or during any other fraction of a second than those when their instrument is functioning. A feel for limits of all sorts comes readily to this assignment. Which means it is time for a further turn.)

13. Compare your last report to your first three or four. Have you come closer to knowing and expressing the nature of the wind? Explain your progress, or your regress if you think that to be the case.

14. Write a proposal for constructing a very different wind-reading instrument, one that will enable you to grasp (?) features of the wind so far missing from your accounts of it.

15. Construct your second wind-reading instrument and be ready to demonstrate it to the class.

(Again I would sort through the proposals, with the class, and work in small groups for assignment 15. That would mean four or five rather than twenty or more instruments to construct and demonstrate. It would be wonderful here if the instruments ran toward the impressionistic rather than toward the mathematical; hence kites and windharps and displays with balloons rather than rotating cups, or a blade pushed back along a scale, or water evaporating from an exposed basin. And such freedom of invention is likely. Many students come to feel confined by their original anemometers and feel the limits of their instruments to be so severe that the wind has escaped their study:

...This is incredibly boring...Thirty-seven times in one hour-long minute the stupid cups go around. I want gusts and swells, evidence of presence.

With the next assignment then we return to individual work and remain in that mode for the rest of the semester.)

16. Conceive of, design, and lavishly illustrate an anemometer that combines features of your first instrument with features of your second, or with a second that didn't come into being through the group projects. Work out a scale of measurement for it and give a name to your Fantasy Anemometer.

17. Write some advertising copy extolling the genius of this most recent invention.

18. Interview a classmate and write a feature story for a local paper on that eccentric inventor and her or his apparatus.

19. Write a proposal to some funding agency arguing for further research and eventual development of your Fantasy Anemometer or that of the person you just interviewed.

> (You'll notice that I'm not asking for this last conception to be built. I'd like to give the freest possible expression to everyone's imagination. In addition, I don't want to run the construction of things into the ground. Twice is probably plenty, perhaps a bit more than plenty.
>
> The assignments that follow from #16 sample different kinds of writing as those opportunities present themselves naturally after the work done so far. Numbers 18 and 19 are both research papers, again, but of very different orders and drawing on different kinds of information, most of which will be well assimilated already and the rest fairly easy to obtain by this point in the course. So to conclude.)

20. What, if anything, is there left to grasp about the wind, what aspect of it can you imagine that your work this semester hasn't captured?

21. Write a short narrative, perhaps a piece of science fiction, even a poem in which the wind plays a part. Might it be a central, or at least an influential character?

> (One could rewrite these two assignments as one, but I'd rather not, so as not to short-circuit the more scientifically adept imaginations in the room. In both cases, the closure of the course is made to rest upon new promise, further potentialities of thought and of study, rather than upon a pretense of wrapping things up. For one of the things that all the students must have imagined by this time is that their work with the wind could, in fact, take over their lives.)

Sequence for a Course in Microbiology
Burke Brown

1. Write about your knowledge of wine. How is it made? Relate any personal experiences with wine (if you wish). Know any historical aspects of wine? Think of all the adjectives you could use to describe wine.

2. Interview three people outside class and ask them about wine. Write a brief summary of their remarks. Which one was the most informative?

3. Make an annotated bibliography of 5-10 articles, books, etc. about wine.

4. Write a detailed set of instructions for making approximately 1 quart to 1 gallon of wine. List equipment and materials needed for the project.

5. Keep a detailed report of the changes that occur in the fermentation of wine.

How does it taste? Smell? Feel? Describe any color changes. What causes these changes?

6. Write a critique of the wine and the winemaking instructions. Are there some improvements you would make in the process?

7. Write a short article about wine for publication in a favorite magazine *(Playboy, Reader's Digest, Ladies Home Journal,* etc.)

8. Write a scientific paper suitable for publication in *Applied and Environmental Microbiology* or in the *Journal of Irreproducible Results* detailing your experiment in making wine. One rough draft will be required for approval prior to turning in the finished paper.

Sequence for a Course in Respiratory Therapy
H. Fred Hill

1. Select an infant with respiratory problems recently admitted into the neonatal intensive care unit. Keep a daily log of this infant's progress, particularly in regards to his/her respiratory problems. Use a problem-oriented record system and keep a list of the infant's problems for reference. Write your log using the format of SOAP notes. For information draw on your clinical observations, physicians' and nurses' notes, laboratory reports, and x-ray reports. Feel free to draw on discussions with nurses, physicians, and instructors, but use care to avoid rumors and speculations. If you do include speculation identify it as such. Follow the infant's progress until either (a) two weeks have passed, (b) the infant's respiratory problems have been resolved, or (c) the infant has died. Your log should be available for daily review and submitted in total at the conclusion of the observation period. (Due at the end of week #4)

2. Research in your textbooks and in professional journals the respiratory problem(s) encountered by the infant you selected in assignment #1. In regards to these problems, describe management techniques, known etiologies, and the rationale for particular treatment modalities. Describe potential hazards and complications of various treatment modalities. (Due at the end of week #5)

3. Compare the management of the infant in assignment #1 to techniques you learned in assignment #2. How closely did the management of this infant compare to methods you have researched? Were any obvious mistakes made? Were differences in management techniques justified? Do management plans differ significantly to the point that a physician must make a choice to pursue one plan of therapy over another? You may consult any experts (physicians, nurses, respiratory therapists) to develop this comparison. (Due at the end of week #6)

4. Critique individual episodes or aspects in the respiratory management of this infant with an eye on improving the management of these problems. Pay particular attention to things that we as respiratory therapists can do, but feel free to comment

on physician and nursing responsibilities as well. (Due at the end of week #7)

5. Write a formal case report on the infant that you followed in assignment #1. Use the format for case study suggested by the respiratory publication *Respiratory Care*. The final form should be in a form suitable for publication (typewritten and proofread carefully). Drafts of this report may be submitted at any time for comments and suggestions from the instructor without penalty. (Due at the end of week #9)

Sequence for a Senior Seminar in Sociology
Marc Matre

1. Go to the library with the list of sociological journals. Search through abstracts and journals in the most convenient and efficient way for yourself. The object of your search is to find at least two articles which meet all of the following tests: (a) The subject matter of the article is very interesting. (b) The article is written so that it can be understood. (c) The research which was done to produce the information for the article is the kind of research which you could do. Carefully read and reread the articles until you are satisfied that you are sure about how well each meets the three tests. Then write a statement telling seminar members why one of the articles best meets the three tests for you. (At least three paragraphs will be necessary, but your statement should not exceed three pages.)

2. Write a (four or five page) proposal telling seminar members about how you imagine doing the kind of research you described in the first assignment. Be sure to cover these points: (a) the purpose (sociological significance), (b) the social setting in which you could do the research, (c) ethical problems you foresee, (d) how you would do the research.

3. Do a simple observation (not less than two or three hours in as unobtrusive, non-participant a fashion as possible) of the aspect of social life which you proposed to study in the second assignment. Revise your proposal. Your revised proposal should be more thorough than your first one. Try to make your revised proposal both more scientific and more realistic in view of what you learned about what you intend to study from your simple observation. Append to your revised proposal a brief (one page) statement telling seminar members about the reasons for the most important revisions in your proposal.

4. Carry out the research you proposed in the third assignment. Write a research report. Your report should include the kinds of information in your revised proposal and the following: (a) results, (b) analysis or synthesis, (c) conclusions, and (d) a brief (one page) statement about the research experience giving seminar members an insider's view of the project.

5. Exchange research reports with another member (or research group) in the seminar. Write a critique of the report and comment on the insider's view of the research. Exchange critiques and write a brief (one page) reponse to the critique.

Appendix
Sample Guidelines for Workshops

Workshop Guidelines for "Experiments in Composing"
Sandra Doe

Writing is a bit like charting new territory—when you look back at the end of the journey, you think you see where you ought to have gone. This is an illusion, since if you were to travel again, it would be a different journey and the writing would be a different piece of work. Most writing ventures are similar to this, a struggle from the beginning to find out what they are and where they are going, an exploration which starts out traveling in the dark. It isn't often that a piece of writing follows a set design, a path fixed with clear sign posts and mile markers; if you try to write along this straight and narrow way, often the piece will collapse, as it strays from the trail for small side trips, piqued by the writer's curiosity, or it changes into something else.

This travel metaphor suggests that writing is a process, a way of exploring yourself and your perceptions, thoughts, and emotions, a way of charting yourself as you travel along.

When you write you find meaning and make meaning in the process of writing itself. One well-known rhetorical question to keep in mind is "How do I know what I think until I see what I've said?" Seeing means understanding as in "I see what you mean." That is, the reader of your work understands the relationships which you've established to make sense out of the world.

The Writers' Workshop in this class will provide a forum for your work, an audience which is response-able, a group of people who also write, explore, ask questions, and respond to your writing efforts in a supportive and sensitive manner. They'll offer feedback as fellow classmates and writers; you'll take your writing into feedforward.

Feedback depends on response in the fullest sense of the word—a generous, sensitive awareness to what is written, its close consideration, a capacity for affirmation and questioning. In this class, we'll use two questions as the basis for feedback: "What do you like about this piece of writing?" and "What suggestions for change do you have for this work?" Feedback requires patience and concern, an involvement in the process, and, as you can see, its language is not limited to the language of computers.

Feedforward is a step-by-step investigation of possibilities, a way of trying out alternatives, a fertile interplay between what others think happened in the writing and what the writer examines in experimenting openly with change. Feedforward is the capacity to formulate the choices you make when you put things together, see relationships, interpret your experience, and make meaning.

At first we'll do some large group feedback and the writing presented will be presented anonomously. After we develop confidence in each other, and response-ableness, we'll break down into small groups. Each individual writer will transfer the feedback into feedforward.

Workshop Guidelines for "Women Writing"
Rebecca Blevins Faery

The text for this course—that is, the source from which you'll learn about writing—will be the writing you all do and what we say about it. With this text and these discussions, you will learn about the whole writing process—not by reading about it, and not by listening to me talk about it, but by writing, by sharing what you've written with me and the rest of the class, by listening to what we say about your writing, and by reading and responding to the writing done by other class members.

As a result of this workshop process, I hope that by the end of the course you will be a more thoughtful writer, aware of your reason for writing any piece and more aware of the audience for whom you intend it; and, finally, that you will have become a better reader and editor of your own writing, able to revise your work to increase its effectiveness.

Here, then, are the guidelines we will follow for our workshop sessions.

Small Groups: I'll divide the class into groups of five people each. I may make some changes in the groups during the first weeks, but after that the groups will stay the same for the rest of the term.

Be conscientious about letting each writer in the group have a chance to have her work discussed.

Read each paper up for discussion at least twice through. If the paper is short, it may be useful to ask the writer to read it aloud.

If you have helpful comments or suggestions which you don't have an opportunity to make in the group, write them down on your copy of the paper and sign your name, and give the copy to the writer.

Remember that the purpose of the workshop is to help all of you become better writers. So make your comments about others' work *constuctive* and *specific*. And remember, too, that while the writer is obligated to listen to what you have to say, she doesn't have to take your advice. It's *her* work.

For The Writer Whose Work Is Being Discussed When something of yours comes up for discussion, write "Discussed in workshop _____(date)" on your copy.

As the group members comment and make suggestions, jot down interesting and helpful comments on your copy of the paper.

After the workshop, give me the copy of your paper with the comments written down so I can see what other readers had to say about it. I will return it to you after I've looked at it. Keep the workshop copy in your portfolio.

Questions for the Writer to Ask to Open Discussion
1. What do you like about my paper?
2. What questions do you want to ask me about my paper?
3. What parts of my paper seem to you to need further work?
4. What would you like to know about how I wrote this paper?

Questions for the Group to Ask the Writer to Continue Discussion
1. What do *you* like about your paper?
2. What part of this paper was easiest to write? What part was hardest?
3. What comments or suggestions in our discussion have you found most helpful? Why?
4. Do you plan to revise this paper? If so, how?

Workshop Guidelines for "Writing to Think and Learn"
Trudy Dittmar

This class will be conducted as a writers'/learners' workshop where you will write about and discuss your writing/learning and the writing/learning of others in the class—sometimes with the class as a whole, sometimes in small groups, and sometimes in pairs.

The workshop setting will help you in many ways. It will help you decide how to get started on a project and how to proceed in your search activity. Once you have finished the search activity, you will write about and discuss your search findings and try to formulate your opinions on them. While doing the research portion of a project you will write about and discuss your research experience. In this case the workshop discussions will answer your questions about research procedures, help solve problems you are having, and help you develop efficient methods of doing research.

Finally, you will discuss your papers in workshop. This will help you see how others react to what you write; you will be able to respond to people's comments and ask questions as your paper is being discussed. You should learn more from this kind of discussion of your work than you would if your instructor's written comments were the only form of response your writing received.

Following are the guidelines that I would like you to use when you are working in small group workshops without my leadership.

General Guidelines
1. Join together in groups of three—no more than four.
2. Change your group each time. Make sure you're with two different people from the time before.

3. If you have trouble deciding whose paper to start with, go in alphabetical order.
4. Read the paper twice. Jot down on your copy of the paper notes in response to the guideline questions below.
5. Discuss your reactions with the group.

Guideline Questions for Commentators

Use the following basic questions to guide you in making responses to the paper:

1. What points does the paper make?
2. What evidence substantiates each point? What is the source of each bit of evidence? How do you know?
3. What questions would you need to have answered in order to understand the paper more thoroughly?
4. What evidence, if any, seems unnecessary or irrelevant? Why?
5. In what ways does the paper accomplish its purpose? How might it do so even more thoroughly?
6. In what ways is the paper suited to its audience? In what ways might the writer make it even more suitable for its audience?

Guideline Questions for Writers (These questions should help you decide what to ask to learn more about the group's opinions of your paper.)

1. What parts of your paper did you have most difficulty with? Spend most time on? Ask the group's opinion on these parts. Find out if you succeeded in your intentions.
2. If commentators say things about your paper that you think are mistaken, push them to give specific reasons (i.e., specific references to your paper) to support their opinions. If they refer to a positive aspect of your paper that you were unaware of, push them there too, to find out just why that aspect of your paper is good. Get as much feedback as you can. Don't let them say the paper is good without making them go into detail. Make them be as specific as possible about *why* it's good.

Procedures for Writers to Keep Track of What They Learned from Workshop Sessions on Their Papers

1. Label your paper (or your dittoed copy of it) "Discussed on _____ _____ " (provide date).
2. As the others comment on what you have written, write interesting or relevant (helpful) comments on your copy. This copy should be kept in your journal.
3. Hand in your copy with the comments you've made on it, so I can see it. On the back, ask any questions you'd like me to answer about the paper.
4. When the paper is returned to you, put it in its proper place in the journal.

Post-Workshop Journal Entry (for all students)

1. At the end of each workshop session, turn to your journal. At the top of a clean page, write "Reflections on Workshop Session for _____

_____ " (give date). Then write down your thoughts about the workshop session you've just been a part of. The following questions may help you write down your reflections:

2. What was accomplished in your session? If your paper was discussed, what ideas did you get about your paper? How would you change it if you had to write it over again? Even if your paper wasn't discussed, what did you contribute to the discussion? What ideas did you get about the paper you wrote for this assignment? What ideas did you get that might help you in writing papers in the future?

3. *You should have a journal entry for each workshop session you take part in, whether your paper was discussed or not.*

Bibliography

Nancy Jones

Like any bibliography, this one is not exhaustive either in its categories or in the items it lists. The categories have been devised to cover topics that are self-evidently related to the explicit concern of this collection with courses and instruction in writing. The items within each category have been chosen because they are pertinent to the set of ideas and practices embodied in this collection.

Educational Theory and Language Learning

Britton, James. *Language and Learning*. Harmondsworth: Pelican, 1972.

Britton, James, Tony Burgess, Nancy Martin, Alex McLeod, and Harold Rosen. *The Development of Writing Abilities (11-18)*. London: Macmillan Education, 1975.

Bruner, Jerome S. *On Knowing: Essays for the Left Hand*. Cambridge, Mass.: Belknap Press of Harvard Univ. Press, 1962.

----------. *The Process of Education*. Cambridge, Mass.: Harvard Univ. Press, 1960.

----------. *Toward a Theory of Instruction*. Cambridge, Mass.: Belknap Press of Harvard Univ. Press, 1966.

Department of Education and Science (Great Britain). *A Language for Life* (Bullock Report). London: HMSO, 1975.

Dewey, John. *Art as Experience*. New York: Minton, Balch, 1934.

----------. *Experience and Education*. New York: Collier Books, 1938.

Emig, Janet. "Writing as a Mode of Learning." *College Composition and Communication*, 28 (1977), 122-128.

Freire, Paulo, *Education for Critical Consciousness*. Trans. Myra Bergman Ramos. New York: Seabury Press, 1973.

Kelly, George A. *A Theory of Personality: The Psychology of Personal Constructs*. New York: Norton, 1963.

Langer, Susanne K. *Feeling and Form*. New York: Charles Scribner's Sons, 1953.

----------. *Philosophy in a New Key: A Study in the Symbolism of Reason, Rite, and Art*. Cambridge, Mass.: Harvard Univ. Press, 1942.

Loban, Walter. *Language Development: Kindergarten through Grade Twelve*. NCTE Research Reports, No. 18. Urbana, Ill.: NCTE, 1976.

Moffett, James. *Teaching the Universe of Discourse*. Boston: Houghton Mifflin, 1968.

Piaget, Jean. *The Language and Thought of the Child*. New York: Harcourt, Brace, and World, 1926.

Polanyi, Michael. *Personal Knowledge: Towards a Post-Critical Philosophy*. London: Routledge & Kegan Paul, 1958.

----------. *The Tacit Dimension*. Garden City, N.Y.: Doubleday, 1966.

Sapir, Edward. "Language." *Encyclopedia of the Social Sciences*. 3rd. ed. New York: Macmillan, 1933, Vol. IX, pp. 155-69. Rpt. in *Culture, Language, and Personality: Selected Essays*. Ed. David G. Mandelbaum. Berkeley: Univ. of California Press, 1956, pp. 1-20.

Vygotsky, Lev. S. *Thought and Language*. Ed. and trans. by Eugenia Hanfmann and Gertrude Vakar. Cambridge, Mass.: MIT Press, 1962.

Whorf, Benjamin Lee. *Language, Thought and Reality*. Ed. John B. Carroll. Cambridge, Mass.: MIT Press, 1956.

Course Design and Instruction in Writing

Baird, Theodore. "The Freshman English Course." *Amherst Alumni News*, 40 (1952), 194-96.

Bartholomae, David. "Teaching Basic Writing: An Alternative to Basic Skills." *Journal of Basic Writing*, 2 (Spring/Summer 1979), 85-109.

Bazerman, Charles. "A Relationship between Reading and Writing: The Conversational Model." *College English*, 41 (1980), 656-61.

Berthoff, Ann E. *Forming/Thinking/Writing: The Composing Imagination*. Montclair, N.J.: Boynton/Cook, 1978.

----------. *The Making of Meaning: Metaphors, Models, and Maxims for Writing Teachers*. Montclair, N.J.: Boynton/Cook, 1981.

Camp, Gerald, ed. *Teaching Writing: Essays from the Bay Area Writing Project*. Montclair, N.J.: Boynton/Cook, 1983.

Coles, William E., Jr. *Composing II: Writing as a Self-Creating Process*. Rochelle Park, N.J.: Hayden, 1981.

----------. *The Plural I: The Teaching of Writing*. New York: Holt, Rinehart and Winston, 1978.

----------. *Teaching Composing*. Rochelle Park, N.J.: Hayden, 1974.

Donovan, Timothy R., and Ben W. McClelland, eds. *Eight Approaches to Teaching Composition*. Urbana, Ill.: NCTE, 1980.

Dowst, Kenneth. *Basic Writing*. Pittsburgh: University of Pittsburgh External Studies Program, 1977.

----------. "Cognition and Composition." *Freshman English News*, 11 (Winter 1983), 1-14.

----------. "Why the Composition Teacher Composes: The Writing Assignment as Teaching Device and Work of Art." *Arizona English Bulletin*, 20 (1978), 99-103.

Emig, Janet. *The Composing Processes of Twelfth Graders*. NCTE Research Reports, No. 13. Urbana, Ill.: NCTE, 1971.

Field, John P., and Robert H. Weiss. *Cases for Composition*. Boston: Little, Brown, 1979.

Friedmann, Thomas. "Teaching Error, Nurturing Confusion: Grammar Texts, Tests, and Teachers in the Developmental English Class." *College English*, 45 (1983), 390-99.

Gibson, Walker. *Seeing and Writing: Fifteen Exercises in Composing Experience*. New York: David McKay, 1959.

Hairston, Maxine. "The Winds of Change: Thomas Kuhn and the Revolution in the Teaching of Writing." *College Composition and Communication*, 33 (1982), 76-88.

Herrmann, Richard, and Diane Tabor. "Expressive Writing: Psychological Development and Educational Setting in a New Language Curriculum." Diss. Harvard University 1974.

Hoffman, Eleanor, and John Schifsky. "Designing Writing Assignments." *English Journal*, 66 (December 1977), 41-45.

Irmscher, William. *Teaching Expository Writing*. New York: Holt, Rinehart and Winston, 1979.

Jones, Nancy. "Design, Discovery, and Development in a Freshman Writing Course: A Case Study." Diss. University of Iowa 1982.

Kelly, Lou. *From Dialogue to Discourse: An Open Approach to Competence and Creativity*. Glenview, Ill.: Scott, Foresman, 1972.

Klaus, Carl H. *Composing Adolescent Experience: An Approach to Writing and Learning in the Junior High Grades*. St. Louis: CEMREL, 1982.

----------. "Research on Writing Courses: A Cautionary Essay." *Freshman English News*, 11 (Spring 1982), 1-14.

Knoblauch, C.H., and Lil Brannon. *Rhetorical Traditions and the Teaching of Writing*. Upper Montclair, N.J.: Boynton/Cook, 1984.

Krupa, Gene. *Situational Writing*. Belmont, Calif.: Wadsworth, 1982.

Labov, William. *The Study of Nonstandard English*. Urbana, Ill.: NCTE, 1970.

Lanham, Richard. *Style: An Anti-Textbook*. New Haven, Conn.: Yale Univ. Press, 1974.

Lindemann, Erika. *A Rhetoric for Writing Teachers*. New York: Oxford Univ. Press, 1982.

Lloyd-Jones, Richard. "Writing Programs and the English Department." *ADE Bulletin*, No. 61 (May 1979), 17-22.

Lunsford, Andrea A. "The Content of Basic Writers' Essays." *College Composition and Communication*, 31 (1980), 278-90.

Manning, Sylvia. "Reflections on Having Separated Freshman Writing from the English Department." *ADE Bulletin*, No. 72 (Winter 1982), 22-25.

Miller, James E., Jr. *Word, Self, Reality: The Rhetoric of Imagination*. New York: Dodd, Mead, 1972.

Moffett, James. "Integrity in the Teaching of Writing." *Phi Delta Kappan*, 61 (1979), 276-79.

Moffett, James, and Betty Jane Wagner. *Student-Centered Language Arts and Reading, K-13: A Handbook for Teachers.* 2nd ed. Boston: Houghton Mifflin, 1968.

Murray, Donald. *A Writer Teaches Writing: A Practical Method of Teaching Composition.* Boston: Houghton Mifflin, 1968.

Neel, Jasper P., ed. *Options for the Teaching of English: Freshman Composition.* New York: The Modern Language Association of America, 1978.

Ohmann, Richard. *English in America: A Radical View of the Profession.* New York: Oxford Univ. Press, 1976.

Pelz, Karen, "Dear Matthew: Letters on Exploratory Writing." Diss. University of Iowa 1981.

Petrosky, Anthony. "From Story to Essay: Reading and Writing." *College Composition and Communication,* 33 (1982), 19-36.

Rose, Mike. "Remedial Writing Courses: A Critique and a Proposal." *College English,* 45 (1983), 109-28.

Sale, Roger. *On Writing.* New York: Random House, 1970.

Steinhoff, Virginia. "Theory and Practice in the Sequencing of Composition Assignments: Issues in Order." Diss. University of Iowa 1980.

Stock, Patricia L., ed. *Fforum: Essays on Theory and Practice in the Teaching of Writing.* Upper Montclair, N.J.: Boynton/Cook, 1983.

Tate, Gary, and Edward P.J. Corbett. *Teaching Freshman Composition.* New York: Oxford Univ. Press, 1967.

Warnock, John. "New Rhetoric and the Grammar of Pedagogy." *Freshman English News,* 5 (Fall 1976), 1-22.

Winterowd, W. Ross. "Developing a Composition Program." In *Reinventing the Rhetorical Tradition.* Ed. Aviva Freedman and Ian Pringle. Conway, Ark.: L & S Books, 1980, pp. 157-71.

Young, Richard, Alton Becker, and Kenneth Pike. *Rhetoric: Discovery and Change.* New York: Harcourt, Brace and World, 1970.

Student Writing and Instructive Response

Bartholomae, David. "The Study of Error." *College Composition and Communication,* 31 (1980), 253-69.

Beaven, Mary H. "Individualized Goal Setting, Self-Evaluation, and Peer Evaluation." In *Evaluating Writing: Describing, Measuring, Judging.* Ed. Charles R. Cooper and Lee Odell. Urbana, Ill.: NCTE, 1977, pp. 135-56.

Brannon, Lil, and C.H. Knoblauch. "On Students' Right to Their Own Texts: A Model of Teacher Response." *College Composition and Communication,* 33 (1982), 157-66.

Brannon, Lil, Melinda Knight, and Vara Neverow-Turk. *Writers Writing.* Montclair, N.J.: Boynton/Cook, 1982.

Bruffee, Kenneth. "The Brooklyn Plan: Attaining Intellectual Growth through Peer-Group Tutoring." *Liberal Education,* 64 (1978), 447-69.

----------. "Collaborative Learning: Some Practical Models." *College English,* 35 (1973), 634-43.

Elbow, Peter. *Writing Without Teachers.* New York: Oxford Univ. Press, 1973.

Graves, Donald. *Balance the Basics: Let Them Write.* New York: Ford Foundation, 1978.

Hawkes, John. "The Voice Project: An Idea for Innovation in the Teaching of Writing." In *Writers as Teachers, Teachers as Writers.* Ed. Jonathan Baumbach. New York: Holt, Rinehart, and Winston, 1970, pp. 89-144.

Hawkins, Thom. *Group Inquiry Techniques for Teaching Writing.* Urbana, Ill.: NCTE, 1976.

Jacobs, Suzanne E., and Adela B. Karlinger. "Helping Writers to Think: The Effect of Speech Roles in Individual Conferences on the Quality of Thought in Student Writing." *College English,* 38 (1977), 489-505.

Kelly, Lou. "Is Competent Copyreading a Violation of the Students' Right to Their Own Language?" *College Composition and Communication,* 25 (1974), 254-58.

----------. "Toward Competence and Creativity in an Open Class." *College English,* 34 (1973), 644-60.

Knoblauch, C.H., and Lil Brannon. "Teacher Commentary on Student Writing: The State of the Art." *Freshman English News,* 10 (Fall 1981), 1-3.

Lloyd-Jones, Richard. "A Garden of Error." In *The Rites of Writing.* Ed. Daniel J. Dieterich. Stevens Point, Wis.: Univ. of Wisconsin-Stevens Point, 1982, pp. 45-52.

Macrorie, Ken. "The Helping Circle." In *Writing to Be Read.* 2nd ed. Rochelle Park, N.J.: Hayden, 1976, pp. 77-86.

Murray, Donald. *Learning by Teaching: Selected Articles on Writing and Teaching.* Montclair, N.J.: Boynton/Cook, 1982.

Rose, Mike. "Rigid Rules, Inflexible Plans, and the Stifling of Language: A Cognitivist Analysis of Writers' Block." *College Composition and Communication,* 31 (1980), 389-401.

Schultz, John. "Story Workshop: Writing from Start to Finish." In *Research on Composing: Points of Departure.* Ed. Charles R. Cooper and Lee Odell. Urbana, Ill.: NCTE, 1978, pp. 151-87.

Shaughnessy, Mina P. *Errors and Expectations: A Guide for the Teacher of Basic Writing.* New York: Oxford Univ. Press, 1977.

Sommers, Nancy. "Responding to Student Writing." *College Composition and Communication,* 33 (1982), 148-56.

Stoll, Patricia. "You Must Begin at Zero: Story Workshop." *College English,* 35 (1973), 256-66.

Williams, Joseph M. "The Phenomenology of Error." *College Composition and Communication,* 32 (1981), 152-68.

Ziegler, Alan. *The Writing Workshop.* Vol. I. New York: Teachers and Writers Collaborative, 1981.

Writing and Learning Across the Disciplines

Adams, James L. *Conceptual Blockbusting: A Guide to Better Ideas*. 2nd ed. New York: W.W. Norton, 1980.

Comley, Nancy, David Hamilton, Carl H. Klaus, Robert Scholes, and Nancy Sommers. *Fields of Writing: Readings Across the Disciplines*. New York: St. Martin's, 1984.

Freisinger, Randall R. "Cross-Disciplinary Writing Workshops: Theory and Practice." *College English*, 42 (1980), 154-66.

Fulwiler, Toby. "Journals Across the Curriculum." *English Journal*, 69 (December 1980), 14-19.

Fulwiler, Toby, and Art Young. *Language Connections: Writing and Reading Across the Curriculum*. Urbana, Ill.: NCTE, 1982.

Griffin, C. Williams, ed. *Teaching Writing in All Disciplines*. San Francisco: Jossey-Bass, 1982.

Hamilton, David. "Interdisciplinary Writing." *College English*, 41 (1980), 780-96.

----------. "Writing Science." *College English*, 40 (1978), 32-40.

----------. "Writing Science II." *Journal of Education*, 162 (1980), 96-113.

Herrington, Anne J. "Writing to Learn: Writing Across the Disciplines." *College English*, 43 (1981), 379-87.

Kinneavy, James. "Writing Across the Curriculum." *ADE Bulletin*, No. 76 (Winter 1983), 14-21.

Kitzhaber, Albert. *Themes, Theories, and Therapy: Teaching of Writing in College*. New York: McGraw-Hill, 1963.

Knoblauch, C.H., and Lil Brannon. "Writing as Learning Through the Curriculum." *College English*, 45 (1983), 465-73.

Lloyd-Jones, Richard. "What We May Become." *College Composition and Communication*, 33 (1982), 202-07.

Maimon, Elaine P. "Cinderella to Hercules: Demythologizing Writing Across the Curriculum." *Journal of Basic Writing*, 2 (Spring/Summer 1980), 3-11.

Maimon, Elaine P., Gerald Belcher, Gail Hearn, Barbara Nodine, and Finbarr O'Connor. *Readings in the Arts and Sciences*. Boston: Little, Brown, 1984.

----------. *Writing in the Arts and Sciences*. Boston: Little, Brown, 1981.

Martin, Nancy, Pat D'Arcy, Bryan Newton, and Robert Parker. *Writing and Learning Across the Curriculum 11-16*. London: Ward Lock, 1976.

Moffett, James. *Active Voice: A Writing Program Across the Curriculum*. Montclair, N.J.: Boynton/Cook, 1981.

Robertson, Linda R. "Stranger in a Strange Land or Stimulating Faculty Interest in Writing Across the Curriculum." Paper presented at the Wyoming Conference on Freshman and Sophomore English, Laramie, Wyo., 1981. (ERIC ED 211 699)

Walvoord, Barbara E. Fassler. *Helping Students Write Well: A Guide for Teachers in All Disciplines*. New York: Modern Language Association, 1982.

Weiss, Robert, and Michael Peich. "Faculty Attitude Change in a Cross-Disciplinary Writing Workshop." *College Composition and Communication*, 31 (1980), 33-41.

Notes on Contributors

Beverly Beem is Professor of English and College Writing Coordinator at Walla Walla College, where she also teaches English Renaissance literature. She is currently designing a cross-disciplinary professional development program in writing for Northwest school teachers.

James Britton has in recent years been a visiting professor at the Ontario Institute for Studies in Education, the University of Calgary, New York University, and the University of Iowa. Prior to his retirement from full time teaching in 1975, he had taught in the British secondary schools and at the University of London, where for sixteen years he was head of the English Department in the Institute of Education and from 1970 on was Goldsmiths' Professor of Education. Among his many publications are *Language and Learning* (Pelican, 1972), *The Development of Writing Abilities (11-18)* (as co-author and editor; Macmillan Education, 1975), and *Prospect and Retrospect* (Boynton/Cook, 1982). In 1977 he was awarded an Honorary Doctorate of Laws by the University of Calgary, and the David H. Russell Award for Distinguished Research in the Teaching of English by the National Council of Teachers of English.

Burke L. Brown is Professor of Biology at the University of South Alabama, specializing in microbiology, particularly virology.

Patricia Carlson is Associate Professor and Writing Program Director at Rose-Hulman Institute of Technology. Her interest in computers and the composing process has led her to do research at NASA/Goddard on the role of writing in advanced computer systems. She is also designing a set of computer programs for instruction in technical writing.

Elizabeth Ciner is Director of the Language Skills Center and a faculty member in the English Department at Carleton College. In addition to directing and participating in a number of cross-disciplinary seminars at the college level, she has worked with secondary school teachers and administrators on their own writing and on the teaching of writing in the schools.

Priscilla Davidson is Associate Professor of English and Director of Freshman Composition at Roosevelt University. She has recently completed work on a Title III grant for which she designed a pilot program to assist city junior college English departments in preparing their graduates for senior college writing experiences and requirements.

Trudy Dittmar was an instructor in charge of the experimental writing program at Brookdale Community College when she devised and implemented the course which appears in this volume. She now maintains a consultative relationship with the college. In 1982-83 she served as fiction editor of *Columbia: A Magazine of Poetry and Prose,* and she is currently at work on a novel.

Sandra Doe is Associate Professor of English at Metropolitan State College, where she has served as Coordinator of the Composition Program. While in residence at the Institute on Writing, she designed a writing center for the College, which she developed and directed upon her return. She is a member of the composition committee, and is active in interdisciplinary efforts on the campus. She is also a performing poet, and has given readings throughout the Denver area.

Tim Donovan is Associate Professor of English and Director of Freshman Composition at Northeastern University. Author of numerous articles on teacher training, composition pedagogy, and writing program administration, he is co-editor of *Eight Approaches to Teaching Composition* (NCTE, 1980), a member of the Executive Committee of CCCC, and since 1980 Co-director of the Martha's Vineyard Summer Institute on Teaching Writing.

Rebecca Blevins Faery is Coordinator of Writing at Hollins College where she teaches beginning and advanced writing courses and directs the Writing Center and the cross-disciplinary writing program. She has published poems, articles, essays, and reviews in a variety of journals, and is a contributor to the forthcoming book by William E. Coles, Jr. and James Vopat, *What Makes Good Writing Good.*

Gracia Grindal is Associate Professor of English at Luther College where, during her tenure as Director of Writing, she designed the College's current writing program. From 1981-1983 she was Visiting Associate Professor of Pastoral Theology and Ministry at Luther Northwestern Seminary in St. Paul, Minnesota where she taught Homiletics using the theory and practice of writing instruction she developed at the Institute.

David Hamilton is Professor of English at the University of Iowa, Editor of *The Iowa Review,* and a staff member of the Institute on Writing. He maintains an interest in writing across the disciplines, stemming from the late 1960's and early 1970's, when he served as assistant editor of the *Michigan Quarterly Review* and took part in Richard Young's interdepartmental seminar on writing and tagmemics. He is the author of articles on interdisciplinary writing and science writing that have appeared in *College English* and *Journal of Education,* and he is co-editor of *Fields of Writing: Readings Across the Disciplines* (St. Martin's Press, 1984).

H. Fred Hill is Instructor in the Department of Respiratory Therapy at the University of South Alabama, specializing in pediatric and neonatal respiratory therapy.

Frank Hubbard is Assistant Professor of English at the University of Wisconsin– Milwaukee, specializing in composition and linguistics. At UWM he has also served as assistant coordinator for business and technical writing and as assistant coordinator for basic writing. His review article on word processors in the teaching of writing recently appeared in *College English*. His critical study, *Style and Theory of Fiction in Conrad*, will be published in 1984 by UMI Press, and he is currently completing work on a freshman rhetoric for St. Martin's Press.

Nancy Jones is Assistant Professor of Rhetoric and English at the University of Iowa, and a staff member of the Institute on Writing. She has conducted writing workshops for school teachers and administrators in the State of Iowa Writing Project, and has served as a consultant to cross-disciplinary projects at both the school and college level. She is currently completing a longitudinal case study of students from one of the courses designed at the Institute.

Philip Keith is Associate Professor of English and Director of Composition at St. Cloud State University. He is Director of the St. Cloud Area Writing Project, a cross-curricular program for university faculty, editor of the first volume of *Minnesota Monographs in Composition,* and a member of the editorial staff of *Rhetoric Society Quarterly.*

Carl Klaus is Professor of English at the University of Iowa and Director of the Institute on Writing. His interest in professional and curricular development dates back to the mid-1960's when he directed three NDEA Institutes in English, and to the mid-1970's when he was director of Iowa's Advanced Writing Program. Co-developer of the Primary Trait System for the assessment of writing, he is editor of *Style in English Prose* (Macmillan, 1968), co-author of *Elements of the Essay* (Oxford, 1969) and *Elements of Writing* (Oxford, 1972), author of *Composing Adolescent Experience* (CEMREL, 1982) and *Composing Childhood Experience* (CEMREL, 1982), and co-editor of *Fields of Writing: Readings Across the Disciplines* (St. Martin's, 1984).

Ruth Lucas is Instructor of Language Arts at Kapiolani Community College, where she has also been chair of the department and coordinator of freshman composition. During a recent leave from the College, she conducted a study of model cross-disciplinary writing programs and served as co-chair of the planning committee for a cross-disciplinary faculty workshop at the University of Hawaii.

Marc Matre is Associate Professor in the Department of Sociology and Anthropology at the University of South Alabama, specializing in minority relations and urban sociology.

Donald Maxwell is Associate Professor of English and leader for composition at J. Sargeant Reynolds Community College. In 1981-82 he taught writing to college instructors and students at the Xi'an Foreign Languages Institute, in the People's Republic of China. He recently received a grant to develop a computer communication network for teaching composition by telephone.

William McCarron is Professor of English and Director of Honors and Enrichment Courses in English at the United States Air Force Academy. During a recent 18-month sabbatical, he also served as a technical writer at Nellis Air Force Base, Nevada. His articles on writing have appeared in *ADE Bulletin, College English,* and *Technical Writing Teacher.* His latest article, "Write as You Fly...Professionally," in the Air Force's *Fighter Weapons Review,* advocates writing as a way of learning more about flying combat aircraft. He is co-compiler of *Lesser Metaphysical Poets: A Bibliography, 1961-1980* (Trinity University Press, 1983), and co-author of a recently completed textbook manuscript on technical writing.

Mary Frew Moldstad is Instructor of English and Director of Developmental Programs at Ashland College. During the 1983-84 academic year, while on leave in England, she investigated student writing practices in the London area.

Karen Pelz is Associate Professor of English at Western Kentucky University, where she directs a pilot program in freshman composition. She has published articles in *Forum for Reading* and the *Journal of Advanced Composition* and is currently president of the Association of Teachers of Advanced Composition. During the summer she teaches in the State of Iowa Writing Project.

Leone Scanlon is Director of the Writing Center at Clark University, where she also coordinates the cross-disciplinary writing program. She has presented papers on peer writing groups at NEMLA, on invention at NYCEA, and has participated in a panel discussion of textbooks at CCCC. Her article, "Invention and the Writing Sequence," recently appeared in *The Writer's Mind: Writing as a Mode of Thinking* (NCTE, 1983).

David Schodt is Assistant Professor of Economics at St. Olaf College, specializing in public finance and Latin American development economics.

Henry Silverman is Professor of American Thought and Language at Michigan State University, and has directed the MSU writing program since 1977. He is author of numerous publications on American literary and social issues, including *American Radical Thought: The Libertarian Tradition* (D.C. Heath, 1970) and "The Old Left and the New Left," in the *Chronicle of Higher Education* (March 1974). His most recent article on writing, "Teaching Writing—An Administrator's View," appeared in the *Michigan English Teacher* (June 1983). He is currently at work on a project involving the use of computers to help in writing classes for developmental students.

Lana Silverthorn has recently been named Director of University Writing Programs at the University of South Alabama, where she previously served as Director of Freshman English. She recently received a grant from NEH to direct summer seminars in writing for faculty at South Alabama, and to co-ordinate a cross-curricular writing project there. A description of the pilot freshman course she designed at the Institute has been published in *The Writing Teacher in Alabama* (October, 1983).

John Thomson is Assistant Professor of English at the United States Air Force Academy. A specialist in Renaissance literature and composition, he prepared and taught his first sequence of writing assignments when he was completing his doctoral studies at the University of Iowa.

Jack H. White is Associate Professor of English and Director of Freshman English at Mississippi State University. Under grants from the Hardin Foundation, he has conducted workshops and seminars in cross-disciplinary writing for faculty at MSU and Meridian Junior College. He also has contributed to the development of additional graduate and undergraduate writing courses at MSU.